Facing the Multi-Age Workforce

Facing the Challenges of a Multi-Age Workforce examines the shifting economic, cultural, and technological trends in the modern workplace that are taking place as a result of the aging global workforce. Taking an international perspective, contributors address workforce aging issues around the world, allowing for productive cross-cultural comparisons. Chapters adopt a use-inspired approach, with contributors proposing solutions to real problems faced by organizations, including global teamwork, unemployed youth, job obsolescence and overqualification, heavy emotional labor and physically demanding jobs, and cross-age perceptions and communication. Additional commentaries from sociologists, gerontologists, economists, and scholars of labor and government round out the volume and demonstrate the interdisciplinary nature of this important topic.

Lisa M. Finkelstein is Professor of Psychology at Northern Illinois University, USA.

Donald M. Truxillo is Professor of Psychology at Portland State University, USA.

Franco Fraccaroli is Professor of Work and Organizational Psychology at University of Trento, Italy.

Ruth Kanfer is Professor of Psychology at Georgia Institute of Technology, USA.

The Organizational Frontiers Series

Series Editor

Richard Klimoski
George Mason University

EDITORIAL BOARD

Neal M. Ashkanasy
University of Queensland

Jill Ellingson
The Ohio State University

Ruth Kanfer
Georgia Institute of Technology

Eden King
George Mason University

Fred Oswald
Rice University

Stephen Zaccaro
George Mason University

Deborah Rupp
Purdue University

Mo Wang
University of Florida

Howard Weiss
Georgia Institute of Technology

Gilad Chen
University of Maryland

SIOP Organizational Frontiers Series

Series Editor

Richard Klimoski
George Mason University

Finkelstein/Truxillo/Fraccaroli/Kanfer: (2015) *Facing the Challenges of a Multi-Age Workforce: A Use-Inspired Approach*
Coovert/Thompson: (2013) *The Psychology of Workplace Technology*
Highhouse/Dalal/Salas: (2013) *Judgment and Decision Making at Work*
Cortina/Landis: (2013) *Modern Research Methods for the Study of Behavior in Organizations*
Olson-Buchanan/Koppes Bryan/Foster Thompson: (2013) *Using Industrial Organizational Psychology for the Greater Good: Helping Those Who Help Others*
Eby/Allen: (2012) *Personal Relationships: The Effect on Employee Attitudes, Behavior, and Well-being*
Goldman/Shapiro: (2012) *The Psychology of Negotiations in the 21st Century Workplace: New Challenges and New Solutions*
Ferris/Treadway: (2012) *Politics in Organizations: Theory and Research Considerations*
Jones: (2011) *Nepotism in Organizations*
Hofmann/Frese: (2011) *Error in Organizations*
Outtz: (2009) *Adverse Impact: Implications for Organizational Staffing and High Stakes Selection*
Kozlowski/Salas: (2009) *Learning, Training, and Development in Organizations*
Klein/Becker/Meyer: (2009) *Commitment in Organizations: Accumulated Wisdom and New Directions*
Salas/Goodwin/Burke: (2009) *Team Effectiveness in Complex Organizations*
Kanfer/Chen/Pritchard: (2008) *Work Motivation: Past, Present and Future*
de Dreu/Gelfand: (2008) *The Psychology of Conflict and Conflict Management in Organizations*
Ostroff/Judge: (2007) *Perspectives on Organizational Fit*

Baum/Frese/Baron: (2007) *The Psychology of Entrepreneurship*
Weekley/Ployhart: (2006) *Situational Judgment Tests: Theory, Measurement and Application*
Dipboye/Colella: (2005) *Discrimination at Work: The Psychological and Organizational Bases*
Griffin/O'Leary-Kelly: (2004) *The Dark Side of Organizational Behavior*
Hofmann/Tetrick: (2003) *Health and Safety in Organizations*
Jackson/Hitt/DeNisi: (2003) *Managing Knowledge for Sustained Competitive Knowledge*
Barrick/Ryan: (2003) *Personality and Work*
Lord/Klimoski/Kanfer: (2002) *Emotions in the Workplace*
Drasgow/Schmitt: (2002) *Measuring and Analyzing Behavior in Organizations*
Feldman: (2002) *Work Careers*
Zaccaro/Klimoski: (2001) *The Nature of Organizational Leadership*
Rynes/Gerhart: (2000) *Compensation in Organizations*
Klein/Kozlowski: (2000) *Multilevel Theory, Research and Methods in Organizations*
Ilgen/Pulakos: (1999) *The Changing Nature of Performance*
Earley/Erez: (1997) *New Perspectives on International I-O Psychology*
Murphy: (1996) *Individual Differences and Behavior in Organizations*
Guzzo/Salas: (1995) *Team Effectiveness and Decision Making*
Howard: (1995) *The Changing Nature of Work*
Schmitt/Borman: (1993) *Personnel Selection in Organizations*
Zedeck: (1991) *Work, Families and Organizations*
Schneider: (1990) *Organizational Culture and Climate*
Goldstein: (1989) *Training and Development in Organizations*
Campbell/Campbell: (1988) *Productivity in Organizations*
Hall: (1987) *Career Development in Organizations*

Facing the Challenges of a Multi-Age Workforce

A Use-Inspired Approach

Edited by

Lisa M. Finkelstein
Northern Illinois University

Donald M. Truxillo
Portland State University

Franco Fraccaroli
University of Trento

Ruth Kanfer
Georgia Institute of Technology

NEW YORK AND LONDON

First published 2015
by Routledge
711 Third Avenue, New York, NY 10017

and by Routledge
27 Church Road, Hove, East Sussex BN3 2FA

Routledge is an imprint of the Taylor & Francis Group, an informa business

© 2015 Taylor & Francis

The right of the editors to be identified as the authors of the editorial material, and of the authors for their individual chapters, has been asserted in accordance with sections 77 and 78 of the Copyright, Designs and Patents Act 1988.

All rights reserved. No part of this book may be reprinted or reproduced or utilized in any form or by any electronic, mechanical, or other means, now known or hereafter invented, including photocopying and recording, or in any information storage or retrieval system, without permission in writing from the publishers.

Trademark notice: Product or corporate names may be trademarks or registered trademarks, and are used only for identification and explanation without intent to infringe.

Library of Congress Cataloging-in-Publication Data
Facing the challenges of a multi-age workforce : a use-inspired approach/ edited by Lisa Finkelstein, Donald Truxillo, Franco Fraccaroli, and Ruth Kanfer.—First Edition.
pages cm.—(SIOP organizational frontiers series)
Includes bibliographical references and index.
1. Age and employment. 2. Ability, Influence of age on. 3. Social mobility.
I. Finkelstein, Lisa M., editor.
HD6279.F33 2015
331.3—dc23
2014043182

ISBN: 978-0-415-83895-5 (hbk)
ISBN: 978-1-84872-518-8 (pbk)
ISBN: 978-0-203-77632-2 (ebk)

Typeset in Minion and Optima
by Florence Production Ltd, Stoodleigh, Devon, UK

Printed and bound in the United States of America by Publishers Graphics, LLC on sustainably sourced paper.

For Rhoda and Kurt, my favorite people.

-LF

For Chip.

-DT

For Pietro, Cecilia, Nicolò, and Alba.

-FF

For Phil and Sarah, whose support inspires my work and outlook on aging.

-RK

Contents

Series Foreword xiii
Preface xv
List of Figures xvii
List of Tables xviii
About the Editors xix
About the Contributors xxii
Acknowledgments xxxiv

PART I   Overview   1

Chapter 1   An Introduction to Facing the Challenges of a
Multi-Age Workforce: A Use-Inspired Approach 3
*Lisa M. Finkelstein, Donald M. Truxillo, Franco Fraccaroli,
and Ruth Kanfer*

PART II   Science Confronts the Global Challenges   23

Issue 1: Organizations and Teams Go Global   25

Chapter 2   Age Diversity and Global Teamwork: A Future
Agenda for Researchers and Practitioners 27
Florian Kunze and Stephan A. Boehm

Chapter 3   Human Resource Management and Sustainability
at Work Across the Lifespan: An Integrative
Perspective 50
*Annet H. de Lange, Dorien T. A. M. Kooij, and
Beatrice I. J. M. van der Heijden*

Issue 2: Patterns of Employment and Unemployment — 81

Chapter 4 The Challenge of Building Human Capital and Benefiting from It: A Person-Centric View of Youth Unemployment and Underemployment 83
José M. Peiró, Ana Hernández, and José Ramos

Chapter 5 The Aging Workforce and the Demands of Work in the 21st Century 108
Margaret E. Beier

Chapter 6 Work Ability and Aging 134
Juhani Ilmarinen and Ville Ilmarinen

Issue 3: Challenges Facing Specific Workforce Sectors — 157

Chapter 7 The Implications of Changes in Job Demands for the Continued and Future Employment of Older Workers 159
Sara J. Czaja, Joseph Sharit, Neil Charness, and Andrew C. Schmidt

Chapter 8 Aging and Emotional Labor Processes 180
James M. Diefendorff, Jennifer Tehan Stanley, and Allison S. Gabriel

Issue 4: Practical Workplace Changes and Challenges — 207

Chapter 9 Workplace Intervention Effectiveness Across the Lifespan 209
Keith L. Zabel and Boris B. Baltes

Chapter 10 Retirement and Bridge Employment: People, Context, and Time 230
Yujie Zhan and Mo Wang

Issue 5: Age Differences and Discrimination — 251

Chapter 11 Intergenerational Perceptions and Conflicts in Multi-Age and Multigenerational Work Environments 253
Cort W. Rudolph and Hannes Zacher

Chapter 12 A Comparison of EEO Law on Workforce Aging Across English-Speaking Countries.................................. 283
Arthur Gutman and Eric Dunleavy

PART III Multidisciplinary Viewpoints 311

Chapter 13 How Individuals Navigate Social Mobility: Changing Capacities and Opportunities in Careers Across Adulthood.. 313
Jutta Heckhausen and Jacob Shane

Chapter 14 Labor Force Transitions in Late Life: Between Agency and Structure.. 321
Kène Henkens

Chapter 15 Optimizing Older Workforces 330
Laura L. Carstensen, Michaela E. Beals, and Martha Deevy

PART IV Editor Viewpoints 337

Chapter 16 Employment Transitions in Late Adulthood................... 339
Ruth Kanfer

Chapter 17 An Aging Workforce: The Contribution of Work, Industrial, and Organizational Psychology 344
Franco Fraccaroli

Chapter 18 Developing "Best Practices" for Organizations: A Gap in the Current Aging Research............................. 350
Donald M. Truxillo

Chapter 19 Now That We Know What . . . *How?* 356
Lisa M. Finkelstein

Author Index.. 363
Subject Index... 366

Series Foreword

This volume focuses on a topic of growing importance in the new age of work. As the 21st century unfolds, it is clear that the nature of work is much different now than the one experienced by our parents. Technical advances and globalization have created the need for a shift in job characteristics to focus more on problem solving, cultural awareness, and interpersonal skills and away from physical demands. These trends have also begun to fundamentally change the work environments, work roles, and tasks that individuals perform.

At the same time, there has been a sea change in the nature of the available workforce. Demographic trends point to continuing age diversity at work, as individuals live longer, healthier lives and seek jobs that provide for satisfaction of basic human motives related to psychological and economic well-being. The focus of this volume—worker age as it affects the individual's experience of work, the workplace, and the organization—addresses the interface between changes in work and changes in the workforce, and some of the most important challenges to face scholars and practitioners concerned with work in the new millennium.

This volume, edited by Lisa Finkelstein, Donald Truxillo, Franco Fraccaroli, and Ruth Kanfer, identifies the key research needs in this area and ways to address them. First, and perhaps most importantly, the volume underscores the many scholarly and practical consequences of growing age diversity in the workplace that is occurring around the world. Research, issues, and controversies related to workforce aging and age-diversity management have appeared with increasing frequency in our field over the past few decades. All too often, however, such work has been scattered across our field, precluding effective information and idea sharing between researchers working in different areas and human resource managers dealing with specific age-related concerns. The editors of this volume have effectively organized these diverse and often disparate lines of research and practice around a "use-inspired" perspective that highlights the synergies that can occur when thinking about employee age and age-diverse workplaces from multiple basic and applied perspectives.

Specifically, this book adopts a framework that organizes scholarly viewpoints and practical problems around four global challenges: (1) changes in the organization and management of work in the 21st century; (2) age-related differences in the meaning and impact of work on workers; (3) specific worker issues; and (4) practical challenges. The inclusion of a final multidisciplinary section that examines the meaning of a multi-age workforce from economic and developmental viewpoints further highlights the value of understanding age diversity from a person-centric perspective that incorporates the role of non-work forces on workplace behavior and attitudes.

The editors have assembled an impressive array of authors to contribute to our understanding of the challenges, solutions, and research needs of the future when it comes to dealing with workers of different ages and a multi-age workforce. In each chapter, authors provide new insights on promising research directions and evidence to support the use of practices that foster employee inclusion and performance in age-diverse workplaces. The emphasis placed on how research findings may be translated into effective organizational and human resource management practices throughout this volume responds to the growing call for an integrative science, and represents a major benefit of this volume for both researchers and practitioners.

On behalf of the SIOP membership and SIOP's Organizational Frontier Series Editorial Board, we thank the editors and contributors for this timely and integrative volume. The framework and aggregation of empirical evidence on this topic make an important contribution to the development of organizational science and practice in this emerging area, and serves as an inspiration to those concerned with the twin goals of promoting employee effectiveness and organizational performance in a world of work increasingly characterized by high levels of age diversity.

Eduardo Salas
Organizational Frontier Series, Past Editor
University of Central Florida

Preface

Although we do not recall actually discussing it with each other directly at the time, looking back it seems this book was "in the air" back in November of 2011 at the University of Trento in Rovereto, Italy. Two of us (Truxillo and Fraccaroli) were organizers of and presenters at the European Association for Work and Organizational Psychology's Small Group Meeting on Aging at Work, and the other two of us (Finkelstein and Kanfer) were keynote speakers at that meeting. This meeting brought together an intimate group of researchers from several countries dedicated to the issues facing the aging workforce. The blend of scholars with different cultural and disciplinary backgrounds, but a shared sense of excitement and passion for this topic, led to an intellectual and collegial experience that exceeded all of our expectations. (The delicious food, wine, and coffee that kept us going did not hurt either.)

All of us left that meeting with a re-energized sense of purpose and a widened perspective for the topic of aging and work. Shortly thereafter, at the SIOP meeting in San Diego in 2012, the seed of a Frontiers Series Book was born, with the goal of capturing the exciting new ideas of I-O psychologists from around the world.

Our vision for this book had five dimensions. We strove for a book that was multicultural, interdisciplinary, use-inspired, person-centric, and future-oriented.

First, there was a palpable sense of urgency regarding this issue from scholars around the globe, even if different countries may have some different societal perspectives and economic priorities around these issues. This emphasized to us the central importance of having a perspective that goes beyond the United States.

Second, we are constantly reminded that the aging workforce is a concern in disciplines beyond I-O psychology. Although this volume contains chapters that build primarily on perspectives dominant in I-O psychology and management, we also invited commentaries from scholars representing other disciplines to weigh in on the issues through their own disciplinary lenses.

Third, we asked that authors take a "use-inspired" approach to their chapters. Though we elaborate more on this in Chapter 1, for those less familiar with this concept, it means that we asked authors to focus on research that is needed to answer pressing societal issues. This is not to say that research for its own sake is not important, but we wanted to emphasize that the aging workforce is a looming crisis that I-O psychology must be prepared to address as it unfolds in the coming decades.

Fourth, we felt strongly about carrying a person-centric focus or theme throughout the chapters in the book. We, as I-O psychologists, have tended to conceptualize people in terms of the variables we are studying at the moment rather than in terms of the whole, complex person. In the case of the aging workforce and work, it means that we need to acknowledge that the person functions not only as an employee within the organization, but within a family, society, culture, and economic system as well; they make decisions within their own, individual framework. For example, retirement decisions are based on a complex set of factors, including the individual's family, economic, and health situation, all operating within larger societal, cultural, and national contexts.

Finally, we took the notion of Frontiers very literally in our vision for this book, and requested that the authors not write a conventional "review and integrate past literature, then make a few suggestions for future needs" type of chapter. Rather, we turned this approach on its head: we wanted the authors just to describe the current state of affairs quite quickly in their chapters, and to spend the majority of their pages on a vision for future research, guided by the changing landscape of our global workforce now and in the coming decades.

Obviously, we see this book as a useful text for graduate seminars in this area. But more importantly, we hope this volume will serve as an inspiration and a roadmap for work and organizational researchers devoting their efforts to both theoretical advancement and practical problem solving in the critical area of aging and work.

Through the completion of this volume, we have all become increasingly aware of the crucial role that work plays in the outcomes of individuals, organizations, and societies. Although this volume focuses largely on the panoply of changes, both internal and exogenous, that occur during later adulthood and their effects on individual well-being, our journey in completing this volume has convinced us that strategies aimed at improving the employability and well-being of older workers has potential benefits that extend to organizations and societies as well. By focusing on the individual, we hope this volume helps to stimulate new research directions for how organizational practices may better promote and make use of the many assets that these mature individuals bring to the workplace.

Lisa Finkelstein, Donald Truxillo, Franco Fraccaroli, and Ruth Kanfer

Figures

1.1	Trajectories of change across the work lifespan	15
2.1	Conceptual model of potential future research on age diversity in teams and companies	28
3.1	Functions of HR bundles of practices in relation to sustainability at work	69
3.2	An integrative perspective on sustainability at work across the lifespan	69
4.1	Main concepts and issues in a person-centric approach to the study of unemployment	103
5.1	Illustration of how age-related changes in knowledge, skills, abilities, and other characteristics (KSAOs) influence PJ fit with work role demands	110
6.1	The work ability house model, describing the different dimensions affecting human work ability	136
6.2	Work ability (Y: WAI-score) and aging (X: Age) in Finnish employed population (extrapolation from age 66 onwards)	140
6.3	Individual distribution of work ability scores by age in small and middle-sized enterprises in Finland	140
6.4	Work well-being index by age and personnel groups	151
8.1	Within-person emotional labor dynamics and stable influences on emotional labor processes	182
11.1	A model of intergenerational conflict	264
11.2	Google Ngram example	268
11.3	Twitter feed sentiment analysis of generation hashtags	269
14.1	Overall graphical representation of agency within structure	326

Tables

3.1	Different Examples of Definitions for the Concept of Sustainability	53
3.2	Results of Empirical (Peer) Reviewed Studies Focusing on "Sustainable Work"	58
3.3	Meaningful HR Bundles and Specific Example Practices to Facilitate Sustainability at Work (cf. Kooij et al., 2014)	65
5.1	Suggested Future Research Topics	126
6.1	Mean Levels of the Work Ability House Structures by Age Group	150
9.1	Future Research Suggestions to Examine the Effectiveness of Workplace Interventions Across the Lifespan	212
10.1	People, Context, and Time Issues in Retirement and Bridge Employment Research	232
11.1	Propositions and Example Future Research Directions	266
12.1	Countries and Age Laws Considered in This Chapter	285
12.2	Six ADEA Dimensions	287
12.3	Mandatory Retirement Exemptions	289
12.4	Recent Settlements Forced by the EEOC	291
12.5	Themes from Our Global Review of Age Discrimination	303

About the Editors

Lisa M. Finkelstein, Northern Illinois University
Lisa M. Finkelstein received her Ph.D. in Industrial-Organizational Psychology from Tulane University in 1996, and has spent her career thus far on the faculty in the Psychology Department at Northern Illinois University. Dr. Finkelstein's main research area is in aging and work, with specific focal areas in age bias, stereotypes, meta-stereotypes, aging and mentoring relationships, and the conceptualization and measurement of age. Her work on aging appears in such journals as the *Journal of Applied Psychology*, the *Journal of Organizational Behavior*, the *European Journal of Work and Organizational Psychology*, *Group and Organizational Management*, and *Experimental Aging Research*. In 2011, she co-edited a special issue on aging and work for the *Journal of Organizational Behavior*, and in that same year delivered a keynote address on age stereotypes at the European Association of Work and Organizational Psychology's Small Group Meeting on Age Cohorts in the Workplace. She serves as an Associate Editor for Group and Organization Management and on the editorial boards of the *Journal of Management*, the *Journal of Business and Psychology*, and *Work, Age, and Retirement*. She is a Fellow of SIOP and in the past decade she has served as program chair, conference chair, and secretary of SIOP. She has supervised more than 25 master's theses and 17 dissertations, has served as program director of the Social-I/O Area at NIU, and has won a university-level award for her undergraduate teaching. Her other research interests include mentoring, stigmas at work, and humor in the workplace.

Franco Fraccaroli, University of Trento
Franco Fraccaroli is a Professor in the Department of Psychology and Cognitive Science, University of Trento, Rovereto, Italy, where he has been Director of the Department and Dean of the Faculty. He has served as President of the European Association of Work and Organizational Psychology and he has been the Co-President of the XIII Congress of EAWOP in Santiago de Compostela (Spain, 2009). He is President of the board of delegates of the Alliance for Organizational Psychology. His main areas of research are transitions to work, experience of joblessness,

psychology of working times, elderly workers and the work exit phase, psychosocial risk, and quality of organizational life. His works have been published in such international journals as the *Journal of Organizational Behavior, Work and Stress*, the *European Journal of Work and Organizational Psychology*, the *European Journal of Psychological Assessment*, and *Violence and Victims*. He has been co-editor of a special issue of the *European Journal of Work and Organizational Psychology* on age in the workplace, and he co-organized the EAWOP Small Group Meeting at the University of Trento in November 2011 on Age at Work.

Ruth Kanfer, Georgia Institute of Technology
Ruth Kanfer is a Professor of Psychology at Georgia Institute of Technology in Atlanta, Georgia, USA. She has published extensively on motivation and self-regulation related to job skill training, academic achievement and job performance, teamwork, and employment transitions. She organized the 2008 SIOP-FBPCS Science Forum on "*The World of Work in the 21st Century: Older Workers, New Work Roles, and Age-Diverse Workplaces,*" and has served on the Scientific Advisory Board of the Center for Lifelong Learning and Development at Jacobs University in Bremen, Germany, and as APA Representative to the Federation for Brain and Behavior Sciences, and currently serves on the editorial boards of *Applied Psychology: An International Review*, the *Journal of Occupational and Organizational Psychology*, and *Human Performance*. She is a Fellow of the American Psychological Association (APA), the Association for Psychological Sciences (APS), and the Society for Industrial and Organizational Psychology (SIOP), and has received the *APA Distinguished Scientific Award for an Early Career Contribution to Psychology in Applied Research*, the *Academy of Management (AoM) Outstanding Publication Award in Organizational Behavior*, the *SIOP William R. Owens Scholarly Achievement Award*, and the *SIOP Distinguished Scientific Contributions Award*.

Donald M. Truxillo, Portland State University
Donald M. Truxillo is a Professor in the Department of Psychology at Portland State University. His work examines aging workforce issues, including age stereotypes and job design for older and younger workers. In addition, his research examines personnel selection methods and applicant reactions to the selection process. His work has been published in outlets such as the *Journal of Applied Psychology, Personnel Psychology*, and the *Journal of Management*. He is a member of six editorial boards and he is an Associate Editor at *Work, Aging and Retirement*. He is a Fellow

of SIOP, Association for Psychological Science, the American Psychological Association, and the International Association for Applied Psychology. He currently serves as Treasurer for the Alliance for Organizational Psychology. He is the recipient of SIOP's 2012 Distinguished Service Contributions Award. Since 2010 he has served on the Doctoral School Committee, Department of Psychological Science and Education, University of Trento, Italy.

About the Contributors

Boris B. Baltes, Wayne State University
Boris B. Baltes is a Professor and the Chair of the Department of Psychology at Wayne State University. His research interests include examining the effects of stereotypes on workplace outcomes, age and workplace issues, and work-family balance. He currently serves as an Associate/Action Editor for the *Journal of Organizational Behavior* and is on the editorial boards of *Organizational Research Methods*, and the *Journal of Business and Psychology*. Dr. Baltes is a Fellow of SIOP (APA Division 14). He received his Ph.D. in I-O Psychology from Northern Illinois University in 1998.

Michaela E. Beals, Stanford University
Michaela E. Beals is a Social Science Research Assistant at the Stanford Center on Longevity. She supports the research, writing, and conference planning needs of the Center. Her work focuses on lifelong individual financial security, including the need to work longer, retirement planning, and avoiding financial fraud. Prior to joining the Center, Beals was a Graduate Research Assistant at the University of Kansas Fragile X Lab. She received an M.A. in Anthropology and a B.A. in Speech-Language-Hearing Sciences and Disorders from the University of Kansas.

Margaret E. Beier, Rice University
Margaret E. Beier is an Associate Professor of Psychology at Rice University in Houston, Texas. She received her B.A. from Colby College (Cum Laude), and her M.S. and Ph.D. degrees from the Georgia Institute of Technology. Margaret's research tests and extends theoretical models of individual differences in age, gender, cognitive ability, personality traits, and motivation as they relate to success in educational and organizational environments. Her work has been published in top-tier journals in both areas (the *Journal of Applied Psychology*, the *Journal of Experimental Psychology: General, Personnel Psychology*, and *Psychological Bulletin*). She serves on the editorial boards of the *Journal of Business and Psychology* and *Work, Aging, and Retirement*, and she is a fellow of the Society for Industrial and Organizational Psychologists (SIOP).

Stephan A. Boehm, University of St. Gallen

Stephan Boehm is an Assistant Professor of Business Administration at the University of St. Gallen, Switzerland, where he also serves as the Director of the Center for Disability and Integration (CDI-HSG). He received his master's and his Ph.D. from the University of St. Gallen. In 2008 and spring 2009, he worked as a Visiting Research Fellow at the Oxford Institute of Ageing at the University of Oxford, UK. His research focuses on leadership, diversity, and human resource management. He has a special interest in the vocational inclusion of employees with disabilities and health-focused leadership, as well as the management of demographic change within companies.

Laura L. Carstensen, Stanford University

Laura L. Carstensen is Professor of Psychology and the Fairleigh S. Dickinson Jr. Professor in Public Policy at Stanford University, where she is also the Founding Director of the Stanford Center on Longevity. She was a Guggenheim Fellow in 2003 and is now a member of the MacArthur Foundation's Research Network on an Aging Society. She currently serves on the National Advisory Council on Aging to NIA. Carstensen has won numerous awards, including the Kleemeier Award, the Distinguished Mentorship Award from the Gerontological Society of America, and the Master Mentor Award from the American Psychological Association. She received a B.S. from the University of Rochester and a Ph.D. in Clinical Psychology from West Virginia University.

Neil Charness, Florida State University

Neil Charness is William G. Chase Professor of Psychology, Interim Director of the Institute for Successful Longevity, and an Associate of the Pepper Institute on Aging and Public Policy at Florida State University. He received his B.A. from McGill University (1969) and his M.Sc. (1971) and Ph.D. (1974) from Carnegie Mellon University in Psychology. He has been an Assistant Professor at Wilfrid Laurier University in Ontario, Canada (1974–1977), then Assistant, Associate, and Full Professor at the University of Waterloo, Ontario, Canada (1977–1994), before joining the Psychology Department at Florida State University in 1994. His research centers on understanding the aging process and its implications for technology use, particularly for health, as well as work performance and expert performance. Dr. Charness is also a member of the CREATE team and the lead investigator for CREATE at the Florida State University site.

Sara J. Czaja, University of Miami

Sara J. Czaja is a Leonard M. Miller Professor of Psychiatry and Behavioral Sciences, and a Professor of Industrial Engineering at the University of Miami. She is also the Scientific Director of the Center on Aging at the University of Miami Miller School of Medicine and the Director of the Center on Research and Education for Aging and Technology Enhancement (CREATE). CREATE is funded by the National Institute on Aging, and involves collaboration with the Georgia Institute of Technology and Florida State University. The focus of CREATE is on making technology more accessible, useful, and usable for older adult populations. Dr. Czaja has extensive experience in aging research and a long commitment to developing strategies to improve the quality of life for older adults. Her research interests include: aging and cognition, aging and healthcare informatics, caregiving, older workers, human-computer interaction, training, and functional assessment. Dr. Czaja is very well published in the field of aging and has written numerous book chapters and scientific articles. She is a fellow of the American Psychological Association, the Human Factors and Ergonomics Society, and the Gerontological Society of America. She is also a member of the National Academy of Science/National Research Council Board on Human Systems Integration.

Martha Deevy, Stanford University

Martha Deevy joined the Stanford Center on Longevity as a Senior Research Scholar in January 2009 and serves as Director of the Financial Security Division. She has over 20 years of management experience in Silicon Valley technology and financial services companies in senior executive positions at Apple, Charles Schwab, and Intuit. Martha has held positions in marketing, business development, product development, strategic planning, finance, and IT. The goal of the Financial Security Division at the Stanford Center on Longevity is to think differently about the perceived problems around an aging population, especially retirement planning and the need to work longer. The Financial Security Division investigates solutions and catalyzes research on how individuals can be assured of a financially secure retirement. She received an M.B.A. from the University of Minnesota and a B.A. in Economics from the University of Illinois.

Annet H. de Lange, HAN University of Applied Sciences

Dr. Annet de Lange works as Professor Human Resource Management (Lector) at the HAN University of Applied Sciences in Arnhem and Nijmegen, and as Visiting Professor at the faculty of Social Sciences of the

University of Stavanger in Norway. Moreover, she is Director of a Dutch Knowledge Center focusing on knowledge exchange on the topic: Sustainability at Work and Human Resource Management (NKDI; including representatives from the Dutch government, municipalities, unions, large-scale and medium-sized companies, Healthy Ageing Northern Netherlands, temporary agencies, and researchers). Her research activities have been focused on "HRM and sustainable work ability of ageing workers." Her research has been successful, culminating in a *cum laude* doctorate, several honorary prizes (IBM Frye Stipendium, André Büssing Memorial Prize, Stichting Praemium Erasmianum Prize, the Journal of Occupational Health Psychology best paper of past ten years Award), national and international grants, and publications in top occupational (health) journals. Furthermore, she serves as Consulting Editor on journals such as *Work and Stress* and the *European Journal Of Work and Organizational Psychology*, and served as Special Guest Editor of several special issues focusing on aging at work (the *Journal of Managerial Psychology*, the *Journal of Organizational and Occupational Psychology*, and *Gedrag & Organisatie*). More information: www.annetdelange.nl.

James M. Diefendorff, University of Akron

Dr. James Diefendorff received his Ph.D. in Industrial-Organizational Psychology from the University of Akron. His research interests include self-regulatory processes, work motivation, and emotional labor. Dr. Diefendorff's research has been funded by the National Science Foundation and his publications have appeared in leading I-O psychology and management journals. Dr. Diefendorff is on the editorial boards of the *Journal of Applied Psychology*, *Organizational Behavior and Human Decision Processes*, *Personnel Psychology*, the *Journal of Vocational Behavior*, and the *Journal of Business and Psychology*. Dr. Diefendorff is currently a Professor of Psychology at the University of Akron. Prior to joining the faculty at the University of Akron, Dr. Diefendorff served on the faculty in the Psychology Department at Louisiana State University and in the Business School at the University of Colorado at Denver. He also has been a Visiting Scholar at Singapore Management University, the University of Osnabrück, and Hong Kong Polytechnic University.

Eric Dunleavy, DCI Consulting Group

Eric Dunleavy received his Ph.D. in Industrial-Organizational Psychology in 2004 from the University of Houston. He is a Principal Consultant at DCI, where he is involved in equal employment audit and litigation consulting. He also serves on staff with the Center for Corporate Equality (CCE), a national nonprofit employer and research association in Washington, DC. He has served as President of the Personnel Testing Council of Metropolitan Washington, DC, and was on the editorial board of *The Industrial-Organizational Psychologist* (TIP), where he co-authored the "On the Legal Front" column with Art Gutman. In 2011, Eric won the first Distinguished Early Career Contributions—Practice award from SIOP.

Allison S. Gabriel, Virginia Commonwealth University
Dr. Allison S. Gabriel is an Assistant Professor of Management in the School of Business at Virginia Commonwealth University. She received her M.A. and Ph.D. in Industrial-Organizational Psychology from the University of Akron and her B.A. in Psychology with honors and highest distinction and a minor in Sociology from the Schreyer Honors College at the Pennsylvania State University. Her research focuses on emotions at work, motivation, job demands, and employee well-being, with an emphasis on within-person processes, and she has been published in leading outlets such as the *Journal of Applied Psychology*, *Personnel Psychology*, and the *Journal of Occupational and Organizational Psychology*. In 2014, her dissertation won the S. Rains Wallace Dissertation Award for the best dissertation in Industrial-Organizational Psychology from the Society for Industrial and Organizational Psychology. Dr. Gabriel currently serves on the editorial board for the *Journal of Occupational and Organizational Psychology*.

Arthur Gutman, Florida Institute of Technology
Arthur Gutman is Professor Emeritus of Psychology and past chair of the I-O Psychology program at Florida Tech. He received his Ph.D. from Syracuse University in 1975 and spent two years at the University of Colorado as an NIMH Postdoctoral Fellow and two years at Georgia State University. He had been at Florida Tech since 1979 before retiring in May 2014. He has consulted with public and private employers, including the Center for Substance Abuse Prevention, the Florida Supreme Court, the Department of Defense's Equal Opportunity Management Institute, the Brevard County Police Testing Center, Intersil Corporation, and Holmes Regional Medical Center. His main teaching interests are in EEO law, personnel selection, statistics, and program evaluation. He has created and validated tests for manufacturing jobs and redesigned selection procedures for police forces. He has served as an expert witness on EEO claims, but his favorite sport is to train employers and employees to detect and prevent illegal workplace discriminatory behaviors so as to prevent the need for

court action. He was on the board of editors of TIP and co-authored a quarterly column called "On the Legal Front" with Eric Dunleavy. He is first author of *EEO Law and Personnel Practices*, 3rd edition, published by Routledge in 2010.

Jutta Heckhausen, University of California Irvine
Jutta Heckhausen is a Professor of Psychology and Social Behavior at the University of California, Irvine, where she heads the Laboratory on Life-Span Development and Motivation. After receiving her Ph.D. from the University of Strathclyde, she was a Senior Research Scientist at the Max Planck Institute for Human Development and Education before joining the University of California, Irvine in 2000. She is a Fellow of the Gerontological Society of America, and has been selected to receive the 2014 Baltes Distinguished Research Achievement Award of the American Psychological Association (APA), Division 20 (Adult Development and Aging). Her research addresses the role of the individual as an active agent in major life-course transitions and when confronted with challenging life events.

Kène Henkens, Netherlands Interdisciplinary Demographic Institute
Kène Henkens is a Sociologist and head of the Themegroup on Work, Aging and Retirement of the Netherlands Interdisciplinary Demographic Institute (NIDI). He is a Professor of Sociology of Retirement at the Department of Sociology, University Of Amsterdam. He is also affiliated with the Department of Health Sciences, University Medical Center Groningen, University of Groningen. He has published extensively on issues regarding the labor supply in an aging workforce. His main research interest is in the area of retirement.

Ana Hernández, University of Valencia
Ana Hernández got her Ph.D. in Psychology in 1998 at the University of Valencia, where she has been Associate Professor since 2003. She has a double affiliation with the Department of Methodology of Behavioral Sciences, and the Research Institute for Personnel Psychology, Organizational Development, and Quality of Working Life (IDOCAL). Since 2012, she is Coordinator of the Studies Section in the Observatory of Job Insertion and Occupational Guidance at the University of Valencia (OPAL). Her main methodological research interests are related to validity of measurement instruments, in general, and scale and item functioning, in particular. She has published about these topics in journals such as *Multivariate Behavioral Research*, the *Journal of Applied Psychology*, and

Structural Equation Modeling, among others. Regarding Work, Organizational, and Personnel Psychology, her main research interests are related to leadership, teamwork and team climate, and underemployment. She has recently published on these topics in journals such as the *Journal of Applied Psychology* and *Computers in Human Behavior*, and the book *Underemployment: Psychological, Economic, and Social Challenges*.

Juhani Ilmarinen, Finnish Institute of Occupational Health
Juhani Ilmarinen received his Ph.D. in Health and Sport Sciences from the University of Cologne, Germany, in 1978. From 1992 to 2005, he was the Professor and Director of the Department of Physiology, and from 2006 to 2008 the Director of the Theme Life Course and Work at the Finnish Institute of Occupational Health, Helsinki, Finland. His research topics are Work Ability and Ageing. Professor Ilmarinen has more than 500 publications, and has published eight books. Ilmarinen was the Secretary of the Scientific Committee Ageing and Work of the International Commission on Occupational Health from 1989 to 2006, and Chairman of the Technical Committee Ageing of the International Ergonomics Association from 1997 to 2007. After retirement in 2009, he is running his own consultancy and working mostly in the European Union.

Ville Ilmarinen, University of Helsinki
Ville Ilmarinen received his M.A. in Psychology at the University of Helsinki in 2012. He is currently working on his doctoral dissertation in the field of Personality and Social Psychology at the Department of Behavioral Sciences in the University of Helsinki. Besides working on his Ph.D., he attempts to contribute to the field of occupational health by studying self-report work ability measurement methods.

Dorien T. A. M. Kooij, Tilburg University
Dr. Dorien Kooij is an assistant professor at the Department of Human Resource Studies of Tilburg University, the Netherlands. Her research focuses on aging at work, and in particular on HR practices for older workers, on how work motivation changes with aging, on age-related factors such as future time perspective, and on job crafting. Her research has been successful, culminating in several awards, such as the HRM Network Best Dissertation Award 2011. She has published in international peer-reviewed journals such as the *Journal of Organizational Behavior*, the *Journal of Occupational and Organizational Psychology*, and *Psychology and Aging*.

Florian Kunze, Universität Konstanz

Florian Kunze is Professor and Holder of the Chair for Organizational Studies at the University of Konstanz, Germany. Before, he was an Assistant Professor at the University of St. Gallen, Switzerland, where he also completed his dissertation in 2010. In 2012, he spent 12 months as a Visiting Scholar at the University of California Los Angeles (UCLA). His main research focus is on processes triggered by the demographic change in companies, diversity management in teams and companies, and evidence-based human resource management.

José M. Peiró, University of Valencia

Jose M. Peiró received his Ph.D. in the University of Valencia in 1977. He is currently Professor of Work and Organizational Psychology and Director of the Research Institute of Human Resources Psychology, Organizational Development and Quality of Working Life (IDOCAL) at the University of Valencia. He is also Senior Researcher at the IVIE (Economic Research Institute) and Director of the Observatory of Spanish Youth Labor Market Entry (Ivie-Bancaja Foundation) since 1995. Dr. Peiró is Founder and served as Director of the Observatory of Graduates' Early Career Development and the Career Service of the University of Valencia (2003–2009). He served as Associate Editor of the *European Journal of Work and Organizational Psychology* (1995–2008) and is currently member of the scientific boards of the *Journal of Management*, the *European Journal of Work and Organizational Psychology*, and *Work and Stress*. His research topics are occupational stress, unemployment, overqualification and employability of youth, psychosocial risk prevention at work, absenteeism, organizational climate and culture, teamwork, leadership, and customer satisfaction in service organizations.

José Ramos, University of Valencia

José Ramos got his Ph.D. in Work and Organizational Psychology in 1993 at the University of Valencia, where he is Full Professor since 2010. Previously, he has served as Associate Lecturer (1993–1999) and Lecturer (1999–2010) in the Department of Social Psychology. He is a member of the Research Institute for Personnel Psychology, Organizational Development, and Quality of Working Life (IDOCAL, University of Valencia) and Associate Researcher at the Valencia Institute of Economic Research (IVIE). He has served as Vice-Dean of Academic Management (1999–2006) and Dean (2006–2012) of the Faculty of Psychology at the University of Valencia. He is a member of the Spanish National Award Committee for the European Diploma in Psychology (EURO-PSY; EFPA) (2007–2010) and is Secretary General of the Committee (2010–). His research interests focus on such topics as service quality, user's satisfaction, organizational climate, occupational stress and health, psychological contract, and more recently on youth unemployment and underemployment. He has published articles in journals such as *Work and Stress*, the *European Journal of Work and Organizational Psychology*, *Psychological Reports*, *Applied Psychology: An International Journal*, *International Labour Review*, *Stress and Health*, and the *International Journal of Stress Management*.

Cort W. Rudolph, Saint Louis University
Cort W. Rudolph, Ph.D., is an Assistant Professor of Industrial and Organizational Psychology at Saint Louis University, where he also serves as the Primary Investigator and Director of the Sustainable Employability Across the Lifespan (S.E.A.L.) Laboratory. He earned a B.A. from DePaul University, and an M.A. and Ph.D. from Wayne State University. Cort's research focuses broadly on issues related to aging and work processes, sustainable employability, and applications of lifespan development theory. Cort is also a member of the editorial board of *Work, Aging and Retirement*.

Andrew C. Schmidt, University of Miami
Andrew Schmidt is a Research Associate at the University of Miami's Center on Aging. He graduated from Florida International University in 2013 with a Bachelor's Degree in Psychology with a focus on Biological Psychology and Neuropsychology and maintains a particular interest in the neural mechanisms of cognitive decline and serious mental illness and how they relate to cognitive rehabilitation. He would like to thank Drs. Czaja and Sharit for the wealth of experience and opportunities they have given them throughout his tenure at the Center on Aging, and also extend his gratitude to his family and loved ones for their love and support along the way.

Jacob Shane, CUNY Brooklyn College
Jacob Shane is an Assistant Professor of Psychology at CUNY Brooklyn College. He received his Ph.D. in Psychology from the University of California, Irvine in 2014, where he worked with Dr. Jutta Heckhausen in the Laboratory on Life-Span Development and Motivation. His dissertation research was funded from the Alison Clarke-Steward Graduate Student Dissertation Award and a grant from the Institute for Research on Labor and Employment. His research focuses generally on the intersection

between motivation and opportunity, and more specifically on career and social mobility goal pursuit across adulthood.

Joseph Sharit, University of Miami
Joseph Sharit is Research Professor of Industrial Engineering, Department of Industrial Engineering at the University of Miami. He received his M.S. and Ph.D. degrees from the School of Industrial Engineering at Purdue University. He holds secondary appointments in the Department of Psychiatry and Behavioral Sciences and in the Department of Anesthesiology at the University of Miami Miller School of Medicine. At the medical school, he is an Investigator responsible for research activities within the Center on Research and Education for Aging and Technology Enhancement (CREATE). He is also affiliated with the Laboratory of E-Learning and Multimedia Research within the Miami VA's Geriatric Research, Education, and Clinical Center (CRECC). His research interests in aging and performance involve older adult interaction with e-health and other technologies such as the Internet and patient portals, as well as other technological systems and work settings.

Jennifer Tehan Stanley, University of Akron
Jennifer Tehan Stanley, Ph.D., is an Assistant Professor of Psychology at the University of Akron. Dr. Stanley received her Ph.D. in Experimental Psychology with a focus in Cognitive Aging from Georgia Institute of Technology. She then completed a postdoctoral fellowship funded by the National Institute on Aging at Brandeis University. Dr. Stanley specializes in adult development and aging, with a particular focus on socio-emotional functioning. She is interested in the mechanisms and consequences of age-related differences in emotion perception and emotion regulation. Dr. Stanley's work has been published in top-tier aging and emotion journals, including *Psychology and Aging*, *Developmental Psychology*, the *Journal of Gerontology*, and the *Journal of Emotion*.

Beatrice I. J. M. van der Heijden, Radboud University Nijmegen
Beatrice I. J. M. van der Heijden is Chair of the Department of Strategic HRM at the Radboud University Nijmegen, Institute for Management Research. She is also affiliated as Professor of Strategic HRM with the Open Universiteit in the Netherlands and with the University of Twente, the Netherlands. Her main research areas are career development, employability, and aging at work. Van der Heijden is Associate Editor of the *European Journal of Work and Organizational Psychology*, and has

published, among others, in the *Journal of Vocational Behavior*, *HRM*, the *Journal of Occupational and Organizational Psychology*, and *Career Development International*.

Mo Wang, University of Florida
Dr. Mo Wang is a tenured Professor at the Warrington College of Business Administration at the University of Florida. He is also the Director of Human Resource Research Center at the University of Florida. He specializes in research areas of retirement and older worker employment, expatriate and newcomer adjustment, occupational health psychology, leadership and team processes, and advanced quantitative methodologies. He has received the Academy of Management HR Division Scholarly Achievement Award (2008), the Careers Division Best Paper Award (2009), and the European Commission's Erasmus Mundus Scholarship for Work, Organizational, and Personnel Psychology (2009) for his research in these areas. He also received Early Career Contribution/Achievement Awards from the American Psychological Association (2013), FABBS (2013), the Society for Industrial-Organizational Psychology (2012), the Academy of Management's HR Division (2011), the Research Methods Division (2011), and the Society for Occupational Health Psychology (2009). He was the Editor of *The Oxford Handbook of Retirement*. He also serves as the Editor-in-Chief for *Work, Aging, and Retirement* and as an Associate Editor for the *Journal of Applied Psychology*. Dr. Wang currently serves as the President of Society for Occupational Health Psychology (2014–2015) and the Director for the Science of Organizations Program at the National Science Foundation (2014–2015).

Keith L. Zabel, Wayne State University
Keith L. Zabel is currently a fifth-year doctoral student at Wayne State University in Detroit, Michigan. In 2011, he was the only I-O graduate student in the United States to receive the three-year National Science Foundation Graduate Research Fellowship. His research interests are broadly around diversified mentoring relationships and aging in the workplace.

Hannes Zacher, University of Groningen
Hannes Zacher is an Associate Professor of Organizational Psychology at the University of Groningen in the Netherlands. He received his Ph.D. in Industrial and Organizational Psychology from the University of Giessen (Germany) in 2009. Subsequently, he was a Postdoctoral Fellow at Jacobs

University (Germany) and Lecturer at the University of Queensland (Australia). His research focuses on different forms of organizational sustainability, with emphases on successful aging at work and career development, proactivity, innovation, leadership, and entrepreneurship, and pro-environmental employee behaviors. He is a member of the founding editorial board of *Work, Aging and Retirement* published by Oxford University Press.

Yujie Zhan, Wilfrid Laurier University
Dr. Yujie Zhan is an Assistant Professor of Organizational Behavior/Human Resource Management in the School of Business and Economics at Wilfrid Laurier University. She holds a Ph.D. in Industrial-Organizational Psychology from the University of Maryland. Her research primarily focuses on older worker employment and retirement, emotion regulation at work, and occupational health psychology. Her research has been published in academic journals including the *Academy of Management Journal*, the *Journal of Applied Psychology*, *Personnel Psychology*, and the *Journal of Occupational Health Psychology*. She has won the Best Paper Award (2009) from the Careers Division of the Academy of Management for her research on retirement.

Acknowledgments

We are most thankful to all of the authors who contributed chapters to this book. We challenged the authors to employ a use-inspired, person-centric lens in addressing their topic and to provide a bold and creative agenda with respect to future research needed on the topic of meeting the challenges of an aging, age-diverse workforce. Each author accepted this challenge and accomplished these goals in interesting and stimulating ways. We are very grateful for the time and energy they devoted to this project and are very proud of the outcome.

We also would like to thank the SIOP Frontiers Board, past and present. This book was accepted under the leadership of Eduardo Salas and his board, and continued to be supported by Richard Klimoski and his board. These board members helped us to crystallize our project goals and provided generously of their time to support the project through all its phases. We thank these individuals for their service to SIOP and to the field.

At Psychology Press, Anne Duffy took on our project and provided the encouragement and guidance we needed to get the project underway. After Anne's retirement, Madeleine Hamlin helped keep things going, and finally Lee Transue and Lauren Verity at Psychology Press, and Amy Wheeler and Andrew Craddock at Florence Production Ltd., brought us to the home stretch. We appreciate the expert guidance of these individuals and Psychology Press in helping us to craft a product that we hope will be of interest to students and faculty alike.

Over the past few years, we have been stimulated by our many conversations with colleagues who have attended the Small Group Meetings on Aging and Work co-sponsored by the Society for Industrial and Organizational Psychology and European Association of Work and Organizational Psychology.

The diversity of perspectives represented at these meetings encouraged us to think about the issues associated with an aging workforce from multiple lenses and reinforced our motivation for producing a volume that brings to bear scientific progress on the important practical issues that currently face policymakers, research scholars, and older workers across the developed world. We also each wish to thank our families and colleagues at our home institutions for their daily support and steadfast encouragement over the past two years. Their support was crucial in creating the space and time for us to produce the integrative volume we sought.

Finally, we wish to thank the many unnamed individuals who have contributed their time in order to provide the data that have so helped advance research in the area. Aging is a difficult topic for most of us to address, and the willingness of these individuals to participate in research and share their thoughts about work life with us has been invaluable and inspiring.

Lisa M. Finkelstein
Donald M. Truxillo
Franco Fraccaroli
Ruth Kanfer

Part I

Overview

1

An Introduction to Facing the Challenges of a Multi-Age Workforce: A Use-Inspired Approach

Lisa M. Finkelstein, Donald M. Truxillo, Franco Fraccaroli, and Ruth Kanfer

This volume addresses what is arguably one of the industrialized world's most pressing challenges at the start of the 21st century; namely, how best to promote employability and well-being in an increasingly older workforce and age-diverse workplace. In North America, Asia, and Europe, aging populations, reductions in birth rates, and new patterns of late life workforce participation have already begun to influence societal norms, public policy, and organizational practices. Organizational and work scholars have also begun to devote systematic attention to the issues associated with these population trends, as evidenced by the growing number of special journal issues and books devoted to effectively managing an aging workforce. In this edited volume, we seek to provide readers with an overview of the substantial progress on this topic and the insights of researchers pursuing these issues pertaining to what needs to be done in the future.

The issues associated with workforce aging demand an interdisciplinary understanding of the psychological, economic, and sociocultural forces that dynamically shape worker behavior and organizational practices. In psychology, accumulating research in developmental lifespan psychology documents the different trajectories of growth, stability, and decline in human cognition, skills, preferences, and competencies over the lifespan. Taken together, these findings portray a complex picture of the individual as a "work in progress," whose contributions to the workplace develop and change over the lifespan as a function of biology and work and non-work conditions.

Research in industrial-organizational (I-O) psychology paints a similarly intricate picture of the role that age diversity may play in managerial practices, in key organizational practices, such as personnel selection and job training, and the impact that organizations have on major life decisions that workers make in later adulthood, such as when and how to retire. Findings in labor economics further show the role that societal laws, social norms, family demands, education, and gender may have on patterns of work participation in midlife and late life, particularly following periods of unemployment. As the contributors to this volume repeatedly suggest, a modern account of work life aging requires the contribution of findings from multiple disciplinary perspectives.

In addition to the aging trend in many national workforces, there have also been dramatic changes in the nature of work. As discussed in several chapters in this volume, jobs that demand heavy physical labor are on the decline and are being rapidly replaced by jobs that demand high levels of problem-solving and interpersonal skill. The near ubiquitous use of teams in organizations, for example, has created strong interest in understanding the role of age in how people get along with others in teams. In the organizationally flatter world of knowledge work, performance is often defined in terms of innovation, spurring new interest in understanding the role of age in divergent thinking.

Accordingly, we argue that it is not possible to study workforce aging without taking into account the changing nature of job demands; that is, that these forces operate in unison to create unique situations in which older workers may experience difficulty maintaining or finding suitable work.

The simultaneous aging of the workforce and changes in the nature of work create a host of new challenges for I-O psychology. Although there is a long history of research from the socio-technical perspective for understanding the impact of new technologies on worker performance, there is far less work directed toward understanding how these changes operate in an age-diverse workforce. Similarly, I-O psychologists have made substantial progress investigating the impact of inter-individual differences in knowledge, skills, and abilities on job performance. What is far less well understood, however, is the impact of intra-individual differences on the antecedents and processes that influence job performance. Understanding how and where these simultaneous trends operate in the vast and volatile modern employment landscape represents a critical first step in developing organizational practices that both promote older worker employability and organizational performance. Thus, a second major objective of this volume is to identify the specific research questions that *need to be asked* and studies that *should be undertaken* in order to practically address the challenges associated with an aging workforce in a changing workplace.

This volume seeks to step into this breach, with the goal of setting an agenda for I-O research to address the coming age-related changes to the workforce. Specifically, our primary goal is not to review past research on age at work, but rather to identify what research we should be doing to address age in the workplace. In this chapter, we set the stage for this book, describing the demographic, economic, societal, and technological changes most relevant to the aging workforce; age-related changes that can affect the workplace; and how a use-inspired approach to I-O research can address these issues.

DEMOGRAPHIC PERSPECTIVES

It is widely recognized that economically developed societies are characterized by an overall process of aging. This process is a combined effect of two demographic trends: a general decline in fertility and an increase in life expectancy. Due to these dynamics, the composition of labor forces in these developed societies is changing, and additional change is expected in the coming 30–50 years. The aging phenomenon is exacerbated by the "baby boomer" generation (persons born between 1946 and 1964) that is now entering into the late career and retirement phases, without a new generation of the same size that is entering the labor market.

To provide some figures, the future scenario of the aging process can be summarized through an index, the *projected old-age dependency ratio* (POADR), widely used in demographic studies that seek to monitor changes in population structure. The POADR is the ratio between the projected total number of people aged 65 and over (usually retired people) and the projected number of people of working age (15–64 years old). The projection makes some assumptions about fertility rate, mortality (or life expectancy), and immigration in different countries. For this reason, the index is a good indicator for comparability across countries, although the overall accuracy is limited because of the high level of uncertainty of the assumptions (Eurostat, 2011; Kinsella & Phillips, 2005; United Nations, 2012).

Eurostat (2012a) produced a scenario based on 2008 data, using changes in the POADR from 1960 to 2060 in 27 European countries. This analysis provides critical insights into the adequacy of pension systems and sustainability of public finances. At the same time, it allows for some forecasts related to the age structure of the working population in the future (Giannakouris, 2008).

These documents can be summarized as follows. First, the portion of people aged 65 years or over is projected to become 30% of the entire population in 2060 from 17.1% in 2008. Second, the POADR is expected to increase to 53% in 2060 from 25.9% in 2010. That means that while today in the EU there are four working people for every retired person, in 50 years this ratio will be two working persons for each retired person. Third, among the EU countries there is strong variability in the aging process. For instance, the POADR will be particularly burdensome (over 60%) for Eastern European countries while it is expected to be lower than 45% for some Nordic countries.

Similar estimates for the USA (Eurostat, 2011) show that the POADR's growth will be from about 19.5 "older dependents" over 100 "workers" in 2010, to 36.8% in 2060; that is, an aging process similar to the European one, but less pronounced. A complete international comparison (Eurostat, 2011) shows that the level of old age dependency is variable between geographical areas, with a more critical situation in Japan and Europe. At the same time, the projections indicate that some developing countries, such as Brazil and China, which now have relatively low old age dependency ratios, will be not immune to the aging phenomenon in the future.

The trends analyzed with POADR assume certain structural processes (fertility, migration, life expectancy) that could potentially be influenced by national governments and international institutions only through long-term policies. But there are some other processes that could exacerbate the age dependency ratio and the sustainability of pension systems. The most crucial one of these is the employment rate for people aged between 55 and 64 years—a rate that, of course, is strongly related to the average age of retirement. In 2000, this rate was around 60% in the USA and Japan, 50% in all the members of the OECD (Organization for Economic Cooperation and Development), which includes more than 30 economically developed countries, and only 37% in the EU (27 countries). The European Commission established a target of 50% for 2010, in an attempt to encourage national governments to adopt policies for postponing retirement. In fact, this objective has not been achieved, considering that in 2011 the employment rate for people aged from 55 to 64 in the EU

(27 countries) was still 47.4%. Only 12 countries (of 27) in 2011 achieved 50%. In the same period, the USA (60%) and Japan (65%) maintain a quite stable rate, whereas the rate for the OECD countries reached 54% in 2011 (OECD, 2012).

Taken together, these data show, first, that there is a general historical trend toward postponing retirement and toward increasing the length of working life. This happened after a long period (during the first three-quarters of the past century) in which the working life has been progressively reduced. This general trend is consistent with improvements in life expectancy (today in Europe and USA the life expectancy at age 65 is 20 and 17 years, respectively, for females and males). This trend is also dictated by public finance constraints. Second, these data show that the pension systems seem still far from financial sustainability in some countries, mostly in Europe. Consider that in 2009 the average age of retirement in the EU was 61.4 years. In the future, the number of people still working at the age of 55–65 will increase in many geographical areas. This trend needs to be accompanied by social policies to improve the quality of working life for elderly people and organizational strategies to manage late careers. Third, there are some substantial differences in the rate of employment between countries and between geographical areas. These differences could have some direct effects on the economic systems of each country in terms of public debt (direct costs to pay pensions) and in terms of general competitiveness. These dynamics could produce intergenerational conflicts and the necessity to improve flexibility in the labor market and employment contracts for older workers.

ECONOMIC ISSUES

Related to these demographic shifts—longer lifespans, a general aging of the population, and, in some countries, a decline in birth rates—there are economic challenges on the horizon for both older and younger workers. These include the need for people to continue to work longer to maintain retirement systems that can no longer be supported by dwindling numbers of younger workers; an increased need for certain job types, such as medical jobs and those requiring post-secondary education; and employment challenges for persons at either end of the age spectrum.

First, longer lifespans, compounded by decreased birth rates in some countries, have the potential to place significant pressures on retirement systems (European Commission and Economic Policy Committee, 2012). These issues have caused many countries to raise the statutory retirement age, although this has also been met with fierce resistance from some workers (e.g., Donadio & Alderman, 2012). Taken together, these events suggest that industrialized societies will need for people to work longer to be able to support their retirement systems; and that employers and societies will need to find ways to keep workers engaged, motivated, and productive, all with sufficient work-life balance and the best health possible. It also suggests that not only will the workforce age, with the workforce participation of those over 55 continuing to increase in both the US and Europe (Eurostat, 2012b; Toossi, 2012), but that people of very different ages will need to work side by side, at a rate previously unseen in industrialized workplaces. At the same time, working longer may be difficult for some older workers: although the number of the most physically demanding jobs may be decreasing—a good sign for older workers—significant numbers of people still work in physically demanding jobs (Johnson, Mermin, & Ressenger, 2011).

At the same time, economic projections indicate changes in certain sectors of the workforce, many of them due to the fact that the general population is living longer. For instance, due to the aging of the population, the number of medical jobs, such as nurses and home healthcare aides, is expected to grow significantly (Lockard & Woolf, 2012). However, many of these jobs require specialized training and have their own sets of physical demands (e.g., nursing and home healthcare aides) (Trinkoff, Lipscomb, Geiger-Brown, Storr, & Brady, 2003), which could pose challenges for older workers. At the same time, the numbers of jobs requiring post-secondary education are expected to continue to grow in the industrialized economies (Lockard & Woolf, 2012), a challenge for many workers both young and old.

In addition, the youngest and the oldest workers may be particularly vulnerable to economic downturns. For instance, the current high unemployment rates in the US and in Europe are producing pressures on workers at both ends of the age spectrum. In the US, older workers who lose their jobs are finding significant challenges with re-employment (U.S. Government Accountability Office, 2012). At the same time, in some European countries, the overall unemployment rates mask substantial differences between the fortunes of older workers versus younger workers (those under 25), whose unemployment rates had exceeded 50% in Greece and Spain as of summer 2012 (Froymovich, 2012; Thompson, 2012). These employment issues are putting pressure on the social safety net, such as many younger people having to live at home. It is also leading to people needing to work in jobs for which they are overqualified (Erdogan, Bauer, Peiró, & Truxillo, 2011) and to older workers needing to continue to work longer or take on bridge employment to have sufficient retirement income. These unemployment issues may also lead to some generational conflict: paradoxically, although older people need to continue to work to support overburdened retirement systems, younger people may perceive that older workers are preventing them from entering the workforce. However, this perception does not seem to fit the economic reality, in that older worker retirements do not necessarily mean more jobs for younger people (Munnell & Wu, 2012).

TECHNOLOGY

When thinking of recent and future changes to the world of work, technology is likely one of the first factors to come to mind, but the impact of changing technologies may affect our work lives in even more ways than we may first realize. For example, rapid technological advances have created entirely new fields of work with increased employment opportunities and required skill sets while also making some long-standing fields obsolete. Even in more traditional jobs, there are continual changes in tools and equipment and increased reliance on the Internet to conduct business. Those increasingly rapid developments require a new mindset geared toward constant training and lifelong learning (Charness, Czaja, & Sharitt, 2007; Czaja & Sharrit, 2009). Moreover, much of the training itself will be delivered via new technologies (Charness et al., 2007; Wolfson, Cavanagh, & Kraiger, 2014). These advances also allow mobility in where people do their work, but at the same time may erase the boundaries of when people are "at" work (Burke & Cooper, 2008). Finally, this same technology provides access to a global workplace with multicultural teams (Olson & Olson, 2000). Each of these issues is given further attention below.

Types of Jobs

Constant and rapid technological developments change the nature of work by creating entirely new fields of work, as well as new jobs within existing fields, while at the same time eliminating others. O*Net continually updates its database service with jobs in "New and Emerging Occupations." Some examples of recent additions include several jobs in tech-heavy occupations such as Geospacial Technology and Bioinformatics (O*Net, 2006). Reports also abound regarding serious decline in growth in more traditional occupations, such as watch/clock repair, camera repair, and postal service work (e.g., AOL, 2011). Interestingly, it is not necessarily technological changes for doing that sort of work that have endangered these occupations, but rather other technological changes in our daily lives that are leading to their demise (e.g., fewer people wear watches because they carry mobile phones with the time; film cameras have largely been replaced by digital cameras or smartphones; and email has severely cut back postal needs). Other occupations have experienced decline because of more direct technological advancements for completing job tasks (such as various machine operators).

Changing Job Processes

Even if certain jobs are not becoming extinct, there are some fundamental changes to the nature of how business is conducted across a wide number of fields, even those not known to be technology-oriented. For example, stock clerks track inventory with more sophisticated scanners, train conductors use scanners to track frequent riders, and warehouse forklift operators use increasingly sophisticated machinery. Small businesses can no longer survive without an active presence on the Internet and on social media (Facebook, Twitter, etc.). There are likely few remaining jobs where technology is not present and evolving.

Lifelong Learning Needs

With these changes comes a constant demand for learning new skills (Czaja & Sharit, 2009). Several challenges are inherent here. First, organizations should be investing in training for all employees regardless of age and tenure if they are likely to come in contact with changing technology. This may be cost-prohibitive, and some leaders may especially doubt the cost-effectiveness of training older employees, who are sometimes believed to have less capacity for development (Finkelstein, Burke, & Raju, 1995). The responsibility for continual learning may fall at least in part on the individual employees, requiring them to be proactive in seeking out developmental opportunities to stay on top of change. Though many employees continue to embrace learning across the lifespan, on average older employees as compared with younger employees may resist learning opportunities out of resentment, fear, or lack of belief that they are truly needed for success, as past experience has not demanded them (Wolfson et al., 2014).

Technology-Based Training

Technology not only creates a need for continual training and learning, but it actually is increasingly likely to also be the medium by which that training is delivered, magnifying challenges. Technology-based instruction (TBI) (Kraiger & Ford, 2006) is a general concept engulfing all training that uses some kind of technological medium (video, computer, etc.) in its delivery. Although there are some aspects to TBI that could potentially level the playing field across age in terms of ease of use (e.g., self-pacing, privacy, and clear and immediate feedback), the features of many TBI programs involve some familiarity with the medium (less likely for older individuals) and cognitive processing capabilities that may on average diminish with age (Czaja, Sharit, Charness, Fisk, & Rogers, 2001; Wolfson et al., 2014).

Expanded Locations of Work

Technological advancement in computers, tablets, smartphones, and their associated software applications have given employees in a variety of fields the "freedom" to work remotely, be it from home, a more conveniently located satellite office, or the local coffee shop (Olson & Olson, 2000). In some ways, this can be advantageous to employees across the lifespan as it may allow for employees to more easily meet childcare or eldercare needs (Czaja & Sharit, 2009). Employees requiring special accommodations— sometimes due to afflictions accompanying aging—could perhaps utilize their current home-based accommodations, requiring less adjustment by employers. However, this "freedom" often comes hand-in-hand with a 24/7 connection culture that dissolves the lines between work and non-work that may be a crucial part of the well-being of employees' health and family lives (Burke & Cooper, 2008). It is interesting to speculate whether older employees who did not go through important life events during this connectivity culture (e.g., forging a new marriage or having children) may have had quite different relationships to those events than currently younger employers who are now embarking on those personal journeys while tethered electronically to work. Aside from the location and times where we do our work, the potential for whom we do it for and with has also expanded tremendously due to technology.

Virtual Teams

The composition of work teams is no longer restricted to those geographically collocated as technology has continually improved our ability to communicate in real time efficiently and inexpensively. Interest in the processes of virtual work has been on the rise, as the advantages to unlimited combinations of talent in a virtual team may be tempered by process loss due to different levels of trust and communication misunderstandings (Olson & Olson, 2000). Leadership of virtually located teams can also create challenges and require new skills among managers (Cascio, 2000; Zaccaro & Bader, 2002). Finally, virtual teams also increase the likelihood of employees from different organizational and national cultures working together on projects. More attention is given to the cultural issue in the following section, but this is truly a place of intersection among workforce trends.

CULTURAL ISSUES

In the previous section, we discussed how technological advancements have begun to break down previous limitations to distributed work teams—and one implication is that we now work with people across vast cultural boundaries. It is no longer just expatriates who must become accustomed to new cultural norms. Some of these norms may be particularly pertinent to our age-diverse workforce. For example, various countries and cultures may have differing age-related expectations regarding things such as how one communicates to elders, as well as differing beliefs and stereotypes about what behavior is appropriate at different ages (Perry & Parlamis, 2006).

Age norms for where one is "supposed" to be on the career ladder have become less stringent over time, but expectations about career timetables still linger (Lawrence, 1996; Pitt-Catsouphes, Matz-Costa, and Brown, 2010). These beliefs also extend into appropriate ages for retirement. Many of these expectations are likely to be at least in part culture-bound. Countries vary in the legal age for retirement, but norms and values—not just laws—likely influence beliefs. Multinational organizations must deal with not only the laws for retirement in their various locales, but also with the beliefs of local employees.

The increased preponderance of global corporations and outsourcing of work has also increased competition among organizations and also among workers vying to promote themselves as adding value, particularly when quality labor may be available less expensively in another part of the world (Frese, 2008). There has been recognition in the careers literature for the past couple of decades that the milieu of a one-organization career is disappearing and being replaced by the expectation of a workforce that is more protean (Briscoe, Hall, & DeMuth, 2006). Those who have a more protean, proactive approach to career management are self-directed and tend to use their internal values, rather than external influences, as a compass to guide their career choices. Interestingly, though, they are not necessarily less committed to the organizations in which they work (Briscoe & Finkelstein, 2009). But there appears to be a growing understanding that the psychological contract between employee and employer is not necessarily as stable as it once was.

Though the career path of the white-collar sector appears more dynamic in today's environment, those in blue-collar jobs may find their career path more fragmented. In order to survive in the current economy, many workers worldwide must work multiple jobs and/or temporary jobs. Though that situation is challenging to juggle anywhere, in some countries, such as some EU countries, this may mean working with temporary and often undesirable or unfair contracts to make ends meet (DeCuyper, Notelaers, & DeWitte, 2009).

Finally, in addition to the ethnic cultural diversity brought about by global corporations, in any one particular country workforce diversity is on the rise. People across ages are working with and for others who are more likely to differ in gender, race, disability status, and sexual orientation than ever before. These issues may relate to age in a multitude of ways. For instance, older workers used to homogenous workforces are now facing a major change. Additionally, what aging means *to* and how it is perceived *by* workers from diverse backgrounds is likely to make the understanding of age effects at work much more complex. For example, within a given culture, the impact of aging in the workforce may differ for minorities and women compared with the majority and men (Goldberg, 2007).

THE WORKER: AGE-RELATED CHANGES

In this section, we briefly summarize basic findings with respect to age-related changes over mid- and late-adulthood that have relevance for the workplace and an individual's employability. Interest in age-related changes that occur during adulthood has burgeoned over the past 30 years. Most studies to date have been cross-sectional, although the number of longitudinal studies that document patterns of intra-individual change over the adult lifespan has been steadily increasing over the past 15 years (e.g., Lucas & Donellan, 2011; van der Velde, Feij, & van Emmerik, 1998). There has also been greater research interest in generational or cohort differences in person attributes (e.g., Hansen & Leuty, 2012; Smits, Dolan, Vorst, Wicherts, & Timmerman, 2011). Studies of cohort differences are particularly germane for understanding the impact of multigenerational workforce on worker relations and teamwork processes. In contrast to research on intra-individual differences in person attributes over the adult lifespan, generational studies focus on contextual factors, such as culture and the common experiences of persons born during a particular period, as they contribute to between-cohort differences on attributes such as work values and attitudes.

Numerous reviews exist on the relationship between chronological age and specific person attributes, including cognitive abilities, knowledge, physical abilities, personality traits, and emotion regulation (e.g., Salthouse, 2012). Comprehensive reviews are also available on the relationship between chronological age and work-related variables, such as work motivation (e.g., Kanfer & Ackerman, 2004), work motives and values (e.g., Kooij, de Lange, Jansen, Kanfer, & Dikkers, 2011), work attitudes (e.g., Ng & Feldman, 2010), and job performance (e.g., Ng & Feldman, 2008). Although these reviews provide comprehensive information on the relationships between chronological age and specific person characteristics, they are difficult to cumulate with respect to how age-related changes operate in unison with work and non-work influences to affect the individual's work experiences and mid- and late-adulthood decisions related to job transitions, including retirement, career transitions, and post-retirement work.

The complexity of findings with respect to age-related changes in person characteristics is illustrated in Figure 1.1. As shown, chronological aging is associated with decline in some characteristics and improvement in other characteristics. Findings in the cognitive aging literature, for example, provide evidence for age-related decline in selective cognitive abilities and processes, though the rate of decline varies considerably from person to person. Although declines in cognitive abilities appear most pronounced with respect to fluid intellectual abilities and memory-related cognitive processes, recent findings also suggest that such declines are not uniform and may importantly depend on the individual's health. Recent findings

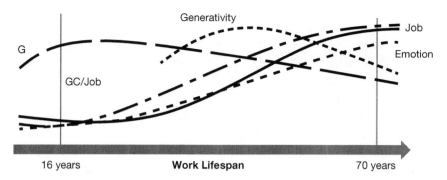

FIGURE 1.1
Trajectories of change across the work lifespan
Source: Kanfer, Beier, and Ackerman (2013)

also suggest that individuals may successfully compensate for gradual age-related declines in cognitive abilities by optimizing abilities such as declarative and job knowledge that tend to increase across the lifespan and to be preserved into late adulthood, and by creating work roles that make lower demands on cognitive abilities that are age-sensitive.

Age-related declines in cognitive abilities have often been interpreted as meaning that older workers are less able learners than younger workers, thus accounting for why older learners often perform more poorly than younger workers in standard job training programs. Recent investigations indicate, however, that older workers continue to learn, albeit sometimes more slowly than younger learners, particularly in training formats that make heavy demands on fluid intellectual abilities (Beier & Ackerman, 2005).

Findings in the social and personality domain also suggest selectivity in the role that chronological age per se plays in social skills and personality. Evidence from cross-sectional and longitudinal studies of personality change over adulthood indicate that although mean trait levels may increase or decrease over the lifespan, the individual's ranking on the trait tends to remain relatively stable across the life course. In the social skills domain, research on age-related changes in emotion regulation shows a gradual age-related increase in these skills.

Historically, person attributes such as physical abilities, cognitive abilities, and personality have been long held to co-vary in part as a consequence of the common role that genetic and psychobiological factors play in their development over the life course. At the same time, however, these person attributes represent only one influence on older adult experience and adjustment. Over the life course, inter- and intra-individual differences in psychological variables interact with family and environmental affordances and constraints. These interactions in turn influence the individual's work history and experiences. In the US, for example, job tenure is typically positively associated with chronological age, higher pay, and increased job responsibility. Although these relations suggest that older workers fare better than younger workers, economic conditions that prompt widespread layoffs may be harder for older workers than younger workers. In contrast to younger workers, older workers who have not engaged in job search or job change for a decade or longer may lack effective job search skills in an increasingly technology-driven marketplace.

Taken together, the reviews on intra-individual change across the lifespan describe a complicated picture of how aging affects an individual's work attitudes, job competencies, and employability in late adulthood. On the one hand, age-related declines in select physical abilities and cognitive processes may encourage early retirement and/or midlife career transition among workers in jobs that place heavy demands on age-sensitive abilities. On the other hand, age-related increases in declarative knowledge, job knowledge, and interpersonal skills may strengthen work attitudes and facilitate performance in jobs that emphasize teamwork and innovation, particularly when working with persons they know well. For other older workers with long job tenures, the same changes in the nature of work and economic conditions may reduce motivation for maintaining employability or making a job transition in late adulthood.

CHANGING PERSON IN A DYNAMIC CONTEXT

As described in the previous sections, people of working age continue to change throughout the work-life span; at the same time, these changes are taking place within a dynamic demographic, economic, and cultural context. In short, psychological structures and processes within the worker are evolving over the life course, and the context within which this is evolving as well. Each of these issues has been discussed independently in this chapter, but the savvy reader can spot the connections among them, and these connections have significant implications for researchers in I-O psychology. For example, how do shifting age demographics impact the treatment of workers of different ages? Does the interplay of changing age demographics and technological demands affect workplace training? Do technological advances, cross-cultural teamwork, and cultural norms differentially affect workers across the life course? These are only a few questions; the permutations of reciprocal influence are abundant.

A USE-INSPIRED, PERSON-CENTRIC APPROACH

Use-Inspired

In 1997, Donald Stokes wrote an influential book in which he argued for "use-inspired" research; namely, research that both informs basic understanding and responds to important practical problems. We believe that the confluence of advances in our understanding of the aging process, improved population health, and the increasing participation of older individuals in the workforce create ideal conditions for conducting research that can inform science, public policy, and human resource practice. Indeed, such work is already underway and beginning to have an impact on public policy, organizational practices, and worker routines. Studies that show age-related improvement in affect regulation, for example, provide evidence for the potential benefit of hiring older workers into customer service positions. Similarly, research on the determinants of retirement has recently broadened beyond the retirement event per se to examine the impact of pre-retirement work and the retirement process on workability and worker well-being after retirement. In countries characterized by a graying workforce, these findings have important implications for public policies that shape social norms for work and retirement, as well as for organizations seeking to develop and maximize workforce investments.

Person-Centric

For much of the 20th century, organizational scholars focused on worker behavior and performance using an organizational lens that emphasized the impact of person characteristics, work design, and managerial practices in terms of maximizing job performance. In the context of industrial economies, in which work products were typically performed on site and during scheduled hours, performance-centric perspectives seemed reasonable. In this perspective, theories of personnel selection, work motivation, and job design were frequently developed and tested using "technical" performance criteria, such as number of units produced. The performance emphasis in organizational science was further supported by workforce demographic trends of the times. As a consequence of the post-WWII baby boom, organizations in the latter part of the 20th century were able to select workers from a large, educated group of younger workers. The ready supply of young talent in many countries along with mandatory retirement legislation during this period encouraged organizations to emphasize selection rather than training, and to develop talent early in the career path rather than during mid or later adulthood.

During the late 20th century, technological advances, globalization, and new demographic trends spurred increased interest in a person-centric perspective on work (e.g., Weiss & Rupp, 2011). In this perspective, work and its outcomes are understood from the worker's viewpoint, and emphasis is placed on sustaining high levels of typical job performance. The person-centric perspective focuses on how workers perceive their tasks and work relations, and perform their job in the broader context of non-work demands. Changes in the nature of work have led to increased use of teams and organizational structures that place a premium on interpersonal relations and "contextual" dimensions of job performance that require further understanding of the events and psychological processes involved in effective worker relations. At the same time, increasing age diversity in the workforce as a consequence of increased longevity, repeal of mandatory retirement legislation, and shifting norms on retirement age have created new organizational challenges with respect to leadership, training and talent development, and the process of work withdrawal in late adulthood. For example, research from the person-centric perspective indicates the key role that organizations play in effective worker transition to retirement and post-retirement adjustment. Conversely, in an increasingly networked economy in which employees are often customers and recruiters, organizations have focused greater attention on identifying human resource practices that sustain employee loyalty to the organization after separation.

In contrast to a performance-centric perspective that clearly demarcates task and non-task behaviors, the person-centric perspective focuses on the interface between work and non-work demands in their effects on worker stress and well-being, that in turn are posited to influence job performance. As applied to older workers, the person-centric perspective allows for greater understanding of the mechanisms through which age-related changes in later adulthood may influence worker motivation, job behaviors, and performance.

The Focal Approach

The adoption of a "use-inspired, person-centric" perspective distinguishes this volume from past work in several ways. First, chapters are organized around issues that have and are expected to emerge as a consequence of changing workforce demographics (e.g., retirement transitions), rather than by substantive topic (e.g., cognitive aging). We have asked the chapter authors to address the implications of findings for enhancing worker well-being in the context of policymaking and organizational practices that sustain competitive excellence.

Second, this volume will adopt a mixed model with respect to the relevance of issues for workers and organizations. Many of the challenges associated with the changing workforce pertain to the factors that contribute to successful aging and adaptation to a changing workplace (e.g., post-retirement job search). To address these issues requires a *person-centric approach* that emphasizes the worker's context and history. Other issues, such as managing an age-diverse workforce, are most relevant for organizational and human resource personnel, and reflect a more traditional *performance-centric perspective*. The proposed volume seeks to address both the person in the organization and the cultural context.

How Can I-O Researchers Address These Issues?

Our approach in this book is to ask: what research should be done in I-O psychology to address these complex patterns of change happening now and in the coming decades? Our distinguished chapter authors were faced with this question, and they accepted the challenge. Again, our approach in this book is not to have authors exhaustively review and catalogue existing research. Rather, in keeping with the spirit of a book chosen to be part of the "Frontiers" series, we use these looming issues as a guide to suggest what our research agenda should be in I-O moving forward in the area of age research. In other words, what research should we be doing to address these demographic, economic, technological, and cultural shifts?

REFERENCES

AOL (2011). *9 Dying Occupations—Thanks to Technology.* Available at: http://jobs.aol.com/articles/2011/10/07 (accessed January 12, 2015)

Beier, M. E., & Ackerman, P. L. (2005). Age, ability, and the role of prior knowledge on the acquisition of new domain knowledge: Promising results in a real-world learning environment. *Psychology and Aging, 20,* 341–355.

Briscoe, J. P., & Finkelstein, L. M. (2009). The "new career" and organizational commitment: Do boundaryless and protean attitudes make a difference? *Career Development International, 14,* 242–260.

Briscoe, J. P., Hall, D. T., & DeMuth, R. L. F. (2006). Protean and boundaryless careers: An empirical exploration. *Journal of Vocational Behavior, 69,* 30–47.

Burke, R. J., & Cooper, C. L. (2008). *The Long Work Hours Culture: Causes, Consequences, and Choices.* Bingley: Emerald Group Publishing.

Cascio, W. F. (2000). Managing a virtual workplace. *Academy of Management Executive, 14,* 81–90.

Charness, N., Czaja, S., & Sharit, J. (2007). Age and technology for work. In K. Shultz & G. Adams (Eds.), *Aging and Work in the 21st Century* (pp. 225–250). Mahwah, NJ: Lawrence Erlbaum Associates.

Czaja, S. J., & Sharit, J. (2009). Emerging challenges for organizations and older workers in the twenty-first century. In S. J. Czaja & J. Sharit (Eds.), *Aging and Work: Issues and Implications in a Changing Landscape* (pp. 1–8). Baltimore, MD: Johns Hopkins University Press.

Czaja, S. J., Sharit, J., Charness, N., Fisk, A. D., & Rogers, W. (2011). The center for research and education on aging and technology for enhancement (CREATE): A program to enhance technology for older adults. *Gerotechnology, 1,* 50–59.

Donadio, R., & Alderman, L. (2012, November). Fragile coalition in Greece narrowly backs austerity. *New York Times.* Available at: www.nytimes.com/2012/11/08/world/europe/greece-austerity-vote.html (accessed November 30, 2012).

DeCuyper, N., Notelaers, G., & DeWitte, H. (2009). Job insecurity and employability in fixed-term contractors, agency workers, and permanent workers: Associations with job satisfaction and affective organizational commitment. *Journal of Occupational Health Psychology, 14,* 193–205.

Erdogan, B., Bauer, T. N., Peiró, J. M., & Truxillo, D. M. (2011). Overqualified employees: Making the best of a potentially bad situation for individuals and organizations. *Industrial and Organizational Psychology: Perspectives on Science and Practice, 4,* 215–232.

European Commission and Economic Policy Committee (2012). *The 2012 Ageing Report: Economic and Budgetary Projections for the EU27 Member States (2010–2060).* Joint report prepared by the European Commission (DG ECFIN) and the Economic Policy Committee (AWG).

Eurostat (2011). European population compared with world population. *European Commission.* Avaialble at: http://epp.eurostat.ec.europa.eu/statistics_explained/index.php/European_population_compared_with_world_population (accessed December 29, 2012).

Eurostat (2012a). Old-age dependency ratio, 1960–2060. *European Commission.* Available at: http://epp.eurostat.ec.europa.eu/statistics_explained/index.php?title=File:Old-age_dependency_ratio,_1960-2060_(1)_(population_aged_65_years_and_over_as_%25_of_population_aged_15-64).png&filetimestamp=20120321111604 (accessed December 29, 2012).

Eurostat (2012b). Employment statistics. *European Commission.* Available at: http://epp.eurostat.ec.europa.eu/statistics_explained/index.php/Employment_statistics (accessed December 1, 2012).

Finkelstein, L. M., Burke, M. J., & Raju, N. S. (1995). Age discrimination in simulated employment contexts: An integrative analysis. *Journal of Applied Psychology, 80,* 652–663.

Frese, M. (2008). The changing nature of work. In N. Chmiel (Ed.). *An Introduction to Work and Organizational Psychology: A European Perspective* (pp. 397–413). Malden, MA: Blackwell.

Froymovich, R. (2012, September). In Europe, signs of a jobless generation. *The Wall Street Journal*. Available at: http://online.wsj.com/article/SB10000872396390444301704 577631391024255180.html (accessed December 1, 2012).

Giannakouris, K. (2008). Ageing characterises the demographic perspectives of the European societies. *Eurostat Statistic in Focus, 72*. Available at: http://epp.eurostat.ec.europa.eu/cache/ITY_OFFPUB/KS-SF-08-072/EN/KS-SF-08-072-EN.PDF (accessed December 29, 2012).

Goldberg, C. (2007). Diversity issues for an aging workforce. In K. Shultz & G. Adams (Eds.), *Aging and Work in the 21st Century* (pp. 51–72). Mahwah, NJ: Lawrence Erlbaum Associates.

Hansen, J. C., & Leuty, M. E. (2012). Work values across generations. *Journal of Career Assessment, 20*, 34–52.

Johnson, R. W., Mermin, G. B. T., & Resseger, M. (2011). Job demands and work ability at older ages. *Journal of Aging and Social Policy, 23*, 101–118.

Kanfer, R., & Ackerman, P. L. (2004). Aging, adult development and work motivation. *Academy of Management Review, 29*, 1–19.

Kanfer, R., Beier, M. E., & Ackerman, P. L. (2013). Goals and motivation related to work in later adulthood: An organizing framework. *European Journal of Work and Organizational Psychology 22*, 253–264.

Kinsella, K., & Phillips, D. R. (2005). Global aging: The challenge of success. *Population Bulletin, 60*, 5–42.

Kooij, D. T. A. M., de Lange, A. H., Jansen, P. G. W., Kanfer, R., & Dikkers, J. S. E. (2011). Age and work-related motives: Results of a meta-analysis. *Journal of Organizational Behavior, 32*, 197–225.

Kraiger, K., & Ford, J. K. (2006). The expanding role of workplace training: Themes and trends influencing training research and practice. In L. Koppes (Ed.), *Historical Perspectives in Industrial and Organizational Psychology* (pp. 281–309). Mahwah, NJ: Lawrence Erlbaum Associates.

Lawrence, B. S. (1996). Organizatinal age norms: Why is it so hard to know one when you see one? *The Gerontologist, 36*, 209–220.

Lockard, C. B., & Woolf, M. (2012). Employment outlook: 2010–2012: Occupational employment projections to 2020. *Monthly Labor Review, 135*, 84–108.

Lucas, R. E., & Donnellan, M. B. (2011). Personality development across the life span: Longitudinal analyses with a national sample from Germany. *Journal of Personality and Social Psychology, 101*, 847–861.

Munnell, A. H., & Wu, A. Y. (2012). Are aging baby boomers squeezing younger workers out of jobs? *Issue in Brief* (pp. 12–18). Chestnut Hill, MA: Center for Retirement Research at Boston College.

Ng, T. W. H., & Feldman, D. C. (2008). The relationship of age to ten dimensions of job performance. *Journal of Applied Psychology, 93*, 392–423.

Ng, T. W. H., & Feldman, D. C. (2010). The relationships of age with job attitudes: A meta-analysis. *Personnel Psychology, 63*, 677–718.

O*Net (2006). New and emerging (N&E) occupations: Methodology development report. National Center for O*Net Development.

OECD (2012). Employment rate of older workers % of population aged 55–64. *OECD ILibrary*. Available at: www.oecd-ilibrary.org/employment/employment-rate-of-older-workers-2012_emp-ol-table-2012-1-en (accessed December 30, 2012).

Olson, G. M., & Olson, J. S. (2000). Distance matters. *Human-Computer Interaction, 15*, 139–178.

Perry, E. L., & Parlamis, J. D. (2006). Age and ageism in organizations: A review and consideration of national culture. In A. Konrad, P. Prasad, & J. Pringle (Eds). *Handbook of Workplace Diversity* (pp. 345–370). London: Sage.

Pitt-Catsouphes, M., Matz-Costa, C., & Brown, M. (2010). The prism of age: Managing age diversity in the twenty-first century workplace. In E. Parry and S. Tyson (Eds.), *Managing an Age Diverse Workforce* (pp. 80–94). London: Palgrave Macmillan.

Salthouse, T. A. (2012). Consequences of age-related cognitive declines. *Annual Review of Psychology, 63*, 201–226.

Smits, I. A. M., Dolan, C. V., Vorst, H. C. M., Wicherts, J. M., & Timmerman, M. E. (2011). Cohort differences in Big Five personality facgtors over a period of 25 years. *Journal of Personality and Social Psychology, 100*, 1124–1138.

Stokes, D. E. (1997). *Pasteur's Quadrant: Basic Science and Technological Innovation.* Washington, DC: Brookings Institution Press.

Toossi, M. (2012). Labor force projections to 2020: A more slowly growing workforce. *Monthly Labor Review, 135*, 43–64.

Thompson, D. (2012, October). Europe's most tragic graph: Greek youth unemployment hits 55%. *The Atlantic Monthly Online.* Available at: http://online.wsj.com/article/SB10000872396390444301704577631391024255180.html (accessed December 1, 2012).

Trinkoff, A. M., Lipscomb, J. A., Geiger-Brown, J., Storr, C. L., & Brady, B. A. (2003). Perceived physical demands and reported musculoskeletal problems in registered nurses. *American Journal of Preventive Medicine, 24*, 270–275.

United Nations (2012). Probabilistic Population Projections: Old-age Dependency Ratio. *Department of Economic and Social Affairs.* Available at: http://esa.un.org/unpd/ppp/Figures-Output/Population/PPP_Old-age-Dependency-Ratio.htm (accessed December 28, 2012).

U.S. Government Accountability Office (2012). Unemployed older workers: Many experience challenges regaining employment and face reduced retirement security. *GAO-12-445,* April 25, 2012.

van der Velde, M. E. G., Feij, J. A., & van Emmerik, H. (1998). Change in work values and norms among Dutch young adults: Ageing or societal trends? *International Journal of Behavioral Development, 22*, 55–76.

Weiss, H. M., & Rupp, D. E. (2011). Experiencing work: An essay on a person_centric work psychology. *Industrial and Organizational Psychology, 4*, 83–97.

Wolfson, N., Cavanagh, T., & Kraiger, K. (2014). Older adults and technology-based instruction: Optimizing learning outcomes and transfer. *Academy of Management Learning and Education, 13*, 26–44.

Zaccaro, S. J., & Bader, P. (2002). E-Leadership and the challenges of leading e-teams: Minimizing the bad and maximizing the good. *Organizational Dynamics, 31*, 377–387.

Part II

Science Confronts the Global Challenges

Issue 1

Organizations and Teams Go Global

2

Age Diversity and Global Teamwork: A Future Agenda for Researchers and Practitioners

Florian Kunze and Stephan A. Boehm

Demographic change is a pressing issue for many industrialized and developing countries today (Peeters & Groot, 2012). From an organizational perspective, the shrinking and aging of the population is most often discussed as a matter of a steady rise of the average age of the organizational workforce. Especially to practitioners in organizations, it is far less clear that the age diversity is also significantly increasing in many teams and departments. As already mentioned in the introductory chapter of this volume, there are multiple causes of growing age diversity in the workforce, including, for example, the phasing out of early retirement programs and increased longevity of workers. In Germany, for example, during the time period 1991–2011, those in the oldest age group (56–65 years) showed the greatest increase in workforce participation of all age groups, with participation in this oldest group more than doubling during the past 20 years (Garloff, Pohl, & Schanne, 2013). In contrast to earlier time periods when companies could solely rely on a homogenous youth- and middle-aged-centered workforce, the trend toward a greater proportion of older workers, especially in the Western industrialized countries, requires that organizations and executives pay greater attention to developing effective strategies for integrating employees from all age groups in order to stay competitive.

This chapter addresses the implications of demographic changes in the workforce for teamwork. To provide a foundation for the chapter, we first offer a condensed overview of recent research findings on the impact of age diversity in teams and organizations. Next, we extend the existing literature by taking a global perspective and examining the durability and

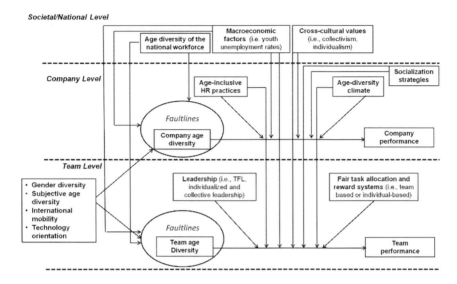

FIGURE 2.1
Conceptual model of potential future research on age diversity in teams and companies

practicality of these findings, which are mainly based on European and/or U.S. perspectives, in the context of a more international/global workforce. In the final section of this chapter, we present a future research agenda aimed at addressing unanswered questions about the interface and consequences of age diversity in the context of global teamwork. In addition, we also outline the core practical implications that can be derived from our conceptual analysis in this chapter. In summary, our goal is to provide a use-inspired, global perspective and future research agenda for dealing with an age-diverse, team-based workforce. The interrelation between the different topics discussed in relation to age diversity in teams and organizations is graphically illustrated in Figure 2.1.

CURRENT STATE OF AGE DIVERSITY RESEARCH AT THE TEAM *AND* ORGANIZATIONAL LEVEL

As with many other diversity facets, age diversity in teams and organizations is a "double-edged sword" (Horwitz & Horwitz, 2007). On the one hand, arguing from an information/decision-making perspective, the combined knowledge and perspectives of employees from different age groups should trigger positive processes and outcomes in teams and organizations, such as better problem-solving competencies, creativity, and overall performance (van Knippenberg & Schippers, 2007; van Knippenberg, de Dreu, & Homan, 2004). On the other hand, a social identity and social categorization perspective (Tajfel & Turner, 1986) would suggest that age diversity leads to age-subgroup formation (i.e., faultlines) within teams and companies. Based on their similarities in terms of life and career stages and their common life experiences, employees of similar ages will tend to group together and form age-based subgroups (Byrne, 1971). Unfortunately, these age-based subgroups are then likely to develop mutual prejudices and decrease their mutual communication (Zenger & Lawrence, 1989) and increase emotional conflict (Pelled, Xin, & Weiss, 2001) and discrimination (Kunze, Boehm, & Bruch, 2011). In turn, following this second theoretical perspective, it seems reasonable to expect that age diversity would be negatively related to processes and outcomes in teams and organizations.

Not surprisingly, given these opposing theoretical rationales, research on the relationship between age diversity and team level performance has produced rather inconsistent results, ranging from negative effects in regular work teams (Jehn & Bezrukova, 2004), to positive effects in top management teams (Kilduff, Angelmar, & Mehra, 2000), to null relationships (for recent overviews, see Kunze & Boehm, 2013; van Knippenberg & Schippers, 2007). Nonetheless, findings of recent meta-analyses by both Joshi and Roh (2009) and van Dijk, van Engen, and van Knippenberg (2012) indicate an overall negative relationship between age diversity and team level performance. To explain these negative meta-analytic findings, one can assume that age-based social identity mechanisms are likely to happen in team settings, with ensuing social-categorization effects serving to dominate information/decision-making processes.

Beyond studies only considering the direct relationships between age diversity and team-level performance outcomes, the last two decades have also produced a reasonable number of studies investigating potential processes and contextual factors that might help to open the "black box of organizational demography" (Lawrence, 1997). In line with the categorization-elaboration model (van Knippenberg et al., 2004), for example, Kearney and Gebert (2009) found that age diversity increased the elaboration of task-relevant information and in turn team performance, but only when the overall transformational leadership climate within the teams was high rather than low. These findings indicate that complex models and analyses are required to fully capture the processes and effects of age diversity on team-level outcomes.

Additionally, the recent years have also seen an increasing interest in studying the effects of age diversity not only at the team level, but also at the organizational level of analysis. A first study in this area by Kunze and colleagues (2011) showed that age diversity triggers rising levels of age discrimination in companies that, in turn, negatively impacts organizational performance, mediated by a company's affective commitment climate. The main theoretical reasoning is that diversity-based subcategorization processes (Tajfel & Turner, 1986) are also likely to occur in whole organizations, negatively affecting outcomes. Additionally, for the special case of age diversity, increasing diversity might also violate traditional organizational age norms (Lawrence, 1988) (e.g., older employees should always have the more senior positions) and thereby impair organizational performance. Another recent study by Kunze, Boehm, and Bruch (2013a) replicated the main findings of the first study (i.e., the negative indirect relationship between age diversity and company performance, mediated through rising age-discrimination climate in companies) and additionally showed that the relationship between age diversity and company performance depends on two organizational-level context factors: age stereotypes of the top management and diversity-friendly HR policies (i.e., workshops and seminars for dealing with diversity). In a similar vein, in a study with a Chinese sample from the insurance industry, Li, Chu, Lam, and Liao (2011) found age diversity to be positively related to objective company performance, but this depended on the contextual factors of country of origin and the firm's market diversification strategies. The results of these organizational-level studies suggest that age diversity plays a decisive role at the organizational level, as well as the team level, in terms of both organizational processes and outcomes.

TAKING A GLOBAL PERSPECTIVE ON AGE DIVERSITY AND TEAMWORK

The previous short literature review indicates that the age composition of teams and organizations matters for performance-related outcomes, as also illustrated in Figure 2.1. The existing research on age diversity, however, has almost exclusively taken a monocultural perspective, focusing primarily on relationships found in Western cultures (using European and US-based research samples). Interestingly, the only study that considered companies with different cultural origins reported variation in the age diversity/

company performance relationship was moderated by the nationality of the firm (Li et al., 2011). Consequently, as we discuss in the following section, there is good reason to assume that both *cultural factors* (i.e., cultural values) as well as *macro-economic factors* (i.e., birth rates, unemployment rates among different age groups) affect the processes by which age diversity affects team performance in different countries. This influence is highlighted in the top level (societal/national level) of Figure 2.1.

Cultural Factors Affecting Age Diversity and Teamwork

As shown in Figure 2.1, we build on cross-cultural research findings (Hofstede, 2001; Schwartz, 1994) to suggest that certain cross-cultural values and associated cultural identities may shape age-based relationships and processes within teams and organizations. In particular, variation in cross-cultural values of *power distance*, defined as the desire of employees for equal power distribution (House, Hanges, Javidan, Dorfman, & Gupta, 2004), and *institutional collectivism*, defined as the degree to which institutions reward and encourage collective actions and collective distributions of resources (House et al., 2004), might affect age-diversity processes in teams and organizations.

First, societies with greater power distance, such as most Asian societies, might be better able to deal with age differences in team settings, especially if the distribution of power and resources is in line with seniority norms (i.e., older employees are more experienced and have higher status represented through hierarchal positions). In these societies, age-based discrimination of older employees, and in consequence impaired team performance, is less likely and age-diverse team members might be able to combine their individual strengths for joint efforts. In contrast, in lower power distance societies, such as in Europe and the US, discrimination against older employees, and thus the negative team-based social categorization processes based on age, are more likely to occur. If, however, the distribution of power and team resources is not in line with seniority norms (i.e., older employees are less experienced and have lower hierarchical positions), societies with lower power distance might be better able to deal with this situation compared to high power distance societies. That is, low power distance may enable an environment that accounts less for seniority or status than individual competence and the contribution of each employee, irrespective of age.

Second, another cultural factor that might work in favor of positive outcomes in age-diverse teams and organizations is the amount of collectivism desired and present in different societies. Again, a significant difference in these collectivism values exists between Asian societies (with relative high collectivism orientation) and U.S. and European societies (with relative low collectivism orientation). In societies with a high collectivism orientation, age-based conflicts and tensions are potentially less likely compared to low collectivism societies, since in high collectivism societies employees can be expected to strive for good collective outcomes and relationships instead of optimizing the outcomes of their individual age subgroup. As such, cultural collectivism might function as a moderator that enables zero or even positive outcomes in age-diverse teams in the same way as collective team identification (i.e., the emotional attachment members have to a given team) (Kearney & Gebert, 2009).

To date, the limited empirical results present inconsistent results on these influences. In line with our conceptual reasoning, studies in Western samples with low power distance and low collectivism show a negative relationship between age diversity and company performance (Kunze et al., 2011, 2013a), while the only study carried out in a Chinese sample, a cultural setting with high power distance and high collectivism, reports a positive main effect between age diversity and company performance (Li et al., 2011). The results of the study by Li and colleagues (2011) are, however, more complex as they show that the country of origin (Western versus Eastern countries) of the companies operating in China matters for the effects of age diversity, in such a manner that the effect is only positive for companies of Western origin and non-significant for Asian companies. Li and colleagues (2011) argue that these effects might be driven by the higher awareness in companies from Western countries for (age) diversity issues. These preliminary contradictory findings of cultural differences in the age diversity/performance relationship show the clear need for further research on the impact of cultural values on the age diversity/organizational performance relation using intercultural samples collected in different countries.

It is also worth considering the impact of potential cross-cultural differences on age identities, and how these differences might yield different age-diversity outcomes in different societies. Some authors (Catterall & Maclaran, 2001) have argued that the attitudes toward age are societally and culturally constructed, and that striving for youthfulness and a lower subjective age is typical only for Western societies. Such a desire for youthfulness might become especially problematic in companies if age diversity rises in companies, based on the increased proportion of older employees. For example, age-based subcategorization might be triggered in organizations where younger and middle-aged employees are reluctant to cooperate with older employees because it reminds them of their own physical decline in the future (Martens, Goldenberg, & Greenberg, 2005).

In general, the dominating deficit hypothesis—i.e., aging is correlated with a general decline in cognitive (Naveh-Benjamin, 2000) and physical (Samson et al., 2000) abilities—in Western cultures also makes age a more salient criterion for differentiation and categorization in organizational settings than in cultures and societies that hold a less negative attitude toward age. In cultures that hold less negative attitudes toward aging, the surface-level criteria of age is less likely to be applied as a main categorization criteria in the workplace, and might be substituted by more information-based criteria, such as tenure, experiences, knowledge, and capabilities that should help age-diverse teams to outperform age-homogeneous teams. Bond and Wang (1986), for instance, propose that Chinese people have a high degree of obeisance toward age. In line with that proposition, Chiu, Chan, Snape, and Redman (2001) found empirical differences in the age stereotypes and discriminatory attitudes between respondents from the UK and Hong Kong. Recent studies, however, have challenged the assumption that strong variations in age identities really exist between cultures. Barak (2009), for example, did a review of studies from 18 different countries and found that the concept of a younger desired subjective age is universal in many Eastern and Western cultures. The desired difference between the chronological and the subjective age, however, differed from only a few months in China to more than 10 years in the UK. These results suggest that feeling younger is a universal desire in many cultures (Schwall, 2012), but that such cultural differences in age identities may offer a fruitful area for new theorizing and research on age-diversity influences on teams and organizations.

Macroeconomic Factors Affecting Age Diversity and Teamwork

The prevalence of Western samples in the research literature on age diversity effects on team and organizational performance is not surprising, as recent demographic trends (i.e., the shrinking and aging of the workforce) are currently most salient in Western industrialized countries. As discussed in Chapter 1, the old-age dependency ratio (OADR), reflecting the ratio between people in retirement age (65+ years) and people of working age (15–64) is projected to change drastically over the next few decades in the European Union (EU), from a current ratio of four people working for every retired person, to only two people working for every retired person by 2060. For the United States, less drastic changes of their population structure are projected, whereas Japan is projected to have the world's fastest aging population (Eurostat, 2013). In contrast, in some developing countries, such as Brazil, India, and China, the population is still relatively young today compared to the Western countries, but also projected to increase in relative terms in the coming decades (Eurostat, 2013).

These trends imply that "real" workforce age diversity is currently mostly found in the Western industrialized world and in Japan, where a large share of younger (i.e., younger than 35) and older (i.e., 55–65) employees are working together. As a consequence, on the one hand, the risk for intergenerational conflicts and tensions within teams, leading to lower output and productivity, is also comparatively high in these countries. On the other hand, the increasing age diversity in these countries might be viewed as a competitive advantage of the industrialized world, especially given the fact that mostly knowledge-based, highly-skilled tasks are still performed in the developed countries, while routine and production tasks are often outsourced to less-developed countries. Complex knowledge-based tasks are situations in which teams might indeed profit from their diverse intergenerational viewpoints and competencies and thus outperform age-homogeneous teams (i.e., Wegge, Roth, Neubach, Schmidt, & Kanfer, 2008), while routine tasks may be better executed by age-homogenous teams. Thus, the globalized labor division might be advantageous for the different age structures in different countries worldwide, and these macroeconomic factors might be important boundary conditions for the relation between team and company diversity and performance, as illustrated in Figure 2.1.

Another interesting aspect of global differences in the population age structure across countries pertains to how these differences might lead to different types of subgroup formation and discrimination processes in age-diverse teams and organizations. For example, in rather youth-focused countries (i.e., India, Indonesia, Brazil), older employees are still the minority group in the workforce, but in many Western developed countries we might soon experience a shift with the younger employees being in a minority position compared to middle-aged and older employees. Favored by very rigid labor market regulations, we can observe tendencies of such a discrimination against younger employees already today in Southern Europe, with youth unemployment rates (16–24 years) over 50% (compared to average rates for all age groups of 25%) in countries such as Greece and

Spain (UNRIC, 2013). In these Southern European countries, younger employees seem to be systematically disfavored in terms of recruiting and career opportunities. Accordingly, in various countries, different age groups might receive a "token status" (Kanter, 1977) within their organization and be especially prone to discrimination by the other dominant age subgroups. This, in turn, has concrete implications, how human resource management and leadership practices have to be designed to successfully deal with an age-diverse workforce. While today many age-adjusted HR measures are directed toward buffering a potential discrimination of older employees (i.e., tailored training programs for older employees, specific career seminars for employees 50+) (Armstrong-Stassen & Templer, 2005), this might change in the future. Companies, especially those operating in drastically aging countries, should keep in mind that such programs should also include specific measures for younger employees. The most promising way for most countries and organizations might be to introduce age-inclusive HR measures (Boehm, Kunze, & Bruch, 2014) that are not directed toward specific age groups, but try to enable fair developing and contribution opportunities for employees from all age groups within an organization.

WHAT WE DO NOT KNOW ABOUT AGE DIVERSITY AND GLOBAL TEAMWORK

Beyond the missing intercultural perspective in the current age-diversity research, there are a number of additional blind spots that might be worth considering in future research endeavors on age-diverse teams and organizations. In this section, we discuss and integrate: (a) ideas about the interaction of age with other diversity facets; (b) the task distribution and reward systems in age-diverse teams; (c) specific leadership strategies for successful age-diverse teams; and (d) the role of organizational factors, which are illustrated in the middle section (company level) and lower section (team level) of Figure 2.1.

Interaction of Age with Other Diversity Facets

An important first step for future research pertains to better integrating the effects of age on team processes with other identity and diversity processes that occur in diverse teams. In fact, an employee's identity is shaped by a number of other surface-level (i.e., gender, tenure, ethnicity) and deep-level (i.e., personality, attitudes, values) criteria, which also might affect his or her emotions and behaviors at the workplace. Unfortunately, the combinations of different diversity facets are rarely considered in management and organizational behavior research (Joshi & Rho, 2009).

One promising way to capture multifaceted diversity processes and outcomes might be to employ the faultline concept. This concept refers to the hypothetical dividing lines that split a group into subgroups based on several demographic criteria aligned with one another (Lau & Murnighan, 1998). For example, a four-person team may have strong faultlines if the memberships on several demographic criteria are aligned (two old women versus two young men) or weak faultlines if some of the demographic criteria are separated (one young woman and one young man versus one old woman and one old man). While in the first example, two separate subgroups are likely to emerge based on the two aligned diversity facets, in the second example such subgroup formation is less likely as the potential faultline is not as clear (the common age or gender might function as a bridge that connects all four people in the team).

In a recent meta-analytic analysis of faultlines, Thatcher and Patel (2011) found that faultlines had positive relations to different kinds of conflict and negative relations to team performance outcomes. Despite these promising results, there is still much debate about theory and methods in that area of research (i.e., Trezzini, 2008), including discussions about the most appropriate way of measuring team faultlines (Meyer & Glenz, 2013). Additionally, the search for context factors that might at least buffer the negative effects of team-faultline formation on team performance is still in its infancy, with only three field studies published to date (Bezrukova, Jehn, Zanutto, & Thatcher, 2009; Kunze & Bruch, 2010; van Knippenberg, Dawson, West, & Homan, 2011).

It might be especially worthwhile in future research to inspect the interaction of age diversity with three other diversity criteria, namely: gender-perceived faultlines, subjective age, and desired mode of work (i.e., travel and career mobility and familiarity with new technologies), as also pictured in Figure 2.1. Research on age/gender faultlines in teams and organizations is especially relevant as demographic trends in many industrialized countries indicate that workforce participation is increasing for both older persons and for females. In particular, in many formerly male-dominated jobs, such as technical or R&D departments or in the top management teams of companies, a slight increase in the proportion of women might have substantial consequences for creating strong, new faultlines. Imagine, for example, a five-person top management team (TMT) that traditionally consisted of five older males. If two of the older males are replaced with two younger females, this might create a strong new faultline within the TMT, as the males and females are not only aligned in terms of age, but also in terms of organizational tenure and potentially also on more personality-based facets (i.e., attitudes toward work-life balance). This risk of a strong faultline creation caused by the increasing workforce participation of women is a challenge that has not yet received enough attention, both from a research perspective and in the public debate on this issue.

A second potentially interesting faultline effect that may have consequences on team or organization performance relates to the combination of age diversity with perceived or subjective age. Subjective age (i.e., how old or young individuals feel compared to their chronological age) is an often-studied research object in the gerontology literature (i.e., Montepare, 2009), but has been relatively neglected in the organizational behavior literature (Schwall, 2012). However, as found for the general population in many countries (i.e., Barak, 2009), we would argue that subjective age should deviate significantly from the chronological age for members of the workforce as well. Based on age marker theory (Montepare, 2009), it can be proposed that certain organizational events and environments (i.e., a very youth-oriented organizational culture, very close identification of the employees with their teams or organizations) affect the employee's perceived age, especially among older employees. If, in an age-diverse team, older team members perceive themselves as being significantly younger, this might serve a protective bridge function that prevents age-subgroup formation in the team. Older employees might thus feel more similar to their younger and middle-aged colleagues, preventing the negative effects of age diversity. At the same time, they would still have the increased knowledge and experience based on their higher chronological age that, in combination with the competencies of their younger colleagues, enables the potential performance gains of age-diverse teams. Accordingly, we strongly encourage further research that goes beyond only considering chronological age, but also assesses and evaluates the effects of subjective age on team processes and outcomes (cf., Kooij, de Lange, Jansen, & Dikkers, 2013).

A third interesting faultline effect may stem from the combination of age diversity with the desired mode of work in different age groups, especially when taking a global perspective. Based on existing research, we would assume that there are, on average, differences in international mobility (Biemann & Andresen, 2010) and technological skills (Cennamo & Gardner, 2008) between different age groups. First, younger workers are often more independent and are thus more willing to travel more or even spend time abroad as expatriates compared to their older colleagues, who have a family or other obligations at home. So, in particular for global teams or local teams operating in global environments, these differences in global mobility in alignment with age might cause potentials for team faultline formation. Second, the experiences and openness to new technologies (i.e., Web-based communication and meeting forms, entering new online distribution channels) might be higher for younger employees in the workforce. Especially members of the youngest generation in the workforce, the so-called Generation Y, are often described as very Web savvy and significantly more experienced with new technology (Reisenwitz & Iyer, 2009) compared to other generations. In consequence, there might be a risk that faultlines in age-diverse teams arise, if this technology orientation is correlated with age. However, for both factors—international mobility and technology orientation—there is limited valid and reliable research so far in their relation to age distributions in teams and organizations. Therefore, these factors might also be used in a stereotypical manner by assigning older employees the roles as being less internationally mobile and technologically skilled, even though there might be older workers who are very willing to move and travel internationally after their children have left home, or who have very high technological skills because they studied information technology. Given the limited empirical evidence of both factors in their relation to age diversity at work, we would encourage more research in the future since both international mobility and technology issues have growing importance in increasingly globalized work environments.

Task Distribution and Reward Systems in Age-Diverse Teams

We believe that one key factor for the success of age-diverse teams might be the issue of task design and distribution, as shown through their moderating role in Figure 2.1. Given the literature on cognitive (i.e., Kanfer & Ackerman, 2004) and physical development (i.e., Ilmarinen, 2001) over the life course, there is little doubt that employees from different age groups have different strengths and capabilities. More experienced employees have, on average, for example, more crystallized, experienced-based cognitive abilities, while younger employees have more fluid information-processing abilities. One key task for successful team management and leadership is to combine the different strengths of team members in a way that maximizes team performance. Assigning specific team roles and tasks to member of different age groups (i.e., a mentoring or consulting role for older employees, and creative product development tasks to younger employees) is, however, a difficult leadership job and should take into account the unique portfolio of the employee's strengths vis-à-vis other team members. One risk of such role assignments based on age is that they rely on age-stereotypical beliefs that might not be true for each individual employee. While, for example, on average, fluid intelligence is lower for older employees, some very smart aging employees might still have higher levels of fluid intelligence than a less intelligent younger employee. Future research is needed to understand the impact of age diversity on leader assessment of employee strengths and the relationship of that assessment to role assignment.

While specific roles for different age groups might make sense from a productive task-allocation perspective, they might violate the diversity-oriented equality rules within organizations. If rules promote that age (or other social category diversity facets) should not be a criterion for promotion and development within the organization, an age-group-oriented task allocation has a high potential to be perceived as age discriminatory. Furthermore, assigning specific team roles to different age groups also has the potential for violating traditional norms of status congruence (Erickson & Grove, 2007). Age is a classical status indicator, and traditionally the oldest employee within a group should receive the highest pay and hold the highest hierarchical position, which is reinforced by the strict seniority-based career systems that are still present in many companies. Having age-specific roles and tasks within a team might interfere with these classical status norms, especially for older employees, and might create negative affective states such as anger and frustration, which in turn might negatively affect their behaviors and also the overall team productivity. In consequence, the main task for leaders in age-diverse teams is to enable a *fair*, age-specified task distribution. In this regard, tasks for more experienced employees should be labeled as equally important for team outcomes as tasks for younger employees. This, however, requires an attitude and team culture toward aging that acknowledges individual age-based strengths and differences, but neglects negative age-based stereotypes and stigmatization.

We would assume, however, that there might be industry-specific differences for the success of fair and age-specific task distribution. While in white-collar jobs it might be easier to find rewarding and meaningful tasks for experienced employees who can profit from their specific strengths, purposeful roles for older employees in physically demanding blue-collar jobs may be less frequent. In sum, we thus highly encourage future research on how a fair task allocation in age-diverse teams and companies should be implemented.

Another related issue that should receive more attention in the future is a differentiation between specific types of goals and reward systems in age-diverse teams. Theoretically, one might assume that team-based reward systems (McClurg, 2001) might be most effective in age-diverse teams, as they foster the completion of collective goals. On the other hand, age-adjusted reward systems might also be needed given the varying motives of employees from different age groups (i.e., Baltes & Baltes, 1990; Kooij et al., 2013). As the findings on age-related changes in motives suggest, younger employees are likely to hold instrumental long-term goals (i.e., career advancement, payment increase), whereas older employees are more likely to hold short-term emotional goals and preferences (i.e., good social relationships at work). The explanation is that younger employees have an open future-time perspective, which makes an investment in long-term instrumental goals subjectively more rewarding, while older employees have a limited future-time perspective, which makes an investment in short-term emotional goals more rewarding. To maintain motivation among employees from different age groups, the goal and reward system needs to be adjusted to these varying motives. From a collective team perspective, however, this age-specific goal and reward system might conflict with the team reward system and reduce alignment between individual-level goals and strengths of the different-aged employees toward a more collective goal focus. Future research might therefore investigate how these potentially conflicting individual and collective reward systems might be integrated into a promising reward structure for age-diverse teams and organizations.

Leadership Strategies for Successful Global Age-Diverse Teams

Another topic that should receive more attention in future studies is effective leadership behavior for age-diverse teams, as also exemplified through its moderating role for the relation between age diversity and team performance outcomes in Figure 2.1. Research findings to date show transformational leadership (TFL) to be a promising strategy for exerting a positive context factor for both the age diversity team outcome relation (Kearney & Gebert, 2009), as well as the relationship between age-based faultlines and team outcomes (Kunze & Bruch, 2010). The explanation for these moderating effects is that a transformational leader, through his or her inspirational role modeling and individual-focused behavior, is able to create a collective identification toward common goals that suppresses all age-based sub-identities within a team and thus prevents the negative subcategorization processes impairing team performance. Recent developments in the TFL literature might offer several ways to further inspect and specify the present finding.

First, some scholars have proposed that the very broad concept of TFL should be better divided into its sub-dimensions, as there is no sound theoretical justification that the six sub-dimensions form one construct (van Knippenberg & Sitkin, 2013). Specifically, the authors argued that many of the reported effects in the TFL literature might only be attributed to the charisma dimensions (providing a role model and vision for the team/company) of TFL, and that the other dimensions (individual consideration, intellectual stimulation, and high performance expectation, fostering common goals) have no effects. We propose that this might also be the case for the moderating effect on age-diverse teams and would encourage further research to investigate the moderating effects of the TFL sub-dimensions separately.

The second current development is to divide the broad TFL construct into a *collective-focused* component, consisting of the sub-dimensions providing a vision and fostering common goals and an *individual-focused* component, consisting of the sub-dimensions intellectual stimulation and individual consideration (Wu, Tsui, & Kinicki, 2010). In several studies (Kunze, de Jong, & Bruch, 2013b; Wu et al., 2010), it was shown that a high average of the collective-focused dimensions is beneficial for team and organizational outcomes, while a high differentiation of the individual-focused dimensions (i.e., a team leader gives more attention and training to one employee than another within teams) impairs team and organizational function. Again, these findings might be also relevant for the age-diversity literature, as one might argue that only a high average of the collective-focused dimension should be beneficial for age-diverse teams, by creating a common understanding and identity. In contrast, a high differentiation of the individual-focused dimension might even increase age-subgroup competition, envy, and mutual prejudices within a team, as the employees of various ages compete for the attention of their leader and necessarily perceive an unfair treatment compared to their differently aged colleagues at some time. On the other hand, age diversity might also sometimes require a differentiation of leadership behavior, especially if some lower-status groups (i.e., young team members) are systematically discriminated against and hence need focused consideration and stimulation from the team leader to productively contribute to the common team goals. In sum, future research should develop and test new and more specified ways on how different dimensions and operationalizations of the broad TFL construct might help in age-diverse teams.

The Role of Organizational Factors

We also think that organizational factors and characteristics should receive more attention in age-diversity research, as illustrated through the moderating role of age-inclusive HR practices, age-diversity climate, and socialization strategies in Figure 2.1. Organizational factors, such as institutionalized diversity management approaches, have only been tested in a limited number of studies for their contextual role for the age diversity and company performance relationship (Choi & Rainey, 2010; Kunze et al., 2013a). In our opinion, these institutionalized practices might also be relevant for processes in age-diverse teams, as the interaction of employees from different age groups within team settings might also be shaped by organizational factors and climates. Of particular interest might be to consider recently published age-related organizational factors, such as an age-inclusive human resource management (HRM) or an age-diversity climate within organizations (Boehm et al., 2014). Age-inclusive HR practices are referring to organizational procedures that should foster the knowledge, skills, abilities, motivation, and opportunities to contribute for all employees irrespective of their age. The implementation of such age-inclusive HR practices throughout a company should be beneficial for the cooperation, communication, and joint behavior of age-diverse teams. In particular, age-inclusive HR practices have been shown to contribute toward a positive age-diversity climate defined as "organizational members' shared perceptions of the fair and nondiscriminatory treatment of employees of all age groups with regard to all relevant organizational practices, policies, procedures, and rewards" (Boehm et al., 2014, p. 6). Such an age-diversity climate may be expected to attenuate age-based subcategorization and discrimination processes within age-diverse teams, while at the same promoting the benefits of age diversity in terms of associated diversity of various information and knowledge resources.

As a further relevant issue, future research might investigate how processes of organizational socialization contribute to the function of age-diverse teams through their impact on newcomers. Organizational socialization is referring to assimilation processes through which new organizational members adjust their mindsets and actions to the existing organizational norms (Morrison, 2002).

In consequence, strong organizational socialization norms are a core prerequisite for developing an organizational culture. From an age-diversity perspective, one might argue that strong socialization norms might be beneficial for age-diverse teams and companies, as new employees are forced to adjust their values to the organizational goals and purposes to be able to stay in the organization. Following this logic, the socialization strategies might be able to create an organization-wide meta-identity that superposes any age-based sub-identities, and categorization processes are less likely to happen. In such companies with dominant newcomer socialization practices, we would expect to at least find a non-significant relationship between age diversity and collective outcomes, as the negative processes of age diversity should be reduced or prevented. If, however, a company aims to gain benefits from age diversity in team and organizational settings, strong organizational socialization strategies might also be counterproductive. We propose that a too strong adjustment to organizational values, goals, and behaviors might suppress the individualized strengths, knowledge, and behaviors of new employees from different age groups that could enrich the collective capabilities of an age-diverse team. Given these competing theoretical rationales, we highly encourage more research on successful socialization strategies in age-diverse teams and companies that enable an equal balance between belongingness and uniqueness (Shore et al., 2011) of members from different age groups.

IMPLICATIONS FOR PRACTITIONERS

Although this chapter is mainly focused on a future research agenda for age diversity in global teams and organizations, our discussion has implications for practitioners as well. These implications are discussed below.

Perhaps the most obvious but important practical implication is that age diversity is a human resource pattern that needs to be actively managed by supervisors and companies. As current studies and especially meta-analyses indicate, age diversity can impair both team and overall company performance. This is still something new for many executives in companies, as the public debate and the practitioner-oriented literature often assumes that just increasing the age diversity will by itself lead to positive processes and outcomes in teams and companies.

Companies should regularly assess the age structure of their workforce on the team, department, and preferably also the organizational level to have an empirical base for focused management and leadership strategies for an age-diverse workforce. This will allow management to monitor changes in age-diversity levels that require special attention. Beyond age diversity, other surface-level (i.e., gender, ethnicity) or deep-level (i.e., personality, subjective age) diversity categories should also be considered when staffing new work teams or departments because the emerging faultline literature shows that the alignment or misalignment of various diversity characteristics has a powerful impact on team processes and outcomes. This is particularly relevant during efforts to increase workforce participation of female employees in formerly male-dominated areas (i.e., top management teams, R&D departments), as in this situation the risk of strong subgroup formation based on missing cross-cutting demographic attributes (i.e., only old male team members and young female team members) increases.

Furthermore, companies should support training and development programs that prevent differences in mobility and the application of new technologies by older and younger employees, which might also spur age-based sub-grouping. For example, participation in multinational projects and expatriate stays should be possible and fostered for employees from all age groups to avoid having the development of an international perspective and network among only specific employee age groups. Additionally, it is crucial that IT competencies are developed for all age groups through training and regular application opportunities to prevent a technology-related "age gap" that might increase the likelihood of age-based subgroup splitting, in particular in virtual team settings.

Leadership strategies and reward systems for an age-diverse workforce should concentrate on creating the right contextual conditions that prevent negative consequences of age-based subgroup formation, while at the same time members of the different age groups should be encouraged to combine their complementary strengths, knowledge, and capabilities. In the empirical literature, TFL has shown to be a promising leadership behavior for age-diverse settings (i.e., Kearney & Gebert, 2009; Kunze & Bruch, 2010). Through the fostering of common goals and visions, role model behavior, intellectual stimulation, and individualized consideration, transformational leaders seem to be able to create a common team identity that superposes age-based sub-identities. This leadership behavior might be especially effective if it is combined with collectively focused goal and reward systems (i.e., team-based goals instead of individual-focused goals) that require interaction of employees from different age groups for joint task completion. Furthermore, based on preliminary empirical results (Kunze, Leicht-Deobald, & Bruch, 2013c), we would assume that a strong differentiation in terms of individualized-focused leadership and individualized reward systems should be the least effective strategy for age-diverse teams.

In addition to team-focused leadership and reward systems, we argue that it is critical that organizational practices and climates be adjusted to an age-diverse workforce. Specifically, we would advise companies to install age-inclusive HR practices in terms of recruiting, development and career opportunities, access to training efforts, and an overall age-friendly organizational culture (Boehm et al., 2014). Through these practices, organizations should be able to create an age-diversity-oriented climate that makes prejudices, discrimination, and conflicts based on the age-group membership less likely.

Finally, we have highlighted the importance of considering age diversity as a global, cross-cultural issue for companies. This is especially relevant for multinational enterprises operating in multicultural environments. For these companies, we would not recommend to roll out a worldwide age-diversity strategy, but rather to customize their practices and interventions to different subsidiaries. While in some countries with a young workforce (e.g., India, Indonesia), teams and departments are most often age-homogenous and thus no special age-diversity measures are needed, in many Western industrialized countries, age diversity is already today a main challenge and needs to be actively managed. Additionally, we would speculate that some cultural values and identities are more favorable for positive outcomes of age diversity than others, and that, for example, a higher respect for seniority and a more collectivistic culture in East Asian countries are a better environment to reap the benefits of age-diverse teams.

CONCLUSION

The goal of this chapter was to develop a forward-looking, global, and use-inspired perspective on dealing with an age-diverse workforce. Building on a short literature review, we developed a conceptual framework on how the empirical research on age diversity might continue in future studies. Most notably, we encourage more research taking a global, cross-cultural perspective on age diversity in teams and companies. Additionally, we suggest that further attention be given to crucial boundary conditions such as task distributions and reward systems, leadership strategies, and organizational factors deserve more attention in future research. In sum, we believe that a lot of interesting avenues lay ahead for age-diversity researchers that will result in effective strategies for practitioners to manage an increasingly age-diverse workplace.

REFERENCES

Armstrong-Stassen, M., & Templer, A. (2005). Adapting training for older employees. *Journal of Management Development*, 24(1), 57–67.

Baltes, P. B., & Baltes, M. M. (1990). Psychological perspectives on successful aging: The model of selective optimization with compensation. In P. B. Baltes & M. M. Baltes (Eds.), *Successful Aging: Perspectives from the Behavioral Sciences* (pp. 1–34). Cambridge: Cambridge University Press.

Barak, B. (2009). Age identity: A cross-cultural global approach. *International Journal of Behavioral Development*, 33(1), 2–11.

Bezrukova, K., Jehn, K. A., Zanutto, E. L., & Thatcher, S. M. (2009). Do workgroup faultlines help or hurt? A moderated model of faultlines, team identification, and group performance. *Organization Science*, 20, 35–50.

Biemann, T., & Andresen, M. (2010). Self-initiated foreign expatriates versus assigned expatriates: Two distinct types of international careers? *Journal of Managerial Psychology*, 25(4), 430–448.

Boehm, S., Kunze, F., & Bruch, H. (2014). Spotlight on age-diversity climate: The impact of age-inclusive HR practices on firm-level outcomes. *Personnel Psychology*, 67, 667–704.

Bond, M. H., & Wang, K. H. (1986). The social psychology of the Chinese people. In M. H. Bond (Ed.). *The Psychology of the Chinese People* (pp. 213–266). Hong Kong: Oxford University Press.

Byrne, D. (1971). *The Attraction Paradigm*. New York: Academic Press.

Catterall, M., & Maclaran, P. (2001). Body talk: Questioning the assumptions in cognitive age. *Psychology & Marketing*, 18(10): 1117–1133.

Cennamo, L., & Gardner, D. (2008). Generational differences in work values, outcomes and person-organisation values fit. *Journal of Managerial Psychology*, 23(8), 891–906.

Chiu, C. K., Chan, A. W., Snape, E., & Redman, T. (2001). Age stereotypes and discriminatory attitudes towards older workers: An East-West comparison. *Human Relations*, 54(5): 629–661.

Choi, S., & Rainey, H. G. (2010). Managing diversity in US federal agencies: Effects of diversity and diversity management on employee perceptions of organizational performance. *Public Administration Review*, 70(1), 109–121.

Erickson, R., & Grove, W. (2007). Why emotions matter: Age, agitation, and burnout among registered nurses. *Online Journal of Issues in Nursing*, 13(1). Available at: http://gm6.nursingworld.org/MainMenuCategories/ANAMarketplace/ANAPeriodicals/OJIN/TableofContents/vol132008/No1Jan08/ArticlePreviousTopic/WhyEmotionsMatterAgeAgitationandBurnoutAmongRegisteredNurses.html (accessed January 12, 2015).

Eurostat (2013). *Old-Age Dependency Ratio, 1960–2060*. European Commission. Available at: http://epp.eurostat.ec.europa.eu/statistics_explained/index.php?File:Oldage_dependency_ratio,_19602060_(1)_(population_aged_65_years_and_over_as_%25_of_population_aged_15-64).png&filetimestamp=20120321111604 (accessed July 13, 2013).

Garloff, A., Pohl, C., & Schanne, N. (2012). Demografischer Wandel der letzten 20 Jahre. *IAB Kurzbericht, 10*(2012), 1–7.

Hofstede, G. (2001). *Cultures Consequences. Comparing Values, Behaviors, Institutions, and Organizations Across Nations*. Thousand Oaks, CA: Sage.

Horwitz, S. K., & Horwitz, I. B. (2007). The effects of team diversity on team outcomes: A meta-analytic review of team demography. *Journal of Management, 33*(6), 987–1015.

House, R. J., Hanges, P. J., Javidan, M., Dorfman, P. W., & Gupta, V. (2004). *Leadership, Culture, and Organizations: The GLOBE Study of 62 Societies*. Beverly Hills, CA: Sage.

Ilmarinen, J. E. (2001). Aging workers. *Occupational and Environmental Medicine, 58*(8), 546–552.

Jehn, K. A., & Bezrukova, K. (2004). A field study of group diversity, workgroup context, and performance. *Journal of Organizational Behavior, 25*(6), 703–729.

Joshi, A., & Roh, H. (2009). The role of context in work team diversity resarch: A meta-analytic review. *Academy of Management Journal, 52*(3), 599–627.

Kanfer, R., & Ackerman, P. L. (2004). Aging, adult development, and work motivation. *Academy of Management Review, 29*(3), 440–458.

Kanter, R. M. (1977). Some effects of proportions on group life: Skewed sex ratios and responses to token women. *American Journal of Sociology, 82*(5), 965–990.

Kearney, E., & Gebert, D. (2009). Managing diversity and enhancing team outcomes: The promise of transformational leadership. *Journal of Applied Psychology, 94*(1), 77–98.

Kilduff, M., Angelmar, R., & Mehra, A. (2000). Top management-team diversity and firm performance: Examining the role of cognitions. *Organization Science, 11*(1), 21–34.

Kooij, D. T., de Lange, A. H., Jansen, P. G., & Dikkers, J. S. (2013). Beyond chronological age. Examining perceived future time and subjective health as age-related mediators in relation to work-related motivations and well-being. *Work & Stress, 27*(1), 88–105.

Kunze, F., & Boehm, S. (2013). Research on age diversity in the workforce: Current trends and future research directions. In C. Cooper, R. Burke, & J. Field (Eds.), *Sage Handbook on Work, Aging, and Society* (pp. 41–60). Thousand Oaks, CA: Sage.

Kunze, F., & Bruch, H. (2010). Age-based faultlines and perceived productive energy: The moderation of transformational leadership. *Small Group Research, 41*(5), 593–620.

Kunze, F., Boehm, S., & Bruch, H. (2011). Age diversity, age discrimination, and performance consequences: A cross organizational study. *Journal of Organizational Behavior, 32*(2), 264–290.

Kunze, F., Boehm, S., & Bruch, H. (2013a). Organizational performance consequences of age diversity: Inspecting the role of diversity-friendly HR policies and top managers' negative age stereotypes. *Journal of Management Studies, 50*(3), 413–442.

Kunze, F., de Jong, S. B., & Bruch, H. (2013b). Consequences of collective-focused and differentiated individual-focused leadership: Development and testing of an organizational-level model. *Journal of Management*. DOI: 10.1177/0149206313498903.

Kunze, F., Leicht-Deobald, U., Bruch, H. (2013c). Age/gender faultlines and team innovation behavior: Exploring the role of differentiated leadership behavior. Paper presented at the Congress of the European Association for Work and Organizational Psychology (EAWOP) in Münster, Germany.

Lau, D. C., & Murnighan, J. K. (1998). Demographic diversity and faultlines: The compositional dynamics of organizational groups. *The Academy of Management Review*, 23(2), 325–340.

Lawrence, B. S. (1988). New wrinkles in the theory of age: Demography, norms, and performance ratings. *Academy of Management Journal*, 31, 309–337.

Lawrence, B. S. (1997). The black box of organizational demography. *Organization Science*, 8(1), 1–22.

Li, J., Chu, C. W. L., Lam, K. C., & Liao, S. (2011). Age diversity and firm performance in an emerging economy: Implications for cross-cultural human resource management. *Human Resource Management*, 50(2), 247–270.

Martens, A., Goldenberg, J. L., & Greenberg, J. (2005). A terror management perspective on ageism. *Journal of Social Issues*, 61, 223–239.

McClurg, L. N. (2001). Team rewards: How far have we come? *Human Resource Management*, 40(1), 73–86.

Meyer, B., & Glenz, A. (2013). Team faultline measures: A computational comparison and a new approach to multiple subgroups. *Organizational Research Methods*, 16(3), 393–424.

Montepare, J. M. (2009). Subjective age: Toward a guiding lifespan framework. *International Journal of Behavioral Development*, 33(1), 42–46.

Morrison, E. W. (2002). Newcomers' relationships: The role of social network ties during socialization. *Academy of Management Journal*, 45(6), 1149–1160.

Naveh-Benjamin, M. (2000). Adult age differences in memory performance: Tests of an associative deficit hypothesis. *Journal of Experimental Psychology: Learning, Memory, and Cognition*, 26(5), 1170–1187.

Peeters, M., & Groot, L. (2012). Demographic change across the globe-maintaining social security in ageing economies. *World Economics*, 13(2), 75–97.

Pelled, L. H., Xin, K. R., & Weiss, A. M. (2001). No es como mi: Relational demography and conflict in a Mexican production facility. *Journal of Occupational and Organizational Psychology*, 74(1), 63–84.

Reisenwitz, T. H., & Iyer, R. (2009). Differences in Generation X and Generation Y: Implications for organization and marketers. *Marketing Management Journal*, 19(2), 91–103.

Samson, M. M., Meeuwsen, I. B., Crowe, A., Dessens, J. A., Duursma, S. A., & Verhaar, H. J. (2000). Relationships between physical performance measures, age, height and body weight in healthy adults. *Age and Ageing*, 29(3), 235–242.

Schwall, A. R. (2012). Defining age and using age-relevant constructs. In J. W. Hedge & W. C. Borman (Eds.), *The Oxford Handbook of Work and Aging* (pp. 169–186). Oxford: Oxford University Press.

Schwartz, S. H. (1994). *Beyond Individualism/Collectivism: New Cultural Dimensions of Values*. Thousand Oaks, CA: Sage.

Shore, L. M., Randel, A. E., Chung, B. G., Michelle, A. D., Holcombe Erhart, K., & Singh, G. (2011). Inclusion and diversity in work groups: A review and model for future research. *Journal of Management*, 37(4), 1262–1289.

Tajfel, H., & Turner, J. C. (1986). The social identity theory of intergroup behaviour. In S. Worchel & W. G. Austin (Eds.), *Psychology of Intergroup Relation* (pp. 7–24). Chicago, IL: Nelson-Hall.

Thatcher, S., & Patel, P. C. (2011). Demographic faultlines: A meta-analysis of the literature. *Journal of Applied Psychology*, 96(6), 1119–1193.

Trezzini, B. (2008). Probing the group faultline concept: An evaluation of measures of patterned multi-dimensional group diversity. *Quality and Quantity*, 42(3), 339–368.

UNRIC (2013). *Mass Immigration to Norway.* Available at: www.unric.org/en/youth-unemployment/27413-mass-immigration-to-norway (accessed July 10, 2013).

van Dijk, H., van Engen, M. L., & van Knippenberg, D. (2012). Defying conventional wisdom: A meta-analytical examination of the differences between demographic and job-related diversity relationships with performance. *Organizational Behavior and Human Decision Processes, 119*(1), 38–53.

van Knippenberg, D., & Schippers, M. C. (2007). Work group diversity. *Annual Review of Psychology, 58,* 515–541.

van Knippenberg, D., & Sitkin, S. B. (2013). A critical assessment of charismatic-transformational leadership research: Back to the drawing board? *The Academy of Management Annals, 7*(1), 1–60.

van Knippenberg, D., de Dreu, C. K. W., & Homan, A. C. (2004). Work group diversity and group performance: An integrative model and research agenda. *Journal of Applied Psychology, 89*(6), 1008–1022.

van Knippenberg, D., Dawson, J. F., West, M. A., & Homan, A. C. (2011). Diversity faultlines, shared objectives, and top management team performance. *Human Relations, 64*(3), 307–336.

Wegge, J., Roth, C., Neubach, B., Schmidt, K. H., & Kanfer, R. (2008). Age and gender diversity as determinants of performance and health in a public organization: The role of task complexity and group size. *Journal of Applied Psychology, 93*(6), 1301–1313.

Wu, J. B., Tsui, A. S., & Kinicki, A. J. (2010). Consequences of differentiated leadership in groups. *Academy of Management Journal, 53*(1), 90–106.

Zenger, T. R., & Lawrence, B. S. (1989). Organizational demography: The differential effects of age and tenure distributions on technical communication. *Academy of Management Journal, 32*(2), 353–376.

3

Human Resource Management and Sustainability at Work Across the Lifespan: An Integrative Perspective

Annet H. de Lange, Dorien T. A. M. Kooij, and Beatrice I. J. M. van der Heijden

> We need to defend the interests of those whom we've never met and never will.
>
> Sachs (2012)

BACKGROUND

The global market has witnessed important changes in the nature of work, as well as in the composition of its workforce (see, for example, Chapter 1, pages 3–22 in this book). These developments have, for example, made the contents of our work more knowledge-intensive, resulted in more flexible workplaces and time schedules, and resulted in a more diverse workforce that has to deal with continuously changing work-related requirements due to constant innovations (Gratton, 2011; Truxillo & Fraccaroli, 2013). One of the most important societal trends affecting our workplace and workforce is the aging of the Western population (Hertel, van der Heijden, de Lange, & Deller, 2013; Truxillo, Cadiz, Rinner, Zaniboni, & Fraccaroli, 2012). The combination of a smaller number of younger workers relative to their older counterparts, and the current "early exit" culture in Europe (Hertel et al., 2013) has resulted in a stronger (financial) need among employers to find ways to enable or "sustain" aging workers into a prolonged working life. In addition, from a management perspective, there is accumulating (research) attention on the question of how we can develop and maintain a *sustainable* aging workforce (Hertel et al., 2013; Shultz & Wang, 2011) aimed at optimizing the person-environment fit (PE fit) between the (changing) worker and his or her (changing) work across time (Edwards, Cable, Williamson, Lambert, & Shipp, 2006; Rudolph, de Lange, & van der Heijden, 2014).

Although the number of studies focusing on the topic "sustainability" has been growing, a critical discussion is needed on human resource management (HRM) conceptualizations of "sustainability at work" (see Ehnert & Harry, 2012; Jackson & Seo, 2010; Jackson, Renwick, Jabbour, & Muller-Camen, 2011 for important reflections on previous definitions and conceptualizations of sustainable HRM). The purpose of this chapter is not to provide an extensive or complete overview on this topic (cf., relevant work of Docherty, Kira, & Shani, 2009 on sustainable work systems), but rather to introduce relevant definitions and new lines of theoretical reasoning directed toward linking sustainability at work and HRM theory and research. More specifically, we aim to extend the current literature on sustainability at work by: (a) discussing what we actually mean by the concept of sustainability at work; (b) discussing the important role that meaningful bundles of human resource (HR) practices can play in developing sustainability at work; and (c) addressing the importance of using an integrated strategic perspective in research, as well as in HRM practice, to facilitate sustainability at work. We will start with a thorough discussion of the concept of sustainability at work.

Sustainability at Work: Concepts and Definitions

We begin with a brief historical overview of the word "sustainability" and its relevant components. In 1972, an important definition of sustainability was introduced by the United Nations (UN) during a conference on the human environment. The UN defined sustainability as "a general worldview according to which people should strive to fulfill their needs in a manner such that the ability of future generations to fulfill their needs is not endangered" (Docherty et al., 2009, p. 3). During the 1980s, we subsequently witnessed a paradigm shift from a focus on the concept of development toward the concept of "sustainable development," defined as "development that meets the needs of the present without compromising the ability of the future generations to meet their own needs" (United Nations Conference on Environment and Development, 1992; Wilkinson, Hill, & Gollan, 2001; World Commission on Environment and Development, 1987).

The notion of human (also labeled as social) sustainability comprises a recent addition to the sustainability debate (Garavan & McGuire, 2010, p. 491). Specifically, Pfeffer (2010, p. 35) referred to human sustainability in the following way: "Just as physical sustainability considers the consequences of organisational activity for material, physical resources: social sustainability might consider how organizational activities affect people's physical and mental health and well-being—the stress of work practices on the human system . . ." (cf., Table 3.1 for a summary of all relevant definitions). A relevant example definition in this regard was provided by Carl Holling (2001, p. 390), who defined human sustainability as "the capacity to create, test and maintain adaptive capability." Holling's definition suggests an important responsibility of the worker (or individual employee) in creating, testing and maintaining his or her own work capacity or ability. Oldham and Hackman (2010), in their discussion of future job design research, signaled a similar trend and stressed the increased importance of personal initiative or responsibility of workers to successfully progress or adjust one's work capacity or ability across time by shaping or customizing their jobs into more sustainable work (e.g., job crafting) (Wrzesniewski & Dutton, 2001).

Obviously, the sustainability concept is highly complex and, as a result, is difficult to capture or operationalize using one specific scale. Nonetheless, Constanza and Patten (1995) suggest that there are three basic questions researchers should tackle when examining sustainability (at work), namely: (1) Which (sub)systems are involved and which parts of these systems need to persist or survive across time (e.g., which included groups of workers do we want to monitor across time, what kind of work will they conduct now and in the future, who are their HR managers and supervisors, and what can we say about the organizations or broader context in which these workers are active)? (2) For how long should they persist or survive (for example, do we want our subgroup of workers to continue working; for a short time frame (e.g., one year), until retirement, or until death)? (3) When do we measure or determine sustainability (depending on the outcomes of questions 1–2)?

The aforementioned definitions, presented in Table 3.1, suggest that the objective of a safe and healthy work environment has become an integrative part of the concept of sustainable development, and both environmental aspects are regarded as important facilitators in making development sustainable, equitable, and sound from an economic, human, social, and even from an ethical point of view (Barling & Griffiths, 2011; Levi, 2011).

TABLE 3.1
Different Examples of Definitions for the Concept of Sustainability

Example Sustainability Definition	Relevant Elements Related to the Four Key Dimensions of Sustainability*	Source
1. A general worldview according to which people should strive to fulfill their needs in a manner such that the ability of future generations to fulfill their needs is not endangered.	• Global perspective • Interconnectedness of different generations • Equal or fair distribution of resources across workers • Current level and future level of work-related requirements	Docherty, Kira, and Shani (2009, p. 3)
2. "Sustainable development," development that meets the needs of the present without compromising the ability of the future generations to meet their own needs.	• Equal or fair distribution of resources across workers • Current level and future level of work-related needs	Wilkinson, Hill, and Gollan (2001)
3. Social sustainability might consider how organizational activities affect people's physical and mental health and well-being—the stress of work practices on the human system.	• Organizational perspective • Relations between organizational practices and individual worker outcomes	Pfeffer (2010, p. 35)
4. The capacity to create, test and maintain adaptive capability.	• Stability as well as progress • Adaptive behavior in times of change • Resource view: capability	Carl Holling (2001, p. 390)

* Four key dimensions: resource preservation and regeneration, priority and fairness, progress and stability, and system-based perspective

Similarly, the International Labour Organization (ILO, 2013, p. 6) defined sustainability at work as decent work that:

> involves opportunities for work that is productive and delivers a fair income, security in the workplace and social protection for families, better prospects for personal development and social integration, freedom for people to express their concerns, organize and participate in the decisions that affect their lives and equality of opportunity and treatment for all women and men.

Another related concept in this regard is "Healthy Work." A joint definition put forward by the ILO and the World Health Organization Committee on Occupational Health defines Healthy Work as "the placing and maintenance of the worker in an occupational environment adapted to his physiological and psychological capabilities; and, to summarize, the adaptation of work to man and of each man to his job."

Four Key Dimensions of Sustainability at Work

Based on earlier work of Docherty et al. (2009), and in accordance with the relevant components of the aforementioned sustainability definitions as summarized in Table 3.1, we argue that the sustainability concept incorporates four key dimensions that can be used in future research to operationalize the concept of sustainability at work into more concrete measurable variables. We describe the first dimension as a *resource-based dimension*. This dimension focuses on sustainability as a process of preservation, as well as regeneration of resources, stating that no generation (e.g., the group of older workers) be allowed to consume all (e.g., job-related) resources at the cost of other generations (e.g., younger workers). The second dimension highlights *priority and fairness*, and emphasizes protecting the needs of all people, now and in the future, instead of satisfying total needs of privileged people, as is the case in the present. This second dimension suggests that the sustainability concept is conceptualized using so-called value-based definitions (i.e., everyone has the right to be engaged in decent work) (Docherty et al., 2009).[1] In other words, this means fairness and equal priority for all and not a privileged few. For example, job-related development as an HR practice is important for all aging workers to sustain a PE fit, but earlier research has shown that contemporary organizational HR practices (e.g., training, etc.) are particularly tailored to the promotion needs of younger workers and less attractive for older workers (Kooij, Jansen, Dikkers, & de Lange, 2014).

The third dimension emphasizes *progress* and refers to the importance of social and technological innovations in relation to the content and type of work (e.g., flexible work), as well as in skills and personal resources of workers (e.g., changing digital skills and level of available knowledge, and future work-related requirements) across time. That is to say, the required innovations make long-term views and proactive investigations regarding the need to focus on stability versus change across time necessary to capture the sustainability part of the (continuously changing) work environment and its included workers. Moreover, *stability in itself*, being an indicator of maintenance (e.g., stable safe work, stable mental health of workers), has become an important new topic or process in the search for sustainability across time, and should therefore be investigated separately instead of controlled for (see future research agenda later in this chapter). Thus, as an example, organizations and aging workers themselves should not only combat skill obsolescence, but should also adapt to future work by developing new necessary skills and knowledge.

The fourth sustainability dimension embedded in previously discussed definitions concerns *system-based aspects that highlight the role and interconnectedness of multiple actors* (i.e., individual workers, employers, organization, and other stakeholders, as well as the role and interconnectedness with the macro-context; cf., Docherty et al., 2009), in relation to the experienced fit between work and individual workers (Edwards et al., 2006; Karasek & Theorell, 1990). The organization is not the only actor responsible for sustainable work; aging workers themselves are responsible as well, and can, for example, craft their job to make sure it continuously fits their (changing) motives and abilities (e.g., Kooij, Tims, & Kanfer, 2015).

The question remains whether the operationalizations used in earlier empirical research meet the aforementioned framework of four key dimensions of sustainability at work. We therefore conducted a literature search using the key term "sustainable work" in the abstract to examine the included concepts and their operationalizations. This literature search resulted in 12 empirical studies, of which six records were excluded after carefully screening the abstract (one dissertation abstract, three abstracts were not based on worker populations, and two abstracts did not include a relevant reference to sustainable work). Table 3.2 presents the results of our review and reveals that sustainability at work has been operationalized in a diverse way using variables that tap the design of work, as well as worker outcomes (e.g., vitality, work ability, lifelong learning; cf., Table 3.2), and even aspects of leadership and HRM. Moreover, from the review of the scholarly literature, it appears that researchers, when examining sustainability at work, refer to a variety of theories, namely:

- leadership and management theory that includes participation of workers (Dellve, Skagert, & Eklöf, 2008);
- job design theory (e.g., Karasek & Theorell, 1990);
- socio-technical system (e.g., Huczynski & Buchanan, 2007);
- chaordic systems theory (e.g., Hock, 1999; van Eijnatten, 2004);
- multidimensional critical human resource management theory (Jabbour & Santos, 2008);
- social exchange theory (Blau, 1964);
- work ability theory (Ilmarinen, 2001);
- conservation of resources theory (Hobfoll, 2001);
- learning theory (Edwards, 2005);
- (lifespan) motivation theory (Deci, Ryan, & Guay, 2013; Heckhausen, Wrosch, & Schulz, 2010; Kanfer & Ackerman, 2004); and
- job crafting theory (Wrzesniewski & Dutton, 2001).

Finally, a perusal of the studies shown in Table 3.2 suggests that sustainability at work is most often defined as work ability (three of the six included studies refer to work ability theory) (Ilmarinen, 2001).

Nonetheless, our review of the nascent empirical literature to date shows that no study includes definitions and operationalizations that fully tap the concept of sustainability at work as shown in Table 3.1, or include the associated four key dimensions: resource preservation and regeneration, priority and fairness, progress and stability, and system-based perspective. For example, studies that build upon work ability theory typically operationalize the sustainability concept using a measure of absence from work instead of the relevant, broader work ability index developed by the Finnish Institute of Occupational Health in the early 1980s of the previous century (Tuomi, Ilmarinen, Jahkola, Katajarinne, & Tulkki, 1998).

Work ability (see also Chapter 6 of this book) expresses the extent to which an employee is capable of working in the present and in the near future, taking his or her own physical and mental resources, as well as the requested level of work demands, into account (Ilmarinen, 2001; Ilmarinen & Tuomi, 1992). The concept of work ability (Ilmarinen, 2001, 2006) includes questions measuring one's abilities and motivation to work, but also includes an assessment of the psychosocial nature of work. According to Ilmarinen (2006), the work ability of employees is assumed to be influenced by micro-, meso-, and macro-level factors (indicating a system approach). At the micro-level, the work ability of workers may be influenced by variables such as general health and individual characteristics (e.g., lifestyle behavior and functional capacities). In contrast, at the meso-level, variables that affect work ability pertain mostly to the work environment (e.g., ergonomics and physical load) and organizational leadership, and in particular to transformational leadership styles aimed at optimizing the fit between the skills, health, motivation of a worker, and his or her changing work environment across time. At the macro-level, network and societal context (i.e., social support, rules, and regulations) are the variables that are posited to most powerfully affect an individual's work ability. Although earlier research has presented criticism concerning the psychometric quality and factor structure of the scale (Radkiewicz & Widerszal-Bazyl, 2005), the systematic and multilevel approach to work ability by Ilmarinen (2009) is consistent with the proposed multidimensional (four) concept of sustainability at work, and we therefore recommend that researchers include measures such as the validated work ability index when seeking to assess sustainability at work.

In addition, Rudolph and colleagues (2014) recently suggested that besides the work ability index, researchers can also examine stability and change in adjustment processes at work through objective and subjective *indices of sustained skills to work and work performance* (e.g., active work participation, job performance), and work *engagement or motivation* as indicators of positive adaptation. As such, Rudolph and colleagues (2014) argue that continued employment participation might be the ultimate criterion for successful psychological adjustment to employment. Second, Rudolph and colleagues (2014) state that more general forms of *subjective success criteria* (e.g., psychological success) may also be considered as indicators of positive adaptation (see van Solinge & Henkens, 2008) (e.g., considerations of subjective well-being and life satisfaction). Furthermore, if we assume that successful adjustment is an objective phenomenon, we could also consider one's perceived success in the adjustment process by measuring factors such as career success and employability (de Lange & van der Heijden, 2013).

In line with the work ability theory and elaborating on the notion of PE fit (Edwards et al., 2006), we assume that worker attitudes and behaviors are sustainable if their (future) needs, abilities, and interests are congruent with aspects and (future) requirements of their current and future work environment. More specifically, we posit that sustainability at work involves a parallel accomplishment of three different objectives, namely: (a) the maintenance of workers' health, motivation, and working capacity or their

TABLE 3.2
Results of Empirical (Peer) Reviewed Studies Focusing on "Sustainable Work"

Studies	Concept(s)	Definitions	Measurement Instrument	Theories	Design or type of paper
1. Dellve, Skagert, and Eklöf (2008)	Sustainable work ability	Sustainable work ability: Long-term work attendance (cf., Dellve, Eriksson, & Vilhelmsson, 2007).	Measured as mean municipal prevalence of long-term work attendance (i.e., no single spell of sick leave exceeding 13 days per year).	Work ability and management theory	Register-based data analyses
2. Hägglund, Helsing, and Sandmark (2010)	Sustainable work ability: Concept can be described as related to high presence at work and no sickness absence.	Sustainable work ability: Referring to *capacity* instead of work, and no definition has been provided of the concept sustainable.	Proxy measure, including sick leave and presence at work.	Work ability theory (Ilmarinen, 2001)	Cross-sectional research
3. Kira and van Eijnatten (2008)	Socially sustainable work organizations	Socially sustainable work organizations: Have a dynamic ability to function both by repeating accustomed and by devising innovative solutions, and they maintain this operational viability by promoting the functional capabilities of their stakeholders. The functional	Not included	Socio-technical system theory	Theoretical paper theory

	Individual sustainability		Chaordic systems	
	Sustainable work abilities	Sustainable work abilities: Long-term adaptive and proactive abilities to work, fare well at work, and contribute through working	Not included	
4. Kira, van Eijnatten, and Balkin (2010)		capability of a sustainable work organization builds on the functional capabilities of its stakeholders, while the stakeholder functional capability is connected to the functional capability of a work organization. On an individual level, sustainability can be defined as the dynamic, sustained capability for 'interior' and 'exterior' functioning. Interior encompasses cognitive (e.g., learning) and affective (e.g., vitality) (cf. Spreitzer, Sutcliffe, Dutton, Sonenshein, & Grant, 2005) functioning, while exterior covers psychophysical or "empirically measurable" functioning.		Job design literature (Hackman and Oldham, 1975; Karasek & Theorell, 1990), resourced-based theories (conservation of resources theory; Hobfoll, 2001)	Conceptual paper with focus on personal crafting and collaborative work crafting affecting both worker and its work.

continued . . .

TABLE 3.2
Continued

Studies	Concept(s)	Definitions	Measurement Instrument	Theories	Design or type of paper
	Versus sustainable work	Sustainable work: Work that promotes the development in personal resources leading to work ability		Crafting theory (Wrzesniewski & Dutton, 2001): job crafting versus collaborative crafting (emphasizing interconnectedness of workers, employees, and other stakeholders) Self-determination theory (Deci & Ryan, 2000) Learning theory (Edwards, 2005) Work ability theory (Ilmarinen, 2001) Lifespan theory (Kanfer & Ackerman, 2004)	
5. Tjulin, MacEhen, and Ekberg (2010)	Sustainable recovery and work ability	Successful return-to-work/post-return phase	Interviewing experiences in post-return-to-work phase. Respondents reported the question of who was responsible for the sustainability in work ability was not formally addressed in policy or even informally acknowledged among all of the workplace actors.	Occupational health theory	Open-ended interview study

6. Vickers (2010)	Sustainability	Sustainability: Development that meets the needs of the present without compromising the ability of future generations to meet their own needs (Wilkinson et al., 2001)	Not included	Multidimensional critical human resource management theory (Jabbour & Santos, 2008)
	Sustainable workplaces	Sustainable workplace: Workplaces that enable workers to keep working, especially those who find themselves working on and around the fringes, with relevant required sustainable work skills: (i) creativity; (ii) long-term focus; cooperative and interdependent behavior; and (iv) high tolerance for ambiguity and unpredictability (Jabbour & Santos, 2008)		
	Sustainable human resource development	Sustainable human resource management: Practices that stimulate workers to think, create, and reflect in original ways about their workplaces and how things are done (fostering innovation).		Introduction of editor

ability to work within their current or other organization, now and in the future (see also van der Heijde & van der Heijden, 2006); (b) the improvement of the working environment to create work settings that are conducive to health, development, motivation, and internal or external mobility of workers; and (c) the development of work organizations and working cultures (i.e., management systems, personnel policy) in a direction that supports worker health, motivation, development, mobility, and safety at work, and in doing so promotes a sound social climate that positively influences organizational performance (de Lange & van der Heijden, 2013). The scholarly discipline and practice of HRM is aimed at understanding how to reach and actually achieve these three objectives.

HUMAN RESOURCE MANAGEMENT

Human resource management refers to all activities associated with the management of work and people within organizations (Boxall & Purcell, 2011). These activities are performed by different actors at different levels (Wright & Nishii, 2013). At the organizational level, the firm's decision-makers (e.g., the board of directors, the HR director) develop *intended HR practices*, which are the result of the development of an HR strategy that is assumed to effectively elicit certain employee outcomes. These intended HR practices are subsequently implemented by line managers, recruiters, and others, and are referred to as *actual HR practices*. Next, at the individual level, these *objective* actual HR practices are perceived and interpreted *subjectively* by employees, and are referred to as *perceived HR practices*. Not surprisingly, earlier research has shown that intended, actual, and perceived HR practices may differ significantly (Khilji & Wang, 2006).

In addition, social exchange (Blau, 1964) and signaling theories (Ostroff & Bowen, 2000) indicate that perceived HR practices will, in turn, influence worker attitudes and behaviors. These theories posit that HR practices have a positive effect on employees by supporting them, or by functioning as "signals" of the organization's good intentions toward them. In this line of reasoning, the general assumption is that individual workers view HR practices as a personalized commitment toward them, as an investment in them, and as a recognition of their contribution, which they will then reciprocate through corresponding positive attitudes and behavior toward the organization (Hannah & Iverson, 2004; Shore & Shore, 1995). In this chapter, we focus on HR practices as *perceived* and *used* by especially older employees.

HR Practices for Aging Workers

Since sustainability at work is associated with workers' ability, health, and motivation to work longer, we briefly review the literature on HR practices for aging workers. There is a large scholarly literature describing many HR practices that have been suggested to be beneficial for especially older workers' motivation and retention (Kooij et al., 2014). These HR practices include, for example, part-time work or retirement, flexible work hours, training programs for older workers, reduced workload, and exemption from shift work and working overtime (Armstrong-Stassen, 2008; Paul & Townsend, 1993; Rau & Adams, 2005; Remery, Henkens, Schippers, & Ekamper, 2003; Saba & Guerin, 2005). However, few studies offer a theoretical explanation for why these HR practices are beneficial for older workers, neither have they examined the influence of these HR practices on older workers' motivation and retention, or their interrelatedness with actual job design (Veth, Emans, van der Heijden, de Lange, & Korzilius, 2011).

One exception comprises Armstrong-Stassen and Ursel's (2009) study on older professionals and nurses, wherein they distinguished between training and development HR practices (e.g., targeting older workers to accommodate their needs and to update their skills) and flexible HR practices (e.g., flexible or reduced work hours, job sharing, and phased retirement). Building upon social exchange theory (Blau, 1964), Armstrong-Stassen and Ursel (2009) hypothesized that these HR practices as perceived by employees would have a positive influence on older workers' intention to remain working, through their mediating effects on perceived organizational support. In line with their expectations, they found that perceived *training and development* HR practices did indeed influence intention to remain working, partly through perceived organizational support, but that perceived *flexible* HR practices did neither affect perceived organizational support nor intention to remain.

Besides these types of HR practices specifically targeting older workers, organizations also offer more *general* HR practices, such as training, career management, and rewards, to their total pool of employees. However, it might be that these general HR practices are less appropriate to motivate and retain older workers (Conway, 2004). Finegold, Mohrman, and Spreitzer (2002) found, for example, that for older workers, job security was more important, while opportunities to develop technical skills were perceived to be less important by this category of workers. In line with these findings, we argue that the influence of these general HR practices on worker outcomes changes with age. More specifically, according to the selection optimization and compensation (SOC) model (Baltes & Baltes, 1990), as losses start to outnumber gains in old age, older people will allocate their resources, such as time, energy, and effort, differently in comparison with younger people.

Evidence on age-related changes in work-related goals and motives provides support for the notion of differences in allocation of resources across the lifespan. Kooij, de Lange, Jansen, Kanfer, and Dikkers (2011), for example, found that work motives pertaining to challenging work, career advancement, working with people, recognition, and compensation (so-called growth and extrinsic motives) were lower among older workers than younger workers, while motives pertaining to interesting work and use of skills, accomplishment, autonomy, helping others, and job security (so-called intrinsic and security motives) were higher among older workers in comparison with their younger counterparts. In other words, intrinsic and security motives appear to increase in strength with age, while growth and extrinsic motives appear to decrease in strength with age. Because motives change, the *utility or value* that particular HR practices have for employees will also change as a function of the worker's age. According to social exchange theory (Blau, 1964), the utility or value of specific HR practices determines to what extent employees repay the organization, in terms of work attitudes and behaviors, for offering them these practices. Therefore, the *influence* of HR practices on employee attitudes and behaviors can be expected to change as a function of age as well.

To further explain how the utility (value) and the influence of HR practices may have different effects on workers of different ages, we argue that it is helpful to categorize HR practices into theoretically meaningful HR bundles, according to their goals (Toh, Morgeson, & Campion, 2008; see also Table 3.3, based on Kooij, 2010). We have used the SOC model (Baltes & Baltes, 1990) to bundle HR practices (see also Kooij, Jansen, Dikkers, & de Lange, 2010, 2014).

The SOC model distinguishes four life goals to which individuals can allocate their resources: (1) growth, which refers to reaching higher levels of functioning; (2) maintenance, which refers to maintaining current levels of functioning in the face of new challenges; (3) recovery, which refers to recovering to previous levels of functioning after a loss; and (4) regulation of loss, which refers to functioning adequately at lower levels. Using the SOC life goals as an organizing scheme, we posit four broad bundles of HR practices for aging workers, of which the influence on worker outcomes changes with age (see Table 3.3):

1. development HR practices, such as training and development on the job, which may help workers to reach higher levels of functioning (growth);
2. maintenance HR practices, such as job security and flexible work hours, which may help workers to maintain current levels of functioning in the face of new challenges (maintenance);
3. utilization HR practices, such as horizontal job movement, task enrichment, and participation in decision-making, which may help workers to *utilize* and broaden relevant existing skills and personal resources; and
4. accommodative HR practices, such as reduced workload and working part-time, which may help workers to function adequately at lower levels when maintenance and recovery are no longer possible by protecting or sparing them.

SOC theory (Baltes & Baltes, 1990) further proposed that losses in old age result in a corresponding shift in one's allocation of resources away from growth and toward maintenance, recovery, and regulation of loss (Hobfoll, 2011). Accordingly, we suggest that, with age, the utility of *development* HR practices will decrease, and the utility of *utilization, maintenance, and accommodative* HR practices will increase. The influence of these HR practices on worker outcomes will therefore also change; specifically, the influence of development HR practices will decrease, and the influence of maintenance, utilization, and accommodative HR practices will increase with age.

In line with this reasoning, results of a meta-analytical approach by Kooij and colleagues (2010) found that the association between the maintenance

TABLE 3.3

Meaningful HR Bundles and Specific Example Practices to Facilitate Sustainability at Work (cf., Kooij et al., 2014)

Development	*Maintenance*	*Utilization*	*Accommodative*
Career planning	Flexible benefits	Participation	Additional leave
Continuous on-the-job development	Ergonomic adjustment	Task enrichment (knowledge transfer)	Long career break; early retirement
Regular training	Performance pay		Demotion
Promotion	Compressed working week		Exemption from overtime working
	Health promotion		

HR practices rewards, information sharing, working in teams, and flexible work hours, on the one hand, and satisfaction and commitment, on the other hand, increased with age, and that the association between the development HR practice promotion and commitment decreased with age. Another study demonstrated that the association between accommodative HR practices and satisfaction and commitment increased with age, among higher-educated and male workers, but not among lower-educated and female workers (Kooij, 2010). In sum, results of empirical work to date suggest that the impact of *development and utilization* HR practices on worker attitudes changes relatively little as a function of age, but that the impact of *maintenance* HR practices increases with age, while the impact of *accommodative* HR practices increases with age among certain groups of employees. Nevertheless, van Dalen, Henkens, and Schippers (2007) found that organizations in the Netherlands and United Kingdom mainly use accommodative HR practices (e.g., additional leave, reduced workload, and part-time retirement) to try to retain their older workers, and hardly invest in the highly important utilization practices and in tailoring development HR practices to older workers. Although lifespan theories (e.g., SOC model) predict that growth and thus development HR practices are less important for older worker motivation, earlier studies found that development HR practices *tailored to older workers* are important for older worker motivation (Armstrong-Stassen & Ursel, 2009) and that general development HR practices are even more important for older worker *performance* compared to younger worker performance, because these practices combat skill obsolescence (Kooij et al., 2013).

In conclusion, the empirical literature on the effects of HR practices among older workers is limited. Although many HR practices have been suggested to be beneficial for older workers' motivation and retention, up to now we lack theoretical ideas underpinning why these HR practices are beneficial for older workers, and, besides, few studies have examined whether these HR practices are indeed beneficial for older workers. Furthermore, organizations already offer their total pool of employees a range of HR practices, but we have little knowledge on whether these HR practices are also suitable for older workers, and how the influence of these HR practices might change with age. Therefore, we need more theoretically and empirically sound scholarly work structuring the literature on HR practices for older workers, and examining the influence of HR practices on older worker outcomes, or on how the influence of HR practices changes with age. We feel that the four HR bundles approach, based on the SOC model that we have proposed in this chapter, can be a fruitful starting point for future research in this field. These four HR bundles also differently influence sustainability at work, or the fit between the changing worker and his or her changing work requirements across the lifespan.

Functions of bundles of HR practices and sustainability at work

Up to now, few studies have focused on HRM in relation to sustainability at work. Recently, Taylor, Osland, and Egri (2012) composed a special issue on HRM's role in sustainability. According to Taylor and colleagues (2012), HRM can be both a means and an end to realizing sustainability at work. Specifically, as a means, HR practices may help directing employee mindsets and behaviors toward achieving the sustainability goals of the organization. As an end, sustainability principles can be embodied in HR practices that are aimed to result in the long-term physical, social, and economic well-being of employees.

There are only a few studies that examine the influence of HR practices on the work ability of older workers. For example, Alavinia, de Boer, Duivenbooden, Frings-Dresen, and Burdorf (2009) examined the work ability of older construction workers. They found that negative physical work-related factors, such as awkward and static back postures, and negative psychosocial work-related factors, such as low job control and high work demands, have a negative influence on their work ability. Moreover, based on SOC theory, Müller, Weigl, Heiden, Glaser, and Angerer (2012) examined interventions aimed at selection (i.e., goal setting and prioritization), optimization (i.e., permanent obtainment, improved and coordinated use of individual means to pursue selected goals), and compensation (i.e., the acquisition and application of alternative individual means or use of external or technological aid to substitute lost means, and the maintenance of a desirable level of functioning in goal attainment). They found that using SOC strategies is positively associated with the work ability of older workers, and that the positive influence of autonomy on work ability is mediated by these SOC strategies.

In sum, the literature on the influence of HR practices on indicators of sustainability at work is scarce. A fruitful avenue for future research is to link the strategic functions of the four HR bundles (see Table 3.3) to different indicators of sustainability at work (e.g., work ability, employability, etc.). Traditionally, HR policies for older workers include measures for distressed or ill workers (curing) or for workers that may suffer from complaints in the near future (prevention). Unlike curing and prevention,

HR practices can also enhance worker skills and health. This so-called "amplition" is not aimed at ameliorating negative worker outcomes, but at enhancing positive worker outcomes (Ouweneel, Schaufeli, & Le Blanc, 2009).

In this regard, and as illustrated in Figure 3.1, we hypothesize that *maintenance* HR practices can stabilize PE fit (or *function as prevention*) by realizing, for example, flexibility in terms of a compressed work week, but can also reflect a lifestyle improvement through participating in a health program. Furthermore, we argue that *accommodative* HR practices can restore a possible PE misfit by making adjustments to the job (e.g., reduce workload, remove shift work, or *function as "curation"*). These HR practices can help aging employees who are experiencing a PE misfit due, for example, to a serious declining health, by offering means to adjust the work situation in line with the health problems or by offering early or part-time retirement to better recover from work. *Development and Utilization* HR practices, on the other hand, could further improve or realize a new PE fit by changing job tasks or increasing personal resources (e.g., through training) necessary for current or future work roles. These HR practices develop employees, but also utilize existing skills and knowledge of employees (or *function as amplition*).

Obviously, we need multiple studies to examine this proposed framework. For example, new longitudinal survey studies are needed that examine the cross-lagged relations and underlying strategic functions of perceived and actual use of HR bundles of practices in relation to indicators of sustainability at work (e.g., work ability, employability, sustained performance, etc.).

TO WRAP IT UP: AN INTEGRATIVE STRATEGIC HRM PERSPECTIVE IN RESEARCH AS WELL AS PRACTICE

In this chapter, we have discussed the concept of sustainability at work in greater detail and have paid attention to the important underlying strategic functions of different HR bundles in facilitating sustainability at work. Nonetheless, our review has indicated that an overarching HRM theory to explain sustainability at work is still missing. We would therefore like to suggest a new integrative strategic HRM perspective (cf., Figure 3.2) that may trigger further theoretical development, and subsequently empirical

Human Resource Management • 69

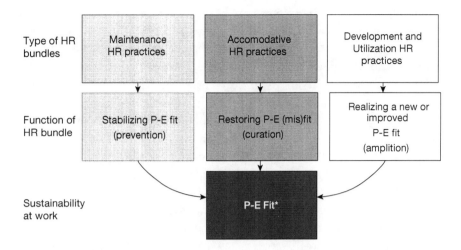

FIGURE 3.1
Functions of HR bundles of practices in relation to sustainability at work

* P-E fit = (future) needs, abilities or skills and interests of worker are congruent with aspects and (future) requirements of their current and future work environment.

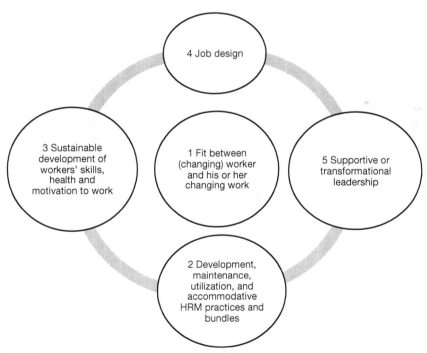

FIGURE 3.2
An integrative perspective on sustainability at work across the lifespan

scholarly work, in this area. More specifically, we argue that both employers' as well as employees' work-related objectives concerning current and future work should be carefully aligned to facilitate sustainability at work (see Figure 3.2, and Dimension 5). We think that to achieve this fit across time, a lifespan-aware and diversity-friendly HRM perspective is important to diagnose reliably what workers need, in terms of specific HR practices and at which stages in their career, as well as their life to grow old successfully or to sustain a PE fit at work (Baltes & Baltes, 1990) (see Chapter 1 of this volume; de Lange et al., 2006; Kooij, de Lange, Jansen, & Dikkers, 2008 for elaborate conceptualizations of meaningful age-related individual changes at work).

More concretely, in line with lifespan theories of control (Heckhausen et al., 2010), the use of SOC strategies may be perceived as a promising strategy to exert control over one's environment, as well as of aligning oneself with it (Heckhausen et al., 2010) (see also Weigl, Müller, Hornung, Zacher, & Angerer, 2013). As humans' capability for control decreases with age, older workers in particular might compensate through using job crafting as an SOC strategy at work. Job crafting in this context is a specific form of proactive work behavior defined as the self-initiated changes individuals make in their tasks or relational boundaries of their work aimed at improving person-job fit (Tims, Bakker, & Derks, 2012; Wrzesniewski & Dutton, 2001). Job crafting thus offers workers a means to continuously adjust their job to intrapersonal changes that are part of their aging process, thereby increasing their sustainability at work by optimizing the fit between the changing worker and his or her changing environment (Kooij et al., 2015). In addition, as there is great diversity in individual characteristics and in the lifespan trajectories of workers, as well as in the (changing) content of their work, we argue that HRM departments and research on these topics should critically examine worker inclusiveness and invest in prevention, curation, and amplition types of HR practices to foster and enhance the work ability of all categories of workers across the lifespan (see Dimensions 2 and 3 of Figure 3.2), and to design sustainable work (Dimension 4).

Besides the effects of HRM, transformational leadership appears to have a positive impact on both followers' development and performance, and on the accomplishment of organizational goals (Bass, Avolio, Jung, & Bernson, 2003; Dvir, Eden, Avolio, & Shamir, 2002) (see also Caldwell, Truong, Linh, & Tuan, 2010), and is herewith hypothesized to be facilitative in sustaining and optimizing a PE fit across time. We would therefore like to stress that transformational leadership styles are needed that are characterized by combining a commitment to helping both individuals and organizations to achieve excellence and sustainability at work (being the fourth dimension of the integrative approach we call for) (Küpers & Weibler, 2006). Only if case management actively engages in human capital management, and is supportive to their employees across their entire careers, alongside more short-term-oriented instrumental leadership, is sustainability enhancement of workers truly stimulated (van der Heijden, 2005). More research is needed to examine the precise role of supervisors, line managers, and leaders in effectively communicating and implementing the different underlying functions of HRM bundles of practices and to actually facilitate stability or positive change among subordinates (in terms of, for example, work ability, employability, performance, or successful adaptation across time).

In this context, we think the following four stages of the HR implementation process suggested by Guest and Bos-Nehles (2013) are important to include in new research examining the role of perceived and used HR practices in relation to sustainability at work. According to Guest and Bos-Nehles (2013), the implementation of HR practices begins with the decision to adopt a particular HR practice; for example, the decision to use a health promotion program to improve the work ability of aging workers who are at risk of developing serious health problems. In the second step, the HR department examines available tests of possible health promotion programs and examines the return on investment of these programs. The third stage involves the decision and selection of using a particular health promotion program. The fourth and final stage concerns the quality of the implementation of the selected health promotion program. The quality of HR implementation is related to factors such as communication and logistics, but also diversity of workers who will use the HR practices. For example, there may not be enough budget to tailor the health promotion program to the needs of different groups of workers (e.g., younger versus older workers, workers with different health problems or educational backgrounds, etc.) or communicate the benefits of using the HR practices to all stakeholders in an organization. We will end this chapter with a short outline of a future research agenda.

Future Research Agenda

Based on our discussion, we conclude that the available research to date has been limited, and we therefore call for the following new types of studies:

1. Studies that include more meaningful measures to tap sustainability at work (see Figure 3.2), and empirically test their psychometric qualities (i.e., their reliability and validity). We recommend taking a broader approach to sustainability at work, incorporating ingredients from the four distinguished key dimensions (see Table 3.1), and taking into account important determinants of sustainability at work, such as individual, job-related, and organizational factors that may enhance or hinder the work ability and successful adaptation of workers across the lifespan. As regards the individual factors, human capital factors, training and development activities, work-home interference, and career involvement may be key. As far as job-related factors are concerned, future work may include the impact of job factors, such as career history and learning value of one's job. Important organizational factors may be the learning climate in one's working organization, leader-member exchange, mentoring and networking opportunities, and age-related HRM policies (van der Heijden, 2005). Only in case an integrative strategic HRM approach is adopted, both employee and organization optimize chances for sustainability at work across the lifespan.
2. More research is needed to empirically distinguish and examine the (strategic) underlying functions of HR bundles in explaining stability versus change in PE (mis)fit across time. More specifically, we should develop more longitudinal field and experimental research to tap processes such as stability and change in the fit between a worker and his or her work environment, and the role different bundles of HRM practices may play in predicting stability or change in PE fit across time. For example, can development HR practices (cf., Table 3.3) such as education and training predict an improved PE fit (amplition), or do these HR practices predict stability in PE fit (operate as a form of prevention)? And further, can development HR practices predict change as well as stability in PE fit among different groups of workers (for example, low-skilled versus high-skilled workers) or from a life course perspective for individual workers at different career stages in their life (junior versus senior career stage)?
3. Studies that provide an overarching HRM theory to explain how to improve sustainability at work, using, for example, our integrative perspective (cf., Figure 3.2) to further develop relevant theoretical argumentation for the relations between perceptions and actual use, or individual needs of HR practices in relation to PE fit across the lifespan.

Which intrapersonal (i.e., age-related psychological, physiological changes or life events) (de Lange et al., 2006), interpersonal (i.e., leadership processes, group processes, etc.), job design-related (i.e., job demands, job resources), or socio-technical explanations (e.g., supportive climate or climate for inclusion) (Nishii, 2009) can be provided and tested in new research to further explain effects of (bundles of) HR practices on sustainability at work across time?

4. Studies that examine whether HR practices can elicit job-crafting behavior among employees. As they are aging, workers can also actively shape their own work to adjust it in line with their changing motives or lifespan needs across time (see also Kira, van Eijnatten, & Balkin, 2010; Kooij et al., 2015). Concrete HR practices, such as extensive training, decentralized decision-making, and information sharing might result in psychological empowerment or new personal resources (Messersmith, Patel, & Lepak, 2011), and thus in increased enhancement of job-crafting behavior. Furthermore, future empirical research, following up on the exemplary work by Weigl and colleagues (2013), may investigate whether organizations providing contextual resources that are conducive for enhanced job control (Heckhausen et al., 2010) are indeed positive in the light of increased sustainability across the lifespan, and whether they facilitate successful aging at work. In sum, future research should not only focus on the direct effects of HR practices (including job design) on sustainability at work, but also on the indirect effect of HR practices via individual characteristics such as job-crafting behavior (being a possible mediator in this regard) (Berg, Wrzesniewski, & Dutton, 2010).

5. So-called HR analytic studies are needed to further examine the cost-effectiveness or the return on investment of bundles of HR practices in terms of prevention, curation, and amplition among aging workers (e.g., de Lange et al., 2006; Kooij et al., 2008). For example, an important question would be whether the bundles of HR practices significantly affect sustainability at work of all workers (and thus result in inclusiveness) or, instead, only affect an exclusive group of workers.

6. Finally, more research in this area can examine the influence of contextual factors (e.g., company size, culture) and the role of leadership style in facilitating effective HR implementation and HR usage among workers (Guest & Bos-Nehles, 2013).

NOTE

1. Obviously, researchers should critically evaluate whether the chosen operationalizations do not result in potential biased interpretations across contexts and cultures (comprising different values and norms).

REFERENCES

Alavinia, S. M., de Boer, G. E., van Duivenbooden, J. C., Frings-Dresen, M. H. W., & Burdorf, A. (2009). Determinants of work ability and its predictive value for disability. *Occupational Medicine, 59*, 32–37.

Armstrong-Stassen, M. (2008). Organisational practices and the post-retirement employment experience of older workers. *Human Resource Management Journal, 18*, 36–53.

Armstrong-Stassen, M., & Ursel, N. D. (2009). Perceived organizational support, career satisfaction, and the retention of older workers. *Journal of Occupational and Organizational Psychology, 82*, 201–220.

Baltes, P. B., & Baltes, M. M. (1990). Psychological perspectives on successful aging: The model of selective optimization with compensation. In P. B. Baltes & M. M. Baltes (Eds.), *Successful Aging: Perspectives from the Behavioral Sciences* (pp. 1–34). New York: Cambridge University Press.

Barling, J., & Griffiths, A. (2011). A history of occupational health psychology. In K. C. Quick & L. E. Tetrick (Eds.), *Handbook of Occupational Health Psychology* (pp. 21–35). Washington, DC: American Psychological Association.

Bass, B. M., Avolio, B. J., Jung, D. I., & Bernson, Y. (2003). Predicting unit performance by assessing transformational and transactional leadership. *Journal of Applied Psychology, 88*, 207–218.

Berg, J. M., Wrzesniewski, A., & Dutton, J. E. (2010). Perceiving and responding to challenges in job crafting at different ranks: When proactivity requires adaptivity. *Journal of Organizational Behavior, 31*, 158–186.

Blau, P. M. (1964). *Exchange and Power in Social Life*. New York: Wiley.

Boxall, P., & Purcell, J. (2011). *Strategy and Human Resource Management*. 3rd ed. New York: Palgrave Macmillan.

Caldwell, C., Truong, D., Linh, P., & Tuan, A. (2010). Strategic human resource management as ethical stewardship. *Journal of Business Ethics, 98*(1), 171–182.

Conway, E. (2004). Relating career stage to attitudes towards HR practices and commitment: Evidence of interaction effects? *European Journal of Work and Organizational Psychology, 13*, 417–446.

Costanza, R., & Patten, B. C. (1995). Defining and predicting sustainability. *Ecological Economics, 15*(3), 193–196.

de Lange, A. H., & van der Heijden, B. I. J. M. (Eds.) (2013). *Handboek: Een leven lang inzetbaar? Duurzame inzetbaarheid op het werk: interventies, best practices en integrale benaderingen. [Handbook: A Life Long Employability? Sustainable Work Participation: Interventions, Best Practices and Integrative Approaches]*. Alphen aan de rijn: Vakmedianet.

de Lange, A. H., Taris, T. W., Jansen, P. G. W., Smulders, P., Houtman, I. L. D., & Kompier, M. A. J. (2006). Age as a factor in the relation between work and mental health: Results from the longitudinal TAS survey. In J. Houdmont & S. McIntyre (Eds.), *Occupational*

Health Psychology: European Perspectives on Research, Education and Practice (Vol. 1) (pp. 21–45). Maia, Portugal: ISMAI Publications.

Deci, E. L., & Ryan, R. M. (2000). The "what" and "why" of goal pursuits: Human needs and the self-determination of behavior. *Psychological Inquiry, 11*(4), 227–268.

Deci, E. L., Ryan, R. M., & Guay, F. (2013). Self-determination theory and actualization of human potential. In D. McInerney, H. Marsh, R. Craven, & F. Guay (Eds.), *Theory Driving Research: New Wave Perspectives on Self Processes and Human Development* (pp. 109–133). Charlotte, NC: Information Age Press.

Dellve, L., Eriksson, J., & Vilhelmsson, R. (2007). Assessment of long-term work attendance within human service organisations. *Work, 29*(2), 71-80.

Dellve, L., Skagert, K., & Eklöf, M. (2008). The impact of systematic occupational health and safety management for occupational disorders and long-term work attendance. *Social Science Medicine, 67,* 965–970.

Docherty, P., Kira, M., & Shani, A. B. (2009). What the world needs now is sustainable work systems. In P. Docherty, M. Kira, & A. B. Shani (Eds.), *Creating Sustainable Work Systems* (pp. 1–23). London: Routledge.

Dvir, T., Eden, D., Avolio, B. J., & Shamir, B. (2002). Impact of transformational leadership on follower development and performance: A field experiment. *Academy of Management Journal, 45,* 735–744.

Edwards, A. (2005). Let's get beyond community and practice: The many meanings of learning by participating. *The Curriculum Journal, 16*(1), 53–69.

Edwards, J. R., Cable, D. M., Williamson, I. O., Lambert, L. S., & Shipp, A. J. (2006). The phenomenology of fit: Linking the person and environment to the subjective experience of person-environment fit. *Journal of Applied Psychology, 91,* 802–827.

Ehnert, I., & Harry, W. (2012). Recent developments and future prospects on sustainable human resource management: Introduction to the special issue. *Management Revue, 23*(3), 221–238.

Finegold, D., Mohrman, S., & Spreitzer, G. M. (2002). Age effects on the predictors of technical workers' commitment and willingness to turnover. *Journal of Organizational Behavior, 23,* 655–674.

Garavan, T. N., & McGuire, D. (2010). Human resource development and society: Human resource development's role in embedding corporate social responsibility, sustainability, and ethics in organizations. *Advances in Developing Human Resources, 12*(5), 487–507.

Gratton, L. (2011). Workplace 2025: What will it look like? *Organizational Dynamics, 40,* 246–254.

Guest, D., & Bos-Nehles, A. (2013). HRM and performance: The role of effective implementation. In J. Paauwe, D. Guest, & P. Wright (Eds.), *HRM and Performance: Achievements and Challenges,* Chichester: Wiley.

Hackman, J. R., & Oldham, G. R. (1975). Development of the job diagnostic survey. *Journal of Applied Psychology, 60*(2), 159–170.

Hannah, D., & Iverson, R. (2004). Employment relationships in context: Implications for policy and practice. In J. Coyle-Shapiro, L. Shore, S. Taylor, & L. Tetrick (Eds.), *The Employment Relationship: Examining Psychological and Contextual Perspectives* (pp. 332–350). Oxford: Oxford University Press.

Heckhausen, J., Wrosch, C., & Schulz, R. (2010). A motivational theory of life-span development. *Psychological Review, 117*(1), 32–60.

Hertel, G., van der Heijden, B., de Lange, A., & Deller, J. (2013). Facilitating age diversity in organizations—part I: Challenging popular misbeliefs. Special issue of the *Journal of Managerial Psychology, 28,* 729–856.

Hobfoll, S. E. (2001). The influence of culture, community, and the nested-self in the stress process: Advancing conservation of resources theory. *Applied Psychology: An International Review, 50*(3), 337–421.

Hobfoll, S. E. (2011). Conservation of resource caravans and engaged settings. *Journal of Occupational and Organizational Psychology, 84*(1), 116–122.

Hock, D. W. (1999). *Birth of the Chaordic Age*. San Francisco, CA: Berrett-Koehler.

Holling, C. S. (2001). Understanding the complexity of economic, ecological, and social systems. *Ecosystems, 4*, 390–405.

Huczynski, A., & Buchanan, D. (2007). *Organisational Behaviour: An Introductory Text*. 6th ed. Harlow: FT/Prentice Hall.

Ilmarinen, J. (2006). The ageing workforce—challenges for occupational health. *Occupational Medicine, 56*(6), 361–364.

Ilmarinen, J. (2009). Aging and work: An international perspective. In J. Sharit (Ed.), *Aging and Work: Issues and Implications in a Changing Landscape* (pp. 51–73). Baltimore, MD: Johns Hopkins University Press.

Ilmarinen, J., & Tuomi, K. (1992). Work ability of aging workers. *Scandinavian Journal of Work, Environment & Health, 18*(2), 8–10.

Ilmarinen, J. E. (2001). Aging workers. *Occupational and Environmental Medicine, 58*(8), 546.

International Labour Organization (2013). *The ILO at a Glance*. Available at: www.ilo.org/wcmsp5/groups/public/@dgreports/@dcomm/@webdev/documents/publication/wcms_082367.pdf (accessed January 10, 2013).

Jabbour, C. J. C., & Santos, F. C. A. (2008). The central role of human resource management in the search for sustainable organizations. *The International Journal of Human Resource Management, 19*, 2133–2154.

Jackson, S. E., & Seo, J. (2010). The greening of strategic HRM scholarship. *Organization Management Journal, 7*, 278–290.

Jackson, S. E., Renwick, D. W. S., Jabbour, C. J. C., & Muller-Camen, M. (2011). State-of-the-art and future directions for green human resource management: Introduction the special issue. *Zeitschrift für Personalforschung, 25*(2), 99–116.

Kanfer, R., & Ackerman, P. L. (2004). Aging, adult development and work motivation. *Academy of Management Review, 29*, 440–458.

Karasek, R., & Theorell, T. (1990). *Healthy Work: Stress, Productivity, and the Reconstruction of Working Life*. New York: Basic Books.

Khilji, S. E., & Wang, X. (2006). "Intended" and "implemented" HRM: The missing linchpin in strategic human resource management research. *International Journal of Human Resource Management, 17*, 1171–1189.

Kira, M., van Eijnatten, F. M., & Balkin, D. B. (2010). Crafting sustainable work: Development of personal resources. *Journal of Organizational Change Management, 23*(5), 616–632.

Kooij, D. T. A. M. (2010). *Motivating older workers: A lifespan perspective on the role of perceived HR practices*. Ridderkerk: Ridderprint (Ph.D. thesis).

Kooij, D. T. A. M., de Lange, A. H., Jansen, P. G. W., & Dikkers, J. (2008). Older workers' motivation to continue work: Five meanings of age. A conceptual review. *Journal of Managerial Psychology, 23*, 364–394.

Kooij, D. T. A. M., Jansen, P. G. W., Dikkers, J. S. E., & de Lange, A. H. (2010). The influence of age on the associations between HR practices and both affective commitment and job satisfaction: A meta-analysis. *Journal of Organizational Behavior, 31*, 1111–1136.

Kooij, D. T. A. M., de Lange, A. H., Jansen, P. G. W., Kanfer, R., & Dikkers, J. S. E. (2011). Age and work-related motives: Results of a meta-analysis. *Journal of Organizational Behavior, 32*, 197–225.

Kooij, D. T. A. M., Guest, D., Clinton, M., Knight, T., Jansen, P. G. W., & Dikkers, J. S. E. (2013). How the impact of HR practices on employee well-being and performance changes with age. *Human Resource Management Journal, 23*, 18–35.

Kooij, D. T. A. M., Jansen, P. G. W., Dikkers, J. S. E., & de Lange, A. H. (2014). Managing aging workers: A mixed methods study on bundles of HR practices for aging workers. *The International Journal of Human Resource Management, 25*(15), 2192–2212.

Kooij, D. T. A. M., Tims, M., & Kanfer, R. (2015). Successful aging at work: The role of job crafting. In P. M. Bal, D. T. A. M. Kooij, & D. M. Rousseau (Eds.), *Aging Workers and the Employee-Employer Relationship* (pp. 145–161). Cham, Switzerland: Springer.

Küpers, W., & Weibler, J. (2006). How emotional is transformational leadership really? Some suggestions for a necessary extension. *Leadership & Organization Development Journal, 27*(5), 368–383.

Levi, L. (2011). Foreword: Narrowing the science-policy gap. In K. C. Quick & L. E. Tetrick (Eds.), *Handbook of Occupational Health Psychology* (pp. x–xvii). Washington, DC: American Psychological Association.

Messersmith, J. G., Patel, P. C., & Lepak, D. P. (2011). Unlocking the black box: Exploring the link between high-performance work systems and performance. *Journal of Applied Psychology, 96*, 1105–1118.

Müller, A., Weigl, M., Heiden, B., Glaser, J., & Angerer, P. (2012). Promoting work ability and well-being in hospital nursing: The interplay of age, job control, and successful ageing strategies. *Work, 41*, 5137–5144.

Nishii, L. H. (2013). The benefits of climate for inclusion for gender-diverse groups. *Academy of Management Journal, 56*, 1754–1774.

Oldham, G. R., & Hackman, J. R. (2010). Not what it was and not what it will be: The future of job design research. *Journal of Organizational Behavior, 31*, 463–479.

Ostroff, C., & Bowen, D. E. (2000). Moving HR to a higher level: HR practices and organizational effectiveness. In K. J. Klein & S. W. J. Kozlowski (Eds.), *Multilevel Theory, Research, and Methods in Organizations: Foundations, Extensions, and New Directions* (pp. 211–266). San Francisco, CA: Jossey-Bass.

Ouweneel, E., Schaufeli, W., & Le Blanc, P. (2009). Van preventie naar amplitie: interventies voor optimaal functioneren [From prevention to amplition: Interventions for optimal functioning]. *Gedrag & Organisatie, 22*, 118–135.

Paul, R. J., & Townsend, J. B. (1993). Managing the older worker—don't just rinse away the gray. *The Academy of Management Executive, 7*, 67–74.

Pfeffer, J. (2010). Building sustainable organisations: The human factor. *Academy of Management Perspectives, 24*(1), 34–45.

Radkiewicz, P., & Widerszal-Bazyl, M. (2005). Psychometric properties of work ability index in the light of comparative survey study. *International Congress Series, 1280*, 304–309.

Rau, B. L., & Adams, G. A. (2005). Attracting retirees to apply: Desired organizational characteristics of bridge employment. *Journal of Organizational Behavior, 26*, 649–660.

Remery, C., Henkens, K., Schippers, J., & Ekamper, P. (2003). Managing an aging workforce and a tight labor market: Views held by Dutch employers. *Population Research and Policy Review, 22*, 21–40.

Rudolph, C., de Lange, A. H., & van der Heijden, B. I. J. M. (2014). Adjustment processes in bridge employment: Where we are and need to go. In P. M. Bal, T. A. M. Kooij, & D. Rousseau (Eds.), *Aging Workers and the Employee-Employer Relationship* (pp. 221–242). New York: Springer.

Saba, T., & Guerin, G. (2005). Extending employment beyond retirement age: The case of health care managers in Quebec. *Public Personnel Management, 34*, 195–214.

Sachs, J. (2012). *The Price of Civilization: Reawakening American Virtue and Prosperity.* New York: Random House.

Shore, L. M., & Shore, T. H. (1995). Perceived organizational support and organizational justice. In R. Cropanzano & K. M. Kacmar (Eds.), *Organizational Politics, Justice, and Support: Managing Social Climate at Work* (pp. 149–164). Westport, CT: Quorum Press.

Shultz, K. S., & Wang, M. (2011). Psychological perspectives on the changing nature of retirement. *American Psychologist, 66*(3), 170–179.

Spreitzer, G., Sutcliffe, K., Dutton, J., Sonenshein, S., & Grant, A. M. (2005). A socially embedded model of thriving at work. *Special Issue: Frontiers of Organization Science, 2*(16), 537–549.

Taylor, S., Osland, J., & Egri, C. P. (2012). Guest editors' introduction: Introduction to HRM's role in sustainability: Systems, strategies, and practices. *Human Resource Management, 51,* 789–798.

Tims, M., Bakker, A. B., & Derks, D. (2012). Development and validation of the job crafting scale. *Journal of Vocational Behavior, 80,* 173–186.

Toh, S. M., Morgeson, F. P., & Campion, M. A. (2008). Human resource configurations: Investigating fit with the organizational context. *Journal of Applied Psychology, 93,* 864–882.

Truxillo, D. M., & Fraccaroli, F. (2013). Research themes on age and work: Introduction to the special issue. *European Journal of Work and Organizational Psychology, 22,* 249–252.

Truxillo, D. M., Cadiz, D. A., Rinner, J. R., Zaniboni, S., & Fraccaroli, F. (2012). A lifespan perspective on job design: Fitting the job and the worker to promote job satisfaction, engagement, and performance. *Organizational Psychology Review, 2,* 340–360.

Tuomi, K., Ilmarinen, J., Jahkola, A., Katajarinne, L., & Tulkki, A. (1998). *Work Ability Index* (2nd ed.). Occupational Health Care 19. Helsinki: Finnish Institute of Occupational Health.

United Nations Conference on the Human Environment (1972). *Report of the United Nations Publication,* Stockholm, June 5–16 1972 (Sales No.E.73.II.A.14 and corrigendum), chap. I. Available at: www.un.org/documents/ga/confl51/aconf15126-1annex1.htm (accessed January 1, 2014).

van Dalen, H., Henkens, K., & Schippers, J. (2007). *Oudere werknemers door de lens van de werkgever.* Nederlands Interdisciplinair Demografische Instituut, Rapport no. 74.

van der Heijden, B. I. J. M. (2005). "No one has ever promised you a rose garden." On shared responsibility and employability enhancing strategies throughout careers. Inaugural address, Open Universiteit in the Netherlands. Heerlen: Open Universiteit in the Netherlands. Assen: van Gorcum.

Van der Heijde, C.M., & Van der Heijden, B.I.J.M. (2006). A competence-based and multidimensional operationalization and measurement of employability. *Human Resource Management, 45*(3), 449–476.

van Eijnatten, F. M. (2004). Chaotic systems thinking: Some suggestions for a complexity framework to inform a learning organization. *The Learning Organization, 11,* 430–449.

van Solinge, H., & Henkens, K. (2008). Adjustment to and satisfaction with retirement: Two of a kind? *Psychology and Aging, 23*(2), 422–434.

Veth, K., Emans, B., van der Heijden, B. I. J. M., Korzilius, H., & de Lange, A. H. (2011). Taking care of older workers: A multi-perspective case study on HRM practices in healthcare organizations for older workers. Paper presented at Dutch HRM network conference 2011, Groningen, Netherlands.

Weigl, M., Müller, A., Hornung, S., Zacher, H., & Angerer, P. (2013). The moderating effects of job control and selection, optimization, and compensation strategies on the age-work ability relationship. *Journal of Organizational Behavior, 34*, 607–628.

Wilkinson, A., Hill, M., & Gollan, P. (2001). The sustainability debate. *International Journal of Operations and Production Management, 21*, 1492–1502.

World Commission on Environment and Development (1987). *Our Common Future.* General Assembly Resolution 42/187. New York: United Nations.

Wright, P. M., & Nishii, L. H. (2013). Strategic HRM and organizational behaviour: Integrating multiple levels of analysis. In J. Paauwe, D. E. Guest, & P. Wright (Eds.), *HRM and Performance Achievements and Challenges* (pp. 97–110). Chichester: Wiley.

Wrzesniewski, A., & Dutton, J. E. (2001). Crafting a job: Revisioning employees as active crafters of their work. *Academy of Management Review, 26*, 179–201.

REVIEWED STUDIES OF TABLE 3.2

1. Dellve, L., Skagert, K., & Eklöf, M. (2008). The impact of systematic occupational health and safety management for occupational disorders and long-term work attendance. *Social Science Medicine, 67*, 965–970.
2. Hägglund, K. M., Helsing, C., & Sandmark, H. (2010). Assistant nurses working in care of older people: Associations with sustainable work ability. *Scandinavian Journal of Caring Studies, 25*, 325–332.
3. Kira, M., & van Eijnatten, F. M. (2008). Socially sustainable work organizations: A chaordic systems approach. *Systems Research and Behavioral Science, 25*, 743–756. Available at: http://dx.doi.org/10.1002/sres.896 (accessed January 1, 2014).
4. Kira, M., van Eijnatten, F. M., & Balkin, D. B. (2010). Crafting sustainable work: Development of personal resources. *Journal of Organizational Change Management, 23*, 616–632.
5. Tjulin, A., MacEachen, E., & Ekberg, K. (2010). Exploring workplace actors experiences of the social organization of return-to-work. *Journal of Occupational Rehabilitation, 20*, 311–321.
6. Vickers, M. H. (2010). From the editor-in-chief's desk: Continuing the discussion on sustainability and work. *Employee Responsibility Rights Journal, 22*, 1–4.

Issue 2

*Patterns of Employment
and Unemployment*

4

The Challenge of Building Human Capital and Benefiting from It: A Person-Centric View of Youth Unemployment and Underemployment[1]

José M. Peiró, Ana Hernández, and José Ramos

Employment status can be viewed as a continuum from the positive pole of being employed in an adequate job to the negative pole of unemployment. In between, situations of underemployment involve mismatches between individuals' human capital, their expectations and preferences, and their job characteristics. Feldman (1996) considered five dimensions of underemployment depending on the type of mismatch: possessing more education than the job requires; having a job outside one's area of formal training; possessing skills that are not utilized in the job; being involuntarily employed in a part-time, temporary, or intermittent job; and earning 20% less than in one's previous job or than one's peers. Both underemployment and unemployment constitute a loss of human capital for economic growth and inhibit individuals' opportunities to fulfill their needs and expectations. Both phenomena are especially worrisome for young people, especially in the current difficult market conditions.

Since 2007, the economic and financial crisis has produced a sharp growth in unemployment rates in most industrialized countries (OECD, 2013), presenting rates for the 15–24-year-old cohort (12.6%) that are twice as high as those for the overall population (6%) (ILO, 2013). Unemployment duration among youth has also increased, as 35% of the young unemployed remained unemployed for more than six months at the end of 2012, compared to the 28.5% observed in 2007. Moreover, during this crisis, youth participation in the labor force decreased because young workers continue with their training or education (OECD, 2013). In spite of this, 12.7% of young people are currently not studying, working, or in training (so-called NEETs), and they will find it very difficult to become employable in the future. Despite large differences across countries, youth unemployment rates are at least twice as high as adult unemployment rates, both in the developed world and in emerging economies (e.g., East Asia or Latin America). These differences are predicted to last at least until 2017 (ILO, 2013). Regarding underemployment rates, although cross-national statistics are lacking or unreliable due to differences in the definition of underemployment and its indicators, it seems that involuntary part-time arrangements in developed economies are increasing (Wilkins & Wooden, 2011), with young people and women showing higher rates. In addition, in developed countries a significant proportion of workers perceive themselves as overqualified, with higher rates among (highly educated) young people. Even if youth underemployment can be seen as a transitory step in professional advancement, young people's unemployment and underemployment are particularly worrisome, as bad entry conditions into the labor market may have long-term effects on career trajectories, especially when individuals stay unemployed or underemployed for relatively long periods of time (García-Montalvo & Peiró, 2008).

Several factors contribute to explaining the prominence of under-employment and unemployment among young adults. First, variation in unemployment rates partly reflects economic cycles. Net employment destruction at the beginning of the current recession could explain higher rates of youth unemployment because work arrangements among youngsters are easier to rescind. In previous recessions, early retirement was a strategy to reduce youth unemployment. However, results of these policies showed that this strategy has been ineffective to increase youth employment. In fact, there is some evidence that older workers do not obstruct young people's access to work; the two act as complements rather than substitutes (Wilkins & Wooden, 2011).

Second, underemployment and unemployment are affected by structural features of the labor market. In fact, economic cycles do not explain why large gaps in overall and youth unemployment also occur during expansive economic periods. Service economies show higher unemployment rates than industrialized ones. Market pressures and competition in the global world lead to increasing work flexibility (e.g., contractual, functional, geographical, schedule, or technological-virtual work). More flexible labor markets (such as the USA, the UK, or Japan) usually show lower rates of youth unemployment compared to more rigid labor markets. Nevertheless, the trend of higher youth unemployment occurs everywhere. In some countries, protectionist policies toward adult (family income providers) and older workers (who are more difficult to reinsert in the labor market) partially account for the differences between adult and youth underemployment and unemployment. Young people frequently gain access to part-time jobs, temporary contracts, or other non-standard jobs, which makes it more difficult for them to remain employed compared to permanent full-time tenured workers.

Third, mismatches in terms of individuals' qualifications and those needed by the production system also contribute to explaining youth underemployment and unemployment. Many countries have not renewed their productive systems to a sufficient degree to provide enough qualified vacancies for the new increasingly educated workers. Human capital literature has often analyzed the misfit from a quantitative (number of education years) perspective, but qualification misfit (type and quality of education and professional competencies) also matters. In addition, the misfit between the labor force available and the one required by companies could involve not only qualifications and skills, but also attitudes and values. Thus, not only education, but also early work socialization would play a role in explaining youth underemployment.

In sum, it has been clearly established that underemployment and unemployment are prominent phenomena among young people that are fostered in some structural and economic contexts. Compared to older ages, youngsters underemployed and unemployed present some specific features since these phenomena can negatively affect early work socialization and even change work ethos. On the other hand, their lack of family responsibilities and the fact that they have shorter or no work experience may mitigate the negative short-term consequences of the phenomena, compared to older ages.

PSYCHOSOCIAL THEORIES OF UNEMPLOYMENT AND UNDEREMPLOYMENT

Unemployment has mainly been explained by two classical theories. The functionalist theory (Jahoda, 1982) considers that employment has latent functions beyond the manifest economic ones, such as time structuring, social relationships, or participation in collective goals. Unemployment precludes satisfaction of these needs, and the unemployed experience negative consequences, such as low psychological well-being. Contrary to Jahoda's theory, which views individuals as mostly reactive, the agency theory (Fryer, 1992) views them as active agents with capacity to plan their actions and decide what to do and how. Unemployment makes it difficult for individuals to implement action plans. When their efforts to plan and organize their lives are frustrated, they experience negative outcomes.

Recent models have expanded agency theory to include not only the effects of unemployment on psychological health and well-being, but also some antecedents, such as motivational factors and job search behaviors, and other employment outcomes, such as speed and quality of re-employment or career development. The dynamic self-regulatory perspective (Wanberg, Zhu, Kanfer, & Zheng, 2012) considers motivational traits and self-regulatory states as antecedents of mental health and job search behaviors of the unemployed, which in turn affect motivational states and self-defeating cognitions in a repeating cycle. Waters (2005, 2007) proposed a conceptual model where protean career attitudes had effects on psychological health that in turn affected job search identity, with effects on re-employment quality and career growth. Moreover, the past decade has witnessed a large body of research on employability, with special attention paid to Fugate, Kinicki, and Ashforth's (2004) model. This model specifies three employability dimensions: career identity, personal adaptability, and human and social capital, all of which are antecedents of individuals' employment status. Extending this framework to consider why a large percentage of young people have difficulties in getting (adequate) jobs could be of interest, as recent cohorts of young people spend many years in education, and job search training is common in many countries. Finally, stress models and equity theory are other interesting frameworks to analyze experiences of unemployment.

Focusing on the main theories used to explain the consequences of underemployment, the relative deprivation theory focuses on the sense of injustice individuals feel when they experience subjective underemployment (Feldman, Leana, & Bolino, 2002). Underemployed individuals believe they should have better jobs than the ones they currently hold, as compared to a specific referent standard (e.g., previous jobs or jobs occupied by individuals with similar experience or education) (Feldman et al., 2002). This sense of injustice leads to less job satisfaction and organizational commitment, and more intention to quit (McKee-Ryan, Virick, Prussia, Harvey, & Lilly, 2009). For human capital theory, individuals and organizations make decisions about investing in their own human capital (e.g., education and training), considering the economic revenues they expect and the outcomes provided by their acquired human capital. For underemployed workers, investments in their own human capital do not pay off, leading to negative job attitudes, intentions to increase the returns for their human capital (i.e., turnover), and reductions in their contributions to the company as a way to recover the investment-return balance (i.e., decreasing job performance and extra-role behaviors). Person-job fit theory (Edwards, 1991) suggests that a mismatch between employees' abilities (i.e., education, skills, and experience) and the actual job requirements could explain the negative outcomes shown by underemployed workers because people perceive that their psychological needs have been ignored, resulting in negative consequences for both employees and organizations (Luksyte & Spitzmueller, 2011). The coping and control theory of re-employment (Latack, Kinicki, & Prussia, 1995) highlights the importance of equilibrium in the job search process and argues that displaced workers do not return to a state of equilibrium until they are re-employed in a job with at least a similar level of quality as the job lost. Workers in unsatisfactory new jobs continue to cope with their job loss as though they were still unemployed (McKee-Ryan & Harvey, 2011).

All these theoretical underemployment frameworks include the concept of a discrepancy between some job features, demands and resources, and individuals' expectations about employment. For all of them, negative outcomes of underemployment involve feelings of inequity or dissatisfaction caused by this discrepancy. Specifically, according to Erdogan, Bauer, Peiró, and Truxillo (2011), equity theory is the framework that explains underemployment effects using deprivation and human capital approaches. In turn, person-job fit and the coping and control theory of re-employment rely on stress as the explanatory process for underemployment's negative outcomes. However, given the increasing frequency of underemployment among young people in its different manifestations, more attention and theoretical elaboration will be required in the near future, not only for the consequences, but also for the antecedents.

UNEMPLOYMENT AND UNDEREMPLOYMENT OUTCOMES

The theories presented contribute to understanding the potential negative consequences of underemployment and unemployment. In fact, recent reviews and meta-analyses of empirical studies have consistently reported detrimental effects of unemployment on different aspects of psychological well-being such as stress, self-esteem, anxiety, and depression (McKee-Ryan, Song, Wanberg, & Kinicki, 2005; Paul & Moser, 2009; Wanberg, 2012), an increase in substance abuse and criminal behaviors (Prause & Dooley, 2011), and in some cases, poor physical health, mortality, and suicide (Wanberg, 2012). The unemployed, especially long-term, miss opportunities to acquire work experience, see their skills and professional competences quickly become outdated, and are worse equipped to re(enter) the job market. Focusing on youth, they frequently enter the labor market by filling jobs under their level of qualification. The longer one is unemployed or underemployed, the greater the possibility of subsequent underemployment.

Underemployment has often been considered partial unemployment (some valued outcomes from work are lacking, despite having a job). Thus, underemployment experiences seem to have similar effects as unemployment, although less severe (Cassidy & Wright, 2008; Kinicki, Prussia, & McKee-Ryan, 2000). Specifically, in their review, Anderson and Winefield (2011) reported negative relationships among underemployment and psychological health, physical health, and job attitudes such as job satisfaction and organizational commitment. Poor person-job fit, one core feature of underemployment, resulted in psychological contract breaches, lack of fulfillment of personal needs, restrictions to training and development, and loss of attachment to meaningful work and relationships, producing stress and lower psychological well-being (Anderson & Winefield, 2011). Erdogan and colleagues (2011) reported that overqualification was related to lower job satisfaction, higher turnover intentions, and lower career and life satisfaction. In a sample of Spanish workers, over-education was negatively related to extra-role behaviors, and the lack of opportunities to express full capacities and update professional competencies acted as barriers to future professional advancement (Agut, Peiró, & Grau, 2009).

However, not all the consequences are necessarily negative. Some types of underemployment may be related to positive outcomes. For example, Bashshur, Hernández, and Peiró (2011) reported that several studies found positive relationships between overqualification and task performance. In addition, overqualification can be an opportunity to further internal career advancement in the organization (Erdogan & Bauer, 2011). In any case, the positive effects for overqualified employees may depend on motivational factors to perform and enrich their jobs in the absence of organizational constraints (Erdogan et al., 2011).

Therefore, it is necessary to clarify the boundary conditions under which overqualification (and other types of underemployment) may produce positive outcomes, as well as the factors that moderate the negative ones. Considering an under-skilled (or partial-time) job an opportunity to gain work experience and progress toward a better job is not the same as considering it a disturbing episode that wastes time and prevents professional advancement. Some recent research has focused on the positive effects of unemployment episodes and job search behaviors on the quality of re-employment and further career development (Wanberg et al., 2012; Waters, 2007). Career planning and some personality variables have been outlined as resources for transforming unemployment episodes into better opportunities for the future (Zikic & Klehe, 2006). Thus, more research is needed on the duration and evolution of underemployment and unemployment, paying attention to individuals' motivational states, action plans, and coping strategies, in order to better understand both detrimental and positive long-term effects of these phenomena. It is necessary to pay attention to the way people give meaning to their underemployment and unemployment, and how they cope with them and shape their outcomes. In other words, it is necessary to take a more person-centric approach.

A PERSON-CENTRIC APPROACH TO YOUTH UNEMPLOYMENT AND UNDEREMPLOYMENT

Underemployment and unemployment have mainly been studied to determine their consequences for people and societies. The study of unemployed or underemployed people, their experiences, and the meaning they give to these situations has been less of an issue. A person-centric approach considers the person living through the experience of underemployment or unemployment and may raise new relevant facets and pose innovative research questions. This approach has clear antecedents linked to the birth of applied psychology in Europe. Since its inception, *applied psychology* has paid attention to the individual in his or her specific real-life contexts, such as the school, the factory, the hospital, etc. (Stern, 1903). Individuals are not just considered organisms surrounded by a bundle of stimuli, but rather as real people in their specific human and social world (Carpintero, 2006). Münsterberg considers the mind as a purposeful reality oriented toward goals, and the different skills and capabilities are components of its whole personality. Stern, in his 'personology' theory, defined the person as a "living totality, individual, unique tending to goals ... open to the surrounding world, and having feelings or lived-through experience" (Stern, 1957, p. 69). The basic components of the person in these conceptions are: uniqueness, openness to the surrounding world and capability to transform it, purposefulness, and intimacy. An additional feature is that the person cannot be considered in a vacuum. As Ortega y Gasset (2004, p. 757) wrote: "I am myself and my circumstance. If I do not save my circumstance, I will not save myself." Moreover, the person is socio-historical (Vygotsky, 1978) and lives in a "human and social world." In this approach, living means an adaptation to and transformation of that world (see Carpintero, 2006 for a more detailed analysis of this tradition). Similarly, Peiró (1990, p. 32) pointed out that the person is:

> responsible, free, creative and capable of developing projects and acting accordingly. He has important potential and capacity for learning, and he is able to anticipate and act in an intentional way and not simply as a mechanical reaction to the stimuli from the environment.

These are essential features of a person-centric approach that need to be considered to understand work and unemployment experiences. More recently, Weiss and Rupp (2011, p. 88) also emphasized the need for an approach of this type in the study of work:

> A person-centric work psychology is a psychology of the self, working. It is a work psychology that preserves the integrity of the person. It is a work psychology that derives its problems and projects from the human experience of working, broadly defined.

Next, we draw on the main aspects of this approach to study underemployment and unemployment.

A Comprehensive Perspective of the Person

Underemployment and unemployment cannot be properly understood without a comprehensive view of the person and his or her circumstances. Therefore, it is important to consider cognitions, affects, habits, values and attitudes, and psychosocial experiences related to the lived-through experiences, as well as the individual's coping strategies and personal projects. One implication of this idea is that when focusing on underemployment or unemployment, subjective measures for capturing psychological processes and intentions are of fundamental importance. These measures may reflect the objective situation, but also individual needs (economic, social, etc.), values, and personal circumstances. In fact, some of these factors have been proposed as moderators in the relationship between objective and subjective underemployment (Virick, 2011). For youth, circumstances such as having finished their formal education or not, having no work experience, dependent or independent living, and having children or not may play a significant role. Moreover, young people may experience dimensions of underemployment in different ways. For example, for an overeducated person with strong economic burdens in an underpaid job, the salient feature will probably be the low salary, while for another person with less economic responsibility, poor job content and no opportunities for career advancement may be more worrisome aspects. Focusing on unemployment, its length may be critical during this stage of life. The longer the unemployment lasts, the more difficult it will be for the young person to find a quality job. Other key variables are having children (taking into account family responsibilities and governmental financial support), their social networks, and the social representation of unemployment in their environment, which may have an effect on their own conception (Archer & Rhodes, 1993). In sum, it is important to take an integrative view of the person in understanding young people's unemployment and underemployment in their daily lives and in their social and cultural context.

The Meaning of Working and Work Socialization

The role work plays in building personal identity is relevant to the way people interpret both work and unemployment. Moreover, both situations contribute to shaping the "work personality" through socialization processes. Research on the meaning of working (MOW, 1987) across cultures identified four different patterns for defining work: "concrete activity" (obtaining money, scheduled, performed in a workplace), "social contribution" (contributing to society, being a member of the community), "burden" (effort, tiredness, physical or psychological fatigue), and "duty" (accountability to others, sense of obligation). The meaning of work has been defined as a multidimensional construct that expresses the sense that people give to work. The dimensions considered are work centrality (both absolute and relative to other life areas such as family, leisure, or the community), societal norms (work as a right and work as duty), work values, and preferred occupational goals (MOW, 1987). Two main orientations were depicted, one "work-centered," embedded in the Protestant ethic, and the other more "leisure-oriented," based on so-called postmodern values. In addition, studies on the work socialization of youth (Whitely, Peiró, & Sarchielli, 1992) pointed out that the quality of work experiences (contract and work arrangements, job demands and duties, social contacts, relationships with supervisors, number and duration of employments) influences young people's work attitudes, occupational and career motivation, and work outcomes. It results in different patterns of occupational roles for young people (more or less oriented toward innovation or conformity) and the configuration of their occupational personality (Feij, Whitely, Peiró, & Taris, 1995).

It is important to note that the meaning of working and work socialization contributes to making sense of unemployment and underemployment situations. The way people interpret and perceive their work situation depends on the extent to which work centrality shapes their personal identity, their orientation toward work as a right or duty, and their own work values and preferred goals. People with a work-centered orientation give more importance to work roles and look for occupational goals to fulfill more personal needs. They are more prone to suffering from unemployment and person-job mismatches because they affect their personal identity more. Those with low work-centered orientation focus more on extrinsic work rewards and are less sensitive to lack of fulfillment through work activity. At the same time, young people who experience more unemployment and underemployment episodes during the transition to work life could develop an occupational personality more aligned to leisure, where work will be less central to their personal identity. Based on this framework, a number of issues could be addressed in future research to answer questions such as the following: Are there changes in the meaning of work among youth compared to the one from previous generations? Does the meaning of work play a significant moderating role in the effects of unemployment and underemployment? Some evidence suggests that negative effects of unemployment on well-being are more pronounced among people with higher work centrality (Ramos & Peiró, 2013). Does the increasing generalization of postmodern values have an effect on the meaning attributed to underemployment? Do the congruence or divergence among individuals' values and the dominant orientation in a given society moderate the effects of work deprivation? Answers to these questions are important from a person-centric approach to the study of youth unemployment and underemployment.

Work Context

The labor market, jobs, and organizations are relevant personal circumstances that help to understand youth underemployment and unemployment experiences. For example, specific labor market and legal conditions may facilitate self-employment and entrepreneurial activities among young people. Regarding jobs, when young people enter the job market for the first time, in contrast to older unemployed people, they do not have any direct work experience. However, when they do have some work experience, their previous jobs may play an important role in attributing meaning to the unemployment situation, and even in the decision to be voluntarily unemployed. When young people first enter the labor market, they often work in non-standard low-quality jobs for which they are overqualified. If this is the case, these experiences may influence subsequent unemployment and work experiences. On the other hand, if young people had previously occupied high-quality jobs in good organizations, this experience might become a standard that would influence the decision to accept or reject a new job in another organization. In fact, in studies about underemployment, the pay level, working time, and other features of the previous job are used to determine whether the new job can be considered underemployment.

Employment policies and practices companies use to manage their human resources are often relevant in unemployment experiences. In fact, some companies sequence periods of unemployment with other periods of employment. Temporary reduction of the work schedule or furloughs can also be used (Halbesleben, Wheeler, & Paustian-Underdahl, 2013). These practices may also influence unemployment experiences and their meaning. Moreover, depending on how work systems are organized and the messages organizations convey about the person-organization relationship, both work and unemployment experiences may vary. In this regard, Weiss and Rupp (2011, p. 87) have pointed out that the collective agenda of the organization is organization-centric, and the overall objective is to find out how "individual behavior can better align with collective purpose." In this situation, people's work experience becomes secondary, which may have an impact on the meaning they assign to work and unemployment. Extending this agenda, a challenge for our discipline is to develop models designed to achieve:

> the compatibility between the need to coordinate and schedule actions, on the one hand, and personal freedom and autonomy of the members, on the other; the compatibility between organizational effectiveness and efficiency

and work satisfaction, and innovation and continuity; free expression of individual creativity and the necessary regulation and structuring of activities; commitment to the organization and a personal and social life; the development and growth of organizations and personal development and self-fulfillment.

(Peiró, 1990, p. 33)

The paradigm inspiring employer-employee relations, human resources management policies and practices, and work arrangements will play an important role in understanding young people's experience of both work and unemployment.

Other Spheres of Life

Work is one out of several interrelated life spheres that constitute human life. The activity system model (Curie, Hajjar, Marquié, & Roques, 1987) defined a system of activity as being composed of work, family, and personal subsystems whose combination constitutes the *model of life* that regulates the connections between these subsystems. The model of life is guided by the obligation to perform activities due to external pressures, as well as personal choices, values, expectations, representations, and main life objectives. The meaning of working study (MOW, 1987) compared work centrality to other life domains, such as the family, leisure and friends, social participation, and religion. Other studies add education and training to these domains. Individuals differ in the extent to which they consider each domain to be a central part of their lives, and the balance among different life spheres is idiosyncratic.

To understand the experiences of youth underemployment and unemployment, it is important to consider the relevance of other life domains in young people's personal and life projects. As Marías (1955, p. 223) has pointed out:

> normally, when one says "to do something" what has to be done is only the doing; in the case of life, one has to make also, and previously, the something, i.e., to decide before hand what one is going to do, what one is going to be; therefore, my life as a possibility must anticipate my real living. This is what is called an intention or project.

Thus, a personal project is not what the person has, but rather what the person does and aims to be. Life tasks focus on highly contextualized, nontrivial problems that are rooted in developmental stages and are made salient by life transitions.

In this context, three issues concerning the relations between different life spheres need further analysis: congruence (versus interference), complementarity and self-regulation, and informal economy work. First, congruence/interference between goals in different life domains (for instance, family or social contacts) may lead to a different appraisal of underemployment or unemployment. Personal experience depends on whether other life domains are impeded or complicated by an unfavorable occupational situation or not. For example, time of underemployment may reduce work-life conflict, and overqualification may lead to more intense involvement in other areas of life, such as caring for relatives, remaining in training, or devoting time to community work.

Second, jobs provide resources for fulfilling personal needs. Agency theory (Fryer, 1992) states that individuals can actively self-direct their behaviors to find alternative ways to fulfill these needs. Therefore, other life domains could act as complementary or alternative ways to fulfill personal needs and contribute to personal projects and expectations. For instance, unemployed or underemployed young people could increase their involvement in domestic tasks, training activities, participation in social or community organizations, and so on. However, if other life domains are also restricted, the consequences of underemployment could be more severe, as in the case of NEET's (who renounced training), young people with no family ties, or those with reduced social networks. If underemployment and unemployment decrease young people's personal resources to maintain activities in the remaining life domains (for instance, making it difficult to maintain activities with friends), their effects could be more detrimental. By contrast, if any of these experiences do not hamper involvement in another domain, or even facilitate it, as in cases of time underemployment, which allows more contact with friends, their effects may be less negative. Recent research on the way people make sense of unemployment has found different patterns of unemployed people (optimist, desperate, discouraged, adapted, and withdrawn) depending on their feelings, attitudes, and behaviors (de Witte, 2012). Thus, when analyzing unemployment (and underemployment), it is important to take into account how young people reorganize the pattern of activities in their different life spheres, and how this affects the way they experience these phenomena. The dynamic self-regulatory framework appears as an interesting theory to design future research on these issues.

Finally, in some countries, unemployment tends to occur simultaneously with high opportunities for informal or black market work. In this context, young adults have opportunities to get involved in this informal economy as a particular form of underemployment. The existence of such alternatives could partly explain the persistence of high rates of long-term unemployment among youth in countries with low rates of social conflict. Nevertheless, although the informal economy may act as a palliative strategy, if young people do not move to a formal economy and get adequate jobs in a relatively short time, the situation may reduce their re-employment opportunities and their well-being. In sum, the interactions among the different life spheres of youth, and their interplay in underemployment and unemployment experiences and consequences, need to be taken into account in a person-centric approach.

Family and Formal Support Systems

Underemployment and unemployment are often seen as a loss, a lack of material, intangible, or symbolic resources, and a reduction in opportunities. Stress theories have paid attention to these phenomena and pointed out that social support plays a buffering role in the effects of these stressful experiences. Thus, a thorough understanding of underemployment and unemployment experiences from a person-centric approach requires the consideration of the main social support systems. Here, we focus on the role of the family and the more formal role of the state.

In the previous section, we paid attention to the family as a significant life sphere of youth. Here, we change the focus and consider the family as the unit of analysis in order to achieve a more comprehensive understanding of unemployment. The family is an important institution all over the world, and in most cultures fulfills protective and supportive functions for its members, although the way it does so may vary from one cultural context to another (e.g., collectivistic versus individualistic). The difficulties that youth encounter in the labor market often have an impact on their families, which frequently act as a system to cope with the situation. Unemployment and the low income that accompanies underemployment in most cases force young people to live in their parents' homes longer, delaying independent living, marriage, and/or having children. The extent to which this is part of their life project could make underemployment and unemployment particularly harmful, especially if greater efforts to find a good job are not rewarded. Nevertheless, the family also provides other types of support, encouraging and supporting mobility, entrepreneurship, or further education. As a collective unit, the family often initiates coping strategies to deal with youth unemployment, or it tries to influence and induce the children to prioritize some coping strategies. However, very little research has focused on the whole family as the unit of analysis of youth unemployment (McKee-Ryan & Maitoza, in press).

Another important social support system is the one provided by the state. Some argue that larger welfare states have a negative impact on growth and employment (Mares, 2007). If young adults can make a reasonable living with unemployment subsidies, the effort they put into finding a job will decrease, as well as the probability of accepting a low-quality job. They might even prefer to not accept any job while they have benefits (Blanch, 1990). However, there is also evidence that unemployment benefits are valuable because they contribute to increasing the chance of re-employment (Kluve, 2010), leading to jobs that last longer (Jacob, 2008), and enhancing job fit (Prause & Dooley, 2011). The question of which unemployment benefits, in terms of time and money, foster an active job search, but without urging the individual to accept just any available job, still needs to be answered. Regarding employment policies and strategies, youth employment protection and employment policies (active and passive) should be pursued. Many social democratic countries have fostered employment protection legislations, overlooking policies for generating employment (Rueda, 2007). This, together with the fact that active policies applied to youth have been neglected or mostly ineffective—see Greenberg, Michalopoulos, and Robins' (2003) meta-analyses and Kluve (2010)—makes it necessary to explore what types of policies and programs are especially beneficial for this vulnerable population, and how to enroll them in specific programs.

In sum, a multilevel analysis of young people's underemployment and unemployment, embedded in their families, will contribute to better understanding these phenomena from a person-centric perspective. Moreover, a contextual approach that takes into account relevant societal elements, such as unemployment subsidies and employment policies, may help to understand how individuals experience and cope with these experiences in different societal and socioeconomic systems. Widening the research focus to include these relevant contextual factors and social actors will provide a more comprehensive view to inspire empirical research and interventions.

Individual's Career and Biography

Apart from the social component, the circumstances that define a person also include temporal and historical components. However, it is not just chronological time that matters, but also psychological time, including expectations, anticipation, and recollection processes (Shipp & Jansen, 2005). When first entering the labor market, the pressure on young people to accept one of the first jobs offered may depend on previous personal or vicarious experience related to work. But it will also depend on their needs, expectations, and employment prospects, considering their career identities, motivations, and life projects, the market demands for their chosen profession, and the labor market situation, among others. As a result, they may or may not accept an underemployment situation. To understand underemployment and unemployment over time, the concepts of magnitude, duration, and trajectory can be useful. For instance, the underemployment experience can be completely different, depending on whether the situation is perceived as a stepping stone to get a better job or lasts a long time and leads the individual to believe that there are no prospects for improvement. Even if underemployment can be a stepping stone to get a better job, especially in organizations that emphasize internal promotions and career paths (see Erdogan & Bauer, 2011), most of the scant research on this topic shows that underemployment has negative pervasive effects on career trajectories (e.g., Büchel & Mertens, 2004; Hernández, Bashshur, & Peiró, 2011; Nabi, 2003), with wage penalties that are maintained throughout individuals' careers, regardless of personal characteristics, background, and economic climate (Prause & Dooley, 2011). Consequently, it is crucial to foster longitudinal research that: (1) clarifies the effects of initial underemployment and unemployment on career paths and the role of education in these paths; and (2) pays attention to the factors that contribute to a good starting point and those that moderate the negative effects of a bad starting point.

Similarly, it would also be interesting to explore the dynamics and effects of possible different sequence patterns of unemployment, underemployment, education and good employment, and the way the subjective experience of underemployment and unemployment can change with this sequence and the labor market conditions. For example, in bad market conditions, people may feel happy to have a job even if they are underemployed, given the lack of available jobs. However, this feeling may depend on whether they were previously unemployed or had a good job. Do particular sequences depend on individuals' career advancement goals? Do particular sequences change individuals' career plans? For example, workers who are not able to progress in their careers tend to become cynical about their chances of succeeding at work by working hard, and they increase careerist behaviors such as impressing management at work (e.g., Feldman & Turnley, 2004). The effects should be exacerbated when education follows a period of underemployment or unemployment and the desired job is not found. If the sequence includes relatively long periods of underemployment or unemployment, individuals may feel discouraged and helpless about their employment experiences (Waters, 2007) and stop actively searching for a good job, thus harming their career identities and plans.

Finally, it is important to note that when young people do not experience a progression to the assumed adult roles through their work trajectories, this can contribute to a change in the traditional young person's biographical plans. As Leccardi (2006) suggests, some young adults seem to be moving from the traditional work path that leads to social and financial independence to a temporary strategy of a "future without a project but not without control." They accept fragmentation and uncertainty as an irreversible reality, and they just concentrate on a very limited temporal area that is subjectively controllable. The meaning of time and future is being transformed through the constraints and opportunities offered at each moment. It is worthwhile to explore how this new view of temporal and biographical plans experienced by younger generations can change their underemployment or unemployment experiences and reactions.

An Agentic Approach

Individuals are not only reactive subjects; they are also purposeful, have projects, and make decisions based on these projects to build the life they want. This is part of building a life project. As Marías (1987, p. 116) points out, "being I consists of exerting a certain pressure on circumstances, compressing them so as to lodge in them—in the future—a programmatic outline of life" Underemployment and unemployment need to be studied taking into account individuals' biography construction, life projects, and the actions individuals can take to prevent, cope with, or improve these typically undesirable situations. Of course, the actions taken will depend on more macro-contextual factors, such as unemployment policies and programs. These macro-strategies interact with micro-level ones (implemented by individuals and, perhaps, their families) not only to reduce the incidence of the phenomena, but also their negative consequences, enhancing the positive ones. Both levels may in fact influence each other, with different results in different contexts. We focus on some of these strategies and actions below.

Geographical mobility of young people: It is often stimulated by governments and regional policies (e.g., the European Union) to reduce unemployment. Migration laws, language issues, and recognition and readability of qualifications across education systems, as well as cultural factors, influence geographical mobility and raise issues about work and organizational socialization in a foreign country. Moreover, at the micro-level, individual characteristics, financial constraints, and previous experiences abroad may influence one's readiness for geographical mobility. Family values and attitudes also influence the decision to move to a different country. In some collectivistic societies, instead of supporting geographical mobility, families favor the extension of the period during which young people live with their parents. As we pointed out in a previous section, the family could be a relevant and productive unit of analysis in this context. Future research should also focus on understanding work socialization and other experiences involved in migratory processes in order to provide insightful inputs about how to make these mobility experiences more productive and beneficial.

Entrepreneurship and self-employment: Young entrepreneurs may create their own jobs and jobs for other people. Some personal factors increase the odds of becoming an entrepreneur (e.g., proactivity) and succeeding in the long run (e.g., stress tolerance). Moreover, some macro-level factors, such as culture (value production versus rent-seeking cultures), economic and legal context, and community resources (e.g., counseling) can foster successful youth entrepreneurship.

Flexicurity: With this strategy, the negative effects of contract flexibility (e.g., increase in temporary contracts) are counteracted by the positive effects of a social support network and active employment schemes. However, the results of different programs promoted in the European Union have not yet been systematically evaluated, and further analysis is required on this type of intervention (García-Montalvo & Peiró, 2008). In fact, it has been suggested that flexicurity regimens may be counterproductive, due to creating a self-perpetuating cycle between living on welfare and underemployment and unemployment, rather than enhancing skills development.

Fostering employability: Apart from investing in *human and social capital*, there are some other personal factors to consider, according to Fugate and colleagues (2004): *adaptability*, which is the "willingness and ability to change behaviours, feelings and thoughts in response to environmental demands" (McArdle, Water, Briscoe, & Hall, 2007, p. 248), and depends on individuals' flexibility, openness to learning, optimism, and self-efficacy; and *career identity*, which refers to who the person is or wants to be in a career context, and which may help individuals to direct, regulate, and maintain their job-seeking behavior. All these factors may affect young people's job search behaviors, which are related to employment success. But some factors, such as adaptability, may be influenced by job seekers' constraints and needs, which also depend on labor market conditions and the support offered by governments and families.

Interventions to improve young adults' self-awareness, intensive job search strategies, and the use of different and efficient channels for getting a job can also contribute to increasing employability and reducing underemployment and unemployment. Furthermore, training and counseling programs designed to improve young people's knowledge of their strengths and opportunities, set goals and monitor progress, discover new trends in the labor market, or redirect their qualifications and career orientations toward emergent job areas should be helpful too. This is especially true when the interventions are customized to fit the personal characteristics of the subjects and their relevant contextual and cultural factors.

The aforementioned strategies are contextual factors aimed to reduce the incidence of underemployment and unemployment, or individual problem-focused coping strategies devoted to altering the cause of distress (Lazarus & Folkman, 1984). Going back to school or getting involved in additional training (i.e., investing in human capital), widening networking (social capital), active job search, and increasing flexibility to accept temporary jobs or look for a job abroad are problem-focused coping behaviors. Of course, individuals can also use emotion-focused coping strategies, by regulating emotional responses to the problem, through cognitive reappraisals or by engaging in counterproductive behaviors, such as drinking alcohol. Even if problem-focused strategies are typically considered more adaptive, self-regulation of emotions also seems to be important in fostering an active job search without getting discouraged or overly affected by possible poor results. Consequently, some emotion-focused coping strategies could facilitate some problem-focused strategies when facing underemployment and unemployment. Although there is some research that supports this idea (Feldman et al., 2002), more research is needed to establish the relative combined efficacy of different strategies, depending on how long the individuals have been underemployed or unemployed, how much effort they put into the job search, or the available coping resources they count on. On this last point, similar to coping with job loss, strategies to cope with underemployment and unemployment may depend not only on financial needs, but also on the coping resources available, both internal, such as self-esteem, and external, such as social support (Kinicki et al., 2000). Future research should clarify the role of these factors in keeping people from becoming discouraged and dropping out of the workforce.

Finally, when focusing on underemployment, especially overqualification, individuals can also use job crafting as a coping strategy, and organizations can contribute to ameliorating the negative consequences of underemployment by fostering empowerment, challenging tasks and advancement opportunities (e.g., Erdogan et al., 2011).

In short, the decision about whether to accept or reject a job is complex. Individuals' decision to remain underemployed or unemployed, actively search for the "perfect" job, or quit a job that does not fit them will depend on multiple factors, such as individual projects (career goals, family plans, etc.), their employment situation so far, their employability and perceived employability, the flexibility of the market and the market conditions, the organizations, their coping resources, their personalities, and unemployment policies, among others. Paying attention to the biographical-context-agentic individual will contribute to improving our understanding of his or her experience and behaviors. These elements offer a complex picture of the phenomena, but in a person-centric approach all these components need to be taken into consideration.

CONCLUDING COMMENTS

Unemployment and underemployment are frequent phenomena that, when experienced by young people for long time periods, may have a lasting impact on the development of their work personality, on human capital availability for companies, and on societal cohesion and inclusion. A person-centric approach to the study of these phenomena will significantly contribute to better understanding them taking into account the specificities for youngsters and to developing policies and coping strategies to make them more productive and positive when they do occur. In this chapter, we aimed to contribute to formulating an agenda for future research (see Figure 4.1 for a graphic overview).

We emphasize that a more thorough understanding of underemployment and unemployment of young people requires a comprehensive perspective of the person and his or her circumstances. Thus, it is important to increase the understanding of young people's meaning of work and their

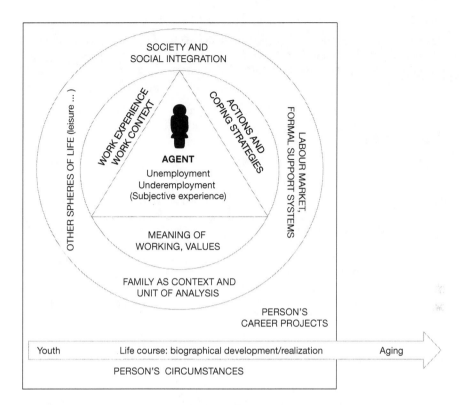

FIGURE 4.1
Main concepts and issues in a person-centric approach to the study of unemployment

work socialization processes. Moreover, their work contexts and experiences need to be more thoroughly considered. In addition, their experience and the value they place on other life spheres are relevant, and special attention should be paid to the role of their families, using a multilevel approach that studies family actions to cope with unemployment. Moreover, the role of policies of other collective systems, such as state subsidy schemes and policies to promote employment, should receive attention. Finally, youth unemployment or underemployment episodes should be considered from a lifespan perspective, taking into account the biographical and career projects, and they should be analyzed along with the coping strategies and behaviors. In this way, youth underemployment and unemployment events can be considered from a more comprehensive approach that uses the person and his or her life circumstances as the focus in studying these phenomena, rather than considering their current status in a limited or undefined time frame and circumstances.

NOTE

1. The present chapter has been prepared with the support of the project PSI2012-36557 funded by DGICYT and the funding of the Generalitat Valenciana for research groups of excellence PROMETEO 2012/048.

REFERENCES

Agut, S., Peiró, J. M., & Grau, R. (2009). The effect of overeducation on job content innovation and career-enhancing strategies among young Spanish employees. *Journal of Career Development*, 36, 159–182.

Anderson, S., & Winefield, A. H. (2011). The impact of underemployment on psychological health, physical health, and work attitudes. In D. C. Maynard & D. C. Feldman (Eds.), *Underemployment: Psychological, Economic, and Social Challenges* (pp. 165–185). New York: Springer.

Archer, J., & Rhodes, V. (1993). The grief process and job loss: A cross-sectional study. *British Journal of Psychology*, 84, 395–410.

Bashshur, M. R., Hernández, A., & Peiró, J. M. (2011). The impact of underemployment on individual and team performance. In D. C. Maynard & D. C. Feldman (Eds.), *Underemployment: Psychological, Economic, and Social Challenges* (pp. 187–214). New York: Springer.

Blanch, J. M. (1990). *Del viejo al nuevo paro. Un análisis psicológico y social*. Barcelona: PPU.

Büchel, F., & Mertens, A. (2004). Overeducation, undereducation, and the theory of career mobility. *Applied Economics*, 36, 803–816.

Carpintero, H. (2006). Towards a history of applied psychology in the 20th century. In Q. Jing, M. R. Rosenzweig, G. d'Ydewalle, H. Zhang, H. C. Chen, & K. Zhang (Eds.), *Progress in Psychological Science Around the World, Vol. II* (pp. 433–442). New York: Psychology Press.

Cassidy, T., & Wright, L. (2008). Graduate employment status and health: A longitudinal analysis of the transition from student. *Social Psychology and Education*, 11, 181–191.

Curie, J., Hajjar, V., Marquie, H., & Roques, M. (1990). Proposition méthodologique pour la description du système des activités. *Le travail humain*, 53, 103–118.

de Witte, H. (2012). On the experience of unemployment: Overview of the international literature and some results from a South African project. Workshop "Experience of Unemployment in Europe and South-Africa," March 30.

Edwards, J. R. (1991). Person-job fit: A conceptual integration, literature review, and methodological critique. In C. L. Cooper (Ed.), *International Review of Industrial and Organizational Psychology, Vol. 6* (pp. 283–357). Chichester: Wiley.

Erdogan, B., & Bauer, T. N. (2011). The impact of underemployment on turnover and career trajectories. In D. C. Maynard & D. C. Feldman (Eds.), *Underemployment: Psychological, Economic, and Social Challenges* (pp. 215–232). New York: Springer.

Erdogan, B., Bauer, T. N., Peiró, J. M., & Truxillo, D. M. (2011). Overqualified employees: Making the best of a potentially bad situation for individuals and organizations. *Industrial and Organizational Psychology*, 4, 215–232.

Feij, J. A., Whitely, W. T., Peiró, J. M., & Taris, T. (1995). The development of career-enhancing strategies and content innovation: A longitudinal study of new workers. *Journal of Vocational Behavior*, 46, 231–256.

Feldman, D. C. (1996). The nature, antecedents and consequences of underemployment. *Journal of Management, 22*, 385–407.
Feldman, D. C., & Turnley, W. H. (2004). Contingent employment in academic careers: Relative deprivation among adjunct faculty. *Journal of Vocational Behavior, 64*, 284–307.
Feldman, D. C., Leana, C. R., & Bolino, M. C. (2002). Underemployment and relative deprivation among reemployed executives. *Journal of Occupational and Organizational Psychology, 75*, 453–471.
Fryer, D. (1992). Psychological or material deprivation: Why does unemployment have mental health consequences? In E. McLaughlin (Ed.), *Understanding Unemployment: New Perspectives on Active Labour Market Policies* (pp. 103–125). London: Routledge.
Fugate, M., Kinicki, A. J., & Ashforth, B. E. (2004). Employability: A psycho-social construct, its dimensions, and applications. *Journal of Vocational Behavior, 65*, 14–38.
García-Montalvo, J., & Peiró, J. M. (2008). *Análisis de la sobrecualificación y la flexibilidad laboral. Observatorio de Inserción Laboral de los Jóvenes 2008*. Valencia: Fundación Bancaja, IVIE.
Greenberg, D. H., Michalopoulos, C., & Robins, P. K. (2003). A meta-analysis of government-sponsored training programs. *Industrial and Labor Relations Review, 57*, 31–53.
Halbesleben, J. R. B., Wheeler, A. R., & Paustian-Underdahl, S. C. (2013). The impact of furloughs on emotional exhaustion, self-rated performance, and recovery experiences. *Journal of Applied Psychology, 98*, 492–503.
Hernández, A., Bashshur, M. R., & Peiró, J. M. (2011). *Overeducation: Permanent or Transitory? The Role of Time and Voluntary Turnover*. Paper presented at 26th annual conference of Society of Industrial-Organizational Psychology. Chicago, IL.
ILO (2013). *Global Employment Trends 2013*. Geneva: International Labour Office.
Jacob, M. (2008). Unemployment benefits and parental resources: What helps the young unemployed with labour market integration? *Journal of Youth Studies, 11*, 147–163.
Jahoda, M. (1982). *Employment and Unemployment: A Social-Psychological Analysis*. Cambridge: Cambridge University Press.
Kinicki, A. J., Prussia, G. E., & McKee-Ryan, F. (2000). A panel study of coping with involuntary job loss. *Academy of Management Journal, 43*, 90–100.
Kluve, J. (2010). The effectiveness of European active labor market programs. *Labour Economics, 17*, 904–918.
Latack, J. C., Kinicki, A. J., & Prussia, G. E. (1995). An integrative process model of coping with job loss. *Academy of Management Review, 20*, 311–342.
Lazarus, R. S., & Folkman, S. (1984). *Stress, Appraisal, and Coping*, New York: Springer.
Leccardi, C. (2006). Redefining the future: Youthful biographical constructions in the 21st century. *New Directions for Child and Adolescent Development, 113*, 37–48.
Luksyte, A., & Spitzmueller, C. (2011). Behavioral science approaches to studying underemployment. In D. C. Maynard & D. C. Feldman (Eds.), *Underemployment: Psychological, Economic, and Social Challenges* (pp. 35–56). New York: Springer.
Mares, I. (2007). The economic consequences of the welfare state. *International Social Security Review, 60*, 65–81.
Marías, J. (1955). *Reason and Life*. London: Hollis & Cárter.
Marías, J. (1987). *The Structure of Society*. Tuscaloosa, AL: University of Alabama Press.
McArdle, S., Water, L., Briscoe, J. P., & Hall, D. T. (2007). Employability during unemployment: Adaptability, career identity and human and social capital. *Journal of Vocational Behavior, 71*, 247–264.
McKee-Ryan, F. M., & Harvey, J. (2011). "I have a job, but . . .": A review of underemployment. *Journal of Management, 37*, 962–996.

McKee-Ryan, F. M., & Maitoza, R. (in press). Job loss, unemployment, and families. In U. C. Klehe & E. A. J. van Hooft (Eds.), *The Oxford Handbook of Job Search and Job Loss*. New York: Oxford University Press.

McKee-Ryan, F. M., Song, Z., Wanberg, C. R., & Kinicki, A. J. (2005). Psychological and physical well-being during unemployment: A meta-analytic study. *Journal of Applied Psychology*, 90, 53–76.

McKee-Ryan, F., Virick, M., Prussia, G. E., Harvey, J., & Lilly, J. D. (2009). Life after the layoff: Getting a job worth keeping. *Journal of Organizational Behavior*, 30, 561–580.

MOW International Research Team (1987). *The Meaning of Working*. London: Academic Press.

Nabi, G. R. (2003). Graduate employment and underemployment: Opportunity for skill use and career experiences amongst recent business graduates. *Education and Training*, 45, 371–382.

OECD (2013). *OECD Employment Outlook 2013*. Paris: Organization for Economic Cooperation and Development.

Ortega y Gasset, J. (2004). *Obras completas, Vol. I*. Madrid: Taurus/Fundación José Ortega y Gasset.

Paul, K. I., & Moser, K. (2009). Unemployment impairs mental health: Meta-analyses. *Journal of Vocational Behavior*, 74, 264–282.

Peiró, J. M. (1990). Expected developments in work and organizational psychology in Europe in the nineties. In P. D. J. Drenth, J. A. Sergeant. & R. J. Takens (Eds.), *European Perspective in Psychology, Vol. 3* (pp. 21–35). Chichester: Wiley.

Prause, J., & Dooley, D. (2011). Youth underemployment. In D. C. Maynard & D. C. Feldman (Eds.), *Underemployment: Psychological, Economic, and Social Challenges* (pp. 59–80). New York: Springer.

Ramos, J., & Peiró, J. M. (2013). Unemployment and well-being in youth transition to the labour market: The role of proactive career approach, work centrality and employability. Paper presented at the Annual Meeting of Belgian Association of Psychological Sciences, Louvain-la Neuve (Belgium), May 28.

Rueda, D. (2007). *Social Democracy Inside Out: Government Partisanship, Insiders, and Outsiders in Industrialized Democracies*, New York: Oxford University Press.

Shipp, A. J., & Jansen, K. J. (2005). *The Temporality of Person-Environment Fit Perceptions: The Role of Retrospection and Anticipation*. Paper presented at the 21st annual meeting of the Society for Industrial Organizational Psychology, Los Angeles, CA.

Stern, W. (1903). Angewandte psychologie [Applied psychology]. *Beitrage zür Psychologie der Aussage*, 1, 4–45.

Stern, W. (1957). *Psicología General desde el punto de vista personalista [General Psychology from a Personalist Point of View]*. Buenos Aires: Paidos (original published in 1938).

Virick, M. (2011). Underemployment and older workers. In D. C. Maynard & D. C. Feldman (Eds.), *Underemployment: Psychological, Economic, and Social Challenges* (pp. 81–104). New York: Springer.

Vygotsky, L. S. (1978). *Mind in Society: The Development of Higher Psychological Processes* (M. Cole, V. John-Steiner, S. Scribner, & E. Souberman, Eds.). Cambridge, MA: Harvard University Press.

Wanberg, C. R. (2012). The individual experience of unemployment. *Annual Review of Psychology*, 63, 369–396.

Wanberg, C. R., Zhu, J., Kanfer, R., & Zhang, Z. (2012). After the pink slip: Applying dynamic motivation frameworks to the job search experience. *Academy of Management Journal*, 55, 261–284.

Waters, L. (2005). The role of protean career attitude during unemployment and re-employment: A literature review and conceptual model. In K. Näswall, J. Hellgren, & M. Sverke (Eds.), *The Individual in the Changing Working Life* (pp. 328–350). Cambridge: Cambridge University Press.

Waters, L. (2007). Experiential differences between voluntary and involuntary job redundancy on depression, job-search activity, affective employee outcomes and re-employment quality. *Journal of Occupational and Organizational Psychology, 80*, 279–299.

Weiss, H., & Rupp, D. E. (2011). Experiencing work: An essay on a person-centric work psychology. *Industrial and Organizational Psychology, 4*, 83–97.

Whitely, W., Peiró, J. M., & Sarchielli, G. (1992). WOSY theoretical framework, research methodology and potential implications. *International Review of Social Psychology, 5*, 9–35.

Wilkins, R., & Wooden, M. (2011). Economic approaches to studying underemployment. In D. C. Maynard & D. C. Feldman (Eds.), *Underemployment: Psychological, Economic, and Social Challenges* (pp. 13–34). New York: Springer.

Zikic, J., & Klehe, U. C. (2006). Job loss as a blessing in disguise: The role of career exploration and career planning in predicting reemployment quality. *Journal of Vocational Behavior, 69*, 391–409.

5

The Aging Workforce and the Demands of Work in the 21st Century

Margaret E. Beier

A recent study of more than 500 executives around the globe by *The Economist* (2011) suggests that organizations are ill-equipped to handle what they term the "Silver Tsunami," referring to the well-documented aging of the labor force. Almost one in three firms report that they are not effective at adapting their HR strategies to meet the demands of an aging workforce (e.g., selection and training) and fewer than one in five firms have policies in place to address the aging of the workforce, such as capitalizing on the knowledge and skills of older workers. Given higher unemployment rates of late, it may be fair to ask whether the projections regarding the aging labor force are still relevant in the context of the "great recession" of 2007–2009. Recent reports suggest that the answer to this question is a resounding "yes." U.S. labor force participation rates continue to increase for workers between the ages of 65 and 69 even in the context of the global recession (Johnson & Butrica, 2012). Moreover, many older workers plan to work past the ages normally slated for retirement in either the same role, in bridge jobs, or encore careers (second careers, which could include a series of different jobs) to satisfy financial, social, or emotional needs. Indeed, a recent survey of workers found that more workers planned to work after retirement in some capacity than planned *not* to work (Sloan Center on Aging and Work, 2012).

The impact of the recession on older workers has been different than for younger workers. For instance, even though younger workers are more likely to be laid off, older workers who are laid off spend more time looking for work before re-employment. Moreover, those older workers who do return to the workforce often do so at lower rates of pay, evidenced by their increased likelihood to move to "bridge employment" of lower status than the job they lost (Sloan Center on Aging and Work, 2012). Many older workers who have difficulty finding work eventually leave the workforce, but these losses are not enough to offset growth in labor participation (Johnson & Butrica, 2012). Otherwise stated, recent economic trends that may have precipitated the loss of older workers in the labor market have also shrunk retirement accounts and kept older people working longer. Managing the aging workforce well will pay off for organizations, but requires understanding how the job demands of 21st century work align with the knowledge, skills, abilities, goals, attitudes, values, and interests (KSAOs) of aging workers.

In this chapter, the relationship between age and work in the 21st century is conceptualized and presented as a function of person-environment fit (the match between a person's attributes and his or her work environment) (Kristof, 1996). Although there are many dimensions of person-environment fit (e.g., person-organization fit, person-supervisor fit, person-team fit), the focus of this chapter is on the alignment between the KSAOs of workers with the task requirements of jobs; that is, person-job (PJ) fit. The underlying thesis is that age-related changes in KSAOs will importantly influence both actual fit (can the person do the job?) and perceptions of fit (does the person/manager/organization think the person can do the job?). Judgments about fit influence worker decisions to engage in their current role when fit is good or to accommodate changes in KSAOs through modifying their current role if possible, through pursuing an entirely new role, or through withdrawal from the workforce (Kanfer & Ackerman, 2004).

This chapter addresses two important questions: (1) What are the needs of the 21st century organization in terms of worker KSAOs and how do these needs align with age-related changes in KSAOs? (2) How can organizations and workers optimize PJ fit to maximize performance, motivation, and continuous development on the job? The chapter is framed around the components outlined as a set of interlocking elements that together form the context for maximizing PJ fit in Figure 5.1. Of particular interest is the relationship between work-role demands and age-related changes in KSAOs (i.e., PJ fit). The elements of PJ fit (worker characteristics and job demands), however, are just two pieces of the larger picture—a picture that includes the larger organizational context and non-work demands. The influence of the organization on PJ fit is through organizational norms and culture. For instance, if there is a culture of age-related bias in the organization as evidenced by a reluctance to train and develop older workers, this will likely impact older worker perceptions of fit.

110 • *Margaret E. Beier*

Likewise, non-work demands such as caring for aging parents can influence the goals of older workers and perceptions of fit within work roles. Moreover, each of the four pieces (work-role demands, age-related changes in KSAOs, organizational factors, and non-work demands) fit within the larger context of the modern workplace, which dictates the types of jobs available and the necessary skills for work in the 21st century.

The chapter is organized into three major parts. The first provides background on the theoretical foundation and importance of examining PJ fit in the context of worker age. It includes a section on theoretical perspectives that inform the discussion, the relationship between age and job performance, and a profile of age-related changes in KSAOs. The next section discusses work in the 21st century, as well as the organizational and non-work environments that will influence PJ fit. The third and final

FIGURE 5.1
Illustration of how age-related changes in knowledge, skills, abilities, and other characteristics (KSAOs) influence PJ fit with work role demands; organizational culture (e.g., existence of age-related bias) and non-work demands are also expected to have an influence on both the person and the work role

section discusses matching work with workers and presents examples of organizational strategies for this task. Finally, a research agenda on age and PJ fit is presented along with conclusions.

THEORETICAL PERSPECTIVES RELEVANT TO AGE AND JOB FIT

Work Design

Job and work role design theories are concerned with describing the process and outcomes of how work is structured, experienced, organized, and enacted, particularly as related to worker motivation and attitudes such as job satisfaction (Morgeson & Humphrey, 2006). Essentially, these theories recognize that what people do at work affects an array of attitudes and behavior (such as motivation, job satisfaction, effort, and engagement) that influence performance and investment in continuous skill development and mastery (Cordery & Parker, 2012; Grant, Fried, & Juillerat, 2011; Hackman & Oldham, 1975; Karasek et al., 1998; Parker, Wall, & Cordery, 2001). Job characteristics considered especially important for increasing motivation are skill variety, task identity (being able to complete a task from beginning to end), task significance (whether the work is important to others either internal or external to the organization), autonomy, and feedback. Two categories of job characteristics have been researched extensively as related to contributing to psychologically engaging work: (a) the psychological demands associated with the work; and (b) the decision latitude afforded the worker (Karasek et al., 1998). Specifically, psychological demands refer to how intellectually engaging job tasks are as related to skill variety, task identity, and task significance; decision latitude is related to worker autonomy in decision-making.

According to work design theories, active and engaging work is high in both psychological demands and decision latitude, and boring work is low in both. Incidentally, jobs that are high in psychological demands but low in autonomy are characteristically stressful. Workers in these types of jobs, for instance, often complain that they have a lot of responsibility to make sure the work gets done, but no actual authority to make anything happen (Karasek et al., 1998). Researchers have only just begun to investigate the influence of job characteristics on the psychological meaning of work and performance for older workers (see Perry, Dokko, & Golom, 2012 for a review of research on age and fit). Recent theory and research suggest that age moderates the relationship between job characteristics and work outcomes such as job satisfaction, work engagement, and job performance (Truxillo, Cadiz, Rineer, Zaniboni, & Fraccaroli, 2012). For instance, jobs high in task variety (i.e., workers perform a wide range of tasks) are more motivating for younger versus older workers because these jobs provide younger workers opportunities to build their skill repertoire. By contrast, jobs that provide the opportunity to use already accumulated skills are more motivating for older workers relative to younger workers because they provide the opportunity to demonstrate expertise (Zaniboni, Truxillo, Fraccaroli, McCune, & Bertolino, 2014). Job complexity is another job characteristic that interacts with age to affect perceptions of work-related opportunities (Zacher & Frese, 2009, 2011). In particular, when jobs are higher in complexity relative to when they are low in complexity, older workers are more likely to perceive growth opportunities within their jobs.

Selection, Optimization, and Compensation (SOC)

SOC theory (Baltes & Baltes, 1990) applies to goal choice at any age, but is considered especially relevant in the context of aging because age-related changes often limit resources, making it essential to focus on, and optimize strengths and to compensate for weaknesses. *Selection* refers to the task of selecting the domains in which the person chooses to operate. Specifically, people will prioritize those domains that are most aligned with their strengths. In the work context, it would be predicted that workers would choose jobs with tasks that correspond to their KSAOs. *Optimization* is related to augmenting those resources that are most relevant to selected goals. These resources could be cognitive, such as knowledge learned through experience, or interpersonal, such as the ability to remain calm in difficult interpersonal interactions. Theoretically, older workers would be predicted to focus on investing in training and development to enhance their perceived strengths rather than to develop new ones. *Compensation* refers to the use of strategies or tools to compensate for age-related losses that affect performance (e.g., documentation strategies to compensate for memory declines; hearing aids). Examples of compensation at work include using large font-type materials to compensate for vision changes and the use of reminder systems to compensate for memory declines. The three components of SOC theory underlie much of the following discussion on age and PJ fit, particularly as it describes the process of gravitating toward work that complements existing KSAOs, optimizing performance in a worker's chosen domain, and compensating for perceived deficiencies when possible.

Socio-Emotional Selectivity (SST)

SST theory (Carstensen, 1998) is also related to goal choice, but unlike SOC theory, it makes more general predictions about how goal content changes with age. Specifically, age-related shifts in goal content are thought to be a function of perceptions of time left in life. When time left is perceived to be extensive (i.e., in youth), people will be more likely to adopt goals related to the acquisition of knowledge (learning and achievement). When time left is perceived to be limited (i.e., in older age), people will be more likely to adopt socio-emotional goals related to emotional fulfillment (spending time with family and close friends). The shift from achievement to socio-emotional goals is thought to influence the value people will assign to an array of work-related activities (including retirement), and as such, will influence motivation and behavior (Vroom, 1964). In the context of PJ fit and aging, SST would predict, for instance, that older workers would be more motivated to engage in jobs that emphasized personally fulfilling rewards such as developing others through mentoring and teaching than they would be to engage in jobs that emphasized extrinsic rewards such as pay and promotion; these predictions have been generally supported in the research literature (Kooij, de Lange, Jansen, Kanfer, & Dikkers, 2011).

Together, these three perspectives provide a theoretical foundation for considering age and PJ fit. From an organizational perspective, work design theories highlight the importance of aligning job tasks with the KSAOs of workers of all ages to ensure a level of psychological challenge that will engage workers. SOC highlights the worker's role in selecting the jobs that best complement their KSAOs, and SST suggests that, in general, the importance of certain job characteristics will change as workers age. These changes could affect the alignment between the work and the worker, which will potentially affect job performance.

AGE AND JOB PERFORMANCE

Meta-analytic research has found no consistent relationship between age and the task dimension of job performance (McEvoy & Cascio, 1989;

Ng & Feldman, 2008; Sturman, 2003; Waldman & Avolio, 1986), although there is evidence that organizational citizenship behavior/contextual performance improves with age (Ng & Feldman, 2008). The lack of a relationship between age and job performance may be one reason why researchers have not focused on the extent to which age-related changes in abilities affect PJ fit. That is, it may be assumed that age-related changes in KSAOs that occur until the age normally slated for retirement do not have an important effect on a worker's PJ fit because they do not seem to affect a worker's ability to do his or her job. There are two problems with this assumption. The first is that the majority of the research on age and job performance has been done using cross-sectional designs, and as such, they include only those workers who have been successful enough in their jobs to be doing those jobs during the time the study is conducted. This is a seemingly obvious point, but it means that cross-sectional studies do not account for workers who select out of jobs and/or careers (whether voluntarily or not) because they are no longer successful or because they no longer fit in the job/career/organization. As such, it is likely that most of the older workers included in these studies are those that have done well in their jobs, which is likely to obscure the true relationship between age and PJ fit (although the extent of this bias is not well understood at present).

The second problem with the assumption that age does not affect PJ fit is that the analyses that have examined the relationship between age and job performance (e.g., meta-analyses by McEvoy & Cascio, 1989; Ng & Feldman, 2008; Sturman, 2003; Waldman & Avolio, 1986) have not considered the KSAO demands of the job as moderators of the age and job performance relation. That is, age may be negatively related to job performance for those jobs that rely heavily on abilities that decline with age, and age may be positively related to job performance for those jobs that rely heavily on abilities that are likely to increase through the lifespan. These shifts in abilities are described below.

PROFILE OF OLDER WORKERS

There is no definitive age at which a worker becomes an "older worker." The Age Discrimination in Employment Act protects workers over the age of 40, but many age researchers would consider 40 to be too young to capture the psychological and physical differences that make a worker an "older" worker. Further complicating matters is the fact that people age differently. Two people at age 50 may have very different memory abilities: one more like a 35-year-old and the other like a 65-year-old (Hertzog, Kramer, Wilson, & Lindenberger, 2008). Moreover, within the same person, different abilities change at different rates. For instance, a person may have similar levels of math and writing skills when younger, but experience in a job that emphasizes writing over math will affect writing skills positively and math skills negatively. For the purposes of this chapter, general trends in KSAOs will be described rather than specifying an age at which a worker becomes an older worker.

A useful framework for conceptualizing age-related changes in abilities is to consider them a function to loss, growth, reorganization, and exchange (Kanfer & Ackerman, 2004). *Loss* refers to the well-documented gradual decline in fluid intellectual abilities (Gf) (Cattell, 1987) that occurs with age. These abilities are most related to working memory capacity, abstract reasoning, processing novel information, and attention. Closely aligned with the decline in Gf abilities is a decline in information processing speed (Salthouse, 1996), which represents a general slowing of the cognitive system. The decline in Gf and processing speed abilities affects the amount of attentional/cognitive resources that a person has available to perform any given task. This decline will potentially affect job performance, particularly for those jobs that rely heavily on Gf abilities such as air traffic control (Ackerman & Kanfer, 1993). Loss in physical abilities such as static strength also occurs with age and is related to the weakening of muscle strength and aerobic capacity (Hedge, Borman, & Lammlien, 2006). These changes will similarly affect performance on jobs with essential tasks that tap these abilities. Moreover, as noted by Kanfer and Ackerman (2004), the cost of expending resources (cognitive and physical) increases with age both in terms of immediate levels of effort and effort over time. As such, older workers may be less able than younger workers to engage in effortful work over extended periods of time.

The *growth* referred to by Kanfer and Ackerman (2004) is related to crystallized intellectual abilities (Gc) (Cattell, 1987), which represent the knowledge acquired through life experiences (educational, vocational, avocational). Measures of Gc show increases in knowledge into middle and older ages. Moreover, broad knowledge assessments intended to measure Gc show that older adults know more than younger adults across academic (history, literature, business) and non-academic (current events, heath-related) knowledge domains (Ackerman, 2000; Beier & Ackerman, 2001, 2003, 2005). Increases in Gc throughout the lifespan suggest that people can compensate for losses in Gf by selecting environments that are aligned with their established knowledge and skills. In some ways, the trajectories of Gf (declining with advancing age) and Gc (remaining stable or improving with age) are functional in the context of adaptation: when people are younger, they are more likely to encounter novel environments and novel problems because they have a limited range of experiences. As people age, however, they acquire both general knowledge about how to behave effectively across a range of situations and specific domain knowledge related to doing their jobs. In essence, because we do it less, solving novel problems becomes less important as we age relative to relying on existing knowledge and experience.

Reorganization and *exchange* refer to changes in motives and values (e.g., shifts from achievement-oriented to social and emotional goals with age) and attitudes. Although personality has typically been thought to remain relatively stable after young adulthood, meta-analytic research that examines mean-level changes in the Big Five traits (i.e., Openness to Experience, Extraversion, Agreeableness, Conscientiousness, and Emotional Stability) finds, for instance, that personality will change well into late life (Roberts, Walton, & Viechtbauer, 2006). In particular, conscientiousness and emotional stability increase on average, although there is individual variability in these findings (i.e., some people will show greater increases in these traits than others).

In terms of motivation, SST (Carstensen, 1998) theory provides a useful framework from which to consider changes in affective and emotional reactions to situations that occur with age. According to SST theory and research that supports it, people learn how to regulate emotions through life experiences and thus develop resiliency in stressful situations (Carstensen & Mikels, 2005). Researchers have also examined strategies for resiliency in what they have termed the *positivity effect* (Mather & Carstensen, 2005), which refers to the tendency for older people to attend to positive rather than negative information in their environment.

In summary, age-related changes in abilities, attitudes, and motives influence older workers' ability to perform effectively at work, the value they place on an array of work-related activities, and the effort they expend toward work. This highlights the dynamic nature of PJ fit in relation to worker age: age-related changes in KSAOs will affect both actual fit (whether or not a person can continue in his or her job) and perceptions of fit (whether workers think they can and whether they want to. Further complicating the picture is that job demands in the 21st century are also dynamic.

WORK IN THE 21ST CENTURY

A shift in the types of jobs available in industrialized countries (from manufacturing/agriculture to knowledge-based jobs) began over the past two decades and promises to continue into the foreseeable future. As a result, fewer jobs in industrialized countries will require physical strength and effort, and more jobs will require working with computers and intense concentration. The technical aspects of jobs in the 21st century will necessitate continuous skill and knowledge updating more than ever before (Johnson, 2004; Johnson, Mermin, & Resseger, 2007). In general, the reduction in the physical demands of jobs should benefit older workers and cognitively demanding jobs may also be better suited for older workers because of the stability and growth of Gc abilities (Sharit & Czaja, 2012). Some cognitively demanding jobs may prove difficult for older workers, however, particularly when the job places heavy demands on Gf abilities (working memory, processing speed, novel problem solving).

In addition to cognitive and physical job characteristics, social and emotional job demands are also changing. Compared with the types of jobs available in the 1970s, current jobs are more likely to require strong interpersonal skills (including dealing with unpleasant people) and the ability to deal with stress caused by interpersonal interactions. Examples are related to job growth in education, social services, and health service sectors (Johnson et al., 2007). Stereotypes of grumpy old people notwithstanding, research suggests that older workers are likely to do well in work contexts that require interpersonal interactions because they seem better able than younger workers to *not sweat the small stuff*. Indeed, research supports the idea that older adults are better able to regulate their emotions in response to disturbing stimuli (Scheibe & Blanchard-Fields, 2009) and experience fewer negative emotions as a result of negative events at work (e.g., Bal & Smit, 2011).

In summary, the shift from manufacturing (i.e., jobs that tap physical capabilities) to knowledge work in most industrialized countries will likely benefit older workers who have acquired vast knowledge (Gc) across a range of domains, including general job-related knowledge about managing a project, interpersonal knowledge about dealing effectively with others, and specific knowledge about a particular job. Older workers are likely to benefit most when jobs do not tax abilities known to decline with advanced age (e.g., Gf, physical abilities, speeded processing), but instead rely on job knowledge. Increases in jobs available in service sectors (e.g., educational, social, and health) are also good news for older workers, who bring a wealth of knowledge about operating in a range of interpersonal situations.

ORGANIZATIONAL AND NON-WORK ENVIRONMENTS

In addition to job tasks, the demands placed on workers from their home environments are also likely to affect their motives, attitudes, and perceptions of PJ fit. Workers overwhelmed with non-work responsibilities, for instance, may be less engaged and effective at work. Although research on how non-work demands change with age is just beginning (see Matthews, Bulger, & Barnes-Farrell, 2010), it may be that older workers will have relatively fewer constraints on their time compared to mid-career workers, who will be more likely juggling an array of outside demands (e.g., childcare and eldercare). Indeed, research suggests that older workers report less work-role conflict and work-role ambiguity than younger workers (Matthews et al., 2010). Even without substantial family demands, workers may choose to increase their investment in their non-work environments relative to their work environments as they age, reflecting the shift from achievement to socio-emotional values suggested by SST theory (Carstensen, 1998). For instance, grandparents may choose to prioritize spending time with their grandchildren over taking on additional responsibilities at work because they consider the development of these interpersonal relationships to be increasingly important as they age. This value shift is likely to affect worker engagement and perceptions of PJ fit, particularly for people working in highly competitive organizational cultures, who may choose to opt out of their current role.

Organizational environments are another important influence on PJ fit through perceptions of person-organization (PO) fit. Explicit age discrimination is typically defined as differential treatment such as would result in the denial of a job or training opportunities because of a person's age. Research on explicit age discrimination suggests that it is becoming less frequent, at least in the United States, most likely because of laws that protect older workers from discrimination. Researchers have also begun to examine subtle forms of bias such as interpersonal discrimination (Hebl, Foster, Mannix, & Dovidio, 2002), which involves subtle verbal (e.g., saying fewer words), paraverbal (e.g., negative tone of voice, less friendliness), and nonverbal (e.g., less eye contact, less smiling, fewer affirmations) behaviors that people exhibit toward a stigmatized group (including older workers). These subtle forms of bias are likely to affect older workers either directly or through its influence on organizational culture. When age-related bias is internalized by older workers, it can affect perceptions of self-efficacy, dependence, depression (Palacios, Torres, & Mena, 2009), and it has the potential to affect job performance (Greller & Stroh, 1995).

Age-related biases seem to be even more insidious than biases related to gender and race (Posthuma & Campion, 2009). This is perhaps because aging affects everyone, although very few people welcome its effects. Indeed, research shows that both younger and older people hold negative age-related stereotypes about the competence of older workers; although older workers are considered reliable, loyal, and productive, they are also thought to be costly, inflexible, hard to train, and unable to keep up with technology (Kite, Stockdale, Whitley, & Johnson, 2005; Posthuma & Campion, 2009). When age-related stereotypes permeate the organizational culture, they will affect perceptions of PJ fit. For instance, the belief that older workers are difficult to train will limit the developmental opportunities they pursue and those that are offered. More generally, being relatively older in organizational cultures that reflect younger values will impact perceptions of PO fit and may affect decisions to remain in a job and/or organization or exit the workforce.

MATCHING WORK TO WORKERS

The process of matching work to workers is challenging because of the continuous updating of skills required by work in the 21st century and the dynamic nature of KSAOs through the lifespan. Further complicating matters is the dynamic nature of learning and skill acquisition on the job. Specifically, the psychological challenge associated with a job will change as a function of experience; challenge is likely to be highest at the start of a new job, and it will decrease over time as workers gain experience and learn how to do their jobs (Murphy, 1989). As such, PJ fit is a dynamic process that should be reconsidered periodically throughout a career as workers seek challenges that best align with their ever-changing KSAOs.

Although many workers select out of jobs that do not align with their KSAOS, movement to new jobs is not always possible due to financial or situational factors. In these cases, it is possible for workers and organizations to employ strategies to improve PJ fit in the current role. In the context of SOC theory (Baltes & Baltes, 1990), worker- and organization-initiated efforts to accommodate aging workers means facilitating *compensation* for declining abilities (physical or cognitive). Some examples of self-initiated accommodations can be found in interviews of workers with jobs high in physical demands (e.g., janitorial, maintenance workers). These interviews suggest that workers modify their approach to work to compensate for age-related limitations, even though they may be unaware of doing it. For instance, older workers tend to be mindful about how much physical effort a task will require (e.g., how much weight they will need to lift and how they might best lift it). They develop strategies for approaching intensely physical activities and are more likely to use tools available to them—tools that they may have rejected or ignored as younger workers (Sanders & McCready, 2009). These employee-initiated compensatory strategies can also be subtler. For instance, a study of young and old typists found that overall typing performance was the same for both groups, even though the older typists were slower on basic speeded tasks. Examination of typing strategies revealed that the older typists were more likely to anticipate upcoming keystrokes by looking ahead in the copy than younger typists (Salthouse, 1984). This compensatory strategy allowed older typists to maintain high levels of performance despite age-related changes in speed. Although not explicitly examined in this study, it is likely that the typists themselves were unaware that their approach differed from that of younger typists. These examples illustrate that the use of compensatory strategies for maintaining proficiency in a job (and PJ fit) is likely pervasive and oftentimes unconscious across all types of jobs.

ORGANIZATIONAL STRATEGIES FOR OPTIMIZING PJ FIT

Organizations can also promote the use of compensatory strategies for maintaining job performance. In many cases, organizationally initiated accommodation can be relatively straightforward, cheap, and easy. For instance, an auto manufacturer in Germany implemented relatively small changes to the physical environment in the manufacturing plant to accommodate older workers on an assembly line. Costs for these changes, which included new wooden platforms, new chairs, and magnifying glasses, were negligible (around US $55,000) and the changes reportedly reduced absenteeism and increased productivity for older workers such that they matched levels of workers 5–10 years younger (*The Economist*, 2011). In addition to increased productivity, these relatively small changes demonstrated that the organization cared about the physical well-being of its workers and likely increased retention for older workers and fostered goodwill between the worker and the organization.

More generally, according to work design theory, the engagement of the aging workforce will likely involve at least three important elements: providing access to flexible work arrangements; providing workers with autonomy by giving them a voice in the decisions that affect their work; and providing opportunities for growth and development to older workers (Tishman, van Looy, & Bruyére, 2012). Increasing flexibility in work arrangements can be relatively straightforward. For instance, older workers may be more amenable to job-sharing and flexible work hours than are younger workers, who may feel that these arrangements would impede their ability to build professional networks, their resumes, and their reputations (likely considered *faits accomplis* for many older workers). Shifting from full-time to part-time work arrangements also may be a reasonable approach to increase worker flexibility. Recent trends in the labor market, however, suggest that older workers are *less* likely to work part-time now than they were a decade ago (Bureau of Labor Statistics, 2008). It may be that the shift from part-time to full-time work is a function of the recent recession, which may have caught many workers financially unprepared for their upcoming retirement. That is, many older workers need to balance their desire for flexible work with the realities of their financial situation.

Autonomy also may be especially important for some older workers. An extreme example of the effect of autonomy on engaging older workers is an approach by some organizations to retain senior leaders by allowing them to customize their own "second career" within the firm (Eyster, Johnson, & Toder, 2008). This policy is mutually beneficial—workers continue to reap the psychological benefits of contributing to the organization they helped build without the intensity of a senior executive schedule and duties; the organization benefits from extensive knowledge and experience of the leader. Facilitating the design of a second career for senior leaders is perhaps not feasible for most organizations. Nonetheless, less extreme and relatively simple steps can be taken to increase employee autonomy.

For instance, workers can provide input about how they might do their jobs better, what skills they might want to develop in the future, and where they feel their skills could most effectively be used in the organization. These conversations could be incorporated into regular performance discussions and could lead to the development of compensatory strategies within the same job and/or working with employees to seek out new roles aligned with their skills and interests (e.g., mentoring, service-oriented functions) (Robson & Hansson, 2007; Yeatts, Folts, & Knapp, 2000).

Some organizations are indeed providing older workers with developmental opportunities that simultaneously optimize older worker KSAOs; for example, moving older knowledge workers into positions that involve training and mentoring younger workers. This is especially important for industries concerned about knowledge transfer to younger generations of workers because they risk losing specialized expertise with the retirement of the baby boomer generation. For manufacturing jobs, some organizations report moving older workers off of assembly lines and into customer service roles, where customers benefit from the expertise and positive perspective of the older worker (Eyster et al., 2008). Although internal moves appear to be a promising approach to retaining older workers and benefiting from their experience and unique KSAOs, an important consideration is that the new opportunity be thought of as a lateral move or promotion. If they are considered demotions, these job changes could backfire by reducing motivation and precipitating older worker exit from the workforce.

Seeking input from workers about their own development through performance discussions should already be happening in organizations, but research suggests that the likelihood of these conversations may depend on the age of the worker. Specifically, older workers are less likely to be offered opportunities to participate in development activities within the workplace (Maurer, Weiss, & Barbeite, 2003). Moreover, decisions about offering development opportunities are influenced by age-related stereotypes about the flexibility and trainability of the older workforce pervasive in many organizations (Cox & Beier, 2014). As such, engaging older workers necessitates an understanding of the age-related stereotypes about development and performance that permeate organizational culture. Even when organizational cultures do support continuous development for workers of all ages, the effect of bias and stereotypes is an important consideration for training the aging workforce.

TRAINING AND DEVELOPMENT STRATEGIES

Changes in skills and abilities with age will affect both the desire to participate and performance in training. Although in-depth treatment of aging and training is beyond the scope of this chapter (see Beier, Teachout, & Cox, 2012), training older workers is relevant to how older workers fit within organizations. A meta-analysis of age and training performance published almost 20 years ago concluded that age is negatively related to performance in work-related training. That is, older people are likely to perform worse and take longer in training than younger people (Kubeck, Delp, Haslett, & McDaniel, 1996). This is not to say, however, that training does not benefit older workers. Indeed, there is ample evidence that older workers do well in training when it is designed to match their unique KSAOs. For instance, training that is self-paced, that connects new learning with existing knowledge, that provides ample models and examples, and that balances structured instruction with less structured discover learning approaches (i.e., starts relatively structured, but becomes less structured with practice) has been shown to be especially effective with older learners (Callahan, Kiker, & Cross, 2003). Self-pacing and structure would help compensate for losses in Gf abilities, connecting new learning to existing knowledge permits optimizing current knowledge, and models serve to increase learner self-efficacy, which positively affect motivation for training and self-regulation during learning.

Although research suggests that older adults have the ability to continually learn and develop, they may not *want* to. Indeed, meta-analytic research suggests that age is negatively related to motivation for career development, engaging in career development behaviors, motivation to learn, and training motivation. Although the effects are weak (e.g., average correlations from –0.22 for engaging in career development behavior to –0.05 for training motivation), these findings suggest that older workers are less likely than other workers to want to engage in work-related development activity (Ng & Feldman, 2012). Like their younger counterparts, older worker motivation for training and development will be a function of the value they assign desired outcomes, the instrumentality of training for obtaining those outcomes, and expectations that they can perform successfully in training (Beier & Kanfer, 2010; Vroom, 1964). Theoretically, the shift from achievement to socio-emotional goals with age (SST) (Carstensen, 1998) will affect the valence of the outcomes related to certain training activities, which will affect motivation for training. Older workers will value training activities related to career advancement and extrinsic outcomes (i.e., increases in pay) *less* than younger workers, but they will value developmental activities that emphasize social and generative motives (e.g., mentoring and managing others) *more* than younger workers. Older workers should also be more likely than younger workers to place a higher value on development activities aligned with their existing knowledge (Gc), and recognized strengths to optimize training outcomes (SOC) (Baltes & Baltes, 1990). Perceptions of changes in abilities with age (especially as related to Gf) are also likely to influence judgments about the effort involved in training. Particularly, if training content is novel and perceived to be difficult and training is fast-paced, older worker motivation for training and development will be negatively affected. Theory and research on motivation for training and development suggests that the manner in which training is positioned influences training motivation. If appropriate, the intrinsic benefits of the training, the links between the training content and existing knowledge, and the tools that will help older learners compensate for age-related losses (e.g., self-pacing, large-font materials) could be highlighted in the training advertisement (Cox & Beier, 2009).

RESEARCH AGENDA

The above discussion paints a complex picture of the trajectories of KSAOs throughout the lifespan and how age-related changes affect both the perception and reality of PJ fit. Although research on age and work has expanded over the past decade, there remains plenty of work to be done. A summary of a research agenda is shown in Table 5.1. The integration of SOC, SST, and work design theories provides the background for much of the discussion above. In reality, however, little empirical research exists that has examined how age-related changes in KSAOs will affect PJ fit (perceptions or reality), job performance, motivation for work, and job attitudes. Moreover, the research that has been conducted on age-related changes has oftentimes shown inconsistent results. This is perhaps a function of the diversity of KSAOs in older workers, given that age-related trajectories are relatively idiosyncratic with respect to chronological age. In general, chronological age may not capture the important psychological variables that account for age-related changes in KSAOs. *As such, the first research recommendation is to include age-related variables that are more psychologically interesting and useful than chronological age in future workplace aging studies.* Many researchers have already begun this effort by examining variables such as relative age (how old a worker feels compared to others in their workgroup) and psychological age (Barnes-Farrell, Rumery, & Swody, 2002; Cleveland & Shore, 1992). Nonetheless, these psychologically meaningful age variables could be used more consistently, which would facilitate research replication and synthesis that will be immensely important in identifying the psychological elements of chronological age that are central to the experience of workforce aging.

In addition to examining the psychological variables associated with age, researchers examining age and work issues seem to have divided the world into two groups of workers—younger and older—and tend to leave out middle-aged workers. Often this grouping reflects study design, especially when only one age group is sampled (usually older workers when the topic is aging) or when there is a comparison between extreme groups. This is problematic because it limits our ability to understand workforce aging. Specifically, examining the full working-age spectrum is necessary to study questions about the factors (both individual differences and environmental) that affect career and developmental trajectories. In an ideal world, research on age and PJ fit would be conducted using longitudinal or cohort sequential designs to address the limits of cross-sectional designs (including issues related to survival and the exclusion of workers who select out of jobs and careers). This is, of course, a tall order given the time and expense of this type of research. But even when longitudinal studies are not possible, researchers can strive to include a full range of working-aged adults in their studies given that factors influencing PJ fit are likely to occur throughout a job or career (not just at the beginning or the end). More generally, the experience of work may be qualitatively different for middle-aged workers relative to older and younger workers; unfortunately, we currently do not know enough about workers of all ages to make this assessment. *Thus, the second recommendation to include a full range of working-aged adults (including middle-aged workers) in their examination of PJ fit.*

The above discussion emphasizes the dynamic nature of PJ fit throughout the work lifespan and suggests that workers who continue to update their skills will remain productive throughout their careers. The necessity to grow and develop at work for workers of all ages highlights the importance of research on training motivation and effectiveness. Although the I-O literature is rife with research on the effectiveness of a variety of training approaches, very little training research has been conducted with working-aged adults (for reviews, see Beier et al., 2012; Wolfson, Cavanagh, & Kraiger, 2013). This is unfortunate because, as discussed above, the KSAO profiles of workers change over the span of a career in

TABLE 5.1

Suggested Future Research Topics

Topic	Description
1. Define age in psychologically interesting and useful ways.	Research on age and work often shows inconsistent results, perhaps because of the variability of changes in KSAOs associated with chronological aging. Including psychologically interesting and useful age variables (e.g., perceived age, relative age) in addition to chronological age in future research will enable researchers to understand what might account for variability in the relationships between age and important outcomes such as job performance and job attitudes.
2. Include longitudinal designs or at minimum the full range of working-aged adults (e.g., from about 16 to about 70).	Longitudinal designs would help illuminate the relationship between age and job performance in the context of job survival. That is, longitudinal research would help answer questions about how the relationship between age and job performance is affected by low performers leaving jobs and high performers staying in jobs. Including middle-aged workers in workforce aging research will provide a more complete picture of development throughout the work lifespan.
3. Examine the best ways to train workers of all ages; process and content.	This recommendation includes investigating the type of training that would be most motivating and interesting to older workers. Considerations include goal relevance and the extent to which training taxes cognitive abilities. Moreover, training processes should be further examined in terms of those training approaches that work best for older workers.

4. Focus on non-work factors that influence older worker perceptions of PJ fit.	Organizational culture will influence worker perceptions of fit, as will outside demands. Examining the balance of work and non-work activity desired by workers at different career stages is an important area of future research. This would include examining the contextual and individual factors that influence decisions to retire from a current work role and/or to exit the workforce completely.
5. Examine job characteristics in relation to the attitudes and performance of workers of all ages.	Job characteristics are an important piece of the PJ fit equation as they can influence job performance and motivation for a job. Research in this area would include understanding how task demands align with changing abilities and motivation throughout the work lifespan, and understanding the characteristics of jobs that are most interesting for older workers.
6. Investigate compensatory strategies (both organizationally and worker-instigated).	Specific questions to be answered relative to compensatory strategies are: (1) How do workers compensate for psychological and physical ability losses with age? (2) Are workers aware of their own compensatory strategies? (3) What can the organization do to augment the use of compensatory strategies to keep workers productive longer? (4) How do these strategies affect worker absenteeism, motivation, and productivity?

ways that will importantly affect training performance, motivation for training, and training outcomes. *The third recommendation for researchers is to redouble their efforts to examine the best ways to train workers of all ages. This includes, but is not limited to, considerations for training design to maximize training outcomes and transfer and considerations regarding maximizing motivation for training and transfer.*

The four parts of PJ fit shown in Figure 5.1 include age-related changes to KSAOs, work-role demands, organizational culture, and non-work demands that together affect important job outcomes such as work performance, motivation for training and development, career development, and job changes. The focus of the discussion above was on person-related KSAOs and job-related task demands, but the extent to which organizational culture and non-work environment also affect the perceptions and realities of PJ fit were also briefly covered. Over the past five years, researchers have begun to understand the impact of age-related bias in organizational culture on an array of outcomes (performance, commitment, motivation for training) (Posthuma & Campion, 2009). Very little is known, however, about the impact of non-work factors on PJ fit, particularly for older workers. It is likely, for instance, that non-work factors such as family demands (whether increasing or decreasing) will change through the work lifespan and will importantly affect worker values and thus PJ fit. Researchers have begun examining issues related to work-life balance and age (Cleveland & Lim, 2008), but there is relatively little work in this area to date. *Therefore, the fourth recommendation is a research focus on the non-work factors that influence older worker perceptions of PJ fit.*

As discussed above, job characteristics are an important element of PJ fit because they influence worker motivation, performance, and attitudes. *The fifth research recommendation is for examining job characteristics in relation to the attitudes and performance of workers of all ages.* This research would include understanding how task demands align with changing abilities and motivation throughout the work lifespan, and understanding the characteristics of jobs that are most interesting for older workers. A related stream of research comprises the *sixth recommendation, which is to investigate the effect of compensatory strategies that are used by older workers and those that are instigated by the organization.* In particular, researchers could identify strategies that are general (used across jobs by many workers) and specific (relevant for relatively few jobs), and worker awareness of strategy use. Moreover, the effect of organizationally initiated compensatory strategies could be examined relative to worker motivation, productivity, health, and absenteeism.

CONCLUSIONS

The aging of the global workforce in industrialized nations has left many business leaders wondering whether older workers will have the knowledge, skills, abilities, motivation, and attitudes to remain effective in the workplace. As of this writing, there is no evidence to suggest that older workers will be at a disadvantage in the 21st century workplace. Indeed, the shift from manufacturing jobs, with their heavy physical labor demands, to knowledge and service jobs aligns nicely with the abilities and attitudes of older workers. Nonetheless, much of the success of older workers will depend on how well their KSAOs match the demands of their jobs. Organizational preparation for the aging workforce will be paramount. One crucial step includes knowing what the ability demands of the jobs they offer are, so organizations can understand how well these jobs fit with the KSAO profile of the aging workforce, and accommodate if necessary. This will be especially important in growth sectors such as health services, education, and technical jobs that must attract more workers in the coming decades. And because workers in the 21st century will need continuous updating throughout their careers to maintain PJ fit, continuing to offer development opportunities for all employees and designing those opportunities so they are effective and appealing for older workers will also be important. Organizations must prepare for the aging of the global workforce to remain competitive, and older workers who can provide input are probably the organization's best resource for this challenge.

REFERENCES

Ackerman, P. L. (2000). Domain-specific knowledge as the "dark matter" of adult intelligence: gf/gc, personality and interest correlates. *Journal of Gerontology: Psychological Sciences, 55B*, 69–84.

Ackerman, P. L., & Kanfer, R. (1993). Integrating laboratory and field study for improving selection: Development of a battery for predicting air traffic controller success. *Journal of Applied Psychology, 78*, 413–432.

Bal, P. M., & Smit, P. (2011). The older the better! Age related differences in emotion regulation after psychological contract breach. *Career Development International, 27*, 6–24.

Baltes, P. B., & Baltes, M. M. (1990). Psychological perspectives on successful aging: The model of selective optimization with compensation. In P. B. Baltes & M. M. Baltes (Eds.). *Successful Aging: Perspectives from the Behavioral Sciences* (pp. 1–34). New York: Cambridge University Press.

Barnes-Farrell, J. L., Rumery, S. M., & Swody, C. A. (2002). How do concepts of age relate to work and off-the-job stresses and strains? A field study of health care workers in five nations. *Experimental Aging Research, 28*, 87–98.

Beier, M. E., & Ackerman, P. L. (2001). Current events knowledge in adults: An investigation of age, intelligence and non-ability determinants. *Psychology and Aging, 16*, 615–628.

Beier, M. E., & Ackerman, P. L. (2003). Determinants of health knowledge in adults: An investigation of age, gender, abilities, personality, and interests. *Journal of Personality and Social Psychology, 84*, 439–448.

Beier, M. E., & Ackerman, P. L. (2005). Age, ability, and the role of prior knowledge on the acquisition of new domain knowledge: Promising results in a real-world learning environment. *Psychology & Aging, 20*, 341–355.

Beier, M. E., & Kanfer, R. (2010). Motivation in training and development: A phase perspective. In S. W. J. Kozlowski & E. Salas (Eds.). *Learning, Training, and Development in Organizations: SIOP Frontiers Book Series* (pp. 65–97). Mahwah, NJ: Erlbaum.

Beier, M. E., Teachout, M. S., & Cox, C. B. (2012). The training and development of an aging workforce. In J. W. Hedge & W. C. Borman (Eds.). *The Oxford Handbook of Work and Aging* (pp. 436–453). New York: Oxford University Press.

Bureau of Labor Statistics, U.S. Department of Labor (2008). The Editor's Desk. More Seniors Working Full Time. Available at: www.bls.gov/opub/ted/2008/aug/wk1/art03.htm (accessed January 7, 2014).

Callahan, J. S., Kiker, D. S., & Cross, T. (2003). Does method matter? A meta-analysis of the effects of training method on older learner training performance. *Journal of Management, 29*, 663–680.

Carstensen, L. L. (1998). A life-span approach to social motivation. In J. Heckhausen & C. S. Dweck (Eds.). *Motivation and Self-Regulation Across the Life Span* (pp. 341–364). New York: Cambridge University Press.

Carstensen, L. L., & Mikels, J. A. (2005). At the intersection of emotion and cognition: Aging and the positivity effect. *Current Directions in Psychological Science, 14*, 117–121.

Cattell, R. B. (1987). *Intelligence: Its Structure, Growth, and Action*. Amsterdam: North Holland.

Cleveland, J. N., & Lim, A. S. (2008). Employee age and performance in organizations. In K. S. Shultz & G. A. Adams (Eds.). *Aging and Work in the 21st Century* (pp. 109–137). Mahwah, NJ: Erlbaum.

Cleveland, J. N., & Shore, L. M. (1992). Self and supervisory perspectives on age and work attitudes on performance. *Journal of Applied Psychology, 77*, 469–484.

Cordery, J., & Parker, S. K. (2012). Work design: Creating jobs and roles that promote individual effectiveness. In S. W. J. Kozlowski (Ed.). *The Oxford Handbook of Organizational Psychology, Vol. 1* (pp. 247–284). New York: Oxford University Press.

Cox, C. B., & Beier, M. E. (2009). The moderating effect of individual differences on the relationship between the framing of training and interest in training. *International Journal of Training and Development, 13*, 247–261.

Cox, C. B., & Beier, M. E. (2014). Too old to train or reprimand: The role of intergroup attribution bias in evaluating older workers. *Journal of Business and Psychology, 29*, 61–70.

Eyster, L., Johnson, R. W., & Toder, E. (2008, January). Current strategies to employ and retain older workers. Washington, DC: The Urban Institute. Available at: www.doleta.gov/reports/Employ_Retain_Older_Workers_FINAL.pdf (accessed February 18, 2014).

Grant, A. M., Fried, Y., & Juillerat, T. (2011). Work matters: Job design in classic and contemporary perspectives. In S. Zedeck (Ed.). *APA Handbook of Industrial and Organizational Psychology, Vol. 1: Building and Developing the Organization* (pp. 417–453). Washington, DC: American Psychological Association.

Greller, M. M., & Stroh, L. K. (1995). Careers in midlife and beyond: A fallow field in need of sustenance. *Journal of Vocational Behavior, 47*, 232–247.

Hackman, J. R., & Oldham, G. R. (1975). Development of the job diagnostic survey. *Journal of Applied Psychology, 60*, 159–170.

Hebl, M. R., Foster, J. B., Mannix, L. M., & Dovidio, J. F. (2002). Formal and interpersonal discrimination: A field study of bias toward homosexual applicants. *Personality and Social Psychology Bulletin, 28*, 815–825.

Hedge, J. W., Borman, W. C., & Lammlein, S. E. (2006). *The Aging Workforce: Realities, Myths, and Implications for Organizations*. Washington, DC: American Psychological Association.

Hertzog, C., Kramer, A. F., Wilson, R. S., & Lindenberger, U. (2008). Enrichment effects on adult cognitive development: Can the functional capacity of older adults be preserved and enhanced? *Psychological Science in the Public Interest, 9*, 1–65.

Johnson, R. W. (2004). Trends in job demands among older workers, 1992–2002. *Monthly Labor Review, 127*, 48–56.

Johnson, R. W., & Butrica, B. A. (2012, May). Age disparities in unemployment and reemployment during the great recession and recovery. Washington, DC: The Urban Institute. Available at: www.urban.org/publications/412574.html (accessed March 4, 2014).

Johnson, R. W., Mermin, G. B. T., & Ressenger, M. (2007). Employment at older ages and the changing nature of work (Research Report No. 2007-20). Available at: www.urban.org/UploadedPDF/1001154_older_ages.pdf (accessed March 4, 2014).

Kanfer, R., & Ackerman, P. L. (2004). Aging, adult development, and work motivation. *Academy of Management Review, 29*, 440–458.

Karasek, R., Brisson, C., Kawakami, N., Houtman, I., Bongers, P., & Amick, B. (1998). The job content questionnaire (JCQ): An instrument for internationally comparative assessments of psychosocial job characteristics. *Journal of Occupational Health Psychology, 3*, 322–355.

Kite, M. E., Stockdale, G. D., Whitley, B. E., Jr., & Johnson, B. T. (2005). Attitudes toward younger and older adults: An updated meta-analytic review. *Journal of Social Issues, 61*, 241–266.

Kristof, A. L. (1996). Person-organization fit: An integrative review of its conceptualizations, measurement, and implications. *Personnel Psychology, 49*, 1–49.

Kooij, D. T. A., de Lange, A. H., Jansen, P. G. W., Kanfer, R., & Dikkers, J. S. E. (2011). Age and work-related motives: Results of a meta-analysis. *Journal of Organizational Behavior, 32*, 197–225.

Kubeck, J. E., Delp, N. D., Haslett, T. K., & McDaniel, M. A. (1996). Does job-related training performance decline with age? *Journal of Applied Psychology, 90*, 677–691.

Mather, M., & Carstensen, L. L. (2005). Aging and motivated cognition: The positivity effect in attention and memory. *Trends in Cognitive Sciences, 9*, 496–502.

Matthews, R. A., Bulger, C. A., & Barnes-Farrell, J. L. (2010). Work social supports, role stressors, and work-family conflict: The moderating effect of age. *Journal of Vocational Behavior, 76*, 78–90.

Maurer, T. J., Weiss, E. M., & Barbeite, F. G. (2003). A model of involvement in work-related learning and development activity: The effects of individual, situational, motivational, and age variables. *Journal of Applied Psychology, 88*, 707–724.

McEvoy, G. M., & Cascio, W. F. (1989). Cumulative evidence of the relationship between employee age and job performance. *Journal of Applied Psychology, 74*, 11–17.

Morgeson, F. P., & Humphrey, S. E. (2006). The work design questionnaire (WDQ): Developing and validating a comprehensive measure for assessing job design and the nature of work. *Journal of Applied Psychology, 91*, 1321–1339.

Murphy, K. R. (1989). Is the relationship between cognitive ability and job performance stable over time? *Human Performance, 2*, 183–200.

Ng, T. W. H., & Feldman, D. C. (2008). The relation of age to ten dimensions of job performance. *Journal of Applied Psychology, 93*, 392–423.

Ng, T. W. H., & Feldman, D. C. (2012). Evaluating six common stereotypes about older workers with meta-analytical data. *Personnel Psychology, 65*, 821–858.

Palacios, C. S., Torres, M. V. T., & Mena, M. J. B. (2009). Negative aging stereotypes and their relation with psychosocial variables in the elderly population. *Archives of Gerontology and Geriatrics, 48*, 385–390.

Parker, S. K., Wall, T. D., & Cordery, J. L. (2001). Future work design research and practice: Towards an elaborated model of work design. *Journal of Occupational and Organizational Psychology, 74*, 413–440.

Perry, E. L., Dokko, G., & Golom, F. (2012). The aging worker and person-environment fit. In J. W. Hedge & W. C. Borman (Eds.). *The Oxford Handbook of Work and Aging* (pp. 187–212). New York: Oxford University Press.

Posthuma, R. A., & Campion, M. A. (2009). Age stereotypes in the workplace: Common stereotypes, moderators, and future research directions. *Journal of Management, 35*, 158–188.

Roberts, B. W., Walton, K. E., & Viechtbauer, W. (2006). Patterns of mean-level change in personality traits across the life course: A meta-analysis of longitudinal studies. *Psychological Bulletin, 132*, 1–25.

Robson, S. M., & Hansson, R. O. (2007). Strategic self-development for successful aging at work. *International Journal of Aging and Human Development, 64*, 331–359.

Salthouse, T. A. (1984). Effects of age and skill in typing. *Journal of Experimental Psychology: General, 113*, 345–371.

Salthouse, T. A. (1996). The processing-speed theory of adult age differences in cognition. *Psychological Review, 103*, 403–428.

Sanders, M. J., & McCready, J. (2009). A qualitative study of two older workers' adaptation to physically demanding work. *Work, 32*, 111–122.

Scheibe, S., & Blanchard-Fields, F. (2009). Effects of regulating emotions on cognitive performance: What is costly for young adults is not so costly for older adults. *Psychology and Aging, 24*, 217–223.

Sharit, J., & Czaja, S. J. (2012). Job design and redesign for older workers. In J. W. Hedge & W. C. Borman (Eds.). *The Oxford Handbook of Work and Aging* (pp. 454–482). New York: Oxford University Press.

Sloan Center on Aging and Work (2012, December). Aging today: Encore careers and bridge jobs. Available at: www.bc.edu/content/dam/files/research_sites/agingandwork/pdf/publications/FS32_EncoreCareers&BridgeJobs.pdf (accessed March 4, 2014).

Sturman, M. C. (2003). Searching for the inverted u-shaped relationship between time and performance: Meta-analyses of the experience/performance, tenure/performance, and age/performance relationships. *Journal of Management, 29*, 609–640.

The Economist (2011, March). A silver opportunity: Rising longevity and its implications for business. London: The Economist Intelligence Unity. Available at: www.manage

mentthinking.eiu.com/sites/default/files/downloads/EIU-Axa_Longevity_Web.pdf (accessed January 7, 2014).

Tishman, F. M., van Looy, S., & Bruyére, S. M. (2012, March). Employer strategies for responding to an aging workforce. Report by the National Technical Assistance and Research Center to Promote Leadership for Increasing the Employment and Economic Independence of Adults with Disabilities. Available at: www.dol.gov/odep/pdf/NTAR_Employer_Strategies_Report.pdf (accessed January 7, 2014).

Truxillo, D. M., Cadiz, D. M., Rineer, J. R., Zaniboni, S., & Fraccaroli, F. (2012). A lifespan perspective on job design: Fitting the job and the worker to promote job satisfaction, engagement, and performance. *Organizational Psychology Review, 2*, 340–360.

Vroom, V. H. (1964). *Work and Motivation*. New York: John Wiley.

Waldman, D. A., & Avolio, B. J. (1986). A meta-analysis of age differences in job performance. *Journal of Applied Psychology, 71*, 33–38.

Wolfson, N., Cavanagh, T., & Kraiger, K. (2013). Older adults and technology-based instruction: Optimizing learning outcomes and transfer. *Academy of Management Learning and Education*. Advance online publication. DOI: 10.5465/amle.2012.0056.

Yeatts, D. E., Folts, W. E., & Knapp, J. (2000). Older workers' adaptation to a changing workplace: Employment issues for the 21st century. *Educational Gerontology, 26*, 565–582.

Zacher, H., & Frese, M. (2009). Remaining time and opportunities at work: Relationships between age, work characteristics, and occupational future time perspective. *Psychology and Aging, 24*, 487–493.

Zacher, H., & Frese, M. (2011). Maintaining a focus on opportunities at work: The interplay between age, job complexity, and the use of selection, optimization, and compensation strategies. *Journal of Organizational Behavior, 32*, 291–318.

Zaniboni, S., Truxillo, D. M., & Fraccaroli, F. (2013). Differential effects of task variety and skill variety on burnout and turnover intentions for older and younger workers. *European Journal of Work and Organizational Psychology, 22*, 306–317.

Zaniboni, S., Truxillo, D. M., Fraccaroli, F., McCune, E. A., & Bertolino, M. (2014). Who benefits from more tasks? Older versus younger workers. *Journal of Managerial Psychology, 29*, 508–523.

6

Work Ability and Aging

Juhani Ilmarinen and Ville Ilmarinen

INTRODUCTION

It is widely accepted, at least at the political level, that most developed countries cannot afford their populations to grow older without working longer. Many governments have therefore connected life expectancy and working life expectancy. However, a question to be answered remains: Is a longer work life an ethically valid goal for everyone (Ilmarinen, 2013)?

In this chapter, we propose that an affirmative answer to this question requires a major reconsideration of how we conceptualize work and work life. Specifically, we argue that work should be designed for the people, not the other way around. Many age-related/aging processes have remained unchanged through the ages. Although healthy aging has improved remarkably in the last hundred years, there are some biological, psychological, and social "rules and laws" of aging. Work life, however, seems to follow a different track in which globalization, new technologies, and finances set the boundaries around length of working life. For example, the need for downsizing, merging, and outsourcing due to economic fluctuations are difficult to predict, but when they happen, older workers are often the target group for fast solutions. As more individuals live longer, the two tracks of human aging and work fit increasingly poorly. That is, in many parts of the world, working life increasingly does not coincide with the track of the aging process. Thus, it is no surprise that many older workers have serious problems remaining and reintegrating in working life, as well as reaching the mandatory retirement age because work does not fit their resources, they have been laid off, or they are not allowed to work any longer due to legislation.

So, what should be done? If the solution is changing the characteristics of working people to help them better fit into the global economy, it is the slow way with limited possibilities and it will take a long time before the aging process has sufficiently changed to follow the track of the working life, which is much more unpredictable than the human aging process and seems to be increasingly driven by profits in the short run. The more sustainable solution would be the adaptation of working life to the human aging process. The nature of work must move with much longer strides toward people, rather than the other way around. As we are very well aware of a spectrum (the good, the bad, the neutral) of non-malleable aging processes over the lifespan, the potential for developing work to become more age-friendly is much greater than the potential to change the aging process. In addition, working life is designed by managers. To maintain the productivity of every generation, those in charge of these arrangements need a new competence to do so. This competence is called "age management" (Ilmarinen, 2006).

WORK ABILITY MODEL

The work ability model is an evidence-based, comprehensive, and systematic model for developing workplaces that facilitate better and longer worker careers. Because of its importance for understanding older individual work ability, we provide a brief overview of the model in this section. The model helps in understanding how different factors of workplace, human resources, and operational environment affect an individual's work ability (Figure 6.1) (Ilmarinen, 2006, 2009, 2013; Lundell et al., 2011).

Extensive international research in recent decades on the work ability of older workers has identified the core factors affecting individual work ability (Gould, Ilmarinen, Järvisalo, & Koskinen, 2008; Ilmarinen, 2006; Kumashiro, 2008; Nygård, Savinainen, Kirsi, & Lumme-Sandt, 2011; Tempel & Ilmarinen, 2013). The research findings can be depicted in the form of a "work ability house" with four floors (Figure 6.1). The three lower floors of the house relate to the individual's resources: (i) health and functional capacities; (ii) competence; and (iii) values, attitudes, and motivation. The fourth floor relates to aspects of (iv) work. Accordingly, we define work ability as the balance between the characteristics and demands of work, and the health, capacities, competencies, values, attitudes, and motivation of the worker. High levels of work ability occur when there is a good fit between the features of work and the individual's resources.

As shown in Figure 6.1, the staircases between the floors indicate that all floors of the house interact. The strongest interaction exists between the floors of "work" and "values & attitudes and motivation" (floors 3 and 4). The third floor represents a worker's subjective perception about themselves at their work—their opinions and feelings about a variety of factors connected with their daily work. Positive and negative experiences at work penetrate into the third floor, which is weighted based on these experiences.

The model also posits a third-floor balcony, from where the worker can see the environment closest to their workplace: (v) family; and (vi) immediate social environment. Both of these affect the worker's work ability. For example, there are negative and positive spillover effects from home to work, and vice versa, that affect well-being across these contexts (Kinnunen, Feldt, Geurts, & Pulkkinen, 2006). In addition, healthy lifestyles and hobbies strengthen health and functional capacities. Therefore, these

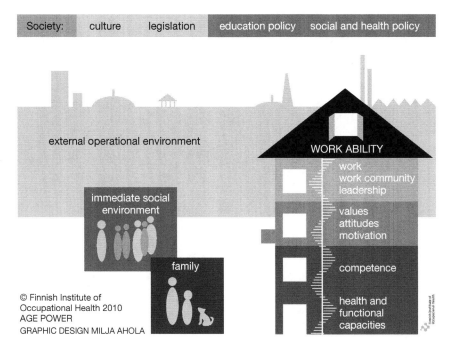

FIGURE 6.1
The work ability house model, describing the different dimensions affecting human work ability

Source: Based on Ilmarinen (2006); translated from Lundell and colleagues (2011) with permission

two factors outside the workplace impact a person's work ability by either improving or worsening the balance between their work and their personal resources.

It is also important to note that an individual's work is under continuous change. The operational environment of work organizations tends to change due to globalization, new technology, and economic situations. Companies today are facing increasing pressure to rationalize production. For example, rationalizing production often leads to downsizing, merging, and outsourcing. As a result of these organizational changes, work intensity increases, workplace security deteriorates, and jobs disappear to low-cost service providers. Simultaneously, the features of the workforce are changing, for example due to aging. Health problems may appear, and the need to update skills and competencies becomes more acute. Unpredictable changes in the work increase the need for updates in the competence domain. The resulting overload and time pressure may then create health problems (Gould et al., 2008). The dynamics between the floors of the house make it challenging to reach a good, sustainable balance between work and a person's resources.

The third floor in Figure 6.1 primarily reflects the work situation. The information flow from different floors and factors outside of work have great potential for affecting workers' attitudes and motivation, as well as their engagement and commitment to their work. The decision of whether to continue working in one's organization until retirement, or even beyond, can be expected to be made largely as a result of these factors. The more positively weighted the third floor is, the more likely it is that one will have a good working life and would be committed to a longer career. Key positive and interacting indicators include appreciation, respect and trust in one's employer, support and feedback from supervisors, fair treatment, and engagement with work.

Regarding the issue of working longer, older workers have several matters to reflect on (before deciding). Worker responses to the question "*Can I* work longer?" involve consideration of first- and second-floor aspects: namely, health resources and competencies. In contrast, answering the question "*Do I want to* work longer?" involves consideration of third-floor factors. A positively loaded third floor is a prerequisite for wanting to work longer. Still further, responses to the question "Should I work longer *if I can* and *others want me* to work longer?" involve fourth-floor factors. In contrast to the previous questions, this is not a question the worker can decide by him or herself, but rather a question that requires input from one's supervisor and employer with respect to making it possible to extend the individual's work beyond retirement age within the current occupation. The puzzle of longer working life at the workplace should first bring all these three pieces (I can, I want, and I may) together. The better the fit between resources and demands, the better the individual's work ability and work-life balance. But there are still some additional factors that may importantly affect working life balance and work ability. These are described in the following section.

Role of Family and Immediate Social Environment

The work ability model explains the work-related factors influencing a person's situation at the workplace. But, as shown in the "yard" in Figure 6.1, there are two more factors affecting work balance—namely, family and close community. Family-related resources, habits, and hobbies affect workers' health. Flexibility in working hours is often requested and evaluated from the standpoint of the needs of the family.

In addition, the values of the younger generations seem to be somewhat different from the values of baby boomers (Twenge, Campbell, Hoffmann, & Lance, 2010). As leisure is valued more among younger generations, the balance between work and other domains of life may become more challenging in the future.

Role of the Operational Environment

Once we have achieved a decent balance in work ability, it may be easily disturbed by several factors in the operational environment. Globalization and new technology impose new demands on work organizations, such as downsizing, merging, and outsourcing, which are almost impossible to avoid. In reality, fighting against these effects at the expense of coping would probably be disastrous for organizations, especially during an economic recession period. Human resource departments are given a task that is impossible to realize in a positive way. We do know that downsizing increases mortality, especially from coronary heart disease, among those who stay at a company (Vahtera et al., 2004). The risk of mortality increased about twofold in companies over a period of seven years following a major downsizing. Therefore, downsizing can have unexpected and negative effects, and is often a dangerous policy both for workers and for the company. Increases in psychosocial work stress (e.g., combinations of high demand/low control or high exhaustion/low gratification) are also associated with greater than twofold increases in the cardiovascular mortality of industrial workers (Kivimäki et al., 2002). Additionally, work stress is known to positively impact the desire to retire earlier (Wahrendorf, Dragano, & Siegrist, 2013). Such negative features of work are risk factors both for work ability and for longer working careers.

WORK ABILITY AND AGING

Work ability can be evaluated by the work ability index (WAI), a subjective survey instrument consisting of seven items (Gould et al., 2008; Rautio & Michelsen, 2013; Tuomi, Ilmarinen, Jahkola, Katajarinne, & Tulkki, 1998). The WAI score ranges from 7 to 49; the higher score, the better the balance, especially between work and health. WAI scores are classified into poor, moderate, good, and excellent categories. The WAI has a high predictive value: of those having a poor WAI at the age of 45–57 years, about 60% were on a work disability pension 11 years later (Tuomi, 1997). The WAI has been translated into 28 languages today and is widely used in different cultures worldwide.

Work ability tends to decline with age (Ilmarinen, Tuomi, & Klockars, 1997), although the mean values of the working population from 20 to 65 years remain at a good or excellent level (Figure 6.2) (Gould et al., 2008). However, about 30% of males and females over 45 years of age in both blue- and white-collar jobs show a marked decline by age in the WAI mean score. In addition, the aging trend of the WAI is different depending on the sector of the economy. Work ability mean scores are lower in farming and agriculture, the wood industry, the metal industry, and transport, as well as in social services, and in some countries among teachers, than in other branches. The best fit between work and individual resources has been found in the electronics and telecommunications sector, and banking and insurance.

Individual differences in work ability increase with age. The over 45-year-old working population in Finnish small and midsize companies is more heterogeneous in work ability compared to younger workers. About 15–30% of 45-year-olds have a moderate or poor WAI. They are at risk of losing their work ability if no preventive or corrective actions are taken (Figure 6.3) (Ilmarinen, 2006).

The declining trend of work ability by age is due to the imbalance between resources and demands, as discussed earlier. Working life seems

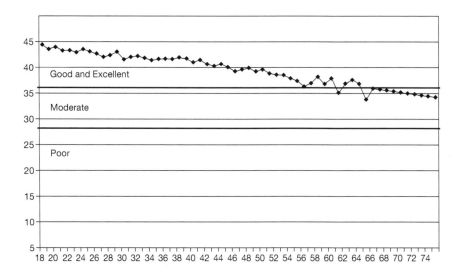

FIGURE 6.2
Work ability (Y: WAI-score) and aging (X: Age) in Finnish employed population (extrapolation from age 66 onwards)

Source: Data derived from Gould and colleagues (2008)

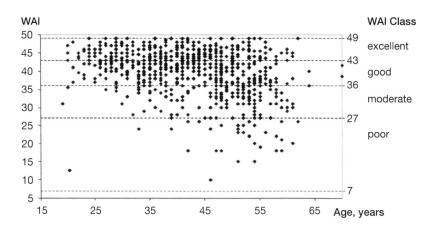

FIGURE 6.3
Individual distribution of work ability scores by age in small and middle-size enterprises in Finland

Source: Ilmarinen (2006)

to develop on its own track, which does not follow the track of normal aging processes. Changes in work do not follow the changes in working people. The most important reasons why the WAI declines with age can be identified on the fourth floor of the model. As a consequence, the third floor is often weighted negatively, and older employees and workers consider their work ability as deteriorating.

PROMOTION OF WORK ABILITY

The work ability house model suggests that actions in the workplace to promote work ability should cover all four floors (Ilmarinen, 2013). Workers and employees are more responsible for their health and competence, and the employer has more responsibility for organizing and arranging the work in ways that support the workers. The promotion concept is therefore based on cooperation between the employer and employee; together, they can create a better balance in the workplace and enhance work ability. Shared responsibility for measures to be taken will make them more acceptable and feasible, and lead to a win-win situation.

Health promotion (first floor) covers a variety of lifestyle habits in terms of eating, drinking, physical activities, recovery, and sleep. Besides a healthy lifestyle, preventive and proactive measures by occupational health services and good treatment of acute health problems play an important role in maintaining good health during the course of life at work. The competence of occupational health experts should therefore also cover aging and health issues. Their understanding of the adjustments needed at work due to changes in health and functional capacities induced by aging is a valuable resource for creating a better working life for older workers. Because many health problems are work-related, the health risks of work should be identified and prevented in the workplace (fourth floor). The strong interactions between health and work demand an active collaboration between occupational health and safety experts, as well as employers and employees.

Maintaining *professional competence* requires the continuous updating of skills and competences (second floor). On-the-job training, together with various types of special staff training courses, gives older workers the opportunity to strengthen their abilities. However, changes in the learning process of older workers should be taken into consideration. Learning strategies, learning conditions, the use of images, relaxation, and timetables for acquiring knowledge vary between younger and older workers (Ilmarinen, 2006). The most important platform for learning is the work and workplace itself. On-the-job learning is possible if the work content and tasks are designed so that they provide learning experiences. Positive learning experiences at work throughout one's career reduce the number of barriers to learning new things and correct negative attitudes toward learning. The attitude of the supervisor is also important; if the supervisor is committed to lifelong learning and supports it by providing training opportunities, an important obstacle to learning for senior employees is removed. Continued learning during aging is an important success factor for active aging and a longer working life.

Values, attitudes, and motivation (third floor) cannot usually be the direct target for intervention. They tend to be indirectly influenced, especially through positive changes on the fourth floor. This means that activities should be focused mainly on the work floor. Several improvements in management and leadership skills impact the features of the third floor. People should feel that they are respected and that they can trust their employer. They expect to be supported by their supervisor in demanding and difficult work situations. They need feedback on whether the work was done well, as well as how to improve their performance. The dialogue between supervisor and workers should be a continuous process, not a one-off annual appraisal interview. Fair treatment and zero tolerance of age discrimination is noted and appreciated among employees. Individual engagement and commitment to work are key indicators of the third floor. It should also be mentioned that employees are ultimately responsible for their own values, attitudes, and other personal factors. Adjusting their own mindset toward work, their internal resources and family issues are necessary to build up a better, sustainable balance in working life. Such a balance creates a positive weighting on the third floor.

The *work floor* is the largest and heaviest floor of the house model. It consists of the work environment (physical, mental, social), work organization and work arrangements, working time, the work community, and work tasks, as well as management. Managers and supervisors play an important role because they have the authority to arrange the work processes and individual work tasks. All decisions and changes in work go through their hands. They are also responsible for occupational health and safety matters, including risk assessments. Risk assessments should take into consideration the large individual differences in functional capacities and health of personnel, disabilities, gender issues, etc. Workers and employees of all age groups are vulnerable to harmful work exposure. Because adapting work to one's abilities, skills, and state of health should be a continuous and dynamic process, based on adequate risk assessment, adapting work to older workers' health status and needs should not present an additional burden. Age is just one aspect of the diversity of the workforce, but the awareness of managers and supervisors of age-related issues needs to be improved. All these age-related actions and improvements needed at workplaces can be termed "age management."

The redesigning of individual work tasks according to the strengths, needs, and capabilities of older workers is crucial for securing the work ability, well-being, and productivity of employees. For example, decreasing the physical workload, introducing short breaks in work processes, and taking account of health risks when scheduling shift work and flexible working arrangements are all age-friendly measures. On the other hand, the strengths of older workers should be better utilized (e.g., strategic thinking, quick-wittedness, considerateness, wisdom, ability to deliberate and rationalize, holistic perception, commitment to work, loyalty toward employer, etc.) (Ilmarinen, 2006; Ruoppila, Huuhtanen, Seitsamo, & Ilmarinen, 2008). The easiest way to identify new needs and ways to redesign the work is to ask older workers how they would like to change and improve their work and its arrangements. Also, human engineering should be utilized to create practical solutions in ergonomics and work arrangements for older workers. Another useful option is to share the work duties between younger and older employees, utilizing and combining their different strengths.

ORGANIZATIONAL BENEFITS OF PROMOTING WORK ABILITY AMONG OLDER WORKERS

Company examples demonstrate that the cost of investments in work ability promotion is outweighed by the benefits. People can continue working productively, the work atmosphere improves, productivity improves, and age-related problems decrease. Cost-benefit analysis shows that the return on investment (ROI) can be very good: the return on €1 amounts to €3–5 after a few years. The positive ROI is based on lower rates of sick leave, lower work disability costs, and better productivity (Näsman & Ahonen, 1999; Näsman & Ilmarinen, 1999).

LONG-TERM EFFECTS OF WORK ABILITY

Recent 28-year follow-up studies of aging workers using a controlled research design showed that work ability at 45–58 years of age significantly predicted daily living independence later in life, between the ages of 73 and 85 years (Von Bonsdorff et al., 2011). The better the work ability was before retirement, the more probable is an active daily living without mobility limitation later on. Therefore, investments in work ability and active aging in workplaces need to be secured during the working years. The investments in work ability, occupational health, and safety in the workplace are also investments in the citizenry across the lifespan. A healthier, limitation-free, and independent-living older generation is an important resource in our society. As a consequence, the old-age dependency ratio becomes less of a burden for taxpayers.

JOB AND SKILL OBSOLESCENCE

Old-fashioned jobs are becoming rare due to new technology and computerization. A study of expected impacts of future computerization on US labor market outcomes shows that from 702 detailed occupations, 47% are in the high-risk category (Frey & Osborne, 2013). These jobs at risk could be automated relatively soon, perhaps over the next decade or two. In addition, computerization can substitute for labor in a wide range of non-routine cognitive tasks. Advance robots are gaining enhanced senses and dexterity, allowing them to perform a broader scope of manual tasks. Frey and Osborne (2013) state that this is likely to change the nature of work across industries and occupations.

The computerization means that the diversity in jobs as well as the polarization between the jobs increases. A substantial part of older workers are today in occupations that will either change remarkably or even disappear from the labor market during the next decades. Their professional competence might be strongly and unilaterally connected with the occupations at highest risk. As a consequence, skill obsolescence may become an acute scenario for these employees. Therefore, we have to find solutions both for job and skill obsolescence for older workers.

New jobs created over the past decades are fundamentally different from the ones that have been lost (Morris & Western, 1999). The new jobs tend to favor educated workers over those with less education and skills; more education translates into higher earnings, but this payoff is most pronounced at the highest educational level. Low-skilled positions are made redundant by technology, which decreases the need for less-educated workers. Creating new jobs at the workplace emphasize the role of management: when technology replaces some tasks in an organization, managers are responsible for organizing the remaining tasks. Therefore, new technology should be married to complementary organizational practices, because it opens up novel possibilities for both discretion and control.

The older workers face the same trends and changes in workplaces as the other age groups. The job they have been recruited to some decades ago has changed remarkably. To avoid skill obsolescence, these workers need to continuously update their skills and to accept and utilize lifelong learning concepts. Skill obsolescence will lead to increasing job insecurity over the life course, making it difficult to maintain adequate level of labor market participation of older workers (Allen & de Grip, 2012).

According to the dynamic model presented by Allen and de Grip (2012), changes in skill requirements and the learning of new skills keep each other roughly in balance. Workers in IT-intensive jobs are not more likely to perceive skill obsolescence than workers in less IT-intensive jobs. But those employed in IT-intensive jobs are more likely to learn on the job. The authors state that skill obsolescence can be a more or less structural characteristic of many jobs. Investments in training as well as on-the-job learning should be a structural characteristic of jobs that are highly challenging and dynamic in implementing new technology. Older workers have longer job tenure, which has a negative effect on the changes of loss employment, indicating that workers accumulate valuable additional human capital through work experience. However, the authors report that this positive effect can decrease after 18 years of additional tenure. Therefore, sustainable training for the oldest workers is also needed. From aging research, we have learned that learning is not dependent on age, but on the way that training is organized. Age-adjusted learning concepts should be utilized for older workers (Ilmarinen, 2006).

OVERQUALIFICATION AND UNDEREMPLOYMENT

There is widespread evidence that many workers possess higher qualifications than are needed for their job. The prevalent rates of overqualification among British graduates in their first job are 36% for men and 41% for women (Brynin, 2002). Society produces more education than the labor market requires. For an individual, the reasons for pursuing education can be social equality, efforts at social closure, and personal demand for social status, as well as calculations that any higher-level education helps job chances later on. Raising the average years of education makes low-skilled workers scarcer, raising their wages, while at the same time increasing supply of highly educated workers, hereby reducing their wages.

Overqualification has positive effects on wages but produces lower returns to education compared with those who are "correctly" placed. Overqualified people achieve higher rewards and generate a premium relative to the job but penalty relative to the qualification. The value of qualification obviously changes over time as the supply and demand for them changes. It would be expected that this growth of qualification would result in an increased demand for appropriate skills, and that the qualification that partly embody these would obtain a greater payback, whether in terms of social status or wage. In fact, this does not appear to be happening, or it is at least subject to counter-forces.

Overqualification can be structural or an individual, life course phenomenon. People start lower down the scale, thus beginning overqualified but subsequently doing work that fits their level of qualification. If this is not true, the overqualification is a structural phenomenon. There is always likely to be at least marginal overqualification because a certain proportion of people choose not to use the full extent of their qualification, for example women who make career sacrifices for family reasons.

Underemployment means working in a job that is below an employee's full working capacity, and it is predicted to become more relevant in the future. For example, 8.8 million workers in the United States are forced to work part-time because they are unable to find suitable full-time jobs. Altogether, the combined proportion of underemployed and overqualified range from 17% to one-third, of which 20% are highly overqualified (McKee-Ryan & Harvey, 2011).

As the average education of workers increases, there is a greater possibility of workers experiencing underemployment. Underemployment is a multidimensional, complex construct that can be described by management scholars, economists, sociologists, and psychologists. In general, it refers to the match between employees' knowledge, skills, and abilities, and the demands of their job. This definition sounds very similar to those described earlier as work ability concept, but the latter have more dimensions for creating the best person-job fitting.

Underemployment is prevalent in all type of jobs: executives, expatriates, faculty member, business school graduates, non-academic university employees, retail sales workers, postal workers, medical and labor technicians, hospital workers; underemployment affects employees across a wide range of occupations. Interestingly, demographic characteristics such as gender, age, and education did not predict underutilization of skills (McKee-Ryan & Harvey, 2011). Age gives a mixed picture: underemployment spiked early (18–24 years of age) and then began to decline, and older workers, as long-tenured employees, faced underemployment because of increased layoffs and age discrimination upon re-employment. Underemployment showed a U-shaped pattern by age.

Underemployment has negative outcomes, and many of them seem to resemble the concepts of the third floor of the work ability house: job and career attitudes, and features of psychological well-being. Job performance can decline, too. Employers may be reluctant to hire overqualified persons because they believe that these workers will move on to more suitable jobs when given opportunity. On the other hand, some performance advantages can be possible, if employees can influence in the situation. Employers can provide challenging tasks, advancement opportunities, and empowerment to prevent withdrawal risk.

Summing up the challenges of job and skill obsolescence, as well as overqualification and underemployment from the viewpoint of work ability concept, these special questions focus into the floors of competence and work. Job obsolescence is a characteristic of work, which has not been developed according to the new demands of operational environment of the enterprises. The solution for avoiding job obsolescence is in the hands of the managers. Competent management can foresee and predict the coming challenges and changes in market, and build up a strategy that can effectively respond, for example, to globalization, new technology, and demographic change. In the strategy, the development of jobs should be combined with development of the competencies of the personnel. If the dynamics binding these two developments together is missing, many older workers will be laid off. The management is in charge not only for the work arrangements, but also for giving opportunities to update the competencies of their manpower. Skill obsolescence should be prevented by sustainable training programs and on-the-job training. Aging is not a problem, and should not be perceived as one, since learning new skills is possible nearly for everyone of working age. As indicated before, valid pedagogic and didactic concepts are necessary for older workers.

Overqualification and underemployment are characteristics often found among younger and older employees, and the reasons and consequences for this pattern give a rather mixed picture. In general, overqualification describes a theoretical and practical compound of skills and knowledge that are not needed (job obsolescence) or cannot be utilized at a given job (underemployment). So, the solution would be to change the job or to develop the job into a direction where these extra competencies can be utilized. Empowering people to develop the content or arrangement of their jobs can lead to better utility of their human capital. In the future, it will perhaps be necessary to have several competencies and skills that can be utilized during the working age. Multiskilled workers are less vulnerable to changes in work life.

Underemployment is both a characteristic of overqualification and lack of appropriate job. People do have a job, but they could and need to work more hours, or they wish for more challenges from the content of their work. The balance in the work ability house is therefore disturbed. The second floor (competence) and fourth floor (work) do not fit well together. The consequences for the imbalance can be recorded on the third floor (attitudes, motivation, and commitment). The solution is first to identify whether there are any possibilities within the company to get more work or to get tasks relevant to one's own competence. Second, older workers should be given the possibility to describe, explain, and show the added value of their aging process: the several dimensions of mental growth should be useful for the employer. Third, job descriptions can be developed into the direction where the older workers are getting stronger. This process of action is not only valid for underemployed or overqualified people, but also to everyone experiencing an imbalance between competence and work.

GOOD WORK—LONGER CAREER PROGRAM 2010–2015

The Finnish technology industries signed a collective agreement with four trade unions in 2009 concerning a program that aimed to maintain work ability and to promote work well-being in the sector (Ilmarinen, Ilmarinen, Huuhtanen, Louhevaara, & Näsman, 2013). Both social partners accepted the work ability house model as a common framework for the program. The goal of the trade unions was to improve working conditions, while the employer wanted to achieve longer working careers. The name "Good Work—Longer Career" (2010–2015) was established, indicating the win-win goal for both program partners. In 2013, the program included 50 companies and some 5,250 workers and employees.

The companies' situations were analyzed using new methods called Work Ability—Person Radar (WA-PR), a survey, and Work Ability—Company Radar (WA-CR), a dialog technique, with which the measures to be taken in each floor were identified and prioritized. WA-PR indicates the strengths and weaknesses in each floor of the work ability house according to the average experiences of the personnel. It shows quantitatively which domains need improvements and enhancements. In addition to WA-PR, WA-CR is a dialogue instrument that is used by a project group at the company specifically selected to be responsible for the program. The project groups consisted of members of the executive board, the human resources team, and representatives of various trade unions active at the workplace. Occupational health, safety officers, and representatives of the supervisor/foreman level were also included. With help of external facilitators, the project group first prioritized the floors, identified the measures needed, and then prioritized the measures to be taken at each given floor. A preliminary plan of action was then drawn up. The benefit of the WA-CR process is that it made the "doing" feasible and concrete; it focused attention on key development goals in the workplace to maintain work ability and to enhance the work well-being, taking into consideration both the opinion of personnel and the tacit knowledge and experiences of the project group.

The preliminary baseline results of the program show, interestingly, that the average results of indicators improved by age, and the age group 55+ show the best mean scores in all other floors except health and functional capacity (Table 6.1). Health and functional capacity showed a decline by age, like the work ability index in earlier studies.

Interesting age trends were also found across different personnel groups. For example, competence (professional competence, job-related training, learning new skills at work; second floor of the work ability house) was at a higher level by age in all personnel groups. However, significant differences in competence existed between blue-collar and white-collar workers. In contrast to white-collar workers, blue-collar workers showed lower mean levels on all indicators of competence. The level of competence indicators of blue-collar workers were close to a "critical" level of score 7 in all age groups except the oldest one.

TABLE 6.1

Mean Levels of the Work Ability House Structures by Age Group (a score below 7 in the scale is a reference for moderate (5.00–6.99) and scores from 7.00 to 8.99 indicate good results)

Work ability house structure	Age group				
	Under 35	35 to 44	45 to 54	Over 54	Total
Health and functional capacity (first floor)	8.47	8.14	8.02	7.83	8.16
Competence (second floor)	7.13	7.28	7.38	7.52	7.30
Attitudes and motivation (third floor)	7.15	7.21	7.34	7.57	7.28
"Work" (fourth floor)	6.79	6.82	6.87	7.07	6.86
Family and close community (nearby environment)	7.50	7.42	7.76	8.09	7.64

In attitudes and motivation (appreciation, trust, commitment, motivation, fair treatment) (third floor of the work ability house), a similar trend was seen: the indicators improved by age but the differences between the personnel groups remained. The level of indicators of blue-collar workers were also in this floor close to the "critical" level of score 7 in all age groups except the oldest one. The critical score 7 is based on predictive power of WAI item 1, which indicated in the 11-year follow-up study that the incidence rate of work disability pension increased among persons showing a poor or moderate work ability at onset of the follow-up study (Tuomi, 1997).

The work (work arrangements, support of supervisor, feedback, support of colleagues) (fourth floor) showed the poorest results across the whole house for all personnel groups. The blue-collar workers were, on average, at a reasonable level in all age groups. Also, employees were close to score 7 in all age groups except the oldest one. The upper employees, including supervisory and managerial occupations, also scored close to the critical levels. The differences between the personnel groups remained, but in the oldest age group the differences across white-collar groups disappeared.

The work well-being index (WWBI), aggregating all indicators from different floors, showed an improvement by age by all personnel groups (Figure 6.4). The blue-collar workers, however, had the lowest scores in all age groups. The employees and upper employees were close to each other across age groups.

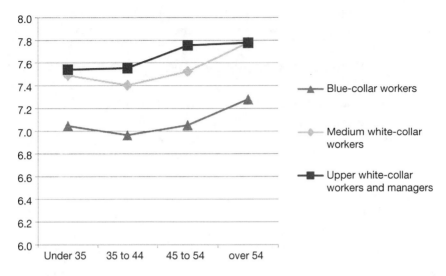

FIGURE 6.4
Work well-being index by age and personnel groups

The results of the WA-PR survey showed that the circumstances in all age groups are considerably poorer on the following indicators: supervisors' feedback, work arrangements (fourth floor), appreciation, trust in employer and fair treatment (third floor), sufficient education (second floor), resources for friends and hobbies (dimensions outside the house), and energy to work until retirement. Altogether, over 150 different development-oriented actions and interventions are underway tackling these issues in 40 companies. The most interesting finding of this study was that several indicators of the work ability house construct improved by age. Research is needed to understand this promising phenomenon better, as well as research clarifying the differences between work ability and the new paradigm of work well-being.

CHALLENGES FOR THE FUTURE

Our societies are getting older and we should be well prepared for it. Work life is also getting more diverse and more demanding than before. Aging means that the growing older population at work is more heterogeneous in various characteristics than before. Therefore, the following general challenges should be met by effective measures in workplaces:

- *Increase the awareness level of age and aging, in society, enterprises, and among individual employees and workers.* The universities and research institution are responsible for creating and delivering the facts about aging. The training institutions should convert the facts of age management into training and coaching programs and courses. In enterprises, both the supervisors and the employees should have a sufficient awareness level in aging matters. In organizing the training, the age-adjusted training concepts should be utilized for older workers.
- *Change the attitude toward age and aging.* Based on a better understanding about aging matters, attitudes can be changed. The benefits of aging in functional capacities, mental growth, and competence should be concretized. Understanding that each developmental phase in the life course has its strengths and weaknesses, emphasize that the added value comes from the differences between people, not from their similarities.
- *Redesign the work for the diversity of the workforce and older workers.* The redesign and arrangements of work are in the hands of supervisors and managers in the company—they have the authority to arrange the work processes. Better awareness levels about aging and fair attitudes toward aging are the prerequisites for age-friendly working life. Age management is a new competence for them. Age management skills and good practices will help them to cope with the varying resources of their teams. Changing of the individual potentials in health and functional capacities, competence, values, attitudes, and motivation makes the difference, not the age. Therefore, with the help of age management tools, more individual solutions can be created for older workers. Promotion of work ability belongs to the competence of the supervisors and managers.

RESEARCH CHALLENGES IN WORK ABILITY AND AGING

Research challenges regarding work ability and aging can be listed as follows (modified according to Gould et al., 2008):

Generally, reliable information about work ability based on follow-up studies is needed. Also, international comparisons of factors maintaining and promoting work ability during aging could improve understanding about the role of cultural factors on work ability. Well-designed intervention studies in organization level are most welcome. More scientific data are needed on all dimensions of work ability, including the dimensions of family and close community, as well as from the operational environment.

- *Role of health and functional capacities in work ability.* Why do some people perceive themselves to be able to work regardless of illnesses and functional limitations? What factors contribute the most to the decreases in work ability among healthy people as they age?
- *Role of competence in work ability.* How does the population level increase in education affect work ability? Why do the indicators of competence have less explanatory power than other dimensions of work ability? How valid are self-reports of occupational competence? The effects of overqualification and underemployment on work ability? Relationships between skill obsolescence, distress, and work ability? How to measure competence as a core dimension of work ability?
- *Role of attitudes in work ability.* What factors of work and management have positive effects on appreciation, trust, fair treatment, and support? Does work commitment always promote work ability? Does commitment produce motivation, or is it the other way around?
- *Role of work, work environment, work arrangement, work community, management in work ability.* Why are there gender differences in work ability? What are the work characteristics that improve and impair work ability by age? How is the functioning of a work community and team reflected in work ability of individual worker? How does the constant change in work life affect work ability? How can we more accurately predict the age-sensitive changes in work life?
- *Role of family and close community in work ability.* In what situations does social support promote work ability? How do the attitudes of close community affect work ability?
- *Work ability among unemployed, handicapped, and disabled people.* A rising part of the workforce will experience periods of unemployment as well as difficulties of return to work. How does work ability change by age during unemployment periods? What is the role of work ability by age in returning to work? Is the work ability of handicapped and disabled people affected by age? How to maintain and promote the work ability of people with impairments?

The theme of work ability and productivity is of great interest for the employer. The investments for promoting the work ability of employees and workers depend on economic implications of these efforts. Therefore, the following research questions are important:

- *Productivity and work ability.* What is the relationship between productivity and work ability, preferably in longitudinal research design? What activities to promote work ability are cost-effective?
- *Work ability at the population level.* Work ability is not only an important measure of situation in workplaces. Also, work ability at the population level is needed for policies, because it has a high predictive power for the employment rates of all generations, but especially for older workers. The possibility to increase the retirement age and to get people working longer depends strongly on the work ability of older workers. The crucial indicators of longer careers are if older workers can, will, and may work longer. In the future, we should be able to follow the work ability of our working population, and to promote it by comprehensive and systematic concepts. Therefore, the following research information is needed:
- *Public policy and work ability.* What are the policies that support high levels of work ability? What are the features of operational environment that support the work ability? What are the best predictors of the development of the population's work ability?

Finally, as mentioned earlier, the ethical and moral issues of prolonging work life should be studied. At least the following question is interesting:

- *Ethics and moral issues of prolonging work life.* Which are the ethical problems in prolonging work life considering workers, employers, and society?

FINAL REMARKS

Work ability is an important human capital of workers throughout their whole career. It is a comprehensive concept requiring continuous processes at workplaces aiming to improve the fitting of human resources and work together. During aging, the diversity of work ability of workers increases. Also, the diversity of work increases. Everybody, regardless of age, needs "good work," at least a decent job. Older workers are heterogeneous working population; thus, standard solutions and designs of work are seldom the best option for the individual or organization. Therefore, age-adjusted equal opportunities are necessary. Plenty of scientific knowledge is available about how to promote work ability of older workers. Managers and supervisors should have the competence to redesign the work for an aging society. A proactive and comprehensive approach according to the work ability house model will avoid obsolescence of job and skill. Also, solutions for overqualification and underemployment for all generations can be created. In the proactive development of better work and longer work careers, both the workers and employers are responsible.

REFERENCES

Allen, J., & de Grip, A. (2012). Does skill obsolescence increase the risk of employment loss? *Applied Economics*, 44(25), 3237–3245.

Brynin, M. (2002). Overqualification in employment. *Work, Employment and Society*, 16(4), 637–654.

Frey, C. B., & Osborne, M. A. (2013). The future employment: How susceptible are jobs to computerisation? Available at: www.oxfordmartin.ox.ac.uk/downloads/academic/The_Future_of_Employment.pdf (accessed September 15, 2013).

Gould, R., Ilmarinen, J., Järvisalo, J., & Koskinen, S. (2008). *Dimensions of Work Ability: Results of the Health 2000 Survey*. Helsinki: Finnish Centre for Pensions, the Social Insurance Institution, National Public Health Institute, Finnish Institute of Occupational Health.

Ilmarinen, J. (2006). *Towards a Longer Worklife: Ageing and the Quality of Worklife in the European Union*. Helsinki: Finnish Institute of Occupational Health, Ministry of Social Affairs and Health.

Ilmarinen, J. (2009). Aging and work: An international perspective. In S. J. Czaja & J. Sharit (Eds.), *Aging and Work: Issues and Implications in a Changing Landscape* (pp. 51–73). Baltimore, MD: Johns Hopkins University Press.

Ilmarinen, J. (2013). Redesign of workplaces for an ageing society. In P. Taylor (Ed.), *Older Workers in an Ageing Society: Critical Topics in Research and Policy* (pp. 133–146). Cheltenham: Edward Elgar Publishing.

Ilmarinen, J., Tuomi, L., & Klockars, M. (1997). Changes in the work ability of active employees over an 11-year period. *Scandinavian Journal of Work, Environment and Health*, 23(1), 49–57.

Ilmarinen, J., Ilmarinen, V., Huuhtanen, P., Louhevaara, V., & Näsman, O. (2013). Good work—longer career: Work well-being in the Finnish technology industry. Conference abstract presented at work, well-being and wealth. Active ageing at work. *Scandinavian Journal of Work, Environment and Health*. August 2013. Available at: www.sjweh.fi/www2013.php (Abstract) (accessed November 20, 2013).

Kinnunen, U., Feldt, T., Geurts, S., & Pulkkinen, L. (2006). Types of work-family interface: Well-being correlates of negative and positive spillover between work and family. *Scandinavian Journal of Psychology*, 47(2), 149–162.

Kivimäki, M., Leino-Arjas, P., Luukkonen, R., Riihimäki, H., Vahtera, J., & Kirjonen, J. (2002). Work stress and risk of cardiovascular mortality: Prospective cohort study of industrial employees. *British Medical Journal, 325*(7369), 857–860.

Kumashiro, M. (2008). Promotion of work ability towards productive aging—selected papers of the 3rd international symposium on work ability. Paper presented at the *Promotion of Work Ability Towards Productive Aging—Selected Papers of the 3rd International Symposium on Work Ability*, Hanoi, Vietnam.

Lundell, S., Tuominen, E., Hussi, T., Klemola, S., Lehto, E., Mäkinen, E., Oldenbourg, R., Saarelma-Thiel, T., & Ilmarinen, J. (2011). *Ikävoimaa työhön [Age Power]*. Helsinki: Finnish Institute of Occupational Health.

McKee-Ryan, F. M., & Harvey, J. (2011). "I have a job, but . . .": A review of underemployment. *Journal of Management, 37*(4), 962–996.

Morris, M., & Western, B. (1999). Inequality in earnings at the close of the twentieth century. *Annual Review of Sociology, 25*, 623–657.

Näsman, O., & Ahonen, G. (1999). The DalBo-project: The economics of maintenance of work ability. In W. J. A. Goedhard (Ed.), *Aging and Work 4. Healthy and Productive Aging of Older Employees* (pp. 171–175). The Hague: Pasmans Offsetdrukkerij.

Näsman, O., & Ilmarinen, J. (1999). Metal-age: A process for improving well-being and total productivity. *Experimental Aging Research, 25*(4), 379–384.

Nygård, C., Savinainen, M., Kirsi, T., & Lumme-Sandt, K. (2011). Age management during the life course. Paper presented at the *4th Symposium on Work Ability, Tampere, 6 to 9 June 2010*, Tampere, Finland.

Rautio, M., & Michelsen, T. (2013). *WAI: How to Use the Work Ability Index(tm) Questionnaire*. Helsinki: Finnish Institution of Occupational Health.

Ruoppila, I., Huuhtanen, P., Seitsamo, J., & Ilmarinen, J. (2008). *Age-Related Changes of the Work Ability Construct and its Relations to Cognitive Functioning in the Older Worker: A 16-Year Follow-Up Study*. Jyväskylä: University of Jyväskylä.

Tempel, J., & Ilmarinen, J. (2013). *Arbeitsleben 2025. Das Haus der Arbeitsfähigkeit im Unternehmen bauen*. Herausgegeben Marianne Giesert. Hamburg: VSA Verlag.

Tuomi, K. (Ed.) (1997). Eleven-year follow-up of ageing workers. *Scandinavian Journal of Work, Environment & Health, 23*(1), 1–71.

Tuomi, K., Ilmarinen, J., Jahkola, A., Katajarinne, K., & Tulkki, A. (1998). *Work Ability Index*. 2nd rev. ed. Helsinki: Finnish Institute of Occupational Health.

Twenge, J. M., Campbell, S. M., Hoffman, B. J., Lance, C. E. (2010). Generational differences in work values: Leisure and extrinsic values increasing, social and intrinsic values decreasing. *Journal of Management, 36*(5), 1117–1142.

Wahrendorf, M., Dragano, N., & Siegrist, J. (2013). Social position, work stress, and retirement intentions: A study with older employees from 11 European countries. *European Sociological Review, 29*(4), 792–802.

Vahtera, J., Kivimäki, M., Pentti, J., Linna, A., Virtanen, M., Virtanen, P., & Ferrie, J. E. (2004). Organisational downsizing, sickness absence, and mortality: 10-town prospective cohort study. *British Medical Journal, 328*(7439), 555–558.

Von Bonsdorff, M. B., Seitsamo, J., Ilmarinen, J., Nygård, C.-H., Von Bonsdorff, M. E., & Rantanen, T. (2011). Work ability in midlife as a predictor of mortality and disability in later life: A 28-year prospective follow-up study. *Cmaj, 183*(4), 235–242.

Issue 3

Challenges Facing Specific Workforce Sectors

7

The Implications of Changes in Job Demands for the Continued and Future Employment of Older Workers

Sara J. Czaja, Joesph Sharit, Neil Charness, and Andrew C. Schmidt

INTRODUCTION

As noted in the introduction to this volume, the demographics of our population are changing dramatically and we are witnessing very unique demographic transitions. One obvious change is the dramatic increase in the number of people living longer; the proportion of persons over the age of 65 in the world is expected to more than double by 2030 and people in this age cohort will reach about 1 billion. Further, people over the age of 85 now represent the fastest-growing portion of many national populations. It is important to distinguish between younger older adults (aged 65–80 years) and those aged 80+ years. Someone who is in their 60s and 70s is typically very different from someone in their 80s. Further, in some countries, such as the United States, the older population is also becoming ethnically diverse, with the greatest growth occurring in Hispanic populations. One obvious implication is the potential need to accommodate differences in language in work systems and training programs.

Overall, this increasing number of older adults in our population presents both opportunities and challenges for our healthcare, the economy, and existing social support systems. For example, in the United States, these demographics, combined with the economic downturn of 2007, had led to vast uncertainties for many Americans, especially those considered to be "older workers." In 2013, nearly 2 million people aged 55 and older in the United States were unemployed, an increase of over 100,000 from the previous year. The decline in fertility rate and policies favoring early retirement have also resulted in a shrinking ratio of workers to unemployed older people in the United States and the EU (referred to as the old-age dependency ratio) (see introductory chapter), and unless there are strategies to promote the employment of older people, the projected old-age dependency ratio (POADR) is expected to continue to increase to about 53% worldwide by 2060. Further, many older people, because of perceptions or actual discrimination due to ageism, find it difficult to secure or maintain employment. A recent meta-analysis (Bal, 2011) found that age was a significantly negative predictor of an employee's chance of advancement, hiring, and their performance appraisal.

However, on the positive side, this picture is beginning to change, and organization and government initiatives are being directed toward increasing the employment rates of older people. A concern in many organizations is that the exodus of the baby boomers from the workforce will result in a depletion of skills and knowledge needed to compete in today's business environment. Thus, organizations are beginning to look to older workers to address the problems of skill and labor shortages and directing efforts to promote the continued employment of older workers. For example, in the power train plant in Dingolfing, Bavaria BMW adapted the design of an assembly line and introduced worker wellness programs to accommodate their older employees. The changes resulted in a 7% increase in productivity in one year. BMW is now implementing the program in other plants in the United States, Germany, and Austria (Loch, Fabian, Bauer, & Mauermann, 2010). In the United States, changes in government and organizational policies such as social security reforms and the decrease in the availability of defined pension plans also favor extending working life (Torres-Gill, 2009). Most countries in the EU are also adopting policies to foster delayed retirement (Sinclair, Watson, & Beach, 2013).

The trend toward early retirement is also beginning to change. Many older people are choosing to remain employed because of an interest in remaining productive or for financial reasons, and others are choosing to work reduced hours, part-time, or looking for opportunities to start a new career. Overall, in the past two decades, there has been a sharp increase in the labor force participation rates of older age groups, including those aged 75+ (Toossi, 2012). Today's U.S. labor force is older, composed of more women, and is more ethnically and culturally diverse. According to the U.S. Bureau of Labor Statistics (2011), in 2010 there were 30 million workers 55 years of age or older in the labor force, representing 19.3% of the total workforce (Toossi, 2012). The Bureau of Labor Statistics (2011) expects this number to reach 41.4 million by 2020, representing a share of 25.2% of the total labor force. The BLS also projects that the roughly 7 million workers 65 or older estimated to be in the current labor force will increase to 19.6 million in 2050, and that over the next 10 years those workers who are 65 or older will grow by 75% as compared to workers between 25 and 54 years of age whose number is only expected to increase by a mere 2%. Similar trends are being observed in other countries. Across almost all EU countries, the growing number of individuals are working longer, and the European Commission projects that the labor force participation rates of people aged 55–64 will increase to about 67% by 2060, and also that the average age of exit from the labor force will increase (Sinclair et al., 2013).

Thus, traditional models of working life where one transitions through three stages: (1) an education period, in which one prepares for work; (2) engagement in one's working career; and (3) retirement, the time of leisure and departure from paid employment, is no longer consistent with the experience of most workers who are making many more transitions throughout their working life and moving in and out of different work experiences. In addition, the current cohort of older adults has generally achieved higher levels of education than previous generations, and many, especially the "baby boomers," have had experience with some forms of technology.

At the same time that we are witnessing demographic changes, there are also dramatic changes in work structures and organizations, which have vast implications for older workers. These include changes in organizational structures, decentralized management, collaborative work arrangements and teamwork, and a greater emphasis on knowledge-based work and jobs that require advanced degrees or training. For example, between 2012 and 2022, occupations that typically require a master's degree for entry are projected to grow the fastest, 18.8%, due to the projected fast growth of jobs within the healthcare and social assistance industries (Bureau of Labor Statistics, 2013). The influx of technology into the workplace is also reshaping work processes, the content of jobs, where work is performed, and training programs. We anticipate that these changes will continue as technology evolves. This implies that workers will have to continually learn new skills and adapt to changes in job demands. Thus, organizations as well as the government will have to develop strategies to ensure that workers of all ages have the opportunities to update their skills to keep pace with changes in work technologies and job demands. Our researchers and that of others has clearly shown that older adults are receptive and able to learn new technologies; however, they have to have access to training and instructional support programs that are designed to accommodate the needs, skills, and abilities of older adults (Czaja & Sharit, 2012). As discussed in a later section of this chapter, aging is associated with plasticity—older adults can experience improvements in physical and cognitive abilities and functional performance, and are capable of learning new skills. They also bring a vast wealth of knowledge, skills, and experience to situations.

Overall, the aging of the population and the shrinking of the number of younger workers, coupled with current economic and policy trends, points to a central fact that governments and organizations will need to be prepared for an aging workforce. The development of strategies to foster successful employment depends on understanding the needs, abilities, and preferences of this age group with respect to work, as well the contextual elements of work organizations and the demands and requirements of current and future jobs. The goals of this chapter are to summarize current knowledge about: (1) changing work practices and organizational structures; (2) changes in job demands and requirements; (3) aging, cognition, and training; and (4) job design and interface issues.

THE CHANGING LANDSCAPE OF THE WORKPLACE

There are a number of factors influencing the extent to which the increasing cohorts of older adults will continue to work, including financial incentives, benefits, health, employment opportunities and socialization, and the ability to adapt to a continually changing work environment. Organizations and work contexts, as well as the types of tasks workers are expected to perform, have undergone major changes in the last few decades, and these changes, which are expected to continue, have created new job demands, knowledge, skill, and ability requirements for workers. The majority of workers use some form of technology at work, and this number will continue to grow, as will the scope and sophistication of technology. For example, workers in the manufacturing industry are increasingly using tools such as Computer Aided Design (CAD), Computer Aided Manufacturing (CAM), Computer Numerical Control (CNC), Direct Numerical Control (DNC), Programmable Logic Control (PLC), Numerical Control (NC), program optimization software, and systems integration software. Workers in the healthcare industry and service industries also need to interface with technology and software applications. Healthcare providers, for example, are now expected to interface with electronic medical record systems to aid patient management activities and to use sophisticated diagnostic tools. Those in the financial services have to use computers and the Internet, and workers in the retail, food service, and travel industries have to work with computers and software programs. An increased emphasis is being placed on knowledge and knowledge management as the key source of competitive advantage for businesses. Knowledge work generally places an emphasis on non-routine cognitive skills such as abstract reasoning, problem-solving, and communication.

Jobs requiring highly skilled workers are also expected to grow. For example, jobs within software and IT services will continue to experience growth, as will jobs in the healthcare industry, medical technology industry, and service sector (Bureau of Labor Statistics, 2013). These types of job typically required highly skilled workers. As noted above, occupations that typically require a post-secondary education are expected to grow at a faster rate than occupations that require a high school diploma or less.

From one perspective, the increased use of technology in the workplace is positive for older workers, as technology-based jobs tend to be less physically demanding. On the other hand, technology-based jobs place higher demands on cognitive processes such as memory, attention, and reasoning (e.g., Czaja & Sharit, 1998; Czaja, Sharit, Ownby, Roth, & Nair, 2001; Sharit & Czaja, 2012). The increased use of technology also creates a need for new learning, which also places demands on cognitive processes such as learning and memory.

Generally, with respect to cognition, many component cognitive abilities, such as working memory, attentional processes, and spatial cognition, important to learning show decline with age, especially under conditions of complexity or when a task represents an unfamiliar cognitive domain. There are also age-related changes in vision, audition, and perceptual/motor skills, which may impact on the ability of older people to learn new skills. However, as discussed later in this chapter, despite these age-related changes in component abilities, older adults do have cognitive plasticity and there is a vast literature (see Bosman & Charness, 1996) on aging and skill acquisition that generally indicates that older adults are able to learn new skills, though it typically takes them longer than younger adults and they require more practice and more environmental support. Older workers are also willing to learn new tasks and skills, and are receptive to using new technologies if they perceive the technology as useful, the technology is easy to use, and they are provided with adequate training and support. To this end, training and retraining opportunities must also be made available to older adults, and, as noted later in this chapter, there is some evidence to suggest that due to age discrimination and stereotypes about older learners, training and retraining opportunities are often less available for older people. Overall, there is a solid evidence base that many age-related declines in cognitive abilities can be compensated for through training and good design practices.

Other changes in work organizations that have implications for the employment of older people are an increased focus on team and collaborative work and changes in organizational hierarchies such that firms are becoming flatter with a focus on decentralized decision-making. In these types of work contexts, workers often need to learn entire processes and be able to communicate effectively with diverse teams of people using new and faster forms of communication such as videoconferencing, email, and instant messaging. Workgroups will also be diverse with respect to the age mix of group members. Thus, strategies must be developed to ensure that workers of different ages can effectively interact with one another and that their skills are maximized. There will also be an increase in the number of workers in nonstandard work arrangements such as self-employment, and the prevalence of home-based work and telecommuting is likely to increase, which raises important issues with respect to training. New training formats such as e-learning also raise a number of issues regarding the design and implementation of training programs. To date, there is little information available on the suitability of e-learning or the optimal e-learning formats for older workers (Czaja and Sharit, 2012; Sharit, Czaja, Hernandez, & Nair, 2009).

IMPLICATIONS OF WORKPLACE CHANGES FOR OLDER WORKERS

As described in the prior section of this chapter, the workplace is changing in response to the historically recent hyper-competitive marketplace. Ironically, formerly staid local markets have been disrupted in part by technological innovations. One way to conceptualize what has happened is a shift from satisficing (Simon, 1956) toward optimizing. That is, both competitive forces and computer technology (which provides inexpensive and powerful computational capabilities) have changed the way that the firm operates. Individuals[1] and firms can use tools (or outsource their use) to maximize their performance. As a result, workers are expected to improve productivity, usually through investing[2] in learning to use new technological tools.

A second notable shift affecting older workers in particular is the introduction of consumer technology into the workplace. The most salient case is the smartphone device, which has led to the "bring your own device" (BYOD) movement, where firms accommodate to their workers' preferences rather than the usual case of firms leading in technology adoption (e.g., the wired telephone) with workers following (Charness, 2008; Charness & Czaja, 2005). However, in the case of BYOD, older workers are likely to be at a disadvantage to their younger counterparts. As Smith (2013) noted, American smartphone ownership declines strikingly with age from the mid-30s or younger at about 80% ownership to less than 40% in the 55–64-year-old age band. For the newly retired older worker aged 65+ years who might be moving back into the labor force for part-time work, the percentage is less than 20%. There are similar age gaps for American tablet computer usage (Zickuhr, 2013), where peak age for ownership is 35–44 years (~50%), with a drop to less than 30% ownership for those 55–64, and below 20% for those seniors aged 65+.

Hence, at the same time that there is a strong premium on adopting productivity tools and requiring workers to train on their own time using technology (e.g., e-learning), the level of familiarity with such tools shows strong age-/cohort-related decline. That is one of the challenges for older workers. However, it is coupled with an additional challenge, namely the slower rate at which older adults can acquire new information and skills.

Age and Learning Rate

Early in the history of research on learning and aging, it was recognized that there was a significant age/cohort gap in acquiring new associations, usually tracked by paired-associate learning experiments. Younger and older adults would be given pairs of unrelated words to learn, usually by presenting them in trial blocks with feedback until the learner had acquired all the pairs. Early studies (see the summary of paired-associate learning in Kausler, 1994) and meta-analytic analyses of memory tasks (Verhaeghen, Marcoen, & Goosens, 1993) show that older adult cohorts are much less effective in such learning than younger cohorts. The same result holds true when memory for text passages has been assessed and the effect size for age differences in such learning is large, with d ~0.7 (Johnson, 2003). It should be noted that many variables impact learning rate, including mode of presentation, testing format, and individual differences such as the prior knowledge that is brought to the learning task (Johnson, 2003). However, age differences in memory performance have held up across time of measurement (Johnson, 2003; Kausler, 1994), suggesting that they represent aging effects rather than cohort effects. A meta-analysis specifically for worker training has shown a similar disadvantage in performance for older compared to younger workers (Kubeck, Delp, Haslett, & McDaniel, 1996).

Such differences in basic learning ability can add up to about a 2:1 old compared to young age difference in the time taken to acquire skill with software applications, such as for self-paced learning of a new word processor (Charness, Kelley, Bosman, & Mottram, 2001). Prior skill was an important predictor variable. Age differences for novice learners were larger than for experienced word processors.

One feature that older workers often bring compared to younger ones is their vast store of acquired experience and knowledge through having competed for jobs for a longer time. Such acquired knowledge and skill ("crystallized ability") is likely to be able to compensate for age-related declines in learning rate and in "fluid ability" (Charness, 2009). The classic example is in the knowledge-computation trade-off for problem-solving performance (Newell, 1990). It demonstrates that a little knowledge can substitute effectively for greater computational capability. One can be much more efficient answering a question by retrieving the answer from memory than from having to compute the answer: knowing $95^2 = 9,025$ rather than doing the problem by hand or punching the problem into a calculator.

If such compensation is present by dint of experience, then older workers should be advantaged compared to younger ones for indicators such as wage rates. As assessed using cross-sectional data, the peak age for work wages is the 55–64-year age band (Bureau of Labor Statistics, 2013), with the second highest band being age 45–54. One must be cautious in interpreting such cross-sectional data given that the result could arise for historical reasons related to employment history and employment sector. However, with an increasing emphasis on new learning, with unfamiliar technology increasingly prevalent, there is a looming question about the potential for age-skill trade-off in the future. In the next section, we focus specifically on training issues given the importance of this topic to the continued employment of older people.

Training and the Employability of Older Workers

Issues related to training or retraining older workers—including the prospects for older workers to receive such training, how to provide or design such training, and the roles of the government and company managers in promoting or creating barriers to the training of these workers—are complex and challenging to resolve. Understanding these issues requires an appreciation of a larger concern, specifically the trend for older workers to increasingly comprise a greater share of the workforce and the implications of this trend for their employability in our current and future economies.

Many factors, mostly economic in nature, are influencing the need and desire for older workers to remain in the workforce past traditional retirement ages. For example, in the United States, these include the Federal Reserve's policy of maintaining low interest rates, which has hurt the retirement savings of many older persons; changes in social security policies that provide greater incentives to continue to work; the fact that half as many employers are offering health insurance plans to retirees as compared to two decades ago, which encourages many workers still too young to qualify for Medicare to remain in the workforce; and remnants of a lingering economic recession that are forcing many older individuals to support children who would normally be in the labor force but cannot obtain employment. These economic factors are also operating in other countries. For example, in the Netherlands, the Dutch government introduced policies to promote continued employment such as a reduction in financial incentives to retire early, the removal of early retirement options, and restrictions to unemployment and disability benefits. Similar policies are being adopted in other EU countries (Sinclair et al., 2013). Improved overall health of older adults and the shifting of jobs way from physical labor, as well as the recognition that staying active and productive can help maintain good health, may also be contributing to a greater willingness to continue working.

Barriers to Older Workers Seeking to Retain or Gain Employment

The current labor market climate, however, is not a positive one for older job seekers. Once an older worker (55+) loses a job, the prospects for rejoining the labor force are lower than that of younger workers (Rix, 2012). In fact, according to a recent study, unemployed older workers were more likely than any other age category of workers to have been without a job for one year or longer (Pew Charitable Trusts, 2012). Although the recent severe recession has altered many company cultures, translating in many instances to a greater reluctance for employers to hire in large numbers workers from any age category, clearly there exist factors that are contributing, directly or indirectly, to decreasing the prospects for older workers to remain employed or gain employment as compared to younger job seekers. Despite attempts to provide a positive portrait of the benefits that older workers can bring to an organization, such as AARP's report (Feinsod, Davenport, & Arthurs, 2005), negative stereotypes or perceptions maintained by employers concerning older workers, as well as, in some cases, unsubstantiated beliefs about the costs that older workers would incur, are still pervasive and impede the prospects for employability of older individuals (Sharit et al., 2009). These include:

1. Older workers are less productive than younger workers, due in part to the perception that slowing with age translates into less efficient work and, in some cases, lower-quality work owing to an inability to process information as extensively or as rapidly.
2. Older workers are less competent working with newer technologies and generally less flexible or willing to adapt to changes in the workplace.
3. Older workers are more costly to train, in terms of investment in time to train and also in having less time available during the course of employment of the older worker to secure the benefits of the investments in training or retraining.
4. Older workers are less likely to have the physical or mental fortitude to endure the continual training and updating of skills and the testing for the demonstration of acquisition of those skills, a training regimen that is being increasingly emphasized by many organizations.
5. Older workers are more expensive in terms of wages, more costly in terms of health insurance, and also more likely to be absent due to health issues.
6. Hiring or retaining older workers blocks career opportunities for younger workers, who may be able to bring with them fresh ideas and newer skills related to performing work and a willingness to work longer hours.

A quotation in a recent article in the *New York Times* (Rampell, 2013) by Daniel Hamermesh, an economics professor at the University of Texas in Austin, encapsulates the challenges that many older workers are likely to confront when seeking employment:

> It just doesn't make sense to offer retraining for people 55 and older ... Discrimination by age, long-term unemployment, the fact that they're now at the end of the hiring queue, the lack of time horizon just does not make it sensible to invest in them.

Many of these perceptions and beliefs, however, can be contested (Posthuma & Campion, 2009), especially for relatively higher-educated older workers. For example, there is evidence that older workers who work with mostly younger workers are often more accepting of new workplace technology than their younger counterparts (Rizzuto, 2011). Older workers also potentially possess a number of positive attributes that can make them assets to employers. These include their increased maturity and emotional stability (Sharit et al., 2009), which can be advantageous in resolving issues in work teams or in sales-related jobs (Smyer & Pitt-Catsouphes, 2009); their judgment in decision-making and in handling various types of issues accrued from their vast experience (Dychtwald, Erickson, & Morrison, 2006); and the fact that they tend to be more reliable (e.g., demonstrate better attendance), conscientious, and persevering in seeking solutions. In addition, if they qualify for Medicare, they are in fact less of a liability with respect to the health insurance burden carried by employers, and older workers have not been found to be larger burdens to their employers in health costs (Grosch & Pransky, 2009).

For older workers seeking employment who possess lower literacy or skill, access to employment opportunities is likely to be especially difficult. Many of these workers may not have the basic skills necessary to participate in community college programs, including those directed at job retraining, and may also be lacking job-hunting techniques (Zhang, 2011), especially with the increasing emphasis in job search processes on use of online or social networking sites if they lack technology or literacy skills. Generally, the evidence indicates that older workers have less access to employer-supported as well as publicly funded training programs, such as those encompassed by the federal Public Workforce System (PWS), as compared to younger workers. Workers 55+ on average were found to receive significantly less hours of employer-sponsored training per year (nine hours) as compared to employers aged 25–34 (37 hours), with the unwillingness of employers to invest in training older workers due to concerns that they would not recoup their investments in training before older workers retire and even age biases cited as possible reasons (Dobbs, Healey, Kane, Mak, & McNamara, 2007; U.S. Department of Labor, 2008).

The Public Workforce System and Training of Older Workers

The PWS, whose primary vehicle is the Workforce Investment Act (WIA) of 1998, has been described by the Government Accountability Office

(GAO) as comprised of more than 47 programs, including its network of One-Stop Career Centers, that are under the administration of nine federal agencies (U.S. Government Accountability Office, 2011). Although the WIA was intended to provide services for people of all ages who are seeking employment, there are only two programs within the PWS dedicated to serving older workers: the Senior Community Service Employment Program, authorized by Title V of the Older Americans Act, and the Alternative Trade Adjustment Assistance (Heidkamp, 2012). These programs have served primarily very low-income older workers or older workers who have been displaced by foreign trade who agree to forgo training. The evidence has indicated that older workers who have received WIA services have lower likelihoods of becoming employed and receiving training than younger WIA participants. However, older WIA participants who accessed training through WIA earn some sort of credential (e.g., high school equivalency, college degree, occupational certificate) at the same or even greater rate than younger WIA participants, and have had some success in obtaining employment after training as compared to people from other age groups.

Motivated by the challenges in finding employment that older workers in WIA-funded programs were facing, the U.S. Department of Labor launched the Aging Worker Initiative in 2009, which, through various pilot sites, is seeking to evaluate the benefits of various strategies. These strategies include offering short-term training to high-demand industries, providing computer training and internships, and use of public messaging and employer dialogues to publicize the potential value of older workers. The results from the evaluation of this initiative, however, are not yet available (Heidkamp, 2012). An abundant learning resource in the United States that can potentially greatly augment the public workforce training system are community colleges. With funding through various grants, the American Association of Community Colleges has launched a number of initiatives, such as the Plus 50 initiative, directed at helping older individuals learn basic occupational skills and obtain certificates and degrees to enhance their employability, but results of the evaluation of such programs are also not yet available (Heidkamp, 2012).

While an increase in knowledge and training beyond post-secondary credentials is critical for improving the employment opportunities of many older workers, especially in occupations such as healthcare and social services, what needs to be acknowledged is the current demand for critical thinking skills and the ability for workers to add value beyond that which is provided by current technologies. These workers will be expected to continuously adapt to the changing conditions that derive largely from globalization and information technology advances, which requires access to more flexible and higher-level training and lifelong learning opportunities. The WIA service delivery system model of the public workforce system is probably not likely to be in a position to address the highly diverse needs of unemployed older workers. As noted by Heidkamp (2012, p. 13):

> Today's public workforce system has to play a dual role—serving as both a safety net for individuals who require income support, literacy, and vocational education and retraining as a result of unemployment, poverty, and long spells out of the labor market—as well as an ongoing support system that provides access to high quality, affordable, and labor market driven education and training to help adults of all ages prepare for and remain in the labor market.

A Framework for a PWS Encompassing Newer Training Strategies

To address the needs of older workers, including learning needs, Heidkamp (2012) has provided a framework for a new PWS, specifically: (1) a reliance on local (e.g., state) labor market data and information to better align educational and training programs with the needs of employers in regional economies; (2) a de-emphasis on short-term educational and training interventions for the purpose of more immediate job placement and greater emphasis on longer-term training (e.g., a year or longer) that is more intensive and encompassing, and thus more likely to enable older workers to overcome gaps in knowledge and more effectively transition to many of the new types of jobs that are emerging or being re-envisioned; (3) more creative delivery of training programs for older adults that are capable of adapting to the learning needs of these individuals; (4) a greater focus on training and development of skilled advisors who not only can properly gauge the potential work skills of the job seekers, but who also have a deep understanding of the skills, knowledge, and abilities needed for the various industries seeking workers, and who understand the relative benefits of different training programs that may be offered for prospective job seekers and can guide these individuals in the use of computer and social media technology to virtually connect to relevant industry personnel; and (5) the use of technology and social media to deliver educational and training programs in addition to other employment services. An example of the latter is the AARP Foundation's WorkSearch Assessment System initiated in 2007, an online system that assesses skills, interests, and abilities and gaps in skill and training, that connects users to training, either online or in the community, as well as to job opportunities, and that uses trained peer volunteers as virtual job coaches to work with users either through discussion groups, email, or telephone.

Designing Training Programs for Older Workers

The implication that training should address the learning styles of older adults, as alluded to above, is critical to the success of such programs and advises that trainers make use of a number of resources that provide recommendations for designing training and instructional programs for older adults. As discussed in detail in Czaja and Sharit (2012), various structures or mechanisms comprising human information processing undergo normal age-related declines, and recognition of the nature of these declines and how they can impede traditional delivery of training is critical for adapting training for older workers. This is especially the case for individuals who may have little prior knowledge stored in their long-term memory, either conceptual or concrete, to use as a basis for taking in new knowledge such as information about new technologies. Declines in working memory capacity, both in the amount of information that can be held or the speed at which information can be negotiated, can greatly impact the ability during training to keep new learning active so that it can be reliably registered in memory and linked to new learning material or previously stored knowledge. This can make older learners particularly susceptible to training that introduces learning materials at an improper rate, in the wrong sequence, with inadequate rest breaks or opportunities to reflect on or rehearse the material, or with inadequate or inappropriate feedback. These and many other information-processing considerations, such as in the speed with which one recognizes or perceives various types of learning materials, ultimately shape and impact the benefits potentially afforded by different instructional methods or strategies, including the use of multimedia training programs. In this regard, many recommendations in the form of principles, guidelines, and suggestions are offered in Czaja and Sharit (2012) that trainers can use to adapt their instructional programs for older workers, depending on the prior experiences, skills, and aptitudes of these workers and the types of jobs the training is being targeted for.

Training Skilled Older Workers

While information-processing capabilities are an important consideration in the training of any older worker, a somewhat different or additional perspective may be needed when the focus is on skilled older workers who are in jeopardy of being displaced, or who are unemployed and possess needed skills but may be resistant to learning new technologies that they feel are unnecessary for performing job functions (e.g., sales) that they feel they are skilled in or qualified for. Many of these workers have critical thinking, judgment, or interpersonal skills, useful knowledge, and are mature, dependable, and loyal, and in some cases may even prove valuable in helping companies service their older customer base (e.g., in the financial services sector). In addition, the removal of these workers may be viewed as a risk to organizations that need the critical knowledge and experience base of these older workers for maintaining knowledge transfer within their organization. However, these workers may also be viewed by management as insufficiently adaptable to the newer workplace information and communication technologies, and for this reason expendable or unappealing. One strategy for dealing with such older workers who are currently employed, especially those who may be willing to curtail their hours in the interest of making themselves more affordable to management, is to make use of mentoring programs (Czaja & Sharit, 2009; Lesser & Rivera, 2007). In these arrangements, younger employees guide the older worker in becoming familiar and competent on work-related technologies, and the older workers in turn guide these younger workers in exercising judgment with regard to establishing business contacts, handling various project-related issues, and gaining deeper insight into business operations.

Assuming one has appropriately adapted instructional techniques for older workers—for example, in teaching software applications such as Microsoft Excel that typically assume learners have some type of transferrable knowledge (e.g., knowledge of Microsoft Word), but which may not be the case for many older workers—there are still many other motivational or attitudinal barriers that need to be overcome to successfully transition these otherwise potentially valuable workers. In a recent article, Searcy (2013) provides four strategies for enabling more senior employees who may be resistant, reluctant, or otherwise averse to adopting newer technologies in the workplace to adapt to these changes. The first strategy is based on the premise that dissatisfaction drives change. For example, identifying complaints that older workers are voicing (e.g., about being able to get useful information on inventory) provides an inroad for demonstrating how a technology (e.g., how a mobile app could provide access to real-time inventory data) could solve their dilemma. The second strategy, which Searcy refers to as the carrot and stick approach, is to make clear—by grounding examples in "harsh reality"—to the resistant older worker what the consequences of not using the technology are, as well as the benefits of using it. For example, an older sales leader could be shown what the cost may be of over-promising and under-delivering of a product if the tablet the company has made available to workers is not being used to check inventory. At the same time, balance the anticipation of negative consequences associated with nonuse of the technology with face-to-face testimonials from coworkers about its benefits—for example, how a new customer relationship management system allowed one to track his or her customer leads more effectively. Often, a company's attempt to address the potential benefits of technologies they are introducing through approaches such as company-wide messages tend to be too distal to provide the intended impact on resistive workers.

A third strategy is to keep the training programs "simple and real" and to avoid "any canned process or training documentation from your vendor [which is] likely geared to the tech-savvy." This point was referred to earlier, and is where many of the research-related or academic recommendations regarding the design of instructional programs are relevant. Part of this strategy, consistent with what the research literature strongly suggests with older learners, is to relate new information to information that may be familiar to the older learner so that associations in memory can be developed that can both benefit the conceptual understanding of the new material, as well as its retention in memory. A simple example of this principle provided by Searcy is to compare instant messaging to yelling over the cubicle wall to a colleague. Finally, Searcy emphasizes the need for ongoing training support using online demonstrations, online tutorials, and easy-to-reach help desks, as well as the importance of building experts within the various teams. For older workers, a useful strategy in training is to train the trainer, who then becomes the resident expert for a group of individuals. Identifying older workers who may desire such roles—as trainers within their teams—may be a particularly useful strategy, as many older employees may feel less threatened listening to instructions or advice about use of technologies from such individuals as compared to much younger and less patient technologically oriented workers.

Overall, it is important to recognize that while many older workers can benefit from training approaches that can successfully accommodate or compensate for normal age-related declines in information processing, the training strategies used to retain or employ older skilled or educated workers who possess critical thinking, judgment, knowledge, or other valuable assets are likely to be very different than the ones needed to employ older less-educated and skilled workers. Transforming the Public Workforce System and educating managers about successful strategies for deriving the benefits older workers have to offer are first steps, albeit very challenging ones, to ensuring that training programs accomplish their goals of employing and retaining older workers.

WORKPLACE AND INTERFACE CONSIDERATIONS

In addition to training, the health and safety of older workers is of utmost importance, and thus consideration needs to be given to ensure that workplaces and interfaces accommodate the needs and preferences of older people. In addition to changes in cognition, aging is also associated with reductions in mobility, strength, dexterity, and visual and sensory acuity. The incidence of chronic conditions such as arthritis increases with age. To accommodate these age-related changes, it is particularly important to adhere to ergonomic guidelines for workplace and interface design (e.g., Fisk, Rogers, Charness, Czaja, & Sharit, 2009; Kroemer, 2009). For example, age-related changes in vision have implications for the design of written instructions and manuals and lighting requirements. There are a variety of strategies available to accommodate people with low vision, such as providing larger monitors, increasing font size, or increasing screen resolution or use of speech as output device. Levels of illumination need to be higher for older adults and potential sources of glare need to be minimized. Many older adults also experience some decline in audition, such as difficulties understanding synthetic speech, detecting high-frequency sound, and locating sound sources. Minimizing background noise in work environments is also an important design consideration. Other important ergonomic guidelines relate to placement of controls and storage units, placement of computers, and workplace layout.

Age-related changes in motor skills may make it difficult for older people to perform tasks, such as assembly work, that require small manipulation or to use current input devices, such as a mouse. New software interfaces and alternative input devices and methods are available to help alleviate problems with mouse control. There are also various software tools to help alleviate problems with vision and hearing, as well as age-related cognitive changes such as declines in memory (e.g., search history tools) and attention (e.g., highlighting). In addition, the National Institute on

Aging has published Web design guidelines for older adults and there are numerous sources of guidelines aimed at "accessible" software (e.g., IBM Special Needs Systems Guidelines, World Wide Web Consortium Web Accessibility Initiative, Trace Research & Development Center: Application Software Design Guidelines).

CONCLUSIONS

The aging of the population and graying of the workforce presents both opportunities and challenges for employers and organizations. Current societal trends indicate that older adults will be a part of the workforce and thus strategies are needed to maximize the productivity, health, safety, and well-being of older workers. The development of these strategies must be based on an understanding of the characteristics, needs, abilities, and preferences of older people, as well as current and future employment and organizational trends. At the same time that the workforce is aging we are witnessing changes in organizational structures, work policies and ongoing developments in technology are also reshaping work processes, the content of jobs, where work is performed, and the delivery of education and training. Taken together, these trends will shape the workplace of the 21st century and result in many emerging challenges for employers and workers that require changes in government and organizational policies, work procedures, and educational and training systems. In our efforts to maximize the effectiveness of workers, workplaces, and organizations, we not only need to accommodate workers of different ages, but also workers with varying skills, attitudes toward work, and cultural and ethnic backgrounds. This is of paramount importance given the changes in the skill requirements of today's jobs and the increased diversity of our workforce. In this regard, it would also be beneficial to understand how strategies to accommodate current workplace and demographics trends could be generalized across countries and populations.

NOTES

1. About 60% of U.S. small businesses in 2007 were single-owner: http://factfinder2.census.gov/faces/tableservices/jsf/pages/productview.xhtml?pid=SBO_2007_00CSCB07&prodType=table (accessed April 30, 2014).

2. That investment is likely to be the responsibility of the employee rather than the employer in small firms (Charness & Fox, 2010).

REFERENCES

Bal, A. C., Reiss, A. E., Rudolph, C. W., & Baltes, B. B. (2011). Examining positive and negative perceptions of older workers: A meta-analysis. *The Journals of Gerontology Series B: Psychological Sciences and Social Sciences, 66*(6), 687–698.

Bosman, E. A., & Charness, N. (1996). Age differences in skilled performance and skill acquisition. In T. Hess & F. Blanchard-Fields (Eds.), *Perspectives on Cognitive Change in Adulthood and Aging* (pp. 428–453). New York: McGraw-Hill.

Bureau of Labor Statistics (2011). Current population survey. Available at: www.bls.gov/cps (accessed December 29, 2013).

Bureau of Labor Statistics (2013). *Table 1. Civilian Labor Force by Age, Sex, Race, and Ethnicity, 1992, 2002, 2012, and Projected 2022.* Bureau of Labor Statistic News Release, November 1, 2013. Available at: www.bls.gov/news.release/pdf/wkyeng.pdf (accessed November 18, 2013).

Charness, N. (2008). Technology as multiplier effect for an aging work force. In K. W. Schaie & R. Abeles (Eds.), *Social Structures and Aging Individuals: Continuing Challenges* (pp. 167–192). New York: Springer.

Charness, N. (2009). Skill acquisition in older adults: Psychological mechanisms. In S. J. Czaja & J. Sharit (Eds.), *Aging and Work: Issues and Implications in a Changing Landscape* (pp. 232–258). Baltimore, MD: Johns Hopkins University Press.

Charness, N., & Czaja, S. J. (2005). Adaptation to new technologies (7.13). In M. L. Johnson (Gen. Ed.), *Cambridge Handbook on Age and Ageing* (pp. 662–669). Cambridge: Cambridge University Press.

Charness, N., & Fox, M. C. (2010). Formal training, older workers, and the IT industry. In J. McMullin & V. W. Marshall (Eds.), *Aging and Working in the New Economy: Changing Career Structures in Small IT Firms* (pp. 143–162). Williston, VT: Edward Elgar.

Charness, N., Kelley, C. L., Bosman, E. A., & Mottram, M. (2001). Word processing training and retraining: Effects of adult age, experience, and interface. *Psychology and Aging, 16*, 110–127.

Czaja, S. J., & Sharit, J. (1998). The effect of age and experience on the performance of a data entry task. *Journal of Experimental Psychology: Applied, 4*, 332–351.

Czaja, S. J., & Sharit, J. (Eds.) (2009). *Aging and Work: Issues and Implications in a Changing Landscape.* Baltimore, MD: Johns Hopkins University Press.

Czaja, S. J., & Sharit, J. (2012). *Designing Training and Instructional Programs for Older Adults.* Boca Raton, FL: CRC Press.

Czaja, S. J., Sharit, J., Ownby, R., Roth, D., & Nair, S. (2001). Examining age differences in performance of a complex information search and retrieval task. *Psychology and Aging, 16*, 564–579.

Dobbs, J., Healey, P., Kane, K., Mak, D., & McNamara, T. (2007). *Age Bias and Employment Discrimination (Fact Sheet, 2007).* Chestnut Hill, MA: Boston College Center on Aging and Work/Workplace Flexibility.

Dychtwald, K. E., Erickson, T. J., & Morrison, R. (2006). *Workforce Crisis. How to Beat the Booming Shortage of Skills and Talent.* Boston, MA: Harvard Business School Press.

Feinsod, R., Davenport, T., & Arthurs, R. (2005). The business case for workers 50+: Planning for tomorrow's talent needs in today's competitive environment. Washington, DC: AARP Public Policy Institute. Available at: http://assets.aarp.org/rgcenter/econ/workers_fifty_plus_1.pdf (accessed December 28, 2013).

Fisk, A. D., Rogers, W. A., Charness, N., Czaja, S. J., & Sharit, J. (2009). *Designing for Older Adults: Principles and Creative Human Factors Approaches* (2nd ed.). Boca Raton, FL: CRC Press.

Grosch, J. W., & Pransky, G. S. (2009). Safety and health issues for an aging workforce. In S. J. Czaja & J. Sharit (Eds.), *Aging and Work: Issues and Implications in a Changing Landscape* (pp. 334–358). Baltimore, MD: Johns Hopkins University Press.

Heidkamp, M. (2012). Older workers, rising skill requirements, and the need for a re-envisioning of the Public Workforce System. New Brunswick, NJ: John J. Heldrich Center for Workforce Development, Rutgers University. Available at: www.cael.org/pdfs/TMT_Reenvision_Public_Workforce_System (accessed December 3, 2013).

Johnson, R. E. (2003). Aging and the remembering of text. *Developmental Review, 23*, 261–346.

Kausler, D. H. (1994). *Learning and Memory in Normal Aging*. San Diego, CA: Academic Press.

Kroemer, K. H. E. (2009). Ergonomic design of workplaces for the aging population. In S. J. Czaja and J. Sharit (Eds.), *Aging and Work: Issues and Implications in a Changing Landscape*. Baltimore, MD: Johns Hopkins University Press.

Kubeck, J. E., Delp, N. D., Haslett, T. K., & McDaniel, M. A. (1996). Does job-related training performance decline with age? *Psychology and Aging, 11*, 92–107.

Lesser, E., & Rivera, R. (2006). *Closing the Generational Divide: Shifting Workforce Demographics and the Learning Function*. Accessed December 3, 2013 from: www-935.ibm.com/services/us/gbs/bus/pdf/g510-6323-00_generational_divide.pdf.

Loch, C. H., Fabian, J. S., Bauer, N., & Mauerman, H. (2010). The globe: How BMW is defusing the demographic time bomb. *Harvard Business Review*, March, 99–102.

Newell, A. (1990). *Unified Theories of Cognition*. Cambridge, MA: Harvard University Press.

Pew Charitable Trusts (2012). Five long-term employment questions. Available at: www.pewtrusts.org/uploadedFiles/wwwpewtrustsorg/Reports/Fiscal_Analysis/Pew_PFAI_Unemployment_Chartbook_print.pdf (accessed December 27, 2013).

Posthuma, R. A., & Campion, M. A. (2009). Age stereotypes in the workplace: Common stereotypes, moderators, and future research directions. *Journal of Management, 35*, 158–188.

Rampell, C. (2013). In a hard economy, older isn't better . . . it's brutal. *New York Times*, February 3, 2013.

Rix, S. (2012). The employment situation, December 2011: Year ends on encouraging note. Washington, DC: AARP Foundation. Available at: www.aarp.org/content/dam/aarp/research/public_policy_institute/econ_sec/2011/fs246.pdf (accessed December 20, 2013).

Rizzuto, T. (2011). Age and technology innovation in the workplace: Does work context matter? *Computers and Human Behavior, 27*, 1612–1620.

Searcy, T. (2013). *Help Older Workers Adapt to Changes*. Available at: www.inc.com/tom-searcy/boomer-workers-help-them-adapt.html (accessed December 3, 2013).

Sharit, J., & Czaja, S. J. (2012). Job design and re-design for older workers. In J. W. Hedge & W. C. Borman (Eds.), *Oxford Handbook of Work and Aging* (pp. 454–482). New York: Oxford University Press.

Sharit, J., Czaja, S. J., Hernandez, M., Yang, Y., Perdomo, D., Lewis, J., Lee, C. C., & Nair, S. (2004). An evaluation of performance by older persons on a simulated telecommuting task. *The Journals of Gerontology: Psychological Sciences, 59B*(6), 305–316.

Sharit, J., Czaja, S. J., Hernandez, M. A., & Nair, S. N. (2009). The employability of older workers as teleworkers: An appraisal of issues and an empirical study. *Human Factors and Ergonomics in Manufacturing*, 19, 457–477.

Simon, H. A. (1956). Rational choice and the structure of the environment. *Psychological Review, 63*(2), 129–138.

Sinclair, D., Watson, J., & Beach, B. (2013). *Working Longer: An EU Perspective.* London: ILC-UK.

Smith, A. (2013). Smartphone ownership—2013 update. Available at: http://pewinternet.org/~/media//Files/Reports/2013/PIP_Smartphone_adoption_2013_PDF.pdf (accessed November 18, 2013).

Smyer, M. A., & Pitt-Catsouphes, M. (2009). Collaborative work: What's age got to do with it? In S. J. Czaja & J. Sharit (Eds.), *Aging and Work: Issues and Implications in a Changing Landscape* (pp. 144–164). Baltimore, MD: Johns Hopkins University Press.

Toossi, M. (2012). Labor force projections to 2020: A more slowly growing workforce. *Monthly Lab. Rev., 135*, 43–64.

Torres-Gil, F. (2009). The politics of work and aging: Public policy for the new elders. In S. J. Czaja & J. Sharit (Eds.), *Aging and Work: Issues and Implications in a Changing Landscape* (pp. 77–89). Baltimore, MD: Johns Hopkins University Press.

U.S. Department of Labor (2008). Report of the taskforce on the aging of the American workforce. Available at: www.doleta.gov/reports/final_taskforce_report_2_27_08.pdf (accessed December 4, 2013).

U.S. Government Accountability Office (2011). Multiple employment and training programs: Providing information on collocating services and consolidating administrative structures could provide efficiencies (GAO 11-92). Available at: www.gao.gov/new.items/d1192.pdf (accessed December 28, 2013).

Verhaeghen, P., Marcoen, A., & Goossens, L. (1993). Facts and fiction about memory aging: A quantitative integration of research findings. *Journal of Gerontology*, 48, 157–171.

Zhang, T. (2011). Workforce Investment Act training for older workers: Toward a better understanding of older worker needs during the economic recovery. Washington, DC: U.S. Department of Labor, Employment Training Administration. Available at: http://wdr.doleta.gov/research/FullText_Documents/ETAOP_2011-10.pdf (accessed December 28, 2013).

Zickuhr, K. (2013). Tablet ownership 2013. Available at: http://pewinternet.org/~/media//Files/Reports/2013/PIP_Tablet%20ownership%202013.pdf (accessed November 18, 2013).

8

Aging and Emotional Labor Processes

James M. Diefendorff, Jennifer Tehan Stanley, and Allison S. Gabriel

Over the past few decades, there has been an increase in service-based jobs within the global economy. In the United States alone, this trend is expected to continue, with projections that the service sector will account for 96% of all new job growth through 2018 (Toosi, 2012), and in the United Kingdom the service sector employs 10% of all employees, with expectations that this percentage will rise (Johnson, Holdsworth, Hoel, & Zapf, 2013; McNair & Flynn, 2006). As a result of these changes, the importance of interpersonal effectiveness on the job is likely to grow. Key contributors to interpersonal effectiveness in service jobs are the ways emotions are experienced, regulated, and expressed by employees (Ashforth & Humphrey, 1993; Rafaeli & Sutton, 1987). Research on these topics is often investigated under the heading of emotional labor, or the management of emotions as part of the work role (Grandey, Diefendorff, & Rupp, 2013; Hochschild, 1983).

Simultaneous to this increase in the service sector is the fact that the working population is getting older, with projections that 25% of the workforce will be older than 55 years by the year 2020 (U.S. Bureau of Labor, 2010). These two trends suggest that the odds of older adults working in service-based occupations may increase. Although separate streams of research have advanced our understanding of emotional labor (Grandey et al., 2013) and aging and emotions (Stanley & Isaacowitz, 2012), little is known about the effects of age on emotional labor processes. The primary purpose of this chapter is to address this gap by reviewing the relevant research, and developing an agenda for investigating age and emotional labor.

OVERVIEW OF EMOTIONAL LABOR

Emotional labor "is performed in response to job-based emotional requirements in order to produce emotion toward—and to evoke emotion from—another person to achieve organizational goals" (Grandey et al., 2013, p. 18). Thus, emotional labor involves the expression of organizationally desired emotions, which may be accomplished by displaying naturally felt emotions, displaying regulated felt emotions (via antecedent-focused emotion regulation or deep acting), or displaying fake emotions (via response-focused emotion regulation or surface acting). The effectiveness of emotional labor depends on a variety of factors that may be categorized as being stable and dynamic attributes of the person (e.g., personality, affective disposition, age, mood resource availability) and situation (e.g., job characteristics, emotional display rules, affective events, customer reactions). Figure 8.1 illustrates some of these general influences by presenting the within-person processes that unfold during emotional labor episodes, as well as stable aspects of the person and situation that can impact event-level variables and relationships. In doing so, the model highlights factors related to *why* individuals may need to regulate their emotions (e.g., display rules, traits, affective events), *how* they regulate their emotions (e.g., antecedent-focused and response-focused), and the *effects* of this regulation on outcomes (e.g., performance, well-being). Our goal with this model was not to comprehensively capture all possible variables related to emotional labor, but to present a model that illustrates the emotional labor process and allows us to highlight points at which age might play a role. For a more detailed account of emotional labor, we recommend recent quantitative and qualitative reviews (Grandey et al., 2013; Hülsheger & Schewe, 2011; Kammeyer-Mueller et al., 2013).

Stable Influences on Emotional Labor: Display Rules and Dispositional Affect

The most commonly examined job-based influence on emotional labor is emotional display rules. Ekman (1973) described display rules as the unwritten norms for how individuals should express emotions in social situations. In the workplace, display rules pertain to the emotions that should be expressed by employees as part of the job (Ashforth & Humphrey, 1993; Diefendorff & Richard, 2003). Display rules in most service-based occupations (e.g., food services, healthcare) require employees to provide

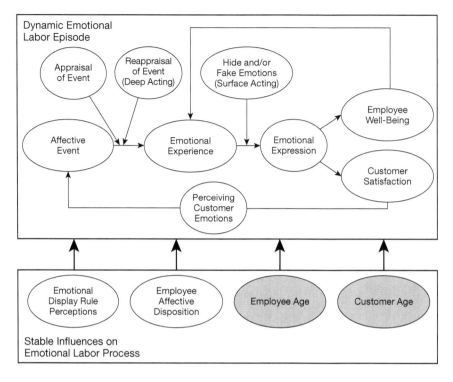

FIGURE 8.1
Within-person emotional labor dynamics and stable influences on emotional labor processes

"service with a smile," which has been interpreted as demands to show positive emotions (i.e., enthusiasm) and hide negative emotions (i.e., anger) (Diefendorff, Croyle, & Gosserand, 2005; Hochschild, 1983). Display rules have been shown to vary across occupations (Brotheridge & Grandey, 2002), to be in-role job expectations (Diefendorff, Richard, & Croyle, 2006), and to exhibit shared, group-level properties (Diefendorff, Erickson, Grandey, & Dahling, 2011). Further, display rules have been shown to correlate with the use of emotion regulation strategies and employee well-being (Brotheridge & Grandey, 2002; Diefendorff & Richard, 2003; Diefendorff et al., 2005).

Dispositional affectivity has been shown to relate to both display rules and emotion regulation strategies (Brotheridge & Grandey, 2002; Gosserand & Diefendorff, 2005). Individuals high in positive affectivity tend to experience high activation positive emotions (e.g., enthusiasm, excitement); individuals high in negative affectivity tend to experience high activation negative emotions (e.g., anxiety, anger) (Watson, Clark, & Tellegen, 1988). Employees who have a dispositional tendency to feel emotions that match display requirements are expected to be able to express naturally felt emotions and engage in less regulation (Côté, 2005; Diefendorff & Gosserand, 2003). Other stable traits, such as the Big Five personality dimensions, emotional expressivity, and customer service orientation (Allen, Pugh, Grandey, & Groth, 2010), have been shown to impact the emotional labor process as well. For instance, individuals who are high in service orientation (i.e., a desire to provide excellent customer service) tend to engage in higher levels of deep acting and lower levels of surface acting (Allen et al., 2010). Additionally, employees who are extraverted are buffered from the negative effects of surface acting (e.g., reduced emotional exhaustion and negative affect) and are able to reap more benefits from deep acting (e.g., increased positive affect, decreased negative affect) (Judge, Woolf, & Hurst, 2009).

Event-Level Emotional Labor Dynamics

Dynamic factors in the person and situation can impact employee emotions and the need to actively regulate feelings and expressions (as depicted in the *Emotional Labor Episode* portion of Figure 8.1). When specific events occur (e.g., a customer encounter), they produce affective reactions that shape subsequent attitudes and behavior (Weiss & Cropanzano, 1996). A commonly studied affective event in service contexts is customer mistreatment, which has been investigated under the headings of workplace incivility and interpersonal injustice (Goldberg & Grandey, 2007; Groth & Grandey, 2012; Rupp & Spencer, 2006; Sliter, Sliter, & Jex, 2012). Customer mistreatment results in negative emotions that deviate from emotional display rules, resulting in the need to actively manage one's emotional experience and expression (Dallimore, Sparks, & Butcher, 2007; Wegge, Vogt, & Wecking, 2007; Yang & Diefendorff, 2009). In contrast, positive customer treatment produces positive emotions in employees (Kim & Yoon, 2012), decreasing the need to actively manage feelings and expressions.

This event-to-emotion linkage can be altered when employees engage in antecedent-focused emotion regulation (Gross, 1998), which are strategies aimed at altering one's emotional reaction to a situation. The emotional labor literature often uses the term *deep acting* to describe these emotion regulation techniques. A common way that antecedent-focused regulation is thought to occur at work is by cognitive reappraisal (Diefendorff, Richard, & Yang, 2008), which involves reinterpreting the situation to change its emotional impact (Gross, 2001). Thus, a person may choose to reappraise mistreatment from a customer as being due to the person having a bad day. Cognitive reappraisal should result in a less negative reaction, making the display of role-appropriate emotions easier. Indeed, a recent meta-analysis (Hülsheger & Schewe, 2011) found that deep acting positively correlated with personal accomplishment ($\rho = 0.27$), emotional performance ($\rho = 0.18$), and customer satisfaction ($\rho = 0.37$), though, fitting with the majority of research, deep acting was not significantly related to emotional exhaustion ($\rho = 0.18$). These results are consistent with experimental research showing that antecedent-focused strategies such as reappraisal are beneficial for well-being and interpersonal effectiveness (Gross & John, 2003; John & Gross, 2004).

Once an emotion is experienced, individuals must determine whether they will show the emotion as is or attempt to alter their expression (Gross, 2001). When feelings match display rules, individuals may simply express their naturally felt emotions (Diefendorff et al., 2005; Zapf, 2002). Though this is desirable, some effort may still be needed to translate the feeling into the script and tenor of a company's service expectation (e.g., saying the company-specific greeting with an intonation described in training materials) (Ashforth & Humphrey, 1993). When feelings do not align with display rules, employees may attempt to modulate their response by hiding their true emotions or faking the desired emotion, actions that are known as response-focused emotion regulation (Gross, 1998), or *surface acting* in the emotional labor literature (Hochschild, 1983). Surface acting leaves experienced emotions intact and only alters outward expressions. In comparison to antecedent-focused regulation, response-focused regulation produces less authentic emotional displays (Grandey, Fisk, Mattila, Jansen, & Sideman, 2005), as well as greater emotional dissonance between feelings and displays. Meta-analytic results have shown that surface acting is negatively correlated with emotional performance ($\rho = -0.14$), task performance ($\rho = -0.11$), and job satisfaction ($\rho = -0.33$), in addition to being positively related to emotional exhaustion ($\rho = 0.44$), psychological strain ($\rho = 0.42$), depersonalization ($\rho = 0.48$), and psychosomatic complaints ($\rho = 0.44$) (Hülsheger & Schewe, 2011). Experimental research also finds that emotion suppression results in decreased well-being, negative social functioning, and performance decrements (Butler et al., 2003; Gross & John, 2003; John & Gross, 2004).

A somewhat overlooked aspect of emotional labor is that it involves a social exchange between employees and customers in which emotions spread from one person to the other in a dynamic way (Côté, 2005; Rafaeli

& Sutton, 1987). That is, employees express emotions consistent with display rules and customers may become "infected" and experience the organizationally desired emotions (Hatfield, Cacioppo, & Rapson, 1993; Pugh, 2001). However, customers may also bring their own emotions to the situation or respond to the employee's emotional displays in unexpected ways. Thus, the emotions that customers feel and express can influence employee emotions and behavior by providing information to employees about whether the service interaction is going well (Côté, 2005; Rafaeli & Sutton, 1987). These feelings can impact subsequent employee emotion regulation, well-being, and performance, as depicted by the feedback loop in Figure 8.1. Similarly, how an employee feels at a given moment will impact how he or she subsequently feels during an interaction or in a future interaction. This idea is also captured by a feedback loop in Figure 8.1.

When viewing emotional labor as a dynamic exchange between employees and customers, it becomes clear that an important determinant of whether this interaction goes well is if employees have the ability to perceive and react to what the customer is feeling (Rafaeli & Sutton, 1987). Such information can come from what the customer says and does, as well as what the customer is expressing emotionally (Hatfield et al., 1993). As such, the ability to perceive emotions likely plays an important role in employees accurately evaluating customer satisfaction and responding accordingly. Thus, the feedback loops and links to performance in Figure 8.1 may be a function of effective emotion recognition. We now turn to a discussion of age differences in emotion with an emphasis on how age might relate to emotional labor processes.

AGE DIFFERENCES IN EMOTION PROCESSES

Despite the dearth of research on age and emotional labor, a consideration of how emotional labor processes operate in late adulthood could be theoretically groundbreaking and practically useful. Although we anticipate that age may influence emotional labor at many points in the process, we focus on three key components of the process for which there is some empirical basis: appraisal, experience, and expression (both display and perception) of emotion. The aging and emotion literature provides a foundation that can be applied to these three areas in the hope of generating propositions for future research. To date, much of the emotions and aging research, and the little that exists on age and emotional labor (Dahling &

Perez, 2010; Scheibe & Zacher, 2013; Sliter, Chen, Withrow, & Sliter, 2013), relies on socio-emotional selectivity theory (SST) (Carstensen, 2006). SST argues that as individuals grow older, they become more motivated to seek positive emotional experiences because of increased salience that their time left in life is limited. These changes are apparent in middle age, with significant differences in future time perspective appearing in the fourth and fifth decades of life (Cate & John, 2007). Given these shifts in the prioritization of emotions and their regulation, it seems likely that age moderates the appraisal (and reappraisal), experience, and expression of emotion within the context of emotional labor.

Appraisal (and Reappraisal)

Stereotypical "older worker" jobs (e.g., nurse, bank teller, receptionist) often involve substantial customer service (Panek, Staats, & Hiles, 2006), suggesting that older workers may frequently experience demands to express positive emotions on the job (i.e., emotional display rules). Though no study has directly assessed whether older workers perceive emotional display rules differently from younger workers, we can extrapolate from SST (Carstensen, 2006) that age-related shifts to prioritize positive emotions may translate into age differences in preferences for showing and experiencing positive emotions at work. Indirect evidence for the potential influence of these preferences on emotional labor comes from work showing that the relationship between scores on the Big Five Personality Inventory and self-reports of positive and negative emotional experiences are weaker for older adults compared to young adults (Ready & Robinson, 2008). The authors suggest that older adults' greater prioritization of emotion regulation (Carstensen, 2006) leads them to appraise situations more positively, trumping the trait-emotional experience relationship seen in younger adults. Thus, older workers may be more likely than their younger counterparts to enter the work environment with emotions and emotional goals that align with the display rules needed to provide "service with a smile." This may mean that older adults: (a) need to engage in *less* emotion regulation than younger adults; and (b) when regulation is needed, they may be more likely to regulate via reappraisal (i.e., deep acting). Indeed, the limited research looking at age in emotional labor has found that deep acting is positively correlated with age, whereas surface acting is negatively correlated (Cheung & Tang, 2010; Dahling & Perez, 2010; Sliter et al., 2013). For instance, Dahling and Perez (2010) found a positive correlation of 0.16 between age and deep acting and a negative correlation between age and surface acting ($\rho = -0.35$), suggesting that older adults may tend to use more adaptive emotion regulation strategies.

Given an age-related reduction in cognitive resources (Park, 2000), the extent to which the appraisal process is automatic versus effortful may determine whether there are age differences in the appraisal of emotion. Empirical work is needed, but it is reasonable to expect that older adults typically may prefer and be more effective when the affective event can be appraised automatically. Evidence consistent with this notion comes from Shiota and Levenson (2009), who demonstrated an age-related improvement for positive reappraisal (i.e., interpreting the situation in a more positive light)—an emotion regulation strategy that could rely on the relatively automatic and effortless top-down goals of SST—but age-related decrements for detached reappraisal (i.e., interpreting the situation in an objective unemotional manner)—an emotion regulation strategy that is thought to require more executive functioning abilities, which decline with age (Salthouse, Atkinson, & Berish, 2003). Thus, the way in which situations are reappraised (e.g., positively, detached) may determine the impact of age.

Moreover, the impact of age on the emotional experience may depend upon when during the emotion process the regulation takes place. Altering feelings once the emotion is already underway requires more regulatory resources than regulation that heads off the emotion before it occurs (Sheppes & Meiran, 2008), and these resources may be less available for older compared to younger adults. Applying these ideas, it may be that older workers will fare worse than younger workers when regulation occurs later in the emotion-generation process, but will perform as well as younger adults when regulation occurs early in the emotion process.

Experience

The aging literature largely supports the idea that there are age differences in the experience of emotions. Cross-sectional and longitudinal data suggest that the experience (frequency) of self-reported negative affect (e.g., depressed, unhappy) decreases with age and the self-reported experience of positive affect (e.g., joy, enthusiasm) is relatively stable across the lifespan (Carstensen et al., 2011; Scheibe & Carstensen, 2010), though some evidence suggests it declines in old age (around 70+ years) (Kunzmann, Richter, & Schmukle, 2013). Additionally, a longitudinal experience-sampling study found improvement in the ratio of positive to negative emotions experienced as individuals age, beginning at age 20 and leveling off at 64 years of age (Carstensen et al., 2011). An important caveat to this pattern of greater experienced positivity with increasing age comes from the strength and vulnerability integration model (SAVI), which posits that older adults have more difficulty than young adults regulating high levels of sustained arousal (whether they are negative or positive) (Charles, 2010). For example, older adults rated low-arousing pictures more pleasant than high-arousing pictures (independent of valence) (Keil & Freund, 2009). Together, these findings suggest a relatively more positive picture for older workers than for young workers in terms of emotional experiences in daily life.

On average, older adults are often better at regulating their emotions than young adults (Gross, 2001; Scheibe & Carstensen, 2010). Older adults tend to be better at avoiding conflict in interpersonal relationships (Birditt, Fingerman, & Almeida, 2005), and compared to their younger counterparts, older adults report greater emotional control (Gross et al., 1997), better perceived emotion regulation skills (Kessler & Staudinger, 2009), and increased mood stability (Williams et al., 2006). Older adults, on average, also exhibit better emotion regulation than young adults in experimental tasks. For example, older adults were better than young adults at down-regulating feelings of disgust without sacrificing performance on a working memory task in a dual-task paradigm (Scheibe & Blanchard-Fields, 2009). Additionally, older adults were more likely to disengage from negative feelings after hearing a person make disparaging remarks about them (Charles & Carstensen, 2008). A recent meta-analysis suggests that this pattern of positive experience extends to the workplace, with older employees reporting greater job satisfaction and less interpersonal conflict than younger employees (Ng & Feldman, 2010).

These age effects can be interpreted within the SST framework. Because older adults perceive their future time as more limited, they minimize negative emotional experiences in order to feel more positively (Carstensen & Turk-Charles, 1994). However, how this is accomplished may matter, as some emotion regulation strategies are more cognitively demanding and older adults tend to have fewer cognitive resources available. Interestingly, the ability to suppress true emotions (akin to surface acting) does not typically show age differences in experimental work (Levenson, 2000). For example, Shiota and Levenson (2009) found no age differences in participants' ability to suppress their emotions when watching sad and disgusting film clips. However, correlational studies have found that age is negatively correlated with surface acting (Dahling & Perez, 2010; Sliter et al., 2013), suggesting that older workers are less likely than younger workers to use surface acting. Further, it appears that older adults, on average, use healthier emotion-regulation strategies than young adults because they prefer reappraisal strategies over suppression strategies (John & Gross, 2004).

In terms of whether there are age differences in antecedent-focused emotion regulation (deep acting), two possible hypotheses emerge. On the one hand, older adults are typically better at regulating their emotions than their younger counterparts (Kessler & Staudinger, 2009; Scheibe & Blanchard-Fields, 2009); so, one might expect older adults to outperform young adults at deep acting. On the other hand, deep acting can require effortful emotion regulation, and older adults have fewer cognitive resources available to do so (Park, 2000). Nevertheless, in one study, older adults outperformed young adults on concurrent cognitive tasks when required to engage in some degree of effortful emotion regulation (Scheibe & Blanchard-Fields, 2009). It is possible that by prioritizing emotion regulation, older adults make emotion regulation less effortful and more automatic, requiring fewer cognitive resources (Gyurak, Gross, & Etkin, 2011). This evidence would suggest that—depending on the level of effort required for engaging in deep acting—older adults might fare quite well.

Expression: Showing Emotions and Perceiving Emotions in Others

Additional components of the emotional labor model in Figure 8.1 where we might expect age differences are in the expression of emotion and the ability to detect customer emotional expressions. Current research suggests some age differences in the expression of emotion. For instance, when watching amusing films, older adults smiled less frequently than young adults, though there were no differences in the frequency of facial expression between young and older adults when watching sad films (Tsai, Levenson, & Carstensen, 2000). However, in another study, there were no age differences in the frequency of expressed target emotion for both positive and negative emotions during a relived emotions task (Levenson, Carstensen, Friesen, & Ekman, 1991). Given these mixed findings, more research is needed on age differences in the frequency of expressed emotions. It is worth noting, however, that when directed to create facial expressions by contracting certain muscles, one study found that the *quality* of older adult facial expressions was not as good as that of young adults as indicated by coders who evaluated the degree to which the directed muscles were contracted (Levenson et al., 1991).

Also part of the emotional labor process is the ability to accurately perceive others' expressions. A handful of studies have found that older adult facial expressions of emotions tend to be more difficult to classify than young adults' expressions (Ebner & Johnson, 2009; Hess, Adams, Simard, Stevenson, & Kleck, 2012; Riediger, Voelkle, Ebner, & Lindenberger, 2011). Age-related changes in the physiognomy of the face (e.g., wrinkles, drooping around the eyes, sagging jowls) (Hooyman & Kiyak, 1996) due to decreased collagen may render older adult facial expressions more difficult to read; alternatively, older adults may tend to simply express emotions less intensely or prototypically than young adults. In a study with videos of angry, sad, and fearful facial expressions, young, middle-aged, and older women were equally poor at identifying emotions expressed by older females (Malatesta, Izard, Culver, & Nicolich, 1987). Furthermore, older women were found to be worse at identifying emotions expressed by their own age group than young adults were at identifying emotions expressed by young posers (Malatesta et al., 1987), supporting the idea that emotions expressed by older adults are difficult to classify for all ages.

In terms of recognizing emotions, on average, older adults are not as accurate as young adults at correctly identifying facial expressions and body cues of emotion, especially anger, sadness, and fear (Ruffman, Henry, Livingstone, & Phillips, 2008). Moreover, older adults are also less accurate, on average, than younger adults at identifying angry, sad, and happy vocal expressions (Ruffman et al., 2008). Although much of this work has used an extreme-groups design (i.e., comparing young adults to older adults), studies that have included middle-aged adults suggest that changes in emotion recognition exhibit a linear decline from young adulthood to old age. For example, middle-aged adults (38–50 years) were worse at identifying emotional prosody (i.e., rhythm, intonation) in speech than young adults (18–28 years) (Paulmann, Pell, & Kotz, 2008). In a study of emotion recognition in lexical and facial stimuli, young adults (18–39 years) were more accurate than middle-aged adults (40–59 years), who were more accurate than older adults (60–85 years) (Isaacowitz et al., 2007). Another study found that recognizing fear in facial expressions was highest among teens (12–19 years), and significantly declined in each subsequent age band: young adults (20–29 years), middle-aged adults (30–49 years), and older adults (50–79 years) (Williams et al., 2006).

Ultimately, age-related deficits in the ability to recognize emotions could lead to a breakdown of the social dynamics of emotional labor if the older worker misses discrepancies between the desired state (happy customer) and the actual experienced state (angry customer) because they fail to accurately identify the customer's emotions. It should be noted, however, that older adults do not have trouble when asked to simply identify the valence (positive, negative, neutral) of an emotional facial expression (Keightley, Winocur, Burianova, Hongwanishkul, & Grady, 2006). Thus, age-related differences in emotion recognition found in the lab may only be a problem in the workplace if it is important to differentiate among discrete negative emotions (e.g., sad versus fear versus anger). Furthermore, experimental work on age differences in emotion recognition has studied this phenomenon devoid of the context usually present in daily life (Barrett & Kensinger, 2010; Barrett, Mesquita, & Gendron, 2011; Isaacowitz & Stanley, 2011). Context has been a critical factor in aging research in other domains, such as intelligence (Colonia-Willner, 1998), helping to determine when age-related deficits in the lab translate to meaningful deficits in real-world scenarios and when they do not. For instance, a typical emotion recognition task requires the participant to identify the emotion expressed in a still photograph by a young adult stranger posing an emotion at maximum intensity. Clearly, this is not how people read emotions in their everyday social partners. Adding context by examining age differences in emotional displays within an emotional labor process would be informative for both theory and practice.

AGING AND EMOTIONAL LABOR: CHALLENGES AND OPPORTUNITIES

Although the research reviewed above offers some promising glimpses into the ways in which aging may impact the emotional labor process, the reality is that there are some hurdles to overcome when merging these two literatures. For example, while much of the aging literature defines an older adult as an individual somewhere between 55 and 85 years old, centering on 65 years old (Baltes & Smith, 2003; Hertzog & Dixon, 1996), the older worker has been described as 40+ (Boerlijst, Munnichs, & van der Heijden, 1998) and 55 years and older (Sterns & Miklos, 1995). This mismatch in each sub-field currently limits the cross-generalizability of findings, especially because longitudinal studies show that linear age-related decline in some aspects of cognitive functioning—such as episodic memory—begins in the sixth decade (Schaie, 1996). Longitudinal data on other cognitive abilities, however, begin a linear age-related decline at earlier ages with significant declines in reasoning, spatial relations, short-term memory, and processing speed appearing as early as the third decade and decreasing thereafter (Salthouse, 2009). This means there may be important differences in the average cognitive ability of studies examining the older worker (40s and 50s) versus studies focusing on the older adult (with an average age of 65 years).

Another challenge to merging the two literatures is the level of analysis examined in each. The aging and emotions literature focuses on the older adult at the individual level, often trying to understand older adults' emotional experiences in a lab context. Emotional labor work takes a more dynamic view, considering how the employee, customer, and organization interact in natural environments. Moreover, embedded within models of emotional labor is the idea that emotional labor processes are dynamic and unfold over time within a given interaction (Beal & Trougakos, 2013), making the influence of age on this dynamic process critical to understand. We believe it is well worth the effort to address these challenges to better understand the unique role of older workers in emotional labor jobs. Building on the work reviewed in the previous sections of this chapter, we develop propositions pertaining to the potential role of age in the emotional labor process. Given the work demonstrating fairly linear age-related changes in cognitive processes (e.g., Salthouse, 2009), we expect that the proposed effects of age on emotional labor may be fairly linear as well, though our propositions highlight the comparison of older versus younger adults. Nonetheless, direct investigation of whether the proposed age-based changes in emotional labor processes are linear or nonlinear is needed.

The Desire to Perform Emotional Labor

Given that older adults have increased desire for positive experiences (Carstensen, 2006), it stands to reason that older adults may have a stronger willingness to follow integrative emotional display rules (i.e., show positive and hide negative emotions) and express positive emotions while on the job. Consistent with this general idea is the observation that older adults tend to have more favorable job attitudes than younger adults (Gibson & Klein, 1970; Michaels & Spector, 1982; O'Brien & Dowling, 1981; Saal, 1978). As a result of this more favorable orientation toward work and the desire to have more positive experiences in general, older adults may be more inclined to commit to integrative display rules (Gosserand & Diefendorff, 2005).

> *Proposition 1*: Older workers are more likely to commit to integrative (i.e., express positive, hide negative) display rules than are younger workers.

Appraisals of Affective Events and the Experience of Emotions in Service Jobs

Customer incivility has been argued to be the most commonly experienced form of workplace mistreatment (Sliter et al., 2012; van Dierendonck & Mevissen, 2002). Thus, employees may need to be prepared to face difficult customers, and may benefit from having a mindset that is open to reappraising difficult interactions. Older adults may be particularly well suited to this task as they come to adopt a perspective on life that suggests that one should not "sweat the small stuff." As such, it is more likely that older individuals will effectively appraise difficult situations as more manageable (i.e., positive reappraisal) (Shiota & Levenson, 2009). Supporting this idea, increased age is associated with more frequent use of cognitive reappraisal and less frequent use of emotion suppression (John & Gross, 2004). Furthermore, older adults are better, on average, at avoiding interpersonal conflicts (Birditt et al., 2005) and less likely to become angry when they hear disparaging remarks (Charles & Carstensen, 2008).

Proposition 2: Older workers appraise difficult customer affective events in a more positive way than younger workers.

Proposition 3: Older adults are more likely to positively reappraise difficult customer affective events than are younger adults.

In terms of felt emotions, given that the experience of negative affect decreases with age (Carstensen et al., 2011), it is expected that older adults will tend to experience fewer negative emotions on the job than young adults. For positive emotional experiences, although evidence suggests that positive emotions are stable across the lifespan (Carstensen et al., 2011), given older adults' improved ability to positively reappraise (Shiota & Levenson, 2009) and down-regulate negative emotions (Scheibe & Blanchard-Fields, 2009), and findings that deep acting (i.e., reappraisal) is related to increased positive affect on a daily basis (Scott & Barnes, 2011), one might expect that older employees will also tend to experience more positive emotions than younger employees.

Proposition 4: Older workers experience fewer negative emotions than younger workers.

Proposition 5: Older workers experience more low-arousal positive emotions (e.g., contentment) than younger workers.

The Expression of Emotions at Work

The above logic suggests that because older adults typically seek out positive experiences and interpret situations more positively (Carstensen, 2006), they will experience higher levels of positive emotions at work. One may initially presume from this that older adults will express positive emotions more often than younger adults. However, as previously discussed, older adults have unique challenges in the actual expression of emotions due to various physiological changes that decrease the quality of facial expressions (Hooyman & Kiyak, 1996; Levenson et al., 1991), in addition to the tendency for older adults to smile less in response to positive stimuli (Tsai et al., 2000). Interestingly, Barger and Grandey (2006) found that for service employees, it was not just smiling that was predictive of customer mood and satisfaction, but the *magnitude* of smiling (e.g., minimal, maximal). The authors argued that maximal smiles are more likely to induce mimicry in customers, helping elicit positive customer experiences. Further, it may be inferred that stronger, or more positive, emotions underlie a maximal smile as opposed to a minimal smile. However, qualities associated with a maximal smile (e.g., up-turning corners of the mouth) may be challenging for older employees. Thus, we propose that older adults may be less likely to produce strong positive emotional expression (i.e., maximal smiles) than younger adults.

> *Proposition 6*: Older workers will express fewer strong positive emotions (i.e., maximal smiles, indicating high activation positive affect) than will younger workers.

As noted earlier in this chapter, display rules in many service occupations prohibit the expression of negative emotions. Nonetheless, such expressions may occur on the rare occasion as when employees "break character" and engage in emotional deviance (Grandey, 2003; Rafaeli & Sutton, 1987). Given findings of age-related decreases in the experience of negative affect (Carstensen et al., 2011; Scheibe & Carstensen, 2010), combined with our previous theorizing that older adults will be more committed to positive display rules, we expect that older adults may be less likely to express negative emotions on the job than younger adults. Thus, given older adults' desire for positive emotions and their ability to regulate emotions, we expect that they may be less likely to express negative emotions on the job than younger adults.

Proposition 7: Older workers will express fewer negative emotions than will younger workers.

The Detection of Customer Emotions in Service Interactions

With regard to emotion detection, the research reviewed suggests that older adults may be at somewhat of a disadvantage. The reason is that while older adults can identify whether a person is experiencing positive or negative emotions, they have difficulty in identifying the specific discrete negative emotion (e.g., angry, afraid, sad) (Ruffman et al., 2008). Of course, in a typical service context, the most likely negative emotion displayed by customers may be anger or a closely related feeling such as frustration. However, knowledge of the context and typical emotional episodes encountered in service jobs may enable older adults to anticipate which negative emotions are likely and compensate for any emotion detection decrement (Isaacowitz & Stanley, 2011). Nonetheless, when an atypical customer expression occurs, older adults may experience greater difficulty in labeling and responding to the emotional expression. Further, this difficulty may be compounded when attempting to identify the emotional expressions of older customers, given the decrease in emotional expression capabilities noted earlier.

Proposition 8: Older workers are less able, on average, to accurately detect discrete emotions in customers than are younger workers.

Proposition 9: It is more difficult to accurately detect the felt emotions of older customers than younger customers.

Furthermore, the dynamic dance of expressing emotions, detecting customer emotions, and responding to those expressions in real time may require significant cognitive resources. Given the general decline in cognitive resources in older adults (Park, 2000), it may be that navigating complex emotional interactions with customers will be more difficult. However, older adults may have more expertise in handling difficult interpersonal situations, and as a result they may have developed compensatory strategies for handling such interpersonal complexity. For instance, older adults may have developed "tried and true" strategies for responding to different complaints and managing difficult customers. Plus, the general orientation toward avoiding conflict and experiencing positive emotions may inoculate the employee from entering into "incivility spirals" (Andersson & Pearson, 1999). In contrast, younger workers may be more affected by difficult customers and get dragged into tit-for-tat negative exchanges.

> *Proposition 10*: Older workers are less affected by customer incivility and less likely to enter into incivility spirals with customers compared to younger workers.

PRACTICAL CONSIDERATIONS

Given that front-line service employees come in contact with customers first (Hochschild, 1983), it is important for organizations to put their "best foot forward." If older adults are better able to: (a) regulate their emotions; (b) experience positive emotions at work; and (c) respond to customer difficulties, managers may consider placing older adults in service roles that possess high levels of customer contact and visibility. Older workers may be more able to establish an initial positive emotional experience for customers than younger workers. This may be especially true when the customer is also older given the finding that customers may prefer to interact with employees of a similar age (Dwyer, Richard, & Shepherd, 1998; Evans, 1963). Additionally, older adults may be better suited than younger adults at handling customer concerns and complaints since customer grievances may trigger negative affective reactions and older adults may be more adept at handling such negative emotional experiences. Moreover, recent research by Johnson and colleagues (2013) found that older workers were less likely to report exposure to negative customer interactions (i.e., unrealistic customer expectations, verbal abuse from customers, disliked customers, customers with ambiguous expectations), suggesting that older adults may be able to more successfully prevent such interactions from occurring or perhaps are less likely to appraise interactions as being negative. In either instance, older adults may be less likely than younger adults to experience the negative effects of emotional labor.

Apart from placing older adults into more visible service roles, research showing that older adults may smile less and have lower-quality positive emotional expressions presents some interesting implications for training. Pugh, Diefendorff, and Moran (2013) highlight the idea that organizations can use training programs to influence "good" emotional labor strategies (i.e., deep acting) and deter individuals from "bad" strategies (i.e., surface acting). Given that older adults may naturally adopt reappraisal, or deep acting, more training could be conducted on the actual physical expressions of emotions because these expressions may not be as naturally strong as the positive expressions of younger adults. Training could be conducted to encourage positive emotional expressions via a variety of additional channels such as eye contact, vocal tone, and vocal quality, which have been considered indicators of "service with a smile" in previous research (Barger & Grandey, 2006; Gabriel, Acosta, & Grandey, in press).

Another intervention would be to train older workers to detect emotional expressions. For example, researchers have found that interventions can improve facial affect recognition accuracy in individuals with conditions linked to emotion detection deficits, such as autism (Bölte et al., 2006), schizophrenia (Russell, Chu, & Phillips, 2006; Silver, Goodman, Knoll, & Isakov, 2004), and learning disabilities (Wood & Kroese, 2007). Emotion recognition training has also been useful for police officers and counseling psychologists (Ennett, 2013; Morrison & Bellack, 1981). For instance, Russell and colleagues (2006) showed improvement in emotion recognition for patients with schizophrenia using the micro-expressions training tool (METT) (Ekman, 2002), a computer-based emotion recognition tool that trains individuals to pay attention to relevant features of an emotional expression. Eye-tracking research suggests that young and older adults do exhibit different gaze patterns during emotion recognition tasks, with older adults looking less at the eyes than young adults (Murphy & Isaacowitz, 2010; Sullivan, Ruffman, & Hutton, 2007). Ideally, better emotion detection skills could assist older employees in responding to customer emotions. However, it should be noted that being able to accurately read emotions may be a double-edged sword. Elfenbein and Ambady (2002) found that employees who were good at detecting negative expressions through "leaky" channels (i.e., the voice) were evaluated more poorly by coworkers and supervisors, suggesting an advantage to *not* detecting subtle emotional cues in others. Indeed, not attending to such cues may be an implicit strategy adopted by older adults for avoiding conflict and managing interpersonal interactions (Gottman & Levenson, 1992).

As a final consideration, research is beginning to identify the importance of emotional labor in electronic interfaces, such as email, instant messaging, and chat room forums (Fife & Pereira, 2001; Turel, Connelly, & Fisk, 2011).

This notion of "e-retailing" (Turel et al., 2011, p. 1) may introduce greater complexity to service encounters as service employees will need to not only manage their own emotions and the emotions of customers, but do so via novel technological interfaces. To the extent that these modes of communication require more cognitive resources, one might expect differences to emerge between older and younger adults (Salthouse, 2009). In addition to resource demands associated with technology, there may be differences in the motivation or desire of younger and older adults to work with such technology. For instance, older adults tend to have more negative attitudes toward technology than young adults, though these attitudes can be mitigated via successful interactions with the technology (Rogers, Stronge, & Fisk, 2005). In a training study of novice computer users aged 19–88 years, increasing age was associated with worse performance and greater time to learn (Charness, Kelley, Bosman, & Mottram, 2001). However, older adults with computer experience took about the same amount of time to learn a new program as inexperienced young adults. In terms of recognizing facial expressions of emotion in video-based computer-mediated communication, older workers may be particularly challenged if the video image is too small, as one study showed that older adults—but not young adults—were slower to respond with the facial expression label when images were small (Roring, Hines, & Charness, 2006). Thus, research is needed to better understand the role of age in technology-mediated customer service interactions.

SUMMARY

The aging population paired with the increasing prominence of the service sector suggests that older adults may be required to engage in emotional labor even more in the future. Building on research showing age-related differences in emotion processes, we make the case for expecting emotional labor differences between older and younger adults. Our review suggests that older adults are well equipped and ready for the challenges presented by emotional labor. However, research that systematically examines these issues is needed before firm conclusions and recommendations on the role of age in service work can be made.

REFERENCES

Allen, J. A., Pugh, S. D., Grandey, A. A., & Groth, M. (2010). Following display rules in good or bad faith? Customer orientation as a moderator of the display rule-emotional labor relationship. *Human Performance, 23,* 101–115.

Andersson, L. M., & Pearson, C. M. (1999). Tit for tat? The spiraling effect of incivility in the workplace. *Academy of Management Review, 24,* 452–471.

Ashforth, B. E., & Humphrey, R. H. (1993). Emotional labor in service roles: The influence of identity. *The Academy of Management Review, 18,* 88–115.

Baltes, P. B., & Smith, J. (2003). New frontiers in the future of aging: From successful aging of the young old to the dilemmas of the fourth age. *Gerontology, 49,* 123–135.

Barger, P. B., & Grandey, A. A. (2006). Service with a smile and encounter satisfaction: Emotional contagion and appraisal mechanisms. *Academy of Management Journal, 49,* 1229–1238.

Barrett, L. F., & Kensinger, E. A. (2010). Context is routinely encoded during emotion perception. *Psychological Science, 21,* 595–599.

Barrett, L. F., Mesquita, B., & Gendron, M. (2011). Context in emotion perception. *Current Directions in Psychological Science, 20,* 286–290.

Beal, D., & Trougakos, J. (2013). Episodic interpersonal emotion regulation: Or, dealing with life as it happens. In A. A. Grandey, J. M. Diefendorff, & D. Rupp (Eds.), *Emotional Labor in the 21st Century: Diverse Perspectives on Emotion Regulation at Work.* New York: Psychology Press/Routledge.

Birditt, K. S., Fingerman, K. L., & Almeida, D. M. (2005). Age differences in exposure and reactions to interpersonal tensions: A daily diary study. *Psychology and Aging, 20,* 330–340.

Boerlijst, J. G., Munnichs, J. M. A., & van der Heijden, B. I. J. M. (1998). The "older worker" in the organization. In P. J. D. Drenth, H. Thierry, & C. J. de Wolff (Eds.), *Handbook of Work and Organizational, Vol. 2: Work Psychology* (2nd ed.) (pp. 183–213). Hove: Psychology Press/Erlbaum.

Bölte, S., Hubl, D., Feineis-Matthews, S., Prvulovic, D., Dierks, T., & Poustka, F. (2006). Facial affect recognition training in autism: Can we animate fusiform gyrus? *Behavioral Neuroscience, 120,* 211–216.

Brotheridge, C. M., & Grandey, A. A. (2002). Emotional labor and burnout: Comparing two perspectives of "people work." *Journal of Vocational Behavior, 60,* 17–39.

Butler, E. A., Egloff, B., Wilhelm, F. H., Smith, N. C., Erickson, E. A., & Gross, J. J. (2003). The social consequences of expressive suppression. *Emotion, 3,* 48–67.

Carstensen, L. L. (2006). The influence of a sense of time on human development. *Science, 312,* 1913–1915.

Carstensen, L. L., & Turk-Charles, S. (1994). The salience of emotion across the adult life span. *Psychology and Aging, 9,* 259–264.

Carstensen, L. L., Turan, B., Scheibe, S., Ram, N., Ersner-Hershfield, H., Samanez-Larkin, G. R., Brooks, K. P., & Nesselroade, J. R. (2011). Emotional experience improves with age: Evidence based on over 10 years of experience sampling. *Psychology and Aging, 26,* 21–33.

Cate, R. A., & John, O. P. (2007). Testing models of the structure and development of future time perspective: Maintaining a focus on opportunities in middle age. *Psychology and Aging, 22,* 186–201.

Charles, S. T. (2010). Strength and vulnerability integration: A model of emotional well-being across adulthood. *Psychological Bulletin, 136,* 1068–1091.

Charles, S. T., & Carstensen, L. L. (2008). Unpleasant situations elicit different emotional responses in younger and older adults. *Psychology and Aging, 23,* 495–504.

Charness, N., Kelley, C. L., Bosman, E. A., & Mottram, M. (2001). Word-processing training and retraining: Effects of adult age, experience, and interface. *Psychology and Aging*, 16, 110–127.

Cheung, F. Y-l., & Tang, C. S-k. (2010). Effects of age, gender, and emotional labor strategies on job outcomes: Moderated mediation analyses. *Applied Psychology: Health and Well-Being*, 2, 323–339.

Colonia-Willner, R. (1998). Practical intelligence at work: Relationship between aging and cognitive efficiency among managers in a bank environment. *Psychology and Aging*, 13, 45–57.

Côté, S. (2005). A social interaction model of the effects of emotion regulation on work strain. *Academy of Management Review*, 30, 509–530.

Dahling, J. J., & Perez, L. A. (2010). Older worker, different actor? Linking age and emotional labor strategies. *Personality and Individual Differences*, 48, 574–578.

Dallimore, K. S., Sparks, B. A., & Butcher, K. (2007). The influence of angry customer outbursts on service providers' facial displays and affective states. *Journal of Service Research*, 10, 78–92.

Diefendorff, J. M., & Gosserand, R. H. (2003). Understanding the emotional labor process: A control theory perspective. *Journal of Organizational Behavior*, 24, 945–959.

Diefendorff, J. M., & Richard, E. M. (2003). Antecedents and consequences of emotional display rule perceptions. *Journal of Applied Psychology*, 88, 284–294.

Diefendorff, J. M., Croyle, M. H., & Gosserand, R. H. (2005). The dimensionality and antecedents of emotional labor strategies. *Journal of Vocational Behavior*, 66, 339–357.

Diefendorff, J. M., Richard, E. M., & Croyle, M. H. (2006). Are emotional display rules formal job requirements? Examination of employee and supervisor perceptions. *Journal of Occupational and Organizational Psychology*, 79, 273–298.

Diefendorff, J. M., Richard, E. M., & Yang, J. (2008). Linking emotion regulation strategies to affective events and negative emotions at work. *Journal of Vocational Behavior*, 73, 498–508.

Diefendorff, J. M., Erickson, R. J., Grandey, A. A., & Dahling, J. J. (2011). Emotional display rules as work unit norms: A multilevel analysis of emotional labor among nurses. *Journal of Occupational Health Psychology*, 16, 170–186.

Dwyer, S., Richard, O., & Shepherd, C. D. (1998). An exploratory study of gender and age matching in the salesperson-prospective customer dyad: Testing similarity-performance predictions. *Journal of Personal Selling & Sales Management*, 18, 55–69.

Ebner, N. C., & Johnson, M. K. (2009). Young and older emotional faces: Are there age group differences in expression identification and memory? *Emotion*, 9, 329–339.

Ekman, P. (1973). *Darwin and Facial Expression: A Century of Research in Review*. Oxford: Academic Press.

Ekman, P. (2002). *Microexpression Training Tool, Subtle Expression Training Tool*. Salt Lake City, UT: A Human Face.

Elfenbein, H. A., & Ambady, N., (2002). Predicting workplace outcomes from the ability to eavesdrop on feelings. *Journal of Applied Psychology*, 87, 963–971.

Ennett, J. (2013). A cop's nonverbal journey: From gut to mind. In D. Matsumoto, M. G. Frank, & H. S. Hwang (Eds.), *Nonverbal Communication: Science and Applications* (pp. 155–162). Thousand Oaks, CA: Sage.

Evans, F. B. (1963). Selling as a dyadic relationship: A new approach. *American Behavioral Scientist*, 6, 76–79.

Fife, E., & Pereira, F. (2001). Small- and medium-size enterprises and the e-economy: Challenges and prospects. *Journal of the Institution of British Telecommunications Engineers*, 2, 173–179.

Gabriel, A. S., Acosta, J. D., & Grandey, A. A. (in press). The value of a smile: Does emotional performance matter more in familiar or unfamiliar exchanges? *Journal of Business and Psychology*.

Gibson, J. L., & Klein, S. M. (1970). Employee attitudes as a function of age and length of service: A reconceptualization. *The Academy of Management Journal, 13*, 411–425.

Goldberg, L. S., & Grandey, A. A. (2007). Display rules versus display autonomy: Emotion regulation, emotional exhaustion, and task performance in a call center simulation. *Journal of Occupational Health Psychology, 12*, 301–318.

Gosserand, R. H., & Diefendorff, J. M. (2005). Emotional display rules and emotional labor. *Journal of Applied Psychology, 90*, 1256–1264.

Gottman, J. M., & Levenson, R. W. (1992). Marital processes predictive of later dissolution: Behavior, physiology, and health. *Journal of Personality and Social Psychology, 63*, 221–233.

Grandey, A. (2003). When "the show must go on": Surface and deep acting as determinants of emotional exhaustion and peer-rated service delivery. *Academy of Management Journal, 46*, 86–96.

Grandey, A. A., Fisk, G. M., Mattila, A. S., Jansen, K. J., & Sideman, L. A. (2005). Is "service with a smile" enough? Authenticity of positive displays during service encounters. *Organizational Behavior and Human Decision Processes, 96*, 38–55.

Grandey, A. A., Diefendorff, J. M., & Rupp, D. E. (2013). *Emotional Labor in the 21st Century: Diverse Perspectives on Emotion Regulation at Work.* New York: Psychology Press/Routledge.

Gross, J. J. (1998). The emerging field of emotion regulation: An integrative review. *Review of General Psychology, 2*, 271–299.

Gross, J. J. (2001). Emotion regulation in adulthood: Timing is everything. *Current Directions in Psychological Science, 10*, 214–219.

Gross, J. J., & John, O. P. (2003). Individual differences in two emotion regulation processes: Implications for affect, relationships, and well-being. *Journal of Personality and Social Psychology, 85*, 348–362.

Gross, J. J., Carstensen, L. L., Pasupathi, M., Tsai, J., Götestam Skorpen, C., & Hsu, A. Y. C. (1997). Emotion and aging: Experience, expression, and control. *Psychology and Aging, 12*, 590–599.

Groth, M., & Grandey, A. A. (2012). From bad to worse: Negative exchange spirals in employee-customer service interactions. *Organizational Psychology Review, 2*, 208–233.

Gyurak, A., Gross, J. J., & Etkin, A. (2011). Explicit and implicit emotion regulation: A dual-process framework. *Cognition & Emotion, 25*, 400–412.

Hatfield, E., Cacioppo, J. T., & Rapson, R. L. (1993). Emotional contagion. *Current Directions in Psychological Science, 2*, 96–99.

Hertzog, C., & Dixon, R. A. (1996). Methodological issues in research on cognition and aging. In F. Blanchard-Fields & T. M. Hess (Eds.), *Perspectives on Cognitive Change in Adulthood and Aging* (pp. 66–121). New York: McGraw-Hill.

Hess, U., Adams, R. B., Jr., Simard, A., Stevenson, Mi. T., & Kleck, R. E. (2012). Smiling and sad wrinkles: Age-related changes in the face and the perception of emotions and intentions. *Journal of Experimental Social Psychology, 48*, 1377–1380.

Hochschild, A. (1983). *The Managed Heart: Commercialization of Human Feeling.* Berkeley, CA: University of California Press.

Hooyman, N., & Kiyak, H. A. (1996). *Social Gerontology: A Multidisciplinary Perspective* (4th ed.). Boston, MA: Allyn & Bacon.

Hülsheger, U. R., & Schewe, A. F. (2011). On the costs and benefits of emotional labor. *Journal of Occupational Health Psychology, 16*, 361–389.

Isaacowitz, D. M., & Stanley, J. T. (2011). Bringing an ecological perspective to the study of aging and emotion recognition: Past, current, and future methods. *Journal of Nonverbal Behavior, 35*, 261–278.

Isaacowitz, D. M., Loeckenhoff, C., Lane, R., Wright, R., Sechrest, L., Riedel, R., & Costa, P. T. (2007). Age differences in recognition of emotion in lexical stimuli and facial expressions. *Psychology and Aging, 22*, 147–159.

John, O. P., & Gross, J. J. (2004). Healthy and unhealthy emotion regulation: Personality processes, individual differences, and life span development. *Journal of Personality, 72*, 1301–1334.

Johnson, S. L., Holdsworth, L., Hoel, H., & Zapf, D. (2013). Customer stressors in service organizations: The impact of age on stress management and burnout. *European Journal of Work and Organizational Psychology, 22*, 318–330.

Judge, T. A., Woolf, E. R., & Hurst, C. (2009). Is emotional labor more difficult for some than others? A multilevel, experience-sampling study. *Personnel Psychology, 62*, 57–68.

Kammeyer-Mueller, J. D., Rubenstein, A. L., Long, D. M., Odio, M. A., Buckman, B. R., Zhang, Y., & Halvorsen-Ganepola, M. D. K. (2013). A meta-analytic structural model of dispositonal affectivity and emotional labor. *Personnel Psychology, 66*, 47–90.

Keightley, M. L., Winocur, G., Burianova, H., Hongwanishkul, D., & Grady, C. L. (2006). Age effects on social cognition: Faces tell a different story. *Psychology and Aging, 21*, 558–572.

Keil, A., & Freund, A. M. (2009). Changes in the sensitivity to appetitive and aversive arousal across adulthood. *Psychology and Aging, 24*, 668–680.

Kessler, E.-M., & Staudinger, U. M. (2009). Affective experience in adulthood and old age: The role of affective arousal and perceived affect regulation. *Psychology and Aging, 24*, 349–362.

Kim, E., & Yoon, D. J. (2012). Why does service with a smile make employees happy? A social interaction model. *Journal of Applied Psychology, 97*, 1059–1067.

Kunzmann, U., Richter, D., & Schmukle, S. C. (2013). Stability and change in affective experience across the adult life span: Analyses with a national sample from Germany. *Emotion*, advance online publication. DOI: 10.1037/a0033572.

Levenson, R. W. (2000). Expressive, physiological, and subjective changes in emotion across adulthood. In S. H. Qualls & N. Abeles (Eds.), *Psychology and the Aging Revolution: How We Adapt to Longer Life, Vol. 9* (pp. 123–140). Washington, DC: American Psychological Association.

Levenson, R. W., Carstensen, L. L., Friesen, W. V., & Ekman, P. (1991). Emotion, physiology, and expression in old age. *Psychology and Aging, 6*, 28–35.

Malatesta, C. Z., Izard, C. E., Culver, C., & Nicolich, M. (1987). Emotion communication skills in young, middle-aged, and older women. *Psychology and Aging, 2*, 193–203.

McNair, S., & Flynn, M. (2006). Managing an ageing workforce in the retail sector: A report for employers. Department for Work and Pensions. Available at: http://statistics.dwp.gov.uk/asd/asd5/rports2005-2006/agepos8.pdf (accessed January 9, 2015).

Michaels, C. E., & Spector, P. E. (1982). Causes of employee turnover: A test of the Mobley, Griffeth, Hand, and Meglino model. *Journal of Applied Psychology, 67*, 53–59.

Morrison, R. L., & Bellack, A. S. (1981). The role of social perception in social skill. *Behavior Therapy, 12*, 69–79.

Murphy, N. A., & Isaacowitz, D. M. (2010). Age effects and gaze patterns in recognising emotional expressions: An in-depth look at gaze measures and covariates. *Cognition & Emotion, 24*, 436–452.

Ng, T. W. H., & Feldman, D. C. (2010). The relationships of age with job attitudes: A meta-analysis. *Personnel Psychology, 63,* 677–718.

O'Brien, G. E., & Dowling, P. (1981). Age and job satisfaction. *Australian Psychologist, 16,* 49–61.

Panek, P. E., Staats, S., & Hiles, A. (2006). College students' perceptions of job demands, recommended retirement ages, and age of optimal performance in selected occupations. *The International Journal of Aging & Human Development, 62,* 87–115.

Park, D. C. (2000). The basic mechanisms accounting for age-related decline in cognitive function. In D. C. Park & N. Schwarz (Eds.), *Cognitive Aging: A Primer* (pp. 3–21). New York: Psychology Press.

Paulmann, S., Pell, M. D., & Kotz, S. A. (2008). How aging effects the recognition of emotional speech. *Brain and Language, 104,* 262–269.

Pugh, S. D. (2001). Service with a smile: Emotional contagion in the service encounter. *The Academy of Management Journal, 44,* 1018–1027.

Pugh, S. D., Diefendorff, J. M., & Moran, C. S. (2013). Emotional labor: Organization level influences, strategies, and outcomes. In A. A. Grandey, J. M. Diefendorff, & D. E. Rupp (Eds.). *Emotional Labor in the 21st Century: Diverse Perspectives on Emotion Regulation at Work* (pp. 199-221). New York, New York: Psychology Press/Routledge.

Rafaeli, A., & Sutton, R. I. (1987). Expression of emotion as part of the work role. *The Academy of Management Review, 12,* 23–37.

Ready, R. E., & Robinson, M. D. (2008). Do older individuals adapt to their traits? Personality-emotion relations among younger and older adults. *Journal of Research in Personality, 42,* 1020–1030.

Riediger, M., Voelkle, M. C., Ebner, N. C., & Lindenberger, U. (2011). Beyond "happy, angry, or sad?" Age-of-poser and age-of-rater effects on multi-dimensional emotion perception. *Cognition & Emotion, 25,* special section, 968–982.

Rogers, W. A., Stronge, A. J., & Fisk, A. D. (2005). Technology and aging. *Reviews of Human Factors and Ergonomics, 1,* 130–171.

Roring, R. W., Hines, F. G., & Charness, N. (2006). Age-related identification of emotions at different image sizes. *Human Factors, 48,* 675–681.

Ruffman, T., Henry, J. D., Livingstone, V., & Phillips, L. H. (2008). A meta-analytic review of emotion recognition and aging: Implications for neuropsychological models of aging. *Neuroscience & Biobehavioral Reviews, 32,* 863–881.

Rupp, D. E., & Spencer, S. (2006). When customers lash out: The effects of customer interactional injustice on emotional labor and the mediating role of discrete emotions. *Journal of Applied Psychology, 91,* 971–978.

Russell, T. A., Chu, E., & Phillips, M. L. (2006). A pilot study to investigate the effectiveness of emotion recognition remediation in schizophrenia using the micro-expression training tool. *British Journal of Clinical Psychology, 45,* 579–583.

Saal, F. E. (1978). Job involvement: A multivariate approach. *Journal of Applied Psychology, 63,* 53–61.

Salthouse, T. A. (2009). When does age-related cognitive decline begin? *Neurobiology of Aging, 30,* 507–514.

Salthouse, T. A., Atkinson, T. M., & Berish, D. E. (2003). Executive functioning as a potential mediator of age-related cognitive decline in normal adults. *Journal of Experimental Psychology: General, 132,* 566–594.

Schaie, K. W. (1996). Intellectual development in adulthood. In J. E. Birren & K. W. Schaie (Eds.), *Handbook of the Psychology of Aging* (4th ed.) (pp. 266–286). San Diego, CA: Academic Press.

Scheibe, S., & Blanchard-Fields, F. (2009). Effects of regulating emotions on cognitive performance: What is costly for young adults is not so costly for older adults. *Psychology and Aging, 24,* 217–223.

Scheibe, S., & Carstensen, L. L. (2010). Emotional aging: Recent findings and future trends. *Journal of Gerontology: Psychological Sciences, 65B,* 135–144.

Scheibe, S., & Zacher, H. (2013). A lifespan perspective on emotion regualtion, stress, and well-being in the workplace. In P. L. Perrewé, J. Halbesleben, & C. C. Rosen (Eds.), *Research in Occupational Stress and Well-Being: The Role of Emotion and Emotion Regulation* (Vol. 11) (pp. 163–193). Bingley: Emerald.

Scott, B. A., & Barnes, C. M. (2011). A multilevel field investigation of emotional labor, affect, work withdrawal, and gender. *Academy of Management Journal, 54,* 116–136.

Sheppes, G., & Meiran, N. (2008). Divergent cognitive costs for online forms of reappraisal and distraction. *Emotion, 8,* 870–874.

Shiota, M. N., & Levenson, R. W. (2009). Effects of aging on experimentally instructed detached reappraisal, positive reappraisal, and emotional behavior suppression. *Psychology and Aging, 24,* 890–900.

Silver, H., Goodman, C., Knoll, G., & Isakov, V. (2004). Brief emotion training improves recognition of facial emotions in chronic schizophrenia. A pilot study. *Psychiatry Research, 128,* 147–154.

Sliter, M., Sliter, K., & Jex, S. (2012). The employee as a punching bag: The effect of multiple sources of incivility on employee withdrawal behavior and sales performance. *Journal of Organizational Behavior, 33,* 121–139.

Sliter, M., Chen, Y., Withrow, S., & Sliter, K. (2013). Older and (emotionally) smarter? Emotional intelligence as a mediator in the relationship between age and emotional labor strategies in service employees. *Experimental Aging Research, 39,* 466–479.

Stanley, J. T., & Isaacowitz, D. M. (2012). Socioemotional perspectives on adult development. In S. K. Whitbourne & M. J. Sliwinski (Eds.), *The Wiley-Blackwell Handbook of Adulthood and Aging* (pp. 236–253). New York: Blackwell.

Sterns, H. L., & Miklos, S. M. (1995). The aging worker in a changing environment: Organizational and individual issues. *Journal of Vocational Behavior, 47,* 248–268.

Sullivan, S., Ruffman, T., & Hutton, S. B. (2007). Age differences in emotion recognition skills and the visual scanning of emotion faces. *Journal of Gerontology: Psychological Sciences, 62B,* 53–60.

Toossi, M. (2012). Labor force projections to 2020: A more slowly growing workforce. *Monthly Labor Review, 135,* 43–64.

Tsai, J. L., Levenson, R. W., & Carstensen, L. L. (2000). Autonomic, subjective, and expressive responses to emotional films in older and younger Chinese Americans and European Americans. *Psychology and Aging, 15,* 684–693.

Turel, O., Connelly, C. E., & Fisk, G. M. (2011). Service with an e-smile: Employee authenticity and customer usage of web-based services. *Proceedings of the 44th Hawaii International Conference on Systems Sciences,* 1–10.

U.S. Bureau of Labor (2010). *Bureau of Labor Statistics Report.* Washington, DC.

van Dierendonck, D., & Mevissen, N. (2002). Aggressive behavior of passengers, conflict management behavior, and burnout among trolley car drivers. *International Journal of Stress Management, 9,* 345–355.

Watson, D., Clark, L. A., & Tellegen, A. (1988). Development and validation of brief measures of positive and negative affect: The PANAS scales. *Journal of Personality and Social Psychology, 54,* 1063–1070.

Wegge, J., Vogt, J., & Wecking, C. (2007). Customer-induced stress in call centre work: A comparison of audio- and videoconference. *Journal of Occupational and Organizational Psychology, 80,* 693–712.

Weiss, H. M., & Cropanzano, R. (1996). Affective events theory: A theoretical discussion of the structure, causes and consequences of affective experiences at work. In B. M. S. L. L. Cummings (Ed.), *Research in Organizational Behavior: An Annual Series of Analytical Essays and Critical Reviews, Vol. 18* (pp. 1–74). Greenwich, CT: Elsevier Science/JAI Press.

Williams, L. M., Brown, K. J., Palmer, D., Liddell, B. J., Kemp, A. H., Olivieri, G., Peduto, A., & Gordon, E. (2006). The mellow years? Neural basis of improving emotional stability over age. *Journal of Neuroscience, 26*, 6422–6430.

Wood, P. M., & Kroese, B. S. (2007). Enhancing the emotion recognition skills of individuals with learning disabilities: A review of the literature. *Journal of Applied Research in Intellectual Disabilities, 20*, 576–579.

Yang, J., & Diefendorff, J. M. (2009). The relations of daily counterproductive workplace behavior with emotions, situational antecedents, and personality moderators: A diary study in Hong Kong. *Personnel Psychology, 62*, 259–295.

Zapf, D. (2002). Emotion work and psychological well-being: A review of the literature and some conceptual considerations. *Human Resource Management Review, 12*, 237–268.

Issue 4

Practical Workplace Changes and Challenges

9

Workplace Intervention Effectiveness Across the Lifespan

Keith L. Zabel and Boris B. Baltes

The purpose of this chapter is to put forth a future research agenda on how workplace interventions can be utilized across the lifespan to increase positive outcomes for both employees and organizations. First, we define workplace interventions and describe the four types we consider throughout the chapter. Second, we describe two aging and development theories, namely socio-emotional selectivity (SEST) theory (Carstensen, 1992) and selection, optimization, and compensation (SOC) theory (Baltes & Baltes, 1990), which we use to develop suggestions for our research agenda. Third, we incorporate several underutilized conceptualizations of age that may impact the effectiveness of workplace interventions across the lifespan. Finally, we focus on each workplace intervention separately and discuss future research possibilities.

WORKPLACE INTERVENTIONS

As noted in Chapter 1 of the book, this chapter will address how workplace interventions can be designed across the lifespan to increase effectiveness through four different lenses of aging, which include *demographic, economic, technological,* and *cultural perspectives*. Workplace interventions have been defined as "the activity through which changes in elements of an organizational work setting are implemented" (Robertson, Roberts, & Porras, 1993, p. 620). Even though there are several other existing frameworks of workplace interventions (e.g., Guzzo, Jette, & Katzell, 1985; Neuman, Edwards, & Raju, 1989), we chose to use Robertson and colleagues' (1993) framework because it included aspects of the other conceptualizations, and added an additional important intervention—physical setting. Robertson and colleagues (1993) defined four types of workplace interventions, including *social* (e.g., team building), *organizing* (e.g., flextime), *technostructural* (e.g., job enrichment) and *physical setting* (e.g., move to an open office space). As we explain a future research agenda for these four types of interventions in regards to aging across the lifespan, we will use two aging theories, namely SOC and SEST, to propose alternative hypotheses around the research agenda.

SOC AND SEST

SOC theory (Baltes & Baltes, 1990) posits that individuals fully capitalize on their development by *selecting* goals, *optimizing* the correct amount and type of resources to achieve the goals, and *compensating* for losses in resources that occur as individuals move toward goal attainment (Baltes & Baltes, 1990). Use of SOC behaviors has been related to numerous beneficial outcomes for individuals across the lifespan, including early adulthood (e.g., partner and career satisfaction in Wiese, Freund, & Baltes, 2000), middle adulthood, and late adulthood (e.g., job performance in Bajor & Baltes, 2003).

SEST (Carstensen, 1992) posits that individuals' motivation for social contact and type of social contact is determined by their goals and life stage. For example, individuals in early and later stages of life are typically motivated to emotionally regulate, whereas individuals at middle life stages are typically motivated to seek information about their world (Carstensen, 1995). Therefore, SEST posits that as individuals move from early adulthood to old age, they become increasingly more selective in how they invest their emotional resources (Carstensen, 1992). Indeed, in her seminal work, Carstensen (1992) found that, starting in early adulthood, individuals began decreasing the number of close friends they invested in emotionally, but increased interaction frequency with their spouse and siblings, a trend that continued throughout adulthood. Because SEST describes how motivation for social contact changes across the lifespan, it is paramount that this theory is incorporated into a future research agenda on how to design workplace interventions across the lifespan.

USING CONCEPTUALIZATIONS OF AGE OTHER THAN CHRONOLOGICAL

Even though scholars nearly always define age as one's age in years (i.e., chronological age), recent reviews (e.g., Kooij, de Lange, & Dikkers, 2008; Kooij, de Lange, Jansen, Kanfer, & Dikkers, 2011) have begun to focus on the other ways age can be conceptualized. For example, age can also be defined as one's *functional age* (e.g., one's health status), *psychosocial age* (e.g., how old one feels, acts), *organizational age* (e.g., job tenure), and *lifespan concept of age* (e.g., number of dependents, marital status) (Kooij et al., 2008). Meta-analytic evidence from Kooij and colleagues (2008, 2011) suggests that the way age is defined has important implications for the relationship between aging across the lifespan and motives to continue working. As one example, Kooij and colleagues (2011) found the negative relationship between chronological age and growth motives was strongest for employees over age 40, and weakest for those aged 36–40. These results suggest that the relationship between age and growth motives is curvilinear in nature when one uses the chronological age conceptualization of age. One explanation for this finding is that the lifespan conceptualization of age (e.g., age of youngest child in the home, marital status) impacts the relationship between chronological age and growth motives.

Recent research also suggests there may be utility in using other conceptualizations of age to study the effectiveness of workplace interventions. Specifically, major U.S. organizations consider organizational age measures (e.g., job tenure, career stage) and the lifespan concept of age to be at least moderately relevant to their organizations' talent management strategies. In contrast, chronological age and generational cohorts are considered less relevant (Sloan Center on Aging & Work, 2010). When one takes into account that most workplace age researchers focus on chronological age, clearly there is an academic-practitioner gap—one that might be closed by research on the relative value of different age constructs in understanding workplace interventions. As we describe a future research agenda for the four types of interventions, please see Table 9.1 for a summary of the future research agenda across all four types of interventions and perspectives.

TABLE 9.1
Future Research Suggestions to Examine the Effectiveness of Workplace Interventions Across the Lifespan

Type of Intervention	Perspectives			
	Demographic	Economic	Technological	Cultural
Social	• Determine how age impacts the effectiveness of team-building interventions based on components of team building. • Determine how age impacts one's interest to be part of team-building interventions.	• Determine how age diversity impacts the success of team-building interventions. • Determine how workgroup size impacts the effectiveness of team building for age-diverse teams, relative to homogenous younger or older workgroups.	• Determine how virtual team building can best be structured across the lifespan.	• Determine how age affects social interventions in non-Western nations through the lens of age diversity.
Organizing	• Determine how flextime culture impacts the decision to recruit mid-/late-career candidates. • Determine why employees with young children are more likely to use flextime than those without young children.	• Determine how eldercare arrangements and flexibility impact recruitment, tenure, and perceptions on the job.	• Determine how organizational age impacts flextime across the lifespan.	• Determine how national culture impacts the success of organizing arrangements across the lifespan.

Techno-structural	• Examine the effectiveness of job enlargement/enrichment interventions across the lifespan, using growth autonomy motives to develop hypotheses. • Determine whether growth or autonomy needs to play a more important role across the lifespan in predicting the success of the intervention.	• Determine how losses in fluid intelligence but gains in crystallized intelligence impact the success of the intervention.	• Determine how functional age impacts the success of the intervention, especially in burgeoning industries.	• Determine how age impacts autonomy/growth motives in non-Western nations, and the impact of that finding on the effectiveness of job-enlargement and job-enrichment interventions.
Physical setting	• Determine how work motives explain older workers' dissatisfaction with moves to open offices.	• Determine how noise explains older workers' dissatisfaction with moves to open offices.	• Determine how privacy and perceptions of physical space explain age-related differences in satisfaction.	• Determine how noise and space perceptions impact the move to open offices in emerging markets.

SOCIAL INTERVENTIONS

As described by Neuman et al. (1989), the purpose of social interventions is to increase organizational performance by valuing employee relations and changing attitudes and perceptions about work-related issues. Even though there are a number of social interventions (e.g., participation in decision-making, training groups) (Neuman et al., 1989), this chapter focuses on team building given it is one of the most popular social interventions (Neuman et al., 1989). Although the context of team-building interventions can vary from outdoor experiential activities to corporate boardrooms, a recent meta-analysis suggests that team-building interventions involve four major components, including goal setting, interpersonal relations, role clarification, and problem-solving (Klein et al., 2009). Team-building interventions can be defined as any workgroup interventions that involve one or all of the aforementioned components, in varying degrees (Salas, Rozell, Mullen, & Driskell, 1999).

Meta-analytic evidence suggests that team building is a successful organizational development intervention, leading to increased job satisfaction (Neuman et al., 1989). Meta-analytic evidence also suggests that all four components of team building lead to increased intervention effectiveness, and that the positive effects of team building are doubled when the size of the group going through the intervention is greater than 10 as opposed to less than 10 (Klein et al., 2009). Our review found no studies that have examined how age impacts the effectiveness of team-building interventions. Using the *demographic perspective*, the fact that older workers will continue to delay retirement to later ages has implications for a future research agenda on team building.

Specifically, future research needs to examine how different conceptualizations of age might differentially predict the success of team building. Our literature review found no studies that have examined the link between age and team building. SEST (Carstensen, 1992) posits that as individuals age, the importance of social motives (e.g., need for affiliation) for working decreases. Meta-analytic evidence (Kooij et al., 2011) and reviews of the literature (e.g., Rudolph, Baltes, & Zabel, 2013) support this proposal. Following this logic, one would argue that as individuals age, their desire to be part of a team-building intervention, or any intervention that requires prolonged social interaction, would decrease. Therefore, future research should examine if this is indeed the case.

Another important future research area is around the different components of team-building interventions. Most notably, SEST would posit the interpersonal relations component of team building to be the least effective component to include for older workers in team-building interventions. On the other hand, SOC would posit that older workers may benefit from a team-building intervention if the intervention relied upon the use of selection, optimization, and compensation strategies. Indeed, the team-building components of goal setting, role clarification, and problem-solving (Klein et al., 2009) map on well to the SOC strategies of selection, optimizing, and compensation. Therefore, future research should examine if there are differences in the effectiveness of team-building interventions across the lifespan based upon the components of team building that are present in the intervention.

Another important and understudied component of team building that uses the *lifespan* conceptualization of age is *age diversity*. Reviews of age diversity (e.g., Wegge & Schmidt, 2009) have agreed that age diversity more often than not is a negative predictor of subjective outcomes such as job satisfaction and objective outcomes such as turnover (e.g., Timmerman, 2000). Research also suggests age diversity negatively impacts health outcomes for younger and older employees, but not middle-aged employees (Liebermann, Wegge, Jungmann, & Schmidt, 2013). Using the *economic perspective*, given that workers need to work longer to support retirement, future research should examine how age diversity impacts the effectiveness of team-building interventions. Currently, no known studies have examined how the age diversity of teams impacts the effectiveness of team-building interventions. Social identity theory (Tajfel, 1978) and similarity attraction theory (Byrne, 1971) suggest that team building will be most effective with a homogenous workgroup as opposed to an age-diverse workgroup. On the other hand, theories on decision-making models in groups suggest that team building will be most effective in age-diverse workgroups (de Dreu, 2006) because diverse workgroups are more likely to have disagreements, which increase the cognitive complexity of the majority viewpoint, and ensure the workgroup is less prone to the social pressures of conformity and polarization (see de Dreu & West, 2001 for a review of relevant findings).

In a similar vein, because team building is most successful for workgroups of 10 or more employees (Klein et al., 2009) relative to fewer than 10 employees, future research should also examine how workgroup size impacts the effectiveness of team building for age-diverse teams, relative to homogenous younger or older workgroups. As workgroups will continue to become more heterogeneous as opposed to homogenous, it is imperative that a future research agenda on team building begins by examining how age diversity impacts the effectiveness of team-building interventions.

Using the *technological perspective*, because of globalization and increased capabilities of technology, virtual teams are more common than ever. Some previous research has begun to examine the formation of virtual team building (e.g., Huang, Wei, Watson, & Tan, 2002). Future research needs to examine how age diversity impacts virtual team building, as well as face-to-face team building (as discussed previously). The intersection of age and team building would seem to have an enhanced effect on virtual team building, given that social motives tend to decrease as individuals age (Kooij et al., 2011) and previous research suggests that older individuals are stereotyped to have much lower willingness to learn and ability to learn new technological skills relative to their younger counterparts (van Dalen, Henkens, & Schippers, 2010). These previous findings would suggest that relative to their younger counterparts, virtual team building would be less successful for older individuals relative to younger individuals. Because team building leads to important outcomes for individuals and organizations when utilized correctly, these kinds of future studies are paramount.

Using the *cultural perspective*, there is an increasing need to examine the effectiveness of team-building interventions across different cultures and ages. The fact that work teams will continue to become more diverse both in terms of age and global origin means the interaction of those factors will also be important in predicting the success of team-building interventions. Given that no known studies have examined how age diversity affects team building, it is not surprising that research has not examined how the interaction of age diversity and global diversity predict the success of team-building interventions. Because previous research suggests that collectivistic cultures pay more respect to elders compared to individualistic cultures (Cuddy, Norton, & Fiske, 2005), it is hypothesized that in age-diverse teams, team building is more successful in collectivistic country cultures or work team cultures than individualistic country or work team cultures.

ORGANIZING INTERVENTIONS

Organizing interventions are utilized in order to provide coordination of activity for employees (Robertson et al., 1993). Organizing interventions are popular because they can often increase the bottom line for organizations, while simultaneously increasing engagement, job satisfaction, and performance, and decreasing turnover (e.g., Baltes, Briggs, Huff, Wright, & Neuman, 1999). Meta-analytic evidence (e.g., Baltes et al., 1999) suggests flextime positively predicts productivity and job satisfaction, and negatively predicts absenteeism. Our search yielded only one academic study that has examined how aging impacts flextime, with findings suggesting that married men and those with preschool-aged children are more likely to use flextime than married females and those with no children under the age of 17 living in the household, respectively (Sharpe, Hermsen, & Billings, 2002).

Given flextime has increased and will only continue to increase because of technological advances, the *demographic perspective* tells us a systematic research agenda that examines how the effectiveness of flextime depends on a conceptualizations of age other than chronological age is warranted. In conjunction with different conceptualizations of age, one particularly useful future research area is examining the effectiveness of flextime policies in the recruitment process, and the ability of age and different conceptualizations of age to moderate that relationship. Specifically, using the *lifespan* concept of age (e.g., number and age of dependents, marital status), future research should examine how the different lifespan variables impact the effectiveness of flextime options during the recruitment process.

Recent research on the recruitment of older workers may provide insight on a future research agenda. Specifically, findings from one study suggest that the age of incumbents is a positive predictor of organizations' decision to recruit older job applicants (Goldberg, Perry, Finkelstein, & Shull, 2013). Therefore, one future research agenda should examine how the flextime use or flextime culture of an organization impacts the decision to recruit mid-career or late-career candidates, who would be more likely to benefit from flextime options relative to younger workers. In addition, future research should examine the reasons why employees with young children are more likely to use flextime than those without young children (Sharpe et al., 2002). Using attraction-selection-attrition theory (Schneider, 1987), one explanation is that employees with young children only apply to organizations with flextime options. Future research should also examine if organizations with flextime options enjoy an advantage to their industry counterparts during the recruitment process, and if that process is impacted by age. If so, then flextime is not only important for retaining talent, but getting it to come through the door in the first place, and age is an important variable to incorporate into future studies.

We can use SOC and SEST to develop hypotheses for this specific future research agenda. Specifically, SEST would posit that as individuals age, flextime options that allow for more flexible work locations (e.g., flexspace) as well as flextime options would be important, because employees will be focused on maintaining their relationships with a small inner circle of friends and relatives. At a young age, SEST would posit that flextime or flexspace is not that important. Therefore, one would expect the importance of flextime/flexspace during the recruitment process to be more important for older workers relative to younger workers. On the other hand, SOC posits that as individuals age, need for security increases (Rudolph et al., 2013). Because older workers seem to place more emphasis on job security relative to younger workers, and feelings of security are more likely to come from actually being in an office work environment as opposed to utilizing flextime or flexspace options, SOC would posit that the effectiveness of flextime during the recruitment process would be more important for younger workers relative to older workers. Because these two robust aging theories give different predictions, this is an important area for future research.

Using the *economic perspective*, future research using the *lifespan* conceptualization of age should examine how eldercare impacts the effectiveness and importance of flextime interventions. Because life expectancy continues to increase and baby boomers are reaching ages where they may need to simultaneously care for an elder parent and child, eldercare will only continue to become an even more important issue for organizations to contend with. As of now, there is limited empirical research on eldercare (e.g., Center on an Aging Society, 2005), and the evidence that is available suggests that eldercare will continue to increase in prevalence (e.g., Center on an Aging Society, 2005).

Much more research is needed to determine how eldercare impacts the importance of flextime interventions during the recruitment process, as well as once individuals are part of the organizations. In addition, it will become increasingly important for organizations to understand how eldercare needs to change across the lifespan in the coming years. Using *chronological age*, SOC and SEST would posit that older or middle-aged workers who have eldercare responsibilities would benefit significantly more by use of flextime interventions relative to their counterparts. Specifically, those theories would posit that the organizing interventions would lead to less resource depletion because workers could use the organizing intervention to use their time most effectively to care for their elders. Given demographic and economic trends, this is an important area for future research.

There are a number of organizations that are utilizing organizing interventions to increase employee effectiveness. One of the more famous programs is the CVS Snowbird program. This particular program allows older employees at numerous different organizational levels and positions to move to a different CVS office location (often in the Southeast United States) for seasonal employment (Sloan Center on Aging & Work, 2012). Results of this program are that CVS has higher retention rates of older workers compared to other organizations. In addition, CVS has increased the proportion of older workers as a part of their organization from 7% to 22%. Indeed, CVS used the *economic perspective* to make this business decision, understanding current demographics made it more likely that both future workers and customers would be more likely to be older as opposed to younger individuals.

Using the *technological perspective*, future research should examine how organizing arrangements help organizations retain employees across the lifespan, focusing on the *organizational age* conceptualization (e.g., job tenure). Previous research suggests over one out of three organizations has done nothing to encourage late-career employees to continue working past retirement age (Pitt-Catsouphes, Matz-Costa, & Besen, 2007). This finding is important given that research suggests employers rate job tenure and career stage as moderately relevant to their organizations' talent management strategies, whereas chronological age and using generational cohorts are viewed as not at all relevant (Sloan Center on Aging & Work, 2010). Using the CVS Snowbird program as an example, clearly there are innovative ways organizations can incentivize late-career employees to continue working. Future research needs to place a greater emphasis on examining organizational age in regard to the success of organizing arrangements.

Finally, future research should use the *cultural perspective* and determine how successful flextime interventions are in non-Western nations, using age as an important moderator. Our literature review found only one academic study that has examined flextime in non-Western nations (Barney & Elias, 2010). Cross-cultural work on flexibility and work-family conflict suggests that while job flexibility reduces work-family conflict the most in Eastern cultures (e.g., China) and the United States, it actually increases work-family conflict in some other Western affluent nations (e.g., Australia) (Hill, Yang, Hawkins, & Ferris, 2004). This research suggests the importance of flextime varies as a function of national culture. The implication of this finding is that the impact of age on the effectiveness of flextime interventions may depend on the context in which it occurs, and that national culture is an important contextual variable to consider.

TECHNO-STRUCTURAL INTERVENTIONS

Techno-structural interventions are utilized in order to influence job design (Robertson et al., 1993) or change work content or method (Neuman et al., 1989). The two most common techno-structural interventions are job enrichment and job enlargement. Job enrichment refers to increasing one's vertical scope of the job while adding more responsibility and autonomy, whereas job enlargement refers to increasing the horizontal scope of one's job by adding more tasks but not responsibility (Hackman & Oldham, 1976). The majority of research on these two types of job design interventions has focused on the positive effects of job design interventions across a number of different sectors, such as education (Firestone, 1991) and the public sector (Raza & Nawaz, 2011). Although more research has focused on job enrichment as opposed to job enlargement, findings suggest both positively predict important outcomes such as self-efficacy (Parker, 1998) and organizational commitment (Raza & Nawaz, 2011). Previous scholars have noted that job enrichment and enlargement interventions likely lead to increased motivation (Chung & Ross, 1977), by increasing task variety (a job characteristic) and autonomy (a psychological state) (Hackman & Oldham, 1976), respectively.

Future research should begin to study job enrichment and enlargement interventions through the lens of career development, using the relationship between age and growth needs and age and autonomy needs as a guide. This future research area is especially important given that many organizations are designing career development programs with an emphasis on age (e.g., Deloitte's Mass Career Customization Initiative) (Sloan Center on Aging & Work, 2010). Previous meta-analytic (Kooij et al., 2011) and review (Rudolph et al., 2013) articles have noted that a small negative correlation exists between age and growth needs, whereas a positive correlation exists between age and autonomy needs (Kooij et al., 2011).

To the extent to which job enrichment interventions fulfill autonomy needs and job enlargement interventions fulfill growth needs, a future research agenda should examine if job enrichment interventions are more effective for older employees relative to younger employees. In addition, future research should examine if job enlargement interventions are more effective for younger employees relative to older employees. Findings from these studies would be paramount using the *demographic perspective* and the fact that older workers will continue to postpone retirement, whereas younger workers find more and more employment challenges.

SOC posits that as individuals age, they are likely to shift their orientation from maximizing gains to minimizing losses. Thus, SOC suggests that job enlargement interventions will be more successful for younger employees relative to older employees because younger employees have higher growth needs and are in the orientation of maximizing gains through increasing the number of tasks they perform, relative to their older counterparts. Similar hypotheses have been developed by Truxillo, Cadiz, Rineer, Zaniboni, & Fraccaroli (2012), who posited that task variety leads to greater job satisfaction, engagement, and job performance for younger workers relative to older workers. These propositions are buttressed by the finding that task variety leads to increased turnover intentions and burnout for older workers relative to younger workers, whereas increased skill variety leads to decreased turnover intentions for older workers relative to younger workers (Zaniboni, Truxillo, & Fraccaroli, 2013). Similarly, recent findings suggest at low levels of task variety, older workers have higher levels of work engagement relative to younger workers. On the other hand, at high levels of task variety, younger workers have higher levels of job satisfaction than older workers (Zaniboni, Truxillo, Fraccaroli, McCune, & Bertolino, in press). Because job enrichment interventions increase autonomy (which older employees desire) but also responsibility (which SOC might posit as less important for older employees), more research is needed to discern how job enrichment and job enlargement interventions impact effectiveness across the lifespan, using SOC to derive different hypotheses for the success of each intervention.

Similarly, future research needs to examine how facets of *functional age*, including health status and physical ability affect the success of techno-structural interventions across the lifespan. As a starting point, research should examine how the health status of employees impacts the effectiveness of all types of interventions that will be discussed in this chapter. Indeed, research suggests approximately 25% of adults have at least one physical disorder (Dewa & Lin, 2000), and that result holds constant across many different levels of work (e.g., unskilled manual employees to professional employees) (Dewa & Lin, 2000). Future research should examine how having a physical or mental disorder impacts the success of techno-structural interventions across the lifespan, especially since the effect of physical disorders is greater later in employees' careers while mental disorders are actually more prevalent earlier in employees' careers (de Girolamo, Dagani, Purcell, Cocchi, & McGorry, 2012).

Using the *economic perspective*, the conceptualization of chronological age has important implications for the success of techno-structural interventions across the lifespan. First, previous research suggests that age is associated with an increase in crystallized intelligence and decrease in fluid intelligence (e.g., Kanfer & Ackerman, 2004). These previous findings suggest that as individuals age chronologically, interventions with success based on prior learning and experiences (i.e., job enrichment) will lead to greater success because individuals can utilize the experience they have gained on similar tasks. On the other hand, these findings suggest that interventions with success based on reasoning abstractly and developing new problem-solving strategies (i.e., job enlargement) will be less successful as individuals age because they require problem-solving in novel situations. Future research needs to examine how crystallized and fluid intelligence impact the success of techno-structural interventions as employees age.

Using both the *economic* and *technological perspectives*, certain industries (e.g., medical) are certain to experience a high demand in jobs in the near future, given the aging workforce. Many of these types of jobs require high levels of physical ability (e.g., caregiver) or specialized training (e.g., doctor). Future research needs to examine the success of techno-structural interventions in different industries that are sure to grow in the future as a result of aging (e.g., medical, technology, construction). Thus, future research needs to examine how the interventions can be formulated across the lifespan to lead to success for employees in certain fields. For example, using functional age, one might posit that younger employers would be most able to complete the physical demands necessary for caregiving work or construction. To motivate younger employees in growing industries, an organization might first use a job enlargement intervention, and back it up with a job enrichment intervention to increase employees' feelings of responsibility and autonomy.

Finally, using the *cultural* perspective, there is a plethora of future research that needs to be done. First, future research needs to examine how the different conceptualizations of age impact motives for working in collectivist cultures. Currently, all research in this area has utilized American and Western European samples (Kooij et al., 2011). Given the focus in collectivist cultures is on the group as opposed to the individual, one might expect different patterns in terms of autonomy needs across the lifespan as one ages, relative to the finding of increasing autonomy needs as individuals age in individualistic cultures (Inceoglu, Segers, & Bartram, 2011).

Such a finding would have important ramifications for how one would expect techno-structural interventions, especially job enrichment, to impact effectiveness for older workers. After a link has been made between aging and work motives in collectivist nations, future research should examine the effectiveness of techno-structural interventions across the lifespan in collectivist countries. Such studies should especially focus on emerging markets (Khanna & Palepu, 2000), such as India, where many large multinational organizations continue to grow their employee base, bringing in the types of career development programs that exist outside of the emerging markets at their corporate headquarters. Answering these questions regarding the success of technostructural interventions for older individuals will be paramount as these emerging markets continue to grow.

PHYSICAL SETTING INTERVENTIONS

Physical setting interventions are utilized in order to change the physical space in which work takes place (Robertson et al., 1993). Research seems to be rather mixed on the effectiveness of physical setting interventions. Some studies find that changes to open offices increase communication (e.g., Sundstrom, Burt, & Kamp, 1980), whereas other studies have found that open office arrangements lead to decreased satisfaction, team member relations, and increased stress (e.g., Brennan, Church, & Kline, 2002). More recent research has examined generational differences in moves to open office arrangements (see Parry & Urwin, 2011 for a review of defining generational cohorts). This research suggests that Generation X and baby boomers are significantly more affected by changes to an open office, in terms of level of distraction and amount of office space perceived, relative to millennials (McElroy & Morrow, 2010).

Future research should examine why there seem to be differences in open office preference based on age and whether the effect holds using different conceptualizations of age other than chronological. SOC and SEST have important predictions for how age impacts moves to open offices. SEST suggests that as individuals age, their need for affiliation decreases because they become more selective in how they utilize their emotional resources. SOC posits that as individuals age, their need for security increases and need for autonomy increases, due to shifts in focusing from growth-related strategies to loss-prevention strategies. The two predictions from SEST and SOC are possible explanations for why older workers dislike moves to open offices relative to younger workers.

Using the *demographic perspective*, a future research agenda needs to test which theory best explains the phenomenon. The cause of age-related decreases in satisfaction with open office systems is important. Specifically, if need for affiliation is the most important moderator, there is very little organizations can do to mitigate the effects of open offices on older workers. On the other hand, if feelings of job security or need for autonomy are the most important moderators, the way the organization frames the move from traditional to open office may be extremely important in older employees' job satisfaction, engagement, and privacy.

Another variable that should be studied in tandem with conceptualizations of age and the success of physical setting interventions is noise. Previous research has found that increased noise is an important factor of the move to open offices that leads to decreased satisfaction and productivity (e.g., Sundstrom, Town, Rise, Osborn, & Brill, 1994). Kanfer and Ackerman's (2004) lifespan work motivation theory posits that four themes of development impact work motivation, including loss, growth, reorganization, and exchange. Specifically related to *loss*, research suggests that as individuals age chronologically, their performance decreases due to decreases in fluid intelligence (Kanfer & Ackerman, 2004). Given fluid intelligence and attention decrease as individuals age, the factor of noise in moving to open offices may be especially important and demotivating for older workers relative to younger workers. Indeed, Kanfer and Ackerman's (2004) work motivation theory would posit that the noise associated with the move to open offices would lead to increased effort needed by older workers to achieve typical performance, at a time when their performance is already decreasing due to decreases in fluid intelligence.

Using both *chronological age* and *functional age*, one explanation for the dissatisfaction with the move to open offices is the increased level of noise associated with the move. Using the *economic perspective*, future research on the intersection of noise and functional age in predicting the effectiveness of physical setting interventions is important for two reasons. First, more and more of the workforce is made up of older workers and the move to open offices continues to increase. Second, if noise level is an important factor that leads to decreased satisfaction for older workers, there is something organizations can actively work on to decrease the effect.

Similar to studying the effects of noise, future studies should examine how other factors of physical setting interventions impact satisfaction. For example, previous research has found that satisfaction after the move to an open-office system is predicted by perceptions of space evaluation and lighting quality (Spreckelmeyer, 1993), as well as privacy (Birnholtz, Gutwin, & Hawkey, 2007). Using the *technological perspective*, SOC and

SEST would posit that variables such as privacy are more important for older employees relative to younger employees given their security needs. Similarly, Kanfer and Ackerman's (2004) work motivation theory would posit that the noise associated with moves to open offices are more important to for older employees relative to younger employees, given the decreases in performance that already exist for older workers due to decreases in fluid intelligence. On the other hand, perceptions of the physical space might be more important for younger employees, who have higher growth needs. Using the lifespan conceptualization of age, employees with children, spouses, or eldercare issues may be more impacted by privacy compared to those without others to care for, given the need to have private conversations about a variety of issues. Future research needs to examine how variables such as privacy and space evaluation in open offices differ across the lifespan using all the conceptualizations of age.

Finally, using the *cultural perspective*, future research should examine how age impacts the effectiveness of physical setting interventions in non-Western nations. This research agenda will become increasingly important in the future as organizations try to take a standardized approach toward managing physical setting interventions in emerging markets in very different corners of the world (e.g., China, Brazil, India, Africa). It is very possible that perceptions of noise and space evaluation after the move to open offices are not as important factors in densely populated emerging markets such as China or India relative to less populated emerging markets such as, generally speaking, the continent of Africa. The different contexts of emerging markets have implications for the impact of age on physical setting intervention effectiveness.

CONCLUSIONS

This chapter described a number of future research areas to examine how four types of workplace interventions impact workplace effectiveness across the lifespan. It is vital that future research incorporates different conceptualizations of age and workplace motives into studying the effectiveness of workplace interventions. Given the widespread use of team building, flextime, and job enlargement/enrichment interventions, it is recommended that future research examine how the four aging perspectives influence the effectiveness of these interventions before moving to the less-studied physical setting interventions. In terms of the aging perspectives, very little work has examined how national culture impacts the effectiveness of workplace interventions. Given that emerging markets are located in many different areas of the world and will be particularly attractive locations for large global companies to build new locations, it is imperative that future research begins to examine how national culture impacts the effectiveness of workplace interventions. Given that the aging of the global workforce will only accelerate in the coming years, capitalizing on the research agendas presented in this chapter is of great importance to academics and practitioners alike.

REFERENCES

Bajor, J. K., & Baltes, B. B. (2003). The relationship between selection, optimization with compensation, conscientiousness, motivation, and performance. *Journal of Vocational Behavior, 63,* 347–367.

Baltes, B. B., Briggs, T. E., Huff, J. W., Wright, J. A., & Neuman, G. A. (1999). Flexible and compressed workweek schedules: A meta-analysis of their effects on work-related criteria. *Journal of Applied Psychology, 84,* 496–513.

Baltes, P. B., & Baltes, M. M. (1990). Psychological perspectives on successful aging: The model of selective optimization with compensation. In P. B. Baltes & M. M. Baltes (Eds.), *Successful Aging: Perspectives from the Behavioral Sciences* (pp. 1–34). New York: Cambridge University Press.

Barney, C. E., & Elias, S. M. (2010). Flex-time as a moderator of the job stress-work motivation relationship: A three nation investigation. *Personnel Review, 39,* 487–502.

Birnholtz, J. P., Gutwin, C., & Hawkey, K. (2007). Privacy in the open: How attention mediates awareness and privacy in open-plan offices. *Proceedings of the 2007 International ACM Conference on Supporting Group Work.*

Brennan, A., Chugh, J. S., & Kline, T. (2002). Traditional versus open office design: A longitudinal field study. *Environment and Behavior, 34,* 279–299.

Byrne, D. (1971). *The Attraction Paradigm.* Orlando, FL: Academic Press.

Carstensen, L. L. (1992). Social and emotional patterns in adulthood: Support for socioemotional selectivity theory. *Psychology & Aging, 7,* 331–338.

Carstensen, L. L. (1995). Evidence for a life-span theory of socioemotional selectivity. *Current Directions in Psychological Science, 4,* 151–156.

Center on an Aging Society (2005). *A Decade of Informal Caregiving: Are Today's Informal Caregivers Different than Informal Caregivers a Decade Ago?* (Data Profile No. 1). Washington, DC: Center on an Aging Society. Available at: http://hpi.georgetown.edu/agingsociety/pubhtml/caregiver1/caregiver1.html (accessed February 12, 2014).

Chung, K. H., & Ross, M. F. (1977). Differences in motivational properties between job enlargement and job enrichment. *Academy of Management Review, 2,* 113–122.

Cuddy, A. J. C., Norton, M. I., & Fiske, S. T. (2005). This old stereotype: The pervasiveness and persistence of the elderly stereotype. *Journal of Social Issues, 61,* 267–285.

de Dreu, C. K. W. (2006). When too little or too much hurts: Evidence for a curvilinear relationship between task conflict and innovation in teams. *Journal of Management, 32,* 83–107.

de Dreu, C. K. W., & West, M. A. (2001). Minority dissent and team innovation: The importance of participation in decision making. *Journal of Applied Psychology, 86*, 1191–1201.

de Girolamo, G., Dagani, J., Purcell, R., Cocchi, A., & McGorry, P. D. (2012). Age of onset of mental disorders and use of mental health services: Needs, opportunities, and obstacles. *Epidemiology and Psychiatric Sciences, 21*, 47–57.

Dewa, C. S., & Lin, E. (2000). Chronic physical illness, psychiatric disorder and disability in the workplace. *Social Science & Medicine, 51*, 41–50.

Firestone, W. A. (1991). Merit pay and job enlargement as reforms: Incentives, implementation, and teacher response. *Educational Evaluation and Policy Analysis, 13*, 269–288.

Goldberg, C. B., Perry, E. L., Finkelstein, L. M., & Shull, A. (2013). Antecedents and outcomes of targeting older applicants in recruitment. *European Journal of Work and Organizational Psychology, 22*, 265–278.

Guzzo, R. A., Jette, R. D., & Katzell, R. A. (1985). The effects of psychologically based intervention programs on work productivity: A meta-analysis. *Personnel Psychology, 38*, 275–291.

Hackman, J. R., & Oldham, G. R. (1976). Motivation through the design of work: Test of a theory. *Organization Behavior and Human Performance, 16*, 250–279.

Hill, E. J., Yang, C., Hawkins, A. J., & Ferris, M. (2004). A cross-cultural test of the work-family interface in 48 countries. *Journal of Marriage and Family, 66*, 1300–1316.

Huang, W. W., Wei, K., Watson, R. T., & Tan, B. C. Y. (2002). Supporting virtual team-building with a GSS: An empirical investigation. *Decision Support Systems, 34*, 359–367.

Inceoglu, I., Segers, J., & Bartram, D. (2012). Age-related differences in work motivation. *Journal of Occupational and Organizational Psychology, 85*, 300–329.

Kanfer, R., & Ackerman, P. L. (2004). Aging, adult development and work motivation. *Academy of Management Review, 29*, 440–458.

Khanna, T., & Palepu, K. (2000). Is group affiliation profitable in emerging markets? An analysis of diversified Indian business groups. *Journal of Finance, 55*, 867–891.

Klein, C., Diazgranados, D., Salas, E., Le, H., Burke, C. S., Lyons, R., & Goodwin, G. F. (2009). Does team building work? *Small Group Research, 40*, 181–222.

Kooij, D., de Lange, A., Jansen, P., & Dikkers, J. (2008). Older workers' motivation to continue to work: Five meanings of age: A conceptual review. *Journal of Managerial Psychology, 23*, 364–394.

Kooij, D. T. A. M., de Lange, A. H., Jansen, P. G. W., Kanfer, R., & Dikkers, J. S. E. (2011). Age and work-related motives: Results of a meta-analysis. *Journal of Organizational Behavior, 32*, 197–225.

Liebermann, S. C., Wegge, J., Jungmann, F., & Schmidt, K. H. (2013). Age diversity and individual team member health: The moderating role of age and age stereotypes. *Journal of Occupational and Organizational Psychology, 86*, 184–202.

McElroy, J. C., & Morrow, P. C. (2010). Employee reactions to office redesign: A naturally occurring quasi-field experiment in a multi-generational setting. *Human Relations, 63*, 609–636.

Neuman, G. A., Edwards, J. E., & Raju, N. S. (1989). Organizational development interventions: A meta-analysis of their effects on satisfaction and other attitudes. *Personnel Psychology, 42*, 461–489.

Parker, S. K. (1998). Enhancing role breadth self-efficacy: The roles of job enrichment and other organizational interventions. *Journal of Applied Psychology, 83*, 835–852.

Parry, E., & Urwin, P. (2011). Generational differences in work values: A review of theory and evidence. *International Journal of Management Reviews*, 13, 79–96.

Pitt-Catsouphes, M., Smyer, M. A., Matz-Costa, C., & Kane, K. (2007). The national study report: Phase II of the national study of business strategy and workforce development. Research Highlight No. 04. Chestnut Hill, MA: The Center on Aging & Work/Workplace Flexibility. Available at: http://agingandwork.bc.edu/documents/RH04_NationalStudy_03-07_004.pdf (accessed December 20, 2013).

Raza, M. A., & Nawaz, M. M. (2011). Impact of job enlargement on employees' job satisfaction, motivation, and organizational commitment: Evidence from public sector of Pakistan. *International Journal of Business and Social Science*, 2, 268–273.

Robertson, P. J., Roberts, D. R., & Porras, J. I. (1993). Dynamics of planned organizational change: Assessing empirical support for a theoretical model. *Academy of Management Journal*, 36, 619–634.

Rudolph, C. W., Baltes, B. B., & Zabel, K. L. (2013). Age and work motives. In J. Field, R. J. Burke, & C. L. Cooper (Eds.), *The Sage Handbook of Aging, Work, and Society*. London: Sage.

Salas, E., Rozell, D., Mullen, B., & Driskell, J. E. (1999). The effect of team building on performance: An integration. *Small Group Research*, 30, 309–329.

Schneider, B. (1987). The people make the place. *Personnel Psychology*, 40, 437–453.

Sharpe, D. L., Hermsen, J. M., & Billings, J. (2002). Factors associated with having flextime: A focus on married workers. *Journal of Family and Economic Issues*, 23, 51–72.

Sloan Center on Aging & Work (2010). Executive case summary series: Talent management and the prism of age. Chestnut Hill, MA. Available at: www.bc.edu/content/dam/files/research_sites/agingandwork/pdf/publications/case_TM.pdf (accessed December 20, 2013).

Sloan Center on Aging & Work (2012). CVS Caremark Snowbird Program. Chestnut Hill, MA. Available at: http://capricorn.bc.edu/agingandwork/database/browse/case_study/24047 (accessed December 20, 2013).

Spreckelmeyer, K. F., (1993). Office relocation and environmental change: A case study. *Environment and Behavior*, 25, 181–204.

Sundstrom, E., Burt, R. E., & Kamp, D. (1980). Privacy at work: Architectural correlates of job satisfaction and job performance. *Academy of Management Journal*, 23, 1101–1117.

Sundstrom, E., Town, J. P., Rice, R. W., Osborn, D. P., & Brill, M. (1994). Office noise, satisfaction, and performance. *Environment and Behavior*, 26, 195–222.

Tajfel, H. (1978). Social categorization, social identify, and social comparison. In H. Tajfel (Ed.), *Differentiation Between Social Groups* (pp. 61–76). New York: Academic Press.

Timmerman, T. A. (2000). Racial diversity, age diversity, interdependence, and team performance. *Small Group Research*, 31, 592–606.

Truxillo, D. M., Cadiz, D. M., Rineer, J. R., Zaniboni, S., & Fraccaroli, F. (2012). A lifespan perspective on job design: Fitting the job and the worker to promote job satisfaction, engagement, and performance. *Organizational Psychology Review*, 2, 340–360.

van Dalen, H. P., Henkens, K., & Schippers, J. (2010). Productivity of older workers: Perceptions of employers and employees. *Population and Development Review*, 36, 309–330.

Wegge, J., & Schmidt, K. (2009). The impact of age diversity in teams on group performance, innovation, and health. In A. S. Antoniou, C. L. Cooper, G. P. Chrousous, C. D. Spielberger, & M. W. Eysenck (Eds.), *Handbook of Managerial Behavior and Occupational Health* (pp. 79–94). Northampton: Elgar.

Wiese, B. S., Freund, A. M., & Baltes, P. B. (2000). Selection, optimization, and compensation. An action-related approach to work and partnership. *Journal of Vocational Behavior, 57,* 273–300.

Zaniboni, S., Truxillo, D. M., & Fraccaroli, F. (2013). Differential effects of task variety and skill variety on burnout and turnover intentions for older and younger workers. *European Journal of Work and Organizational Psychology, 22,* 306–317.

Zaniboni, S., Truxillo, D. M., Fraccaroli, F., McCune, E. A., & Bertolino, M. (2014). Who benefits from more tasks? Older versus younger workers. *Journal of Managerial Psychology, 29,* 508–523.

10

Retirement and Bridge Employment: People, Context, and Time

Yujie Zhan and Mo Wang

The workforce is aging. This demographic change in the workforce has greatly shaped and facilitated research on older workers' career decisions such as retirement and working after retirement. Today, retirement is defined as a process that occurs over a period of time, starting with planning and decision-making a long time before the actual exit from the workforce, and not completed until one adjusts to retirement (Beehr, 1986; Wang & Shi, 2014). On the one hand, due to the increase in life expectancy, people do not view retirement as approaching the end of life anymore. Rather, many people have started to view retirement as a new life stage when they can pursue goals that cannot be reached while working (Shultz & Wang, 2011; Wang & Shultz, 2010; Wang, Henkens, & van Solinge, 2011). This also provides the opportunity for working longer and working in a different industry to those who desire to do so (Wang, Zhan, Liu, & Shultz, 2008). On the other hand, the increased life expectancy combined with the rising healthcare costs also brings financial challenges to individuals who expect a longer period of retirement (Adams & Rau, 2011). Some older workers may face the necessity of working longer to secure the financial aspects of their retirement life. From the employers' perspective, because of the aging trend, some employers may experience labor force shortages. They could potentially benefit from hiring older workers given older workers' experiences and reliability (Ng & Feldman, 2008, 2013). Therefore, the recent years have witnessed an increase in the labor force participation exhibited by older workers as they leave their career jobs and move toward complete work withdrawal, namely bridge employment (Shultz, 2003; Wang & Shi, 2014).

These changes have generated a number of studies in industrial-organizational (I-O) psychology research that have attempted to understand retirement and bridge employment. In spite of the existing findings, there are still many important questions that need to be addressed in the research area of retirement and bridge employment.

In this chapter, we focus on issues that we believe will move the research area of retirement and bridge employment forward in the near future. First, we discuss research questions in this research area in terms of three key elements, people, context, and time, in understanding the retirement process. We organize research questions in this way rather than based on different retirement stages because: (a) research effort focusing on different retirement stages should be better integrated to provide complete knowledge about the retirement process; and (b) it might be fruitful to systematically examine people, context, and time as three key elements for *any* retirement stage. Next, given the changes in socioeconomic background and the aging trend globally, we discuss research questions that are specific to bridge employment, which is believed to be one of the critical areas in future retirement research (Shultz & Wang, 2011). Finally, we conclude with general thoughts about theoretical and methodological advancements in this research area.

PEOPLE, CONTEXT, AND TIME

People, context, and time are three key elements that drive our understanding of the retirement process and bridge employment. Following the person-centered approach, we suggest that studying individuals' experiences, including individual characteristics that shape their experiences, the situations in which experiences occur, and the patterns of how experiences change across time, is important in deriving research questions in the literature of retirement and bridge employment (Liu, Zhan, & Wang, 2011; Weiss & Rupp, 2011). Accordingly, we propose several directions for future research in this area based on these three elements and their combinations (see Table 10.1).

People: Subjective Voluntariness and Motives

Retirement research has often viewed retirement as a normative life transition that has similar impacts across people. Thus, to explore the consequences of retirement, past research has relied on the comparisons between retirees and older workers. However, retirement and bridge

TABLE 10.1

People, Context, and Time Issues in Retirement and Bridge Employment Research

	Research Questions	*Methodological Issues*
People	Subjective experiences of voluntariness of retirement and bridge employment	Better measurement of subjective experiences; configural analysis
	Motivational mechanisms of taking bridge employment	
	Identification of sub-populations of older workers and retirees	
Context	Work context: age composition at work, ageism climate, organizational policies and practices related to aging workers, organizational and occupational norms	Data collection from multiple sources; multiple levels of analysis
	Interpersonal context: interpersonal relationships, social networks	
	Family context: financial condition, caring obligations, marital status and quality, spouse employment status	
	External context: macroeconomic trend, labor market demands, government policies related to pension and old-age security systems	
Time	Change patterns of attitudes, intentions, behaviors, and well-being in retirement	Longitudinal design; repeated measures
	Interrelations among different stages throughout the retirement process	
People × Context	Context that raises the salience of situational features	
	Context that serves as situational strength	
	Person-environment fit approach that explains retirement and bridge employment decisions	
People × Time	Different change patterns based on sub-populations	

employment could carry different meanings for older adults with different experiences. As suggested by the person-centered approach, individuals form perceptions and take actions based on their reflections of personal experiences (Weiss & Rupp, 2011). Thus, even when retirement decisions and/or bridge employment decisions are made by older adults themselves, some may perceive their retirement and/or bridge employment to be less voluntary than others, and thus engage in different adjustment patterns based on different interpretations of retirement motives. For example, when some older workers feel that they have to retire due to health concerns or dependent care obligations, they are likely to perceive themselves to be forced into retirement (Szinovacz & Davey, 2005). Similarly, when some retirees feel they have to go back to the workplace under financial pressure, they are likely to perceive themselves to be forced into bridge employment.

To our knowledge, although voluntariness has been demonstrated to have an important influence on retirees, only a few studies have compared voluntary and involuntary retirees' retirement decision and adjustment. For example, Shultz, Morton, and Weckerle (1998) identified a set of push (i.e., negative considerations for retirement decision) and pull (i.e., positive considerations for retirement decision) factors that distinguished retirees who felt they were forced to retire from those who viewed their early retirement decision as voluntary, and found that voluntary retirement was associated with higher life satisfaction and better health. Given the difference in people's feelings of voluntariness of retirement and bridge employment, subjective voluntariness could be an important factor that might assist in explaining inconsistent findings in prior literature. For example, voluntary versus involuntary retirees are expected to engage in retirement planning to a different extent, set different goals for retirement, hold different attitudes toward retirement transition, and exhibit different coping strategies and transition trajectories in adjusting to post-retirement life. Therefore, rather than treating retirement and bridge employment as normative career transitions that have universal meanings for every older adult and simply comparing retirees with workers, future research should carefully take older adults' subjective feelings about their retirement and bridge employment situations into consideration.

Related to subjective voluntariness, the motivation behind retirement and bridge employment also warrants greater attention (Quick & Moen, 1998; Wang et al., 2011). Many age-related changes in motivation have been documented (Kanfer & Ackerman, 2004). According to the socio-emotional selectivity theory (Carstensen, 1995), with an increase in age, people's behaviors are more likely to be driven by building gratifying social relationships and short-term goals, and less likely to be driven by competitive goals and long-term achievement and advancement. In addition, generativity motives (i.e., focusing on developing or coaching future generations) become more important among older workers who have already established success in their midlife age period (Mor-Barak, 1995). Bridge employment provides a great opportunity for studying these motivational shifts among older workers. Moreover, despite the age-related motivational shift tendency, studies have already shown that retirees engage in bridge employment due to both extrinsic (e.g., financial needs and social relatedness needs) and intrinsic (e.g., personal satisfaction, growth needs, and generative needs) reasons (Dendinger, Adams, & Jacobson, 2005). It may be fruitful to examine how different motivations influence retirees' choices of bridge jobs and whether retirement and bridge employment have the same impact for retirees motivated by different needs.

People: Configural Approach

Past research on retirement and bridge employment has made great progress in examining the effects of many individual attributes in affecting older workers' employment and retirement processes. Most studies seek explanation by associating certain individual attributes (e.g., demographic characteristics and personality traits) with retirement-related outcomes (e.g., retirement intentions, decisions, and adjustment). This variable-centered approach capitalizes on the relationships among different properties of people, but neglects the existence of distinct and internally cohesive sub-populations based on the synergistic combination of multiple properties (Zyphur, 2009). This is suggested by a configural approach to research, which aims to identify such sub-populations, or unobservable groups of people, that may exhibit different attitudinal and behavioral patterns in the retirement process.

We provide two examples to illustrate the potential implications that can be derived from taking the configural approach. First, sub-populations of older workers may be identified based on their commitment to their organization and commitment to their occupation. Past research has examined the roles of organizational commitment and occupational commitment separately and demonstrated different effects of these two work-related commitment types in predicting older workers' retirement and bridge employment decisions (Adams, Prescher, Beehr, & Lepisto, 2002; Zhan, Wang, & Yao, 2013). Given the commonalities and differences between these two constructs, it is important to explore their mutual or synergistic effects (Meyer & Allen, 1997; Sinclair, Tucker, Cullen, & Wright, 2005). Depending on the shared similarities within sub-populations and the distinctions between different sub-populations, latent profile analysis (i.e., a statistical method for identifying subtypes of related cases from multivariate continuous data) (Wang & Hanges, 2011) can be used to identify older workers in different commitment profiles. They may have different preference for retirement timing and the industry and/or company in which they continue working after retirement. They may also show different patterns in the role transition process.

Second, sub-populations of older adults may be identified based on their perceived rank orders of different work motives. Past research has shown that older adults' work engagement may be driven by multiple reasons (e.g., financial needs, interpersonal needs, personal needs, and generative needs) (Dendinger et al., 2005), and the relative importance of each reason may differ across individuals. Simply examining the main effect of each work motive may miss the opportunity to capture the potential complexity of one's priority consideration in the decision-making process. Thus, latent class analysis, which is a statistical method for identifying subtypes of related cases from multivariate categorical data (Wang & Hanges, 2011), could be used to classify older adults based on their ordered work motives.

Context: Domains of Context and Person × Context Dynamics

Studying personal experiences in the retirement process cannot overlook the role of context because context usually defines the conditions and boundaries of experiences, and it may have powerful effects on attitudes, decisions, and behaviors (Johns, 2006). In the retirement and bridge employment literature, prior research has largely focused on the focal individual's demographic status and attitudes toward work and retirement, but rarely studied the characteristics of situations, which warrant future research attention.

Contextual factors include factors from different levels and domains. First, work context indicates the company's attitudes toward older employees and impacts the older employees' fit to their job positions and company. Specifically, age composition or age diversity may serve as signals to older workers and influence their identification to their work unit or company and attitudes toward work in general (e.g., Avery, McKay, & Wilson, 2007; Kunze, Boehm, & Bruch, 2011). Workplace policies and practices related to the treatment of older workers may also be critical in forming an ageism climate or an aging-friendly climate that may influence older employees' attachment to organization and retirement intention (Boehm, Kunze, & Bruch, 2013; Goldberg, Perry, Finkelstein, & Shull, 2013). For example, Boehm and colleagues (2013) surveyed a sample of German companies and found that age-inclusive human resource practices (e.g., equal opportunities to training and promotion for all age groups) promoted the age diversity climate, and ultimately increased performance and reduced turnover intentions at the company level.

Another much understudied work context is the occupation to which people are affiliated. Different occupations may be characterized by different levels of physical and cognitive demands, different levels of preferences for experience, and expertise versus cutting-edge technologies and innovation, as well as different norms for hiring older and retired employees. Some of the occupational characteristics may strongly relate to aging and older workers' particular needs in the workplace (Wang & Zhan, 2012). Therefore, future research should take a closer look at how work context, including task demands, work unit/organizational policy and climate, and occupational norms, shapes one's decisions in the retirement process.

Second, the workplace as a social community also provides important interpersonal context. Research on employee retention has emphasized the role of interpersonal links in reducing employees' withdrawal behaviors (Lee, Mitchell, Sablynski, Buron, & Holtom, 2004). The impact of interpersonal context might be stronger for older employees. As discussed earlier, older adults value social goals such as maintaining and building satisfying social relationships to a greater extent than younger ones (Carstensen, 1995). Therefore, studying the system of social relationships within work units may contribute to our understanding of older employees' motivation and decision-making for retirement and bridge employment. For example, having a dense and strong friendship network in the workplace may enhance one's sense of social belongingness and acceptance, likely serving as a key contextual factor in retaining older employees. In addition, due to social observation and social comparison, strong social connections within workgroups may also encourage collective attitudes or elicit contagious behaviors (Felps et al., 2009), which has rarely been discussed in retirement literature.

Third, family provides the most important context outside of the work domain. Some studies have been conducted to explore the effects of family-related factors in the retirement process. For example, family financial pressure and obligation for supporting dependents have been suggested to impede the likelihood of retirement and bridge employment decisions (e.g., Szinovacz, DeViney, & Davey, 2001). However, many findings regarding the effects of family-related factors (e.g., marital status and marital quality) on retirement processes remain inconsistent across studies (Wang & Shultz, 2010). Another stream of research related to family context is the crossover effects, which refer to the influence of older worker attitudes on the spouse's attitudes and vice versa (Westman & Etzion, 1995). In the retirement literature, it is suggested that partners may influence each other in the retirement decision-making process and adjustment process (Henkens & van Solinge, 2002; Smith & Moen, 1998), but the crossover influences between partners have not been consistently supported either (van Solinge & Henkens, 2005; Szinovacz & Davey, 2004). Several possible explanations for the inconsistency have been proposed. For example, due to government policies regarding the pension and old-age security systems and retirement age limits in different countries, many couples may have limited opportunity and autonomy to retire at the same time (van Solinge & Henkens, 2005). It is also likely that many family-related factors are relatively distal in influencing people's retirement processes and their effects may be modified by other proximal factors (Wang et al., 2008). Another possible explanation is that studying the effects of family context needs to go beyond the mere demographics such as marital status, but also examine partners' health condition and psychological characteristics. At this stage, it is difficult to understand the mixed results since there are only a small number of studies examining the family contextual influences on retirement process. Future work should pay greater attention to the interdependence of work and family domains.

Fourth, the role of the external environment has been understudied in retirement literature. The external environment includes but is not limited to macroeconomic trends and labor market demands, as well as government policies on pension and old-age security systems (Feldman, 1994). Although this might be less of the focus in I-O psychology literature, the external environment may have powerful impacts on older adults' retirement and employment decisions (Shultz & Wang, 2011). For example, different countries often endorse different social institutions for retirement support. Therefore, across different societies, older workers may exhibit different retirement-planning behaviors. Specifically, Hershey, Henkens, and van Dalen (2007) examined the psychological and cross-cultural precursors to financial planning for older workers in the United States and the Netherlands. They found that Dutch workers were less involved in retirement-planning activities and had lower levels of goal clarity for retirement planning than U.S. workers. This is not surprising given that the majority of older Dutch workers are still covered by guaranteed defined benefit pension plans, whereas the vast majority of US organizations now offer more volatile and uncertain defined contributions plans.

Existing studies predicting retirement and bridge employment decisions have been largely focused on predictive effects of individual characteristics and/or work-related factors (Topa, Moriano, Depolo, Alcover, & Morales, 2009). Little attention has been paid to interactions between factors from different conceptual categories (Wang & Shultz, 2010). More research attention should be paid to the person × context dynamics in retirement process. We highlight three mechanisms where context may modify the effects of individual attributes in retirement literature. First, context indicates the salience of certain situational features that may influence people's sensitivity to retirement and re-employment (Johns, 2006). For example, one's family financial pressure may direct a worker's attention to realistic factors in making retirement and employment decisions, and constrain workers' ability to carry out a preferred path to retirement (Zhan et al., 2013). External environmental factors, such as economic crisis and high unemployment rate, may also serve as salient contextual features that heighten people's sensitivity to bridge employment opportunities (Gobeski & Beehr, 2009). The second mechanism highlights the strength of situation, that is, the capacity of situations in abetting or constraining human agency (Mischel, 1968). In strong versus weak situations, there are obvious norms and rigid role expectations, and there is limited latitude or opportunity for people to express individual differences. Strong organizational climate and occupational norms may function in this way by defining the more appropriate retirement pathway for employees. Third, person-environment fit approach may be applied to and benefit the research on retirement and bridge employment (Wang & Shultz, 2010). It has been suggested to contribute to the retention and well-being of employees in the workplace. Person-environment fit can be represented by different types of joint relationship between person and environmental characteristics (Muchinsky & Monahan, 1987). For example, an older worker may fit into a workgroup because he or she possesses similar demographic attributes, needs, values, and goals to other employees in the group, or because he or she possesses unique attributes, abilities, and skills that complement others'. Promoting the perceived fit requires to study people and context jointly. In sum, in studying the role of context, future research should: (a) identify impactful contextual factors in different domains; and (b) examine the mechanisms of person × context dynamics from different aspects.

Time: Longitudinal Perspective

Although time could be considered as a contextual factor, we discuss it as a unique element in studying retirement because it provides an additional and critical dimension to describe retirement as a process. Today, retirement has been increasingly conceptualized as a process instead of an event (Shultz & Wang, 2011; Wang & Shultz, 2010). In other words, different stages are involved in defining the retirement process, including retirement planning, retirement and bridge employment decision-making, and retirement adjustment. This process-focused conceptualization suggests that a static perspective of viewing retirement as a one-time working status shift may fail to provide a comprehensive understanding about the determinants and outcomes of retirement. Rather, researchers are encouraged to study retirement from a longitudinal perspective. This not only suggests methodological advancements, but also highlights the opportunity offered by taking a longitudinal perspective in helping address important research questions that could not be clearly answered otherwise. Specifically, we suggest that two important research questions can be better addressed with a longitudinal approach.

First, it is important to study the change patterns of attitudes, intentions, behaviors, and well-being related to retirement and bridge employment. During the pre-retirement period, older workers' perceptions and considerations of retirement may gradually change as they approach retiring age and prepare for retirement (Ekerdt, Kosloski, & DeViney, 2000), which may relate to changes of retirement attitudes and intentions. During the post-retirement period, retirees may experience fluctuations or systematic changes in their psychological well-being and post-retirement activities, including bridge employment, voluntary work activities, and leisure activities. Applying a longitudinal perspective, we are able to better describe the change trajectories in terms of the linearity and change rate. The change trajectories may manifest in different patterns across different time periods, such as the increase of satisfaction during the honeymoon period immediately after retiring, the decrease of satisfaction during the following disenchantment period, and the recovery of well-being thereafter (Reitzes & Mutran, 2004). Better understanding about these change patterns may help us reconcile the inconsistent findings in prior studies because relationships between constructs might vary depending on when these constructs are measured along the retirement process. In addition, studying the change patterns of attitudes, intentions, behaviors, and well-being in retirement process in a longitudinal perspective also calls for future research exploring factors that may modify the trajectories. For example, it is theoretically and practically important to identify factors that may buffer the well-being drop after retirement and smooth one's transition process.

Second, given the different stages of the retirement process, future research should better examine the interrelations among these stages. Previous individual studies tend to view stages as separate and independent, and focus on examining phenomena and relationships related to a certain stage. It is not difficult to identify separate sets of studies that examine individual and work-related predictors of retirement planning, retirement decision, bridge employment decision, and post-retirement adjustment, but little is known about how these stages connect to each other. Studying the connections among stages will lead to a more comprehensive understanding of one's transition from career to retirement. For example, individuals' decision on retirement and bridge employment during the later career stage might be influenced by their earlier work histories, and individuals' post-retirement activities and well-being might be influenced by pre-retirement planning. Related to the first point of taking longitudinal perspective regarding change patterns, such influences may occur in a dynamic pattern such that earlier stage experiences not only define the starting point of later stage experiences, but also shape how experiences change during a later stage (Elder, 1995; Kim & Hall, 2013).

Considering the longitudinal perspective and configural perspective together, some pioneering work has been done to capture the unobserved sub-populations who exhibit different patterns of pathways in retirement process. For example, Pinquart and Schindler (2007) and Wang (2007) both identified three latent classes of retirees based on repeated assessment of retirees' retirement satisfaction and psychological well-being. Their findings highlighted the existence of different trajectories of retirement adjustment, and directed future studies to examine correlates of retirement adjustment for different retiree sub-populations and search for potential interventions that may help different retirees transit to retirement successfully.

FUTURE DIRECTIONS FOR BRIDGE EMPLOYMENT RESEARCH

The external context within which employees retire has changed significantly in the past couple of decades. The changes in pension and old-age security policies and the economic depression, as well as the increased employable years due to improved health and longevity, have directed more research attention to bridge employment. Compared to research on retirement intentions and decisions, many questions on bridge employment still need to be addressed, and they are different from questions associated with retirement. In addition to the research trends discussed earlier in this chapter, below we propose research questions that are specific to bridge employment.

Bridge Employment and Successful Aging

Literature so far has suggested bridge employment having positive impacts on older individuals. Most existing research has focused on its positive influences on retirement satisfaction and well-being. Given the aging trend, we believe it is important to study bridge employment as a contributor to successful aging in a broader sense given that bridge employment may help individuals to maintain an active and productive life (Hansson, DeKoekkoek, Need, & Patterson, 1997). As suggested by the model of selective optimization with compensation, three fundamental processes, selecting goals in fundamental domains on which to focus one's resources, optimizing developmental potential in selected domains, and compensating for health-related constraints and losses, are essential for successful aging (Baltes, Staudinger, & Lindenberger, 1999). They help to maintain effective functioning and minimize losses associated with the aging process. Thus, an interesting research question is how bridge employment may facilitate these fundamental processes, fulfill personal goals, and effectively reallocate resources during later adulthood. Further, linking bridge employment to successful aging is not only meaningful in the work domain (e.g., helping older adults maintain important job competencies and fulfill mastery goals), but also relevant to understanding people's overall life satisfaction and health in the non-work domain. This suggests that future research on bridge employment may be benefited by incorporating constructs from motivation and self-regulation literature and examining a wider range of correlates of those constructs. The outcomes of bridge employment could broadly include attitudes, activities, and well-being in both work and non-work domains.

In addition, the reasons why bridge employment has beneficial impacts on retirement transition should be studied. Multiple theoretical models, such as continuity theory (Atchley, 1989) and role theory (Ashforth, 2001), have been borrowed to explain the effects, but it is still not clear what kinds of changes happen to individuals working in bridge jobs, or how bridge jobs prepare individuals for retirement. Specifically, bridge employment may take many different forms, including full-time, part-time, and self-employed work. Therefore, bridge employment does not necessarily relate to lower task demands or fewer working hours. Since it may not be a gradual work withdrawal, does it just provide extra time for older adults to prepare for retirement? How does one's identity change in the transition from a career job to a bridge job? How does one's attitude toward work-family balance change in the transition from a career job to a bridge job? Given that previous theoretical review (e.g., Wang & Shi, 2014; Wang & Shultz, 2010) has conceptualized bridge employment as a career development stage, it might mean that the boundary between the career job and the bridge job is blurrier than traditionally thought. This points to the possibility of older workers actively planning their bridge employment to continuously fulfill their career goals after retirement.

Further, it becomes more complicated but intriguing when different motivations of bridge employment are considered in exploring the different change patterns. For individuals taking bridge employment driven by intrinsic motivation (e.g., enjoyment and challenges), the bridge jobs they choose are more likely to be aligned with their career identity and foster their self-worth, thus ultimately benefitting their satisfaction in both the work and non-work domain. For individuals driven by extrinsic motivation (e.g., financial needs), they may also be satisfied with their bridge jobs since these jobs may help financially. However, these individuals may not benefit as much from their bridge jobs in terms of health and psychological well-being. This could be because they have to take bridge jobs that are not necessarily what they actually want, adding to their life demand instead of enjoyment (Zhan, Wang, Liu, & Shultz, 2009). So far, little research has been done to address these questions. Addressing these questions will contribute to our understanding of the mechanisms underlying the facilitative effect of bridge employment on retirement transitions and successful aging.

Implications of Bridge Employment for Employers

While most bridge employment research has taken the employees' perspective in studying the antecedents and outcomes of bridge employment, studies examining the implications of bridge employment from employers' perspective are greatly needed. First, there is a lack of research on how to retain and attract older workers. Given the experiences and expertise of older workers, hiring retired workers may be viewed as a cost-effective strategy for companies that need to alleviate their specific labor force shortage. Meanwhile, because of the age-related changes in terms of workers' abilities, needs, and work motivations (Kanfer & Ackerman, 2004; Ng & Feldman, 2013; Wang & Zhan, 2012), human resource management practices, such as recruitment, training, and job design, should be designed and delivered accordingly. One of the few empirical studies that examined bridge employment from the employers' perspective is Rau and Adams' (2005) study, in which they used experimental design to test the interactive effect between different policies and practices (i.e., targeted recruitment directed at increasing employment of older workers, work-time flexibility, and mentoring opportunity) in attracting older workers. This line of research should be further developed given the aging trend of the workforce and organizations' mission to maintain critical human resources.

Second, there is a lack of research on the potential benefits to employers who provide bridge job positions. This relates to research of bridge employees' task performance and organizational citizenship behaviors. Bridge employment may indicate a different type of employee-organization relationship, and organizations are likely to expect unique contributions from employees on bridge job positions compared to regular employees, such as the knowledge transfer from older to younger employees (Wang & Zhan, 2012). Ng and Feldman (2008) reported positive correlations between age and multiple organizational citizenship behaviors, and Mathieu and Zajac (1990) also reported positive correlations between age and commitment to organizations. However, given the unique type of job contract and psychological contract introduced by bridge employment, it is likely that bridge employees are not very committed to organizations because they may simply view bridge jobs as temporal transitions toward complete work withdrawal, and it is also likely that bridge employees are highly committed to organizations, especially when they stay with the same employer from career job to bridge job. Thus, it would be interesting to explore how employees in bridge job positions compare to other employees in terms of their attachment to organization and their organizational citizenship behaviors. In addition to the employee-organization relationship, motivation of bridge employment again comes into play. Comparing people who want to take bridge employment versus those who have to, the level of work engagement and task performance may significantly vary. The former ones are likely to devote themselves to the job that they are passionate about, whereas the latter ones are likely to invest minimum effort to just keep the paycheck coming. These differences are practically important to employers who provide bridge jobs and need to be studied in future research.

THEORIES AND METHODOLOGY: GENERAL RECOMMENDATIONS

Theoretical Perspectives

Earlier empirical research on retirement and bridge employment has rarely been grounded in well-developed theories. We believe that this research will benefit from applying multiple theoretical perspectives. Different theoretical perspectives may suggest a variety of variables that contribute to our understanding of retirement and bridge employment. Wang and Shultz's (2010) article provides a great review for the four types of conceptualizations of retirement: retirement as decision-making, retirement as an adjustment process, retirement as a career development stage, and retirement as a part of human resource management, and the corresponding theories that support each conceptualization. Bridge employment as a unique phenomenon during the retirement process can be similarly conceptualized in these four ways. Researchers should choose their theoretical perspectives based on how they conceptualize retirement and bridge employment.

Recent retirement research has started adopting new theoretical frameworks to explain the transition process. Responding to the recommendation of applying resource perspective to retirement research (Wang & Shultz, 2010; Wang et al., 2011), Leung and Earl (2012) developed the retirement resources inventory, and found multiple sets of key retirement resources, including tangible resources, mental capacity, and social resources. Their results supported the resource perspective of retirement, demonstrating that resource accessibility is critical to retirees' well-being. Kubicek, Korunka, Raymo, and Hoonakker (2011) further showed the gender differences in the influences of resources on retirees' well-being. Applying a resource perspective to retirement research raises new research questions. It calls for more research effort to clarify the taxonomy of retirement resources, explore the change in resources during the retirement process, and identify activities that may help retirees maintain critical resources and avoid resource losses.

Research on aging workers and retirement has also been advanced by theories of lifespan development, such as the socio-emotional selectivity theory (Carstensen, 1995) and the selective optimization with compensation model (Baltes et al., 1999) mentioned earlier in the chapter. These theoretical models inspire new explanations for retirement process by integrating future time perspective, motivation, and regulatory focus into retirement research (Bal, Jansen, van der Velde, de Lange, & Rousseau, 2010; de Lange, van Yperen, van der Heijden, & Bal, 2010). Taking a life-span developmental perspective highlights the potential changes in perceptions, attitudes, and motivations from early to late adulthood. This is consistent with the research trend in retirement literature toward a more longitudinal and dynamic approach, thus providing a necessary theoretical aspect for understanding the nature and mechanisms of psychological transition for people moving from complete employment to complete work withdrawal.

Methodological Advancement

The above research questions provide opportunity to further improve research methodologies in this field. Specifically, studying the retirement process from a longitudinal perspective requires collecting longitudinal data and measuring key variables on multiple time points along the retirement process in order to capture the dynamic change patterns. In particular, to sufficiently capture the fluctuations in attitudes, behaviors, and well-being states during the retirement process, measurement should be conducted for at least four repeated times. This way, nonlinear changes in variables that are not monotonic can be modeled. Further, given pre-retirement status may offer a useful baseline to understand changes that happen during retirement transition and post-retirement employment, we recommend researchers to start their longitudinal data collection before retirement happens. Finally, selecting appropriate time lag is crucial. If the time lag is too long between consecutive measurement points (e.g., five years), the observations over time may miss important change trends that happen within shorter time windows (Wang, 2007). Based on previous longitudinal studies in this field (e.g., Pinquart & Schindler, 2007; Wang, 2007), it seems that a time lag ranging from six months to 24 months may provide the most opportunities to observe meaningful changes during the retirement process.

Similarly, studying different domains of contextual impacts may involve collecting data from multiple sources and measuring contextual constructs at multiple levels. For example, different composition models (Chan, 1998) may be used to capture the contextual constructs based on individual-level measures, such as work design characteristics (Wöhrmann, Deller, & Wang, 2013). Further, archival data, such as data from the Bureau of Labor Statistics, may help to establish socioeconomic contexts (e.g., macroeconomic trends and labor market demands).

In addition, retirement and bridge employment research may also benefit from findings of qualitative studies. The retirement process is complex. There are many possible pathways to retirement, and the process may be characterized by multiple exits and re-entries into the workforce depending on individual differences and contextual characteristics (Feldman, 1994; Wang, 2007). Given the complexity of the retirement process, a narrative perspective could be particularly helpful in providing rich information regarding how people identify turning points in the transition process, how people make critical career-related decisions, and what strategies people use to adjust to retirement.

REFERENCES

Adams, G. A., & Rau, B. L. (2011). Putting off tomorrow to do what you want today: Planning for retirement. *American Psychologist, 66*, 180–192.

Adams, G. A., Prescher, J., Beehr, T. A., & Lepisto, L. (2002). Applying work-role attachment theory to retirement decision-making. *International Journal of Aging & Human Development, 54*, 125–137.

Ashforth, B. (2001). *Role Transitions in Organizational Life: An Identity-Based Perspective.* Mahwah, NJ: Erlbaum.

Atchley, R. C. (1989). A continuity theory of normal aging. *Gerontologist, 29*, 183–190.

Avery, D. R., McKay, P. F., & Wilson, D. C. (2007). Engaging the aging workforce: The relationship between perceived age similarity, satisfaction with coworkers, and employee engagement. *Journal of Applied Psychology, 92*, 1542–1556.

Bal, P. M., Jansen, P. G. W., van der Velde, M. E. G., de Lange, A. H., & Rousseau, D. M. (2010). The role of future time perspective in psychological contracts: A study among older workers. *Journal of Vocational Behavior, 76*, 474–486.

Baltes, P. B., Staudinger, U. M., & Lindenberger, U. (1999). Life span psychology: theory and application to intellectual functioning. *Annual Review of Psychology, 50*, 471–507.

Beehr, T. A. (1986). The process of retirement: A review and recommendations for future investigation. *Personnel Psychology, 39*, 31–55.

Boehm, S. A., Kunze, F., & Bruch, H. (2013). Spotlight on age-diversity climate: The impact of age-inclusive HR practices on firm-level outcomes. *Personnel Psychology, 67*, 667–704.

Carstensen, L. L. (1995). Evidence for a life span theory of socioemotional selectivity. *Current Directions in Psychological Science, 4*, 151–156.

Chan, D. (1998). Functional relations among constructs in the same content domain at different levels of analysis: A typology of composition models. *Journal of Applied Psychology, 83*, 234–246.

de Lange, A. H., van Yperen, N. W., van der Heijden, B. I. J. M., & Bal, P. M., (2010). Dominant achievement goals of older workers and their relationship with motivation-related outcomes. *Journal of Vocational Behavior, 77*, 118–125.

Dendinger, V. M., Adams, G. A., & Jacobson, J. D. (2005). Reasons for working and their relationship to retirement attitudes, job satisfaction and occupational self-efficacy of bridge employees. *International Journal of Aging & Human Development, 61*, 21–35.

Ekerdt, D. J., Kosloski, K., & DeViney, S. (2000). The normative anticipation of retirement by older workers. *Research on Aging, 22*, 3–22.

Elder, G. H. (1995). The life course paradigm: Social change and individual development. In P. Moen, G. H. Elder, & K. Luscher (Eds.), *Examining Lives in Contexts: Perspectives on the Ecology of Human Development* (pp. 101–139). Washington, DC: American Psychological Association.

Feldman, D. C. (1994). The decision to retire early: A review and conceptualization. *Academy of Management Review, 19*, 285–311.

Felps, W., Mitchell, T. R., Hekman, D. R., Lee, T. W., Holtom, B. C., & Harman, W. S. (2009). Turnover contagion: How coworkers' job embeddedness and job search behaviors influence quitting. *Academy of Management Journal, 52*, 545–561.

Gobeski, K. T., & Beehr, T. A. (2009). How retirees work: Predictors of different types of bridge employment. *Journal of Organizational Behavior, 30*, 401–425.

Goldberg, C. B., Perry, E. L., Finkelstein, L. M., & Shull, A. (2013). Antecedents and outcomes of targeting older applicants in recruitment. *European Journal of Work and Organizational Psychology, 22*, 265–278.

Hansson, R. O., DeKoekkoek, P. D., Need, W. M., & Patterson, D. W. (1997). Successful aging at work: Annual review, 1992–1996: The older worker and transitions to retirement. *Journal of Vocational Behavior, 51*, 202–233.

Henkens, K., & van Solinge, H. (2002). Spousal influences on the decision to retire. *International Journal of Sociology, 32*, 55–74.

Hershey, D. A., Henkens, K., & van Dalen, H. P. (2007). Mapping the minds of retirement planners. *Journal of Cross-Cultural Psychology, 38*, 361–382.

Johns, G. (2006). The essential impact of context on organizational behavior. *Academy of Management Review, 31*, 386–408.

Kanfer, R., & Ackerman, P. L. (2004). Aging, adult development, and work motivation. *Academy of Management Review, 29*, 440–458.

Kim, N., & Hall, D. T. (2013). Protean career model and retirement. In M. Wang (Ed.), *The Oxford Handbook of Retirement* (pp. 102–116). New York: Oxford University Press.

Kubicek, B., Korunka, C., Raymo, J. M., & Hoonakker, P. (2011). Psychological well-being in retirement: The effects of personal and gendered contextual resources. *Journal of Occupational Health Psychology, 16*, 230–246.

Kunze, F., Boehm, S. A., & Bruch, H. (2011). Age diversity, age discrimination climate and performance consequences: A cross organizational study. *Journal of Organizational Behavior, 32*, 264–290.

Lee, T. W., Sablynski, C. J., Burton, J. P., & Holtom, B. C. (2004). The effects of job embeddedness on organizational citizenship, job performance, volitional absences, and voluntary turnover. *Academy of Management Journal, 47*, 711–722.

Leung, C. S. Y., & Earl, J. K. (2012). Retirement resources inventory: Construction, factor structure and psychometric properties. *Journal of Vocational Behavior, 81*, 171–182.

Liu, S., Zhan, Y., & Wang, M. (2011). Person-centric work psychology: Additional insights on its tradition, nature, and research methods. *Industrial and Organizational Psychology: Perspectives on Science and Practice, 4*, 105–108.

Mathieu, J. E., & Zajac, D. M. (1990). A review and meta-analysis of the antecedents, correlates, and consequences of organizational commitment. *Psychological Bulletin, 108*, 171–194.

Meyer, J. P., & Allen, N. J. (1997). *Commitment in the Workplace: Theory, Research, and Application.* Thousand Oaks, CA: Sage.

Mischel, W. (1968). *Personality and Assessment.* New York: Wiley.

Mor-Barak, M. E. (1995). The meaning of work for older adults seeking employment: The generativity factor. *International Journal of Aging and Human Development, 41*, 325–344.

Muchinsky, P. M., & Monahan, C. J. (1987). What is person-environment congruence? Supplementary versus complementary models of fit. *Journal of Vocational Behavior, 31*, 268–277.

Ng, T. W. H., & Feldman, D. C. (2008). The relationship of age to ten dimensions of job performance. *Journal of Applied Psychology, 93*, 392–423.

Ng, T. W. H., & Feldman, D. C. (2013). How do within-person changes due to aging affect job performance? *Journal of Vocational Behavior, 83*, 500–513.

Pinquart, M., & Schindler, I. (2007). Changes of life satisfaction in the transition to retirement: A latent-class approach. *Psychology and Aging, 22*, 442–455.

Quick, H. E., & Moen, P. (1998). Gender, employment, and retirement quality: A life course approach to the differential experiences of men and women. *Journal of Occupational Health Psychology, 3*, 44–64.

Rau, B. L., & Adams, G. A. (2005). Attracting retirees to apply: Desired organizational characteristics of bridge employment. *Journal of Organizational Behavior, 26*, 649–660.

Reitzes, D. C., & Mutran, E. J. (2004). The transition into retirement: Stages and factors that influence retirement adjustment. *International Journal of Aging and Human Development, 59*, 63–84.

Shultz, K. S. (2003). Bridge employment: Work after retirement. In G. A. Adams & T. A. Beehr (Eds.), *Retirement: Reasons, Processes, and Results* (pp. 215–241). New York: Springer.

Shultz, K. S., & Wang, M. (2011). Psychological perspectives on the changing nature of retirement. *American Psychologist, 66*, 170–179.

Shultz, K. S., Morton, K. R., & Weckerle, J. R. (1998). The influence of push and pull factors on voluntary and involuntary early retirees' retirement decision and adjustment. *Journal of Vocational Behavior, 53*, 145–157.

Sinclair, R. R., Tucker, J. S., Cullen, J. C., & Wright, C. (2005). Performance differences among four organizational commitment profiles. *Journal of Applied Psychology, 90*, 1280–1287.

Smith, D. B., & Moen, P. (1998). Spousal influence on retirement: His, her, and their perceptions. *Journal of Marriage and the Family, 60*, 734–744.

Szinovacz, M. E., & Davey, A. (2004). Honeymoons and joint lunches: Effects of retirement and spouse's employment on depressive symptoms. *Journal of Gerontology: Psychological Sciences, 59B*, 233–245.

Szinovacz, M. E., & Davey, A. (2005). Predictors of perceptions of involuntary retirement. *The Gerontologist, 45*, 36–47.

Szinovacz, M. E., DeViney, S., & Davey, A. (2001). Influences of family obligations and relationships on retirement: Variations by gender, race, and marital status. *Journals of Gerontology: Social Sciences, 56B*, 20–27.

Topa, G., Moriano, J. A., Depolo, M., Alcover, C., & Morales, J. F. (2009). Antecedents and consequences of retirement planning and decision-making: A meta-analysis and model. *Journal of Vocational Behavior, 75*, 38–55.

van Solinge, H., & Henkens, K. (2005). Couples' adjustment to retirement: A multi-actor panel study. *Journals of Gerontology: Social Sciences, 60B*, 11–20.

Wang, M. (2007). Profiling retirees in the retirement transition and adjustment process: Examining the longitudinal change patterns of retirees' psychological well-being. *Journal of Applied Psychology, 92*, 455–474.

Wang, M., & Hanges, P. (2011). Latent class procedures: Applications to organizational research. *Organizational Research Methods, 14,* 24–31.

Wang, M., & Shi, J. (2014). Psychological research on retirement. *Annual Review of Psychology, 65,* 209–233.

Wang, M., & Shultz, K. S. (2010). Employee retirement: A review and recommendations for future investigation. *Journal of Management, 36,* 172–206.

Wang, M., & Zhan, Y. (2012). Employee-organization relationship in older workers. In L. M. Shore, J. A.-M. Coyle-Shapiro, & Tetrick, L. (Eds.), *The Employee-Organization Relationship: Applications for the 21st Century* (pp. 427–454). New York: Psychology Press.

Wang, M., Zhan, Y., Liu, S., & Shultz, K. S. (2008). Antecedents of bridge employment: A longitudinal investigation. *Journal of Applied Psychology, 93,* 818–830.

Wang, M., Henkens, K., & van Solinge, H. (2011). Retirement adjustment: A review of theoretical and empirical advancements. *American Psychologist, 66,* 204–213.

Westman, M., & Etzion, D. (1995). Crossover of stress, strain and resources from one spouse to the another. *Journal of Organizational Behavior, 16,* 169–181.

Weiss, H. W., & Rupp, D. E. (2011). Experiencing work: An essay on a person-centric work psychology. *Industrial and Organizational Psychology: Perspectives on Science and Practice, 4,* 83–97.

Wöhrmann, A. M., Deller, J., & Wang, M. (2013). Outcome expectations and work design characteristics in post-retirement work planning. *Journal of Vocational Behavior, 83,* 219–228.

Zhan, Y., Wang, M., Liu, S., & Shultz, K. (2009). Bridge employment and retirees' health: A longitudinal investigation. *Journal of Occupational Health Psychology, 14,* 374–389.

Zhan, Y., Wang, M., & Yao, X. (2013). Domain specific effects of commitment on bridge employment decisions: The moderating role of economic stress. *European Journal of Work and Organizational Psychology, 22,* 362–375.

Zyphur, M. J. (2009). When mindsets collide: Switching analytical mindsets to advance organization science. *Academy of Management Review, 34,* 677–688.

Issue 5

Age Differences and Discrimination

11

Intergenerational Perceptions and Conflicts in Multi-Age and Multigenerational Work Environments

Cort W. Rudolph and Hannes Zacher

One underappreciated consequence of the aging population phenomenon is that we are now experiencing what is arguably the most age-diverse workforce in modern history (Hanks & Icenogle, 2001; Newton, 2006; Toossi, 2004). As our workforce continues to age, shifts in the age demographic composition (i.e., the age diversity) of organizations and their subunits will become more apparent (Roth, Wegge, & Schmidt, 2007). Several factors have influenced and will continue to drive this trend. For example, in Western countries, younger people entering the workforce are more educated than ever before (Hussar & Bailey, 2013; Ryan & Siebens, 2012; Stoops, 2003) and could feasibly rise to positions of power in organizations more quickly than others have in the past (e.g., promotion rates vary as a function of age) (Rosenbaum, 1979; see also Clemens, 2012 conceptualization of the "fast track effect"). Furthermore, older workers are increasingly delaying retirement beyond the normative retirement age (Baltes & Rudolph, 2012; Burtless, 2012; Flynn, 2010), and already retired individuals are seeking re-employment in bridge employment roles in higher numbers than before (e.g., Adams & Rau, 2004; Kim & Feldman, 2000; Weckerle & Shultz, 1999).

An important and understudied consequence of this shift toward greater age diversity is the increased level of interpersonal exchange between younger and older workers within organizations. Such exchanges may represent fertile ground for skewed intergenerational perceptions to drive misunderstandings and conflicts between younger and older workers. Investigating such interactions represents an important opportunity to better understand how perceived age and generational differences manifest in teams and organizations and affect valued outcomes at various levels of abstraction (e.g., individual well-being, interpersonal relationships, team performance). Furthermore, there is a substantial gap in our understanding of the interplay between age demographic shifts and other broad-scale changes to the nature of work, such as those alluded to in Chapter 1 of this volume (e.g., changing technologies, redefining when, where, and how work gets done). We feel that this gap represents an opportunity for researchers and practitioners to jointly inform our empirical knowledge base to bolster the understanding of these complex issues.

THE PRESENT CHAPTER

In this chapter, we attempt to achieve several goals. First, we define the emerging issues of intergenerational perceptions and conflict within organizations, and review both theoretical support and empirical evidence that explains the presence of negative intergenerational exchanges in the workplace with a focus on future research directions (for a summary, see Table 11.1). Then, given the lack of an integrative framework for understanding these processes and the use-inspired nature of this text, we propose a new theoretically grounded model of intergenerational exchanges in the workplace (Figure 11.1). The development of this model was challenging given the psychological and person-centric focus of this text. Indeed, there is an inherent contradiction that must be addressed here, in that one cannot readily adopt a person-centric approach to understanding generational phenomena. The application of generational theory to understanding the behavior of individuals may even represent an ecological fallacy (i.e., wherein inferences about the nature of individuals are drawn from inferences about the group to which these individuals belong). Thus, the primary focus of this model is to delineate the processes that underlie intergenerational conflict—that is, negative experiences that result from intergenerational exchanges in the workplace. The model specifies how external societal processes (e.g., the social construction of generational differences) and intra-organizational social processes (e.g., implicit organizational age grading) operate in tandem to influence individual expectations and intergenerational conflicts in the workplace. The goal of this model is to direct research efforts and practical applications in this area. As such, we offer several testable propositions and implementable ideas throughout this work that should serve to guide future research and practice efforts. Finally, given recent research suggesting that intergenerational contact can be mutually beneficial in certain circumstances (e.g., Kessler & Staudinger, 2007; Zacher, Rosing, Henning, & Frese, 2011), we end our discussion by briefly considering empirical evidence that explores the possibility of positive potentials arising from intergenerational exchange in work contexts, and discuss how these findings can inform contemporary research and practice to benefit employers and society.

GENERATIONAL THEORY, INTERGENERATIONAL EXCHANGE, AND CONFLICT

To gain an understanding of how cross-age interactions could lead to intergenerational conflict, we must first address the common use of the concept of "generations" as a nominal classification system. At its most basic conceptualization, the term "generation" refers to a group of people born during a common time span, who by virtue of their chronological age proximity have shared the same general life experiences (e.g., major historical events) (see Eyerman & Turner, 1998; Mannheim, 1970). Proponents of generational theory have argued that such shared life experiences drive collective assumptions and values that translate into common attitudes, beliefs, and a cohesive sense of group identity. Membership in a generational cohort is often invoked as an explanation for observed or experienced differences between people of various ages. Importantly, many have argued that "generational differences" are cause for concern in the design and implementation of various workplace policies and practices, and business strategies should be aligned to effectively manage such differences (e.g., Blythe et al., 2008; Cennamo & Gardner, 2008; Kowske, Rasch, & Wiley, 2010; Weston, 2001).

We and others (e.g., Joshi, Dencker, & Franz, 2010; Joshi, Dencker, Franz, & Martocchio, 2011) generally eschew the notion of classifying individuals into broadly defined generational groups for several reasons. Primarily, the classification of people into groups on the basis of either their chronological age (e.g., younger versus middle aged versus older) or various generational cohorts (e.g., silent generation, baby boomers, Generation X, millennials) serves only as a proxy for perceived differences in attitudes, values, cognitive process, and motives. That is, while there are likely some broadly defined differences in historical experiences that might drive generational homogeneity in some respects (e.g., cohort-based effects), the fundamental importance of individual developmental experiences cannot be overemphasized (e.g., Rosow, 1978; Stewart & Healy, 1989). Moreover, operationalizing age in terms of generational groups is often achieved by artificially dividing continuous chronological ages into broader generational categories. The bifurcation of continuous data into categories and the resulting loss of information is generally frowned upon in methodological circles (see MacCallum, Zhang, Preacher, & Rucker, 2002). A related concern is that many studies adopting this approach rely on cross-sectional data, making it impossible to untangle generational, cohort, and aging-related differences (Baltes, 1968).

This issue is further complicated by the application of generational theory to the workplace, as many organizational processes (e.g., organizational entry and socialization, promotion, tenure) may serve as a proxy for cohort experiences, and can affect the formation of generation-like cohort groups within organizations (see Lawrence & Zyphur, 2011). Considering support for generational theory, several recent comprehensive reviews have suggested that there is rather weak empirical support for the notion of generational differences, both in terms of work-relevant outcomes (i.e., Costanza, Badger, Fraser, Severt, & Gade, 2012; Parry & Urwin, 2011; Real, Mitnick, & Maloney, 2010; however, see Twenge, 2010) and beyond (e.g., narcissism) (Trzesniewski, Donnellan, & Robins, 2008).

One reason people hang onto the notion of generational differences is that generational groupings represent convenient categories for classifying and capturing the complexities of age (see Kooij, de Lange, Jansen, & Dikkers, 2008; Pitt-Catsouphes, Matz-Costa, & James, 2012; Schwall, 2012; Sterns & Doverspike, 1989). We argue here that a more likely cause of intergenerational conflicts are differences in the *expectations* people hold regarding individuals of different ages (i.e., based upon their assumptions regarding generational cohort membership) and the way that such expectations define patterns of behavior in cross-age interactions. We conceptualize intergenerational exchanges in this chapter as representing a variety of possible interactive social exchanges between members of the multi-age workforce, and intergenerational conflict to represent the tension, friction, disagreement, or discord that can arise from such intergenerational exchanges (see Lyons & Kuron, 2014).

We classify these conflicts as "intergenerational" because people often incorrectly assume that such conflicts arise from actual generational differences in work attitudes and behavior. Arguably, the popular focus on managing intergenerational exchanges in the workplace and beyond (e.g., Dols, Landrum, & Wieck, 2010; Wieck, 2007) has overemphasized the role that actual generational differences play in such intergenerational exchanges and exacerbated the assumption that real differences between age groups are the root of such conflict (see also Joshi et al., 2010, 2011). This rather social-constructivist perspective on intergenerational conflict suggests that generational differences exist insomuch as people believe and expect that they do, and allow such beliefs and expectations to affect how they interact across various situations with other people of different ages. A related issue, age stereotyping, further fuels such conflicts.

REVIEW OF AGE STEREOTYPES AS CROSS-AGE PERCEPTIONS

Stereotypes involved in cross-age perceptions can be classified as either other-referenced (i.e., perceptions of "others," meaning people in age categories different from one's own) or self-referenced (i.e., perceptions of one's own age category). While a majority of research has focused on other-referenced age stereotypes, their content, and their implications, a growing body of research is focusing on self-referenced stereotypes in the form of both meta-stereotypes and intra-generational stereotyping processes. Furthermore, while research on cross-age perceptions generally focuses on older-younger differences, some empirical attention has been paid to other age groups (e.g., middle-aged/career/life).

Other-Referenced Age Stereotypes

A primary driver of perceived cross-age differences is the prevalence of age-related stereotypes. Generally, stereotypes are defined as expectations and beliefs about the characteristics of out-group members (Fiske, 1998). As aging is a universal phenomenon, the experience and application of age stereotypes can vary within persons over time. This makes studying the endorsement and application of age stereotypes particularly interesting compared to stereotypes about stable categories such as gender and race. Most academic research has conceived age stereotypes in terms of descriptions and characteristics indicative of *older* individuals (as opposed to those of younger or other-aged individuals). Given this, it is perhaps not surprising that a great deal of the literature on age stereotypes in the workplace has focused on the influence of older worker stereotypes on various processes and outcomes (e.g., Hassel & Perrewe, 1995; see Posthuma & Campion, 2009 for a review). However, it is worth noting that there is no shortage of evidence from more mainstream outlets to suggest the presence of stereotypes against *younger* adults, particularly in the workplace (e.g., Gilbert, 2011; Graves, 2012; Smith, 2013).

Relatively little attention has been paid to stereotypical characterizations of other age groups besides older workers (e.g., younger workers or middle-aged workers) (however, see Bertolino, Truxillo, & Fraccaroli, 2013; Truxillo, McCune, Bertolino, & Fraccaroli, 2012). However, some empirical work outside of the organizational sciences has attempted to codify and differentiate stereotypes about younger versus older people (e.g., Hummert, 1990; Kite, Stockdale, Whitley, & Johnson, 2005; Williams & Nussbaum, 2001), and stereotypical expectations of middle-aged individuals surrounding normative beliefs about midlife-appropriate development and behavior (e.g., Krueger, Heckhausen, & Hundertmark, 1995). Interestingly, while older worker stereotypes tend to pit the capabilities and characteristics of older workers against those of younger workers, evidence from a variety of sources suggests that younger worker stereotypes are not simply the opposite of older worker stereotypes (e.g., Myers & Sadaghiani, 2010; Strauss & Howe, 2000; Wilson & Gerber, 2008; Zacher & Gielnik, 2014). Furthermore, older worker stereotypes can reflect both negative and positive generalizations and perceptions. For example, older workers are generally seen as more reliable than younger workers—a positive yet perhaps overgeneralized assumption (see Bal, Reiss, Rudolph, & Baltes, 2011 for a meta-analytic review).

Posthuma and Campion (2009) review and generally qualitatively refute many of the most common older worker stereotypes. Going further, Ng and Feldman (2012) meta-analytically evaluated empirical evidence for six common older worker stereotypes to test the validity of these stereotypical generalizations. Controlling for the effects of tenure, the only stereotype-consistent evidence that was garnered was for the idea that older workers are generally less willing or motivated to participate in training and career development activities. Notably, these relationships were quite weak and there was no appreciable relationship between age and *actual* participation in training (i.e., older workers were no more or less likely to participate in training than younger workers). Recent reviews further substantiate the mixed evidence for age differences in work motivation (Kooij et al., 2008; Rudolph, Baltes, & Zabel, 2013).

Descriptive versus Prescriptive Age Stereotypes

A recent distinction has been made between *descriptive* and *prescriptive* age stereotypes (North & Fiske, 2012, 2013). It is argued that descriptive age stereotypes entail expectations about what older people typically "do," whereas prescriptive age stereotypes entail what older people "should do," particularly with respect to using, sharing, and divesting themselves of valued resources (North & Fiske, 2012, 2013). Three distinct prescriptive dimensions that younger individuals are likely to endorse are outlined by North and Fiske (2012, 2013): (1) active *succession* of enviable positions and influence; (2) minimizing passive shared-resource *consumption*; and (3) age-appropriate, symbolic *identity* maintenance.

Generally, prescriptive stereotypes define other-referenced normative expectations for behaviors, and inattention to or violation of these expectations can drive intergenerational conflicts. For example, if older individuals postpone retirement, and remain in the workforce beyond their statutory retirement age, younger workers might perceive violations of succession, consumption, and identity-based prescriptive norms. It is also possible that these ideas work both ways; for example, it might be that older workers see younger workers' fast advancements through the organization as violations of consumption, resource, and identity norms. This could drive similar contempt between older and younger workers insomuch as older workers perceive that younger workers are "skipping ahead" in line and not "acting their age" (cf., Lawrence, 1984, 1988). It bears mentioning here that the applicability of this perspective to work contexts remains untested and should serve as a basis for future study concerning intergenerational perceptions.

Self-Referenced Age Stereotypes

Age stereotypes can also take self-referenced forms, including age meta-stereotypes and intra-generational stereotypes. Meta-stereotypes are assumptions that people hold about what other people might think about their social group (Vorauer, Main, & O'Connell, 1998), and recent research by Finkelstein, Ryan, and King (2013) has highlighted the existence of age meta-stereotypes in the workplace. In terms of future research, it seems important to draw a connection between the idea of meta-stereotypes and the established paradigm surrounding stereotype threat. Stereotype threat involves concerns of confirming or being reduced to a negative stereotype about one's social group (Steele & Aronson, 1995). The experience of stereotype threat may negatively impact on older workers' job attitudes and behaviors (Kalokerinos, von Hippel, & Zacher, 2014). For instance, a recent study showed that stereotype threat among older—but not younger—workers predicted negative job attitudes and poorer mental health, which in turn were associated with intentions to resign and intentions to retire (von Hippel, Kalokerinos, & Henry, 2012). Given the nascent nature of the literature on self-referenced age stereotypes, it would be wise for researchers to adopt a stereotype threat paradigm for investigating the deleterious effects of age meta-stereotypes on task performance, job attitudes, and other work outcomes.

Intra-Generational Stereotypes

Research has also examined intra-generational stereotypes among older adults, which encompass older adults' lack of positive attitudes or even negative attitudes and beliefs about people of their own age (Bodner, 2009). Such intra-generational stereotypes and intra-generational ageism (Butler, 1969) may lead older adults to disidentify with other older adults (i.e., to see them as a derogated out-group) and to consider the group of younger adults their preferred in-group (Bodner, 2009). In the work context, older workers who hold negative beliefs about their own age group may distance themselves from other older workers, describe themselves as younger or middle-aged workers, and prefer to interact more frequently with workers from other age groups.

Research findings on intra-generational stereotypes suggest that negative information and stereotypes about one's own age group can lead to lower well-being and performance among older adults, and to a tendency to disidentify with their same-aged peers and to seek contact with members of other age groups (e.g., Weiss & Lang, 2009, 2012). What is unclear is how intra-generational stereotype processes might play out in work contexts, and what effect such processes would have on social interactions in the workplace. Future research also must address the myriad contextual factors that either elicit intra-generational stereotypes, or serve as conditional influences to their effects on indicators of work performance (e.g., older adults who categorized themselves as older as opposed to younger had reduced performance on cognitive ability tests) (see Haslam et al., 2012). Future investigations might further consider how social networks emerge within age-diverse workgroups under the presence of negative age-related information (see Weiss & Freund, 2012).

THEORETICAL PERSPECTIVES ON INTERGENERATIONAL CONFLICT

Beyond stereotyping processes, several theoretical perspectives can be borrowed from to explain the underlying causes of intergenerational conflict. Below, we introduce relational demography as an organizing framework to understand comparative age processes in organizations, and then briefly review three theories (i.e., social identity and self-categorization theories, implicit organizational age grading, and leader-member exchange theory) that support comparative age processes. Then, we tie these theories into our broader argument regarding the nature of and processes leading to intergenerational conflict.

Relational Demography

Relational demography addresses how comparative demographic characteristics impact various outcomes within organizations and is a useful theoretical framework to understand intergenerational exchanges and conflicts in the workplace (cf., Kunze, Böhm, & Bruch, 2011; Lawrence, 1997). Research and theory in this area suggest that the comparative demographic makeup of teams and other organizational subunits can meaningfully impact important organizational outcomes, particularly those rooted in social-interactive processes (e.g., Tsui & O'Reilly, 1989). Along these lines, relational demography seeks to understand how comparative demographic characteristics of individuals at the within-group level can explain outcomes at the individual level of analysis (e.g., how does the comparative age between team members and their leader influence individual teamwork perceptions?) (see Tsui, Egan, & O'Reilly, 1991; Zenger & Lawrence, 1989).

Given relevant empirical findings (e.g., Collins, Hair, & Rocco, 2009; Kearney, 2008; Liden, Stilwell, & Ferris, 1996), future investigations of age-based relational demography should take advantage of advances in mixed-effects statistical methods and address complimentary calls for multilevel theory development. Indeed, the relative ease of representing individual-within-group processes represents an opportunity to gain a better picture of how relational age differences affect outcomes for individuals and workgroups, and to untangle the likely and potentially interesting interactive effects of multiple category membership (e.g., relational age and sex; relational age and organizational age). It also seems prudent to expand the criterion space to include performance- and non-performance-related outcomes in studies of relational age effects. Given the focus of the present work, interpersonal conflict seems an obvious choice, however given the potential outcomes of intergenerational exchanges, studies of relational age and workgroup trust, cohesion, and climate-like variables would also be informative contributions to this literature. Future studies could examine relational age effects adopting a person-environment (or person-person) fit perspective, which considers not only supplementary fit (i.e., similarity), but also complementary fit (i.e., mutual fulfillment of demands and needs) (Perry, Dokko, & Golom, 2012).

Leader-Member Exchange Perspective on Intergenerational Conflict

One interesting area for future research to apply age-based relational demography perspectives is in the area of leader-subordinate relationships. The study of the nature of social interaction between leaders and their subordinates has a long history in the organizational sciences. For example, leadership research (e.g., Dansereau, Cashman, & Graen, 1973; Graen, Novak, & Sommerkamp, 1982) has long suggested that leaders do not use the same leadership style with all of their subordinates, and that unique in-group/out-group exchange relationships develop between leaders and their subordinates over time (Graen, 1976). Age categorization represents one possible source of classification into in-groups versus out-groups.

A variety of social comparison theories suggest that similarities in attitudes and demographic characteristics may bolster the process of developing trust (e.g., Byrne, 1961). Expectations regarding other age groups are likely to exacerbate this process based upon the assumptions that underlie constructed generational differences. Thus, in multigenerational workgroups, it is possible that the formation of in-groups and out-groups falls along the lines of leader-subordinate age similarity (see Rudolph, 2011). While seemingly tenable, research is needed to specifically tease out when and through what process this categorization occurs, and how it specifically drives in-group/out-group formation.

Social Identity and Self-Categorization Theory Perspectives on Intergenerational Conflict

Both social identity theory (Ashforth & Mael, 1989; Tajfel & Turner, 1985) and self-categorization theory (Turner & Oakes, 1989) posit that people classify themselves and others into groups using salient and personally relevant criteria, such as age. People generally respond unfavorably when their social identity (i.e., the aspect of our self that involves a membership in a social group) is threatened. Such threats may engender negative effects, such as in-group bias (or in-group favoritism) and discrimination against those who are members of social out-groups (Hogg & Terry, 2000; Randel, 2002). One possible source of identity threat in work contexts is perceived age dissimilarity to one's coworkers, which may increase one's age-relevant identity salience (i.e., the extent to which one's age group membership is a central component of the self-concept) (see Ng, 1998; Thompson, 1999). Research suggests that the presence of similarly aged coworkers is likely to affirm age-group identity, thereby heightening identification with one's coworkers (Kearney & Gebert, 2009). On the contrary, the salience of age differences in multigenerational workgroups might serve as a catalyst for the negative consequences associated with this social comparison process— the result could be increased intergenerational conflict and decreased team performance.

Lawrence's Implicit Organizational Age Grading Theory

Implicit organizational age grading theory suggests that an active self-contextualization process occurs by which people gain personal insight via comparisons with similar others in the workplace. Lawrence (1984) argued that people's perception of age distributions within organizations are salient factors in the construction of such implicit age norms, and that people actively use such age norms as indicators of their career progression. Lawrence (1984) demonstrated that people who see themselves as "behind time" (i.e., in terms of their perceived career progression) with respect to others tend to have more negative attitudes toward work than others who are "on time." The (in)equity perspective on workplace justice suggests that people who perceive that they are not getting their fair share of valued resource allocations may retaliate in subversive ways in order to compensate for this discrepancy (e.g., Adams, 1965; Walster, Walster, & Bersheid, 1978). People who see themselves as "behind time" may perceive such resource discrepancies (e.g., not getting their fair share of resources, such as job promotions and consequent benefits) and as such may subtly change their behavior to rectify such inequities. The manifestation of such behaviors may drive intergenerational conflict to the extent that such actions are attributed to age-specific generalizations (e.g., subtle changes in productivity could be ascribed to age-related declines in functioning), however this notion remains untested, and represents yet another venue for future research.

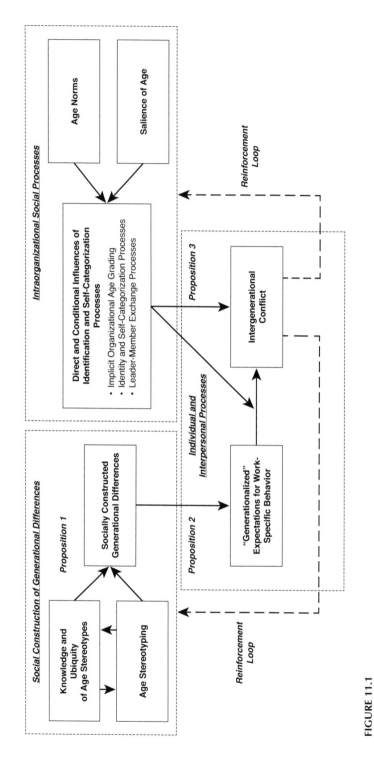

FIGURE 11.1
A model of intergenerational conflict

A MODEL OF INTERGENERATIONAL CONFLICT

Given the lack of a coherent, workable, and theoretically justified model for studying intergenerational conflict in the workplace, we coalesce the ideas presented above into an integrative framework to guide future research on this topic. To this end, our arguments for the processes underlying intergenerational conflict are depicted in Figure 11.1 and summarized in Table 11.1 In essence, this model suggests that intergenerational conflict is fueled indirectly by the social construction of generational differences at the societal level, and directly *and* conditionally through various intra-organizational social processes. First, considering our earlier discussion of the perceptual and constructed nature of generational differences, our model suggests that generational differences are largely a social artifact. Thus:

> *Proposition 1*: Generational differences are socially constructed via: (a) the knowledge of common age stereotypes, which are supported by the popular overemphasis on the existence of generational differences; and (b) their application via cognitive stereotyping processes.

Several ideas are contained within this proposition. First, more research is needed to address the ubiquity of age stereotypes in the workplace. That is to say, we need to know more about the collective prevalence of contemporary age stereotypes, and how engrained such stereotypes are insomuch as they influence thoughts and actions. This includes the need for more research on the content and potentially mixed nature of generationalized expectations, as we have defined them. Our understanding of age stereotypes across the lifespan is relatively narrow at this point (i.e., we generally focus on negative characterizations of *older* individuals), and a broader understanding of these phenomena rests on understanding multiple forms of age stereotypes. We suggest that more attention needs to be paid to understanding multiple forms of positive and negative age characterizations at various points across the lifespan (e.g., younger and middle-aged/career/life, as opposed to solely older).

Proposition 1 further suggests the need for more research on the sociocultural ubiquity and pervasiveness of the generational differences construct. These are admittedly not particularly easy issues to address, and they perhaps beg for the creative application of emerging research methodologies. One particularly intriguing possibility for studying this

TABLE 11.1
Propositions and Example Future Research Directions

Proposition #1

"Generational differences are socially constructed via: (a) the knowledge of common age stereotypes, which are supported by the popular overemphasis on the existence of generational differences; and (b) their application via cognitive stereotyping processes."

Research Area	Example Future Research Questions
Age and Aging Stereotypes	• What is the specific content and implication of "younger" and "middle-aged" worker stereotypes? • How do age stereotypes relate to beliefs about when someone is a "younger", "middle-aged," or "older" worker? • What is the specific content and implication of prescriptive age stereotypes in work contexts? • How can we integrate meta-stereotype processes into the stereotype threat paradigm? • How do "shared" age stereotypes in teams and organizations affect the formation of "organizational age cultures?"
The Construction of Generational Differences	• What is the content and the extent/ubiquity of (e.g., popular belief in/support for) generational difference in work-relevant outcomes? • What sociocultural mechanisms support and propagate the idea of generational differences in work-related behaviors, attitudes, and motivations? • How is the idea of generational differences in the workplace represented, and how do such representations fuel the myth of generational differences in the workplace?

Proposition #2

"The perception of constructed generational differences facilitates intergenerational conflict via 'generationalized expectations' for work-specific behavior."

Research Area	Example Future Research Questions
Intergenerational Exchanges and Conflicts	- How can we integrate relational demography with person-environment fit perspectives (i.e., supplementary and complementary fit)? - Can we expand the criterion space to include performance- and non-performance-based outcomes of intergenerational conflict? - What are "intergenerational potentials" and their relations to conflict (i.e., positive consequences of exchanges and conflicts)? - What factors lead to the creation of intergenerational potential in the work context?

Proposition #3

"Organizational and job-specific age norms and the salience of age influence age-related identification and self-categorization processes. In turn, such processes directly and conditionally drive intergenerational conflict."

Research Area	Example Future Research Questions
Age Norms and Age Salience	- How does age similarity affect the creation of social in-groups/out-groups within organizations? - How can we link perceptions of organizational age distributions and norms to intergenerational conflict? - Can we untangle the influence of multiple age category membership via mixed effects modeling and relational demography perspectives? - How does age (dis)similarity affect the formation and maintenance of leader-follower exchange relationships?
Social Identity Perspectives	- How can social identity and self-categorization perspectives explain the emergence and maintenance of age stereotypes in the workplace? - How can we best define and study age identity complexity (e.g., organizational identification and "older worker"/"younger worker" identities)? - How do age norms and the salience affect age group identification? - How do intra-generational stereotypes serve an identity maintenance and enhancement mechanism in the workplace?

phenomenon is to take advantage of the so-called "big data" trend by mining the contents of large-scale, publicly available databases for evidence of trends in the emergence and prevalence of related phenomena. For example, Google's Ngram database and Twitter's feed database can be queried to investigate trends in the usage and appearance of ideas that are related to intergenerational exchanges in popular literature and social discourse (see Michel et al., 2011 for an example). Such databases offer researchers access to vast amounts of information, and allow for interesting applications of emerging data analytic methods to address these types of research questions.

Google's Ngram database contains yearly counts of selected words and phrases found in over 5.2 million books digitized by Google, and the open-source R environment for statistical computing offers a package called

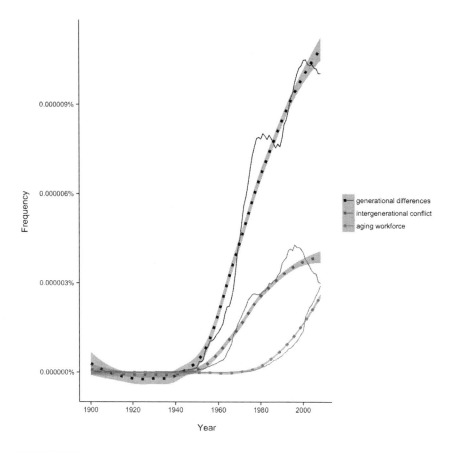

FIGURE 11.2
Google Ngram example

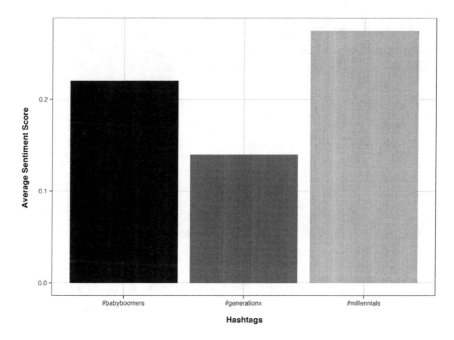

FIGURE 11.3
Twitter feed sentiment analysis of generation hashtags

"ngrmr" (Carmody, 2013) that allows for this database to be accessed and its contents analyzed with relative ease. An example of this type of analysis can be found in Figure 11.2. Here, we have queried the Google Ngram database for the following terms: generational differences, intergenerational conflict, and aging workforce. We queried the database for the appearance of these terms for the years 1900 to 2008, and limited the search to English texts. The resulting data can be represented as the frequency of occurrence of these phrases (i.e., non-cumulatively and relative to other phrases present in the same time frame) over time. Figure 11.2 suggests the emergence of some interesting patterns—most notably the rise in the concepts of generational differences and intergenerational conflicts as represented in popular literature over time.

Another R package, "twitteR" (Gentry, 2013) allows researchers to query and analyze trends (e.g., hashtags, tweet contents) directly from the Twitter database. These trends can be compiled and subjected to any number of qualitative analyses, including qualitative sentiment analysis (Pang & Lee, 2008). To illustrate this, we ran a basic sentiment analysis on Tweets containing generation-related hashtags (i.e., #babyboomers, #generationx,

#millennials). We queried the Twitter application programming interface (API) for these hashtags, and ran sentiment analyses on the content of the resulting tweets using a lexical corpus of positively and negatively valenced words developed by Hu and Liu (2004). We then constructed a bar plot (see Figure 11.3) depicting the average sentiment score of tweets containing these generational hashtags (i.e., average sentiment values above zero indicate that the valence of tweets containing these hashtags was *positive*). The results indicate that tweets about generations are on average generally positive, but that tweets about "Generation X" seem to be less positively valenced than tweets about "baby boomers." The valence of tweets about millennials appears to be highest, which is perhaps not surprising considering the medium.

The proposed model next specifies the mechanism by which socially constructed generational differences drive intergenerational conflict. Consistent with Joshi and colleagues (2010, 2011), we suggest that constructed generational differences influence intergenerational conflict by setting up behavioral expectations (i.e., prescriptions) for members of various age groups at the individual level—we term these expectations "generationalized" as they dictate how individuals are likely to interact and behave at work by virtue of their membership in a particular generationally defined age category.

Proposition 2: The perception of constructed generational differences facilitates intergenerational conflict via "generationalized expectations" for work-specific behavior.

Given the relative novelty of this proposition to research in I-O psychology, further research is needed to explicate the nature of these generationalized expectations. Specifically, research should address how such generationalized expectations are formed and shaped by stereotypes (i.e., descriptions), how they are applied and operate at various levels of abstraction, and their affective, behavioral, and cognitive components.

Finally, our model specifies various processes that both directly and conditionally affect the unfolding process of intergenerational conflict. More specifically, we argue that various intra-organizational social processes associated with identification and self-categorization—fueled by organizational age norms and the salience of age—can directly affect intergenerational conflict. Furthermore, these social processes can have a conditional influence of the effects of the aforementioned generationalized expectations for work-specific behavior that either mitigate or exacerbate intergenerational conflict.

> *Proposition 3*: Organizational and job-specific age norms along with the salience of age influence age-related identification and self-categorization processes, which in turn directly and conditionally drive intergenerational conflict.

Of note here, when conceptualized in a conditional sense, age-related identification and self-categorization processes might contribute to an organization's climate for aging (e.g., Kunze et al., 2011; Noack & Staudinger, 2009; Zacher & Gielnik, 2014). Psychological climate is generally defined as individual employee perceptions of their work environment (Baltes, Zhdanova, & Parker, 2009). Psychological climate *for* aging constitutes employee perceptions of the age-friendliness of their work environments, and employees' shared (i.e., agreed-upon) perceptions constitute the organization's climate for aging. While some research has addressed this idea, there is a need for future investigations that more fully explain factors that drive positive versus negative climates for aging in organizations. For example, our model specifies that age norms and the salience of age within organizations constitute important facets that support age climate through identification and self-categorization processes.

CONSEQUENCES OF INTERGENERATIONAL CONFLICT

Our model further suggests that intergenerational conflict can in turn impact the social construction of generational differences and intra-organizational social processes via reinforcement loops (Figure 11.1). Thus, the occurrence of conflicts among workers of different ages may further stabilize the construction of generational differences in different psychological characteristics (i.e., age stereotypes) and strengthen social categorization processes based on age group and cohort memberships, leading to the possibility of a negative intergenerational conflict spiral. That is to say, it is likely that such processes are negatively accruing and cyclical—intergenerational conflict reinforces both the social construction of generational differences and intra-organizational social processes, which in turn further support intergenerational conflict. For example, age stereotypes that define socially constructed generational differences and generationalized expectations for work-specific behavior are likely to lead to intergenerational conflict. Such conflicts likely reinforce age stereotypes, which in turn feed back into this deleterious cycle.

Intergenerational conflict is also likely to negatively affect individual worker and organizational outcomes via inefficient or disrupted communication and coordination processes. For instance, intergenerational conflict may negatively influence the job attitudes and organizational identification of both younger and older workers and lead to declines in individual and team performance, as well as turnover. On the part of younger workers, intergenerational conflict may further have detrimental effects on their attitudes toward older people in general, as well as their own aging process (i.e., health and aging satisfaction) (Levy, Slade, Kunkel, & Kasl, 2002). Among older workers, intergenerational conflict may lead to decreased organization-based self-esteem, as well as reduced intentions to continue working past normative retirement age (Armstrong-Stassen, 2008). Because of the salience of age differences, and the role of self-referenced and meta-stereotyping processes, such conflict may further induce stereotype threat (von Hippel et al., 2012).

Future research is needed that investigates these potential effects of intergenerational conflict in workplaces, as well as their boundary conditions. For instance, the nature of different levels of the work environment (cf., Edwards & Shipp, 2007), including the job, organizational, and vocational context, may make certain age stereotypes more or less salient and thus enhance or mitigate detrimental effects of intergenerational conflict. On the one hand, older workers may be impacted most by intergenerational conflicts in work environments that emphasize the stereotypical strength of younger workers (e.g., the use of up-to-date technology). On the other hand, work environments that make older workers' stereotypical strengths salient (e.g., counseling, mentoring, or other generative processes) may lead younger workers to suffer more from intergenerational conflicts.

CONSIDERING THE POSITIVE CONSEQUENCES OF AGE DIVERSITY

The preceding sections of the chapter have presented an admittedly bleak view of the possible outcomes of increased age diversity in work contexts.

Our focus on intergenerational conflict necessitated this negative stance. Lest we leave the reader with the notion that increased age heterogeneity can *only* be a bad thing, we provide here a glimpse at the possibility for positive effects of age diversity within organizations and their subunits. The notion of positive intergenerational exchanges is not a new idea (see Peacock & Tailey, 1984). Indeed, contemporary scholarship from the diversity literature (e.g., van Knippenberg, de Dreu, & Homan, 2004) acknowledges that workgroup diversity can have both positive and negative consequences (e.g., increased team performance). For example, the categorization-elaboration model (van Knippenberg et al., 2004) suggests that the primary process underlying the positive effects of diversity on team performance is elaboration of task-relevant information (i.e., the sharing and processing of diverse information and viewpoints among team members). This general idea is also reflected in diversity theories that stem from the communications and decision-making literatures (e.g., de Dreu, 2006; Kerschreiter, Mojzisch, Schulz-Hardt, Brodbeck, & Frey, 2003).

Research has shown that high levels of certain team characteristics (i.e., average team need for cognition) and leadership characteristics (e.g., transformational leadership) can boost the favorable outcomes of high age diversity in teams, including the elaboration of task-relevant information, collective team identification, and, subsequently, leader ratings of team performance (Kearney & Gebert, 2009; Kearney, Gebert, & Voelpel, 2009). Along these lines, Kessler and Staudinger (2007) found that when interacting in intergenerational task performance settings that were characterized by high levels of support for generativity (i.e., the concern for the next generation) (McAdams & de St. Aubin, 1992; Zacher et al., 2011) and identity formation, young adults exhibited more prosocial behaviors, while older adults where better able to regulate their emotions, and exhibited higher levels of cognitive fluency. More recently, Iweins, Desmette, Yzerbyt, and Stinglhamber (2013) showed that intergenerational contact at work and organizations' appreciation of different age groups improved workers' job attitudes by creating a sense of dual identity (i.e., being a member of both one's generation and organization). Thus, it appears that there is at least some evidence to suggest that intergenerational interactions can be mutually beneficial, and in particular malleable facets of the context of such interaction can facilitate this process.

Research in the field of communications has also shed some light on the possible positive implications of intergenerational exchanges that are driven by positive stereotypes (see Harwood, Giles, & Ryan, 1995; Williams & Nussbaum, 2001). For example, McCann, Dailey, Giles, and Ota (2005) found that young adults who characterized older adults as benevolent and personally vital were also more likely to report positive communication with older adults. In their intergenerational contact model, Fox and Giles (1993) proposed that the individual characteristics, goals, and expectations of younger and older persons, as well as external factors such as social norms, power, and salience of age, influence the characteristics of the intergenerational contact situation, which in turn impacts the quality of contact, attributions, and possible change of intergenerational attitudes. While the focus of our conceptual model (Figure 11.1) is currently exclusively on intergenerational conflict, future research could attempt to integrate intergenerational potential into such a model.

REMEDIATING INTERGENERATIONAL CONFLICT

An important area for future research and organizational practice is how intergenerational conflicts can be prevented or their negative consequences remediated. The literature on intergroup contact may be useful in this regard (Allport, 1954; Pettigrew, 1998). Specifically, the contact hypothesis (Allport, 1954) posits that the relationships between groups that hold stereotypes about and experience conflict with each other can be improved through frequent and positive interactions. For instance, more opportunities for communication and teamwork among workers from different age groups could be a way to reduce stereotypes and to enhance understanding of different viewpoints. According to intergroup contact theory (Allport, 1954), factors that further facilitate the effects of intergroup contact include common goals, leadership support, and shared social norms. Recent scholarship regarding understanding and managing relational identities (e.g., Shapiro, 2010; Sluss & Ashforth, 2007) reflects similar sentiments. As shown by Iweins and colleagues (2013), intergenerational contact may, alongside organizational support for different age groups, diminish ageism and improve job attitudes. At the organizational level, Kunze, Böhm, and Bruch (2013) found positive effects of age diversity (which potentially allows for more intergenerational contact to occur) on organizations' age discrimination climate, which in turn negatively impacted on firm performance (see also Kunze et al., 2011). Important here, the study also showed that top managers' age stereotypes increased and age-inclusive HR practices weakened these associations. Considering these ideas, practitioners could aim to implement these factors as part of formal interventions in age-diverse teams.

Preliminary support for the importance of leadership support comes from a study by Kearney and Gebert (2009), who found that transformational leadership buffered the negative effect of age diversity on team performance. Research in lifespan psychology showed that social comparisons with younger people resulted in lower cognitive task performance among older adults only when prior intergenerational contact had not been positive (Abrams, Eller, & Bryant, 2006). Thus, this research suggests that positive contact between different age groups might weaken older workers' vulnerability to the negative performance consequences of intergenerational comparisons. A promising avenue for future research is to conduct field- or quasi-experiments in which the age diversity of workgroups, contact between workers of different ages, and group-level influences such as leadership behaviors are manipulated, and intergenerational conflict and positive intergenerational potentials (e.g., mutual learning) are assessed as outcome variables.

CONCLUSION

In this chapter, we reviewed various theories and empirical evidence on intergenerational perceptions and conflict within organizations, and proposed an integrative conceptual model of the processes leading to intergenerational conflict. It is our hope that this model will stimulate further research on the social exchanges among different age groups at work, with a particular focus on how intergenerational conflicts can be prevented and their negative effects mitigated. While the viewpoint taken here suggests the inevitability of intergenerational conflict, emerging evidence suggests that positive intergenerational exchanges can be facilitated through relatively straightforward interventions aimed at manipulating facets of the work environment. While increased age heterogeneity in the workplace is inevitable, our hope is that the ideas presented here serve as a catalyst for mitigating the negative impact of intergenerational conflict on organizations, their processes, and constituents.

REFERENCES

Abrams, D., Eller, A., & Bryant, J. (2006). An age apart: The effects of intergenerational contact and stereotype threat on performance and intergroup bias. *Psychology and Aging, 21*(4), 691–702.

Adams, G., & Rau, B. (2004). Job seeking among retirees seeking bridge employment. *Personnel Psychology*, 57(3), 719–744.
Adams, J. S. (1965). Inequity in social exchange. *Advances in Experimental Social Psychology*, 2, 267–299.
Allport, G. W. (1954). *The Nature of Prejudice*. Cambridge, MA: Perseus Books.
Armstrong-Stassen, M. (2008). Organisational practices and the post-retirement employment experience of older workers. *Human Resource Management Journal*, 18(1), 36–53.
Ashforth, B. E., & Mael, F. (1989). Social identity theory and the organization. *Academy of Management Review*, 14(1), 20–39.
Bal, A. C., Reiss, A. E., Rudolph, C. W., & Baltes, B. B. (2011). Examining positive and negative perceptions of older workers: A meta-analysis. *The Journals of Gerontology Series B: Psychological Sciences and Social Sciences*, 66(6), 687–698.
Baltes, B. B., & Rudolph, C. W. (2012). The theory of selection, optimization and compensation. In M. Wang (Ed.), *The Oxford Handbook of Retirement* (pp. 88–101). New York: Oxford University Press.
Baltes, B. B., Zhdanova, L. S., & Parker, C. P. (2009). Psychological climate: A comparison of organizational and individual level referents. *Human Relations*, 62(5), 669–700.
Baltes, P. B. (1968). Longitudinal and cross-sectional sequences in the study of age and generation effects. *Human Development*, 11(3), 145–171.
Bertolino, M., Truxillo, D. M., & Fraccaroli, F. (2013). Age effects on perceived personality and job performance. *Journal of Managerial Psychology*, 28(7/8), 867–885.
Blythe, J., Baumann, A., Zeytinoglu, I. U., Denton, M., Akhtar-Danesh, N., Davies, S., & Kolotylo, C. (2008). Nursing generations in the contemporary workplace. *Public Personnel Management*, 37(2), 137–159.
Bodner, E. (2009). On the origins of ageism among older and younger adults. *International Psychogeriatrics*, 21(6), 1003–1014.
Burtless, G. (2012). Who is delaying retirement? Analyzing the increase in employment at older ages (white paper). Available at: https://appam.confex.com/.../Burtless_APPAM_Complete_Nov-2012.pdf (accessed February 1, 2014).
Butler, R. N. (1969). Age-ism: Another form of bigotry. *The Gerontologist*, 9(4), 243–246.
Byrne, D. (1961). Interpersonal attraction and attitude similarity. *The Journal of Abnormal and Social Psychology*, 62(3), 713–715.
Carmody, S. (2013). ngramr: Retrieve and plot Google n-gram data. R package version 1.4.2. Software. Available at: http://CRAN.R-project.org/package=ngramr (accessed February 1, 2014).
Cennamo, L., & Gardner, D. (2008). Generational differences in work values, outcomes, and person-organisation values fit. *Journal of Managerial Psychology*, 23(8), 891–906.
Clemens, A. (2012). Position-specific promotion rates and the "fast track" effect. *Research in Labor Economics*, 36, 77–107.
Collins, M. H., Hair, J. F., & Rocco, T. S. (2009). The older-worker-younger-supervisor dyad: A test of the Reverse Pygmalion effect. *Human Resource Development Quarterly*, 20(1), 21–41.
Costanza, D. P., Badger, J. M., Fraser, R. L., Severt, J. B., & Gade, P. A. (2012). Generational differences in work-related attitudes: A meta-analysis. *Journal of Business and Psychology*, 27(4), 375–394.
Dansereau, F., Cashman, J., & Graen, G. (1973). Instrumentality theory and equity theory as complementary approaches in predicting the relationship of leadership and turnover among managers. *Organizational Behavior and Human Performance*, 10(2), 184–200.

de Dreu, C. K. W. (2006). When too little or too much hurts: Evidence for a curvilinear relationship between task conflict and innovation in teams. *Journal of Management, 32*, 83–107.

Dols, J., Landrum, P., & Wieck, K. L. (2010). Leading and managing an intergenerational workforce. *Creative Nursing, 16*(2), 68–74.

Edwards, J. R., & Shipp, A. J. (2007). The relationship between person-environment fit and outcomes: An integrative theoretical framework. In C. Ostroff & T. A. Judge (Eds.), *Perspectives on Organizational Fit* (pp. 209–258). San Francisco, CA: Jossey-Bass.

Eyerman, R., & Turner, B. S. (1998). Outline of a theory of generations. *European Journal of Social Theory, 1*(1), 91–106.

Finkelstein, L. M., Ryan, K. M., & King, E. B. (2013). What do the young (old) people think of me? Content and accuracy of age-based metastereotypes. *European Journal of Work and Organizational Psychology, 22*(6), 633–657.

Fiske, S. T. (1998). Stereotyping, prejudice, and discrimination. In D. T. Gilbert, S. T. Fiske, & G. Lindzey (Eds.), *The Handbook of Social Psychology, Vol. 2* (4th ed.) (pp. 357–393). Boston, MA: McGraw-Hill.

Flynn, M. (2010). Who would delay retirement? Typologies of older workers. *Personnel Review, 39*(3), 308–324.

Fox, S., & Giles, H. (1993). Accommodating intergenerational contact: A critique and theoretical model. *Research on Aging, 7*(4), 423–451.

Gentry, J. (2013). twitteR: R based Twitter client. R package version 1.1.7. Software. Available at: http://CRAN.R-project.org/package=twitteR.

Gilbert, J. (2011). The millennials: A new generation of employees, a new set of engagement policies. Available at: http://iveybusinessjournal.com/topics/the-workplace/the-millennials-a-new-generation-of-employees-a-new-set-of-engagement-policies#.Ut VsUxayPcM (accessed January 14, 2014).

Graen, G. B. (1976). Role making processes within complex organizations. In M. D. Dunnette (Ed.), *Handbook of Industrial and Organizational Psychology* (pp. 1201–1245). Chicago, IL: Rand-McNally.

Graen, G. B., Novak, M. A., & Sommerkamp, P. (1982). The effects of leader-member exchange and job design on productivity and satisfaction: Testing a dual attachment model. *Organizational Behavior and Human Performance, 30*(1), 109–131.

Graves, J. A. (2012). Millenial workers: Entitled, needy, self-centered? Available at: http://money.usnews.com/money/careers/articles/2012/06/27/millennial-workers-entitled-needy-self-centered (accessed January 14, 2014).

Hanks, R. S., & Icenogle, M. (2001). Preparing for an age-diverse workforce: Intergenerational service-learning in social gerontology and business curricula. *Educational Gerontology, 27*(1), 49–70.

Harwood, J., Giles, H., & Ryan, E. B. (1995). Aging, communication, and intergroup theory: Social identity and intergenerational communication. In J. F. Nussbaum (Ed.), *Handbook of Communication and Aging Research* (pp. 133–159). Hillsdale, NJ: Lawrence Erlbaum & Associates.

Haslam, C., Morton, T. A., Haslam, S. A., Varnes, L., Graham, R., & Gamaz, L. (2012). "When the age is in, the wit is out": Age-related self-categorization and deficit expectations reduce performance on clinical tests used in dementia assessment. *Psychology and Aging, 27*(3), 778–784.

Hassell, B. L., & Perrewe, P. L. (1995). An examination of beliefs about older workers: Do stereotypes still exist? *Journal of Organizational Behavior, 16*, 457–468.

Hogg, M. A., & Terry, D. J. (2000). Social identity and self-categorization processes in organizational contexts. *Academy of Management Review, 25*, 121–140.

Hu, M., & Liu, B. (2004). Mining and summarizing customer reviews. Proceedings of the ACM SIGKDD International Conference on Knowledge Discovery and Data Mining (KDD-2004), Seattle, Washington, USA.

Hummert, M. L. (1990). Multiple stereotypes of elderly and young adults: A comparison of structure and evaluations. *Psychology and Aging*, 5(2), 182–193.

Hussar, W. J., & Bailey, T. M. (2013). Projections of education statistics to 2021. National Center for Education Statistics: U.S. Department of Education. Available at: http://nces.ed.gov/pubs2013/2013008.pdf (accessed February 1, 2014).

Iweins, C., Desmette, D., Yzerbyt, V., & Stinglhamber, F. (2013). Ageism at work: The impact of intergenerational contact and organizational multi-age perspective. *European Journal of Work and Organizational Psychology*, 22, 331–346.

Joshi, A., Dencker, J. C., Franz, G., & Martocchio, J. J. (2010). Unpacking generational identities in organizations. *Academy of Management Review*, 35(3), 392–414.

Joshi, A., Dencker, J. C., & Franz, G. (2011). Generations in organizations. *Research in Organizational Behavior*, 31, 177–205.

Kalokerinos, E. K., von Hippel, C., & Zacher, H. (2014). Is stereotype threat a useful construct for organizational psychology research and practice? *Industrial and Organizational Psychology: Perspectives on Science and Practice*, 7(3), 381–402.

Kearney, E. (2008). Age differences between leader and followers as a moderator of the relationship between transformational leadership and team performance. *Journal of Occupational and Organizational Psychology*, 81, 803–811.

Kearney, E., & Gebert, D. (2009). Managing diversity and enhancing team outcomes: The promise of transformational leadership. *Journal of Applied Psychology*, 94(1), 77–89.

Kearney, E., Gebert, D., & Voelpel, S. C. (2009). When and how diversity benefits teams: The importance of team members' need for cognition. *Academy of Management Journal*, 52(3), 581–598.

Kerschreiter, R., Mojzisch, A., Schulz-Hardt, S., Brodbeck, F. C., & Frey, D. (2003). Informationsaustausch bei Entscheidungsprozessen in Gruppen: Theorie, Empirie und Implikationen für die Praxis [Information exchange in decision processes of groups: Theory, data and practical implications]. In S. Stumpf & A. Thomas (Eds.), *Teamarbeit und Teamentwicklung [Team Work and Team Development]* (pp. 85–118). Göttingen: Hogrefe.

Kessler, E. M., & Staudinger, U. M. (2007). Intergenerational potential: Effects of social interaction between older people and adolescents. *Psychology and Aging*, 22, 690–704.

Kim, S., & Feldman, D. C. (2000). Working in retirement: The antecedents of bridge employment and its consequences for quality of life in retirement. *Academy of Management Journal*, 43(6), 1195–1210.

Kite, M. E., Stockdale, G. D., Whitley, B. E., & Johnson, B. T. (2005). Attitudes toward younger and older adults: An updated meta-analytic review. *Journal of Social Issues*, 61(2), 241–266.

Kooij, D. T. A. M., de Lange, A. H., Jansen, P. G. W., & Dikkers, J. S. E. (2008). Older workers' motivation to continue to work: Five meanings of age. *Journal of Managerial Psychology*, 23(4), 364–394.

Kowske, B. J., Rasch, R., & Wiley, J. (2010). Millennials' (lack of) attitude problem: An empirical examination of generational effects on work attitudes. *Journal of Business and Psychology*, 25, 265–279.

Krueger, J., Heckhausen, J., & Hundertmark, J. (1995). Perceiving middle-aged adults: Effects of stereotype-congruent and incongruent information. *The Journals of Gerontology Series B: Psychological Sciences and Social Sciences*, 50(2), 82–93.

Kunze, F., Böhm, S. A., & Bruch, H. (2011). Age diversity, age discrimination climate and performance consequences: A cross organizational study. *Journal of Organizational Behavior, 32*(2), 264–290.

Kunze, F., Böhm, S., & Bruch, H. (2013). Organizational performance consequences of age diversity: Inspecting the role of diversity-friendly HR policies and top managers' negative age stereotypes. *Journal of Management Studies, 50*(3), 413–442.

Lawrence, B. S. (1984). Age grading: The implicit organizational timetable. *Journal of Organizational Behavior, 5*(1), 23–35.

Lawrence, B. S. (1988). New wrinkles in the theory of age: Demography, norms, and performance ratings. *Academy of Management Journal, 31*(2), 309–337.

Lawrence, B. S. (1997). Perspective: The black box of organizational demography. *Organization Science, 8*(1), 1–22.

Lawrence, B., & Zyphur, M. (2011). Identifying organizational faultlines with latent class cluster analysis. *Organizational Research Methods, 14*, 32–57.

Levy, B. R., Slade, M. D., Kunkel, S. R., & Kasl, S. V. (2002). Longevity increased by positive self-perceptions of aging. *Journal of Personality and Social Psychology, 83*, 261–270.

Liden, R. C., Stilwell, D., & Ferris, G. R. (1996). The effects of supervisor and subordinate age on objective performance and subjective performance ratings. *Human Relations, 49*(3), 327–347.

Lyons, S., & Kuron, L. (2014). Generational differences in the workplace: A review of the evidence and directions for future research. *Journal of Organizational Behavior, 35*, 139–157.

MacCallum, R. C., Zhang, S., Preacher, K. J., & Rucker, D. D. (2002). On the practice of dichotomization of quantitative variables. *Psychological Methods, 7*, 19–40.

Mannheim, K. (1970). The problem of generations. *Psychoanalytic Review, 57*(3), 378–404.

McAdams, D. P., & de St. Aubin, E. (1992). A theory of generativity and its assessment through self-report, behavioral acts, and narrative themes in autobiography. *Journal of Personality and Social Psychology, 62*(6), 1003–1015.

McCann, R. M., Dailey, R. M., Giles, H., & Ota, H. (2005). Beliefs about intergenerational communication across the lifespan: Middle age and the roles of age stereotyping and respect norms. *Communication Studies, 56*(4), 293–311.

Michel, J. B., Shen, Y. K., Aiden, A. P., Veres, A., Gray, M. K., The Google Books Team, Pickett, J. P., Hoiberg, D., Clancy, D., Norvig, P., Orwant, J., Pinker, S., Nowak, M. A., & Aiden, E. L. (2011). Quantitative analysis of culture using millions of digitized books. *Science, 331*(6014), 176–182.

Myers, K. K., & Sadaghiani, K. (2010). Millennials in the workplace: A communication perspective on millennials' organizational relationships and performance. *Journal of Business and Psychology, 25*(2), 225–238.

Newton, B. (2006). Training an age-diverse workforce. *Industrial and Commercial Training, 38*(2), 93–97.

Ng, S. H. (1998). Social psychology in an ageing world: Ageism and intergenerational relations. *Asian Journal of Social Psychology, 1*(1), 99–116.

Ng, T. W., & Feldman, D. C. (2012). Evaluating six common stereotypes about older workers with meta-analytical data. *Personnel Psychology, 65*(4), 821–858.

Noack, C. M. G., & Staudinger, U. M. (2009). Psychological age climate: Associations with work-related outcomes. Poster presented at the Annual Meeting of the Society for Industrial and Organizational Psychology, New Orleans, LA.

North, M. S., & Fiske, S. T. (2012). An inconvenienced youth? Ageism and its potential intergenerational roots. *Psychological Bulletin, 138*(5), 982–997.

North, M. S., & Fiske, S. T. (2013). A prescriptive intergenerational-tension ageism scale: Succession, identity, and consumption (SIC). *Psychological Assessment*, 25(3), 706–713.

Pang, B., & Lee, L. (2008). Opinion mining and sentiment analysis. *Foundations and Trends in Information Retrieval*, 2(1–2), 1–135.

Parry, E., & Urwin, P. (2011). Generational differences in work values: A review of theory and evidence. *International Journal of Management Reviews*, 13(1), 79–96.

Peacock, E. W., & Talley, W. M. (1984). Intergenerational contact: A way to counteract ageism. *Educational Gerontology*, 10(1), 13–24.

Perry, E. L., Dokko, G., & Golom, F. D. (2012). The aging worker and person-environment fit. In J. W. Hedge & W. C. Borman (Eds.), *The Oxford Handbook of Work and Aging* (pp. 187–212). New York: Oxford University Press.

Pettigrew, T. F. (1998). Intergroup contact theory. *Annual Review of Psychology*, 49, 65–85.

Pitt-Catsouphes, M., Matz-Costa, C., & James, J. (2012). *Through a Different Looking Glass: The Prism of Age*. Chestnut Hill, MA: Sloan Center on Aging & Work, Boston College.

Posthuma, R. A., & Campion, M. A. (2009). Age stereotypes in the workplace: Common stereotypes, moderators, and future research directions. *Journal of Management*, 35(1), 158–188.

Randel, A. E. (2002). Identity salience: A moderator of the relationship between group gender composition and work group conflict. *Journal of Organizational Behavior*, 23, 749–766.

Real, K., Mitnick, A. D., & Maloney, W. F. (2010). More similar than different: Millennials in the US building trades. *Journal of Business and Psychology*, 25(2), 303–313.

Rosenbaum, J. E. (1979). Organizational career mobility: Promotion chances in a corporation during periods of growth and contraction. *American Journal of Sociology*, 85, 21–48.

Rosow, I. (1978). What is a cohort and why? *Human Development*, 21(2), 65–75.

Roth, C., Wegge, J., & Schmidt, K.-H. (2007). Konsequenzen des Demographischen Wandels für das Management von Humanressourcen [Consequences of demographic changes for the management of human resources]. *Zeitschrift für Personalpsychologie*, 6, 99–116.

Rudolph, C. W. (2011). A meta-analytic framework for understanding how leader-subordinate age differences impact leadership effectiveness ratings: A novel approach to relational demography. *ETD Collection for Wayne State University*. Paper AAI3466678. Available at: http://digitalcommons.wayne.edu/dissertations/AAI346678 (accessed February 1, 2014).

Rudolph, C. W., Baltes, B. B., & Zabel, K. L. (2013). Age and work motives. In J. Field, R. J. Burke, & C. L. Cooper (Eds.), *The Sage Handbook of Aging, Work, and Society*. Thousand Oaks, CA: Sage.

Ryan, C. L., & Siebens, J. (2012). Educational attainment in the United States: 2009. *Current Population Reports*. Available at: www.census.gov/prod/2012pubs/p20-566.pdf (accessed February 1, 2014).

Schwall, A. R. (2012). Defining age and using age-relevant constructs. In J. W. Hedge & W. C. Borman (Eds.), *The Oxford Handbook of Work and Aging* (pp. 169–186). New York: Oxford University Press.

Shapiro, D. L. (2010). Relational identity theory: A systematic approach for transforming the emotional dimension of conflict. *American Psychologist*, 65(7), 634–645.

Sluss, D. M., & Ashforth, B. E. (2007). Relational identity and identification: Defining ourselves through work relationships. *Academy of Management Review*, 32(1), 9–32.

Smith, K. (2013). Disadvantages of hiring younger employees. Available at: http://under30ceo.com/disadvantages-of-hiring-younger-employees/ (accessed January 14, 2014).

Steele, C. M., & Aronson, J. (1995). Stereotype threat and the intellectual test performance of African Americans. *Journal of Personality and Social Psychology, 69*(5), 797–811.

Sterns, H. L., & Doverspike, D. (1989). Aging and the training and learning process in organizations. In I. Goldstein & R. Katze (Eds.), *Training and Development in Work Organizations* (pp. 299–332). San Francisco, CA: Jossey-Bass.

Stewart, A. J., & Healy, J. M. (1989). Linking individual development and social changes. *American Psychologist, 44*(1), 30–42.

Stoops, N. (2004). Educational attainment in the United States: 2003. U.S. Census Bureau. Available at: www.census.gov/prod/2004pubs/p20-550.pdf (accessed February 1, 2014).

Strauss, W., & Howe, N. (2000). *Millennials Rising: The Next Great Generation*. New York: Vintage Books.

Tajfel, H., & Turner, J. C. (1985) The social identity theory of intergroup behavior. In S. Worchel & W. G. Austin (Eds.), *Psychology of Intergroup Relations* (2nd ed.) (pp. 7–24). Chicago, IL: Nelson-Hall.

Thompson, V. L. S. (1999). Variables affecting identity salience among African Americans. *Journal of Social Psychology, 139*, 748–761.

Toossi, M. (2004). Labor force projections in 2012: The graying of the US workforce. *Monthly Labor Review, 127*, 37–57.

Truxillo, D. M., McCune, E. A., Bertolino, M., & Fraccaroli, F. (2012). Perceptions of older versus younger workers in terms of Big Five facets, proactive personality, cognitive ability, and job performance. *Journal of Applied Social Psychology, 42*(11), 2607–2639.

Trzesniewski, K. H., Donnellan, M. B., & Robins, R. W. (2008). Do today's young people really think they are so extraordinary? An examination of secular trends in narcissism and self-enhancement. *Psychological Science, 19*(2), 181–188.

Tsui, A. S., & O'Reilly, C. A. (1989). Beyond simple demographic effects: The importance of relational demography in superior-subordinate dyads. *Academy of Management Journal, 32*(2), 402–423.

Tsui, A. S., Egan, T., & O'Reilly, C. (1991). Being different: Relational demography and organizational attachment. *Administrative Science Quarterly, 37*(4), 549–579.

Turner, J. C., & Oakes, P. J. (1989). Self-categorization theory and social influence. In P. B. Paulus (Ed.), *Psychology of Group Influence* (2nd ed.) (pp. 233–275). Hillsdale, NJ: Lawrence Earlbaum & Associates.

Twenge, J. M. (2010). A review of the empirical evidence on generational differences in work attitudes. *Journal of Business and Psychology, 25*(2), 201–210.

van Knippenberg, D., de Dreu, C. K., & Homan, A. C. (2004). Work group diversity and group performance: An integrative model and research agenda. *Journal of Applied Psychology, 89*(6), 1008–1022.

von Hippel, C., Kalokerinos, E. K., & Henry, J. D. (2012). Stereotype threat among older employees: Relationships with job attitudes and turnover intentions. *Psychology and Aging, 28*(1), 17–27.

Vorauer, J. D., Main, K. J., & O'Connell, G. B., (1998). How do individuals expect to be viewed by members of lower status groups? Content and implications of meta-stereotypes. *Journal of Personality and Social Psychology, 75*(4), 917–937.

Walster, E., Walster, G., & Berscheid, E. (1978) *Equity: Theory and Research*. Boston, MA: Allyn & Bacon.

Weckerle, J. R., & Shultz, K. S. (1999). Influences on the bridge employment decision among older USA workers. *Journal of Occupational and Organizational Psychology, 72*(3), 317–329.

Weiss, D., & Freund, A. M. (2012). Still young at heart: Negative age-related information motivates distancing from same-aged people. *Psychology and Aging, 27*, 173–180.

Weiss, D., & Lang, F. R. (2009). Thinking about my generation: Adaptive effects of a dual identity in later adulthood. *Psychology and Aging, 24*(3), 729–734.

Weiss, D., & Lang, F. R. (2012). "They" are old but "I" feel younger: Age-group dissociation as a self-protective strategy in old age. *Psychology and Aging, 27*(1), 153–163.

Weston, M. (2001). Coaching generations in the workplace. *Nursing Administration Quarterly, 25*(2), 11–21.

Wieck, K. L. (2007). Motivating an intergenerational workforce: Scenarios for success. *Orthopaedic Nursing, 26*(6), 366–371.

Williams, A., & Nussbaum, J. F. (2001). *Intergenerational Communication Across the Life Span*. London: Routledge.

Wilson, M., & Gerber, L. E. (2008). How generational theory can improve teaching: Strategies for working with the "millennials." *Currents in Teaching and Learning, 1*(1), 29–44.

Zacher, H., & Gielnik, M. (2014). Organizational age cultures: The interplay of chief executive officers' age and attitudes toward younger and older employees. *International Small Business Journal*. Published online first. DOI: 10.1177/0266242612463025.

Zacher, H., Rosing, K., Henning, T., & Frese, M. (2011). Establishing the next generation at work: Leader generativity as a moderator of the relationships between leader age, leader-member exchange, and leadership success. *Psychology and Aging, 26*(1), 241–252.

Zenger, T. R., & Lawrence, B. S. (1989). Organizational demography: The differential effects of age and tenure distributions on technical communication. *Academy of Management Journal, 32*(2), 353–376.

12

A Comparison of EEO Law on Workforce Aging Across English-Speaking Countries

Arthur Gutman and Eric Dunleavy

The purpose of this chapter is to examine age discrimination employment laws around the globe using the Age Discrimination Employment Act of 1967 (ADEA) in the United States (US) as a focal point. We will compare ADEA case law to case law in Canada, Australia, New Zealand, the United Kingdom (UK) (England, Northern Ireland, Scotland, and Wales), and Ireland. We will also consider the legal context in forecasting what I-O psychology research and practice could do to address legal issues with the aging workforce.

The ADEA and relevant implications for I-O psychologists are covered in other resources (e.g., Gutman, Koppes, & Vodanovich, 2010; Sterns, Doverspike, & Lax, 2005). However, no resource to our knowledge is available that summarizes age protection and enforcement across multiple countries. Three things stood out to us as we studied the other countries. First, the ADEA is an *older workers* statute; other countries protect older and younger workers alike. Second, the ADEA was part of a well-orchestrated plan based solely on issues relating to older workers; age discrimination proscriptions in other countries were woven into proscriptions based on other classifications (e.g., race, religion, and ethnicity) and, for the most part, still are. Third, the ADEA was born with strong enforcement and regulatory controls that are unmatched in any other country.

The ADEA was not developed overnight. It traces to no single event or edict. Rather, it was the product of years of congressional debate and study that began in the early 1950s. Congress took no action on age discrimination until the debates surrounding Title VII of the Civil Rights

Act of 1964, a statute that proscribes discrimination based on race, color, religion, sex, and national origin, and serves as a statutory and regulatory model for all other major anti-discrimination laws in the US.

At the time of the Title VII debates, serious consideration was given to including age as a protected class. However, Congress wanted more information on age-specific issues. For example, it was commonly believed that discrimination against the Title VII classes was intentional, and often a by-product of animus, whereas age discrimination was a by-product of false beliefs and stereotypes, and rarely the result of animus. Congress also wanted more information on how age discrimination affects older workers and the economy. Therefore, rather than including age as a Title VII class, Congress directed the Secretary of the Department of Labor (DOL) to study age discrimination with the purpose of creating what we now know as the ADEA.

The strong enforcement and regulatory authority in the ADEA was also part of the congressional plan. Originally, the DOL was charged with enforcing the ADEA, including authorship of regulations and guidelines for employers and the courts. In 1978, enforcement of the ADEA was passed onto the Equal Employment Opportunity Commission (EEOC), whose own birth was part of the Title VII plan. Although all the major countries we examined have regulatory human rights commissions, none of these commissions have the amount of authority established in the EEOC. Table 12.1 shows the countries and laws considered in this chapter.

Among the other countries we studied, Canada is the only one with a history of proscribing age discrimination that is as old as that in the US. However, unlike the US, where the proscriptions flowed from the federal government to the states, the proscriptions in Canada flowed from its provinces and territories to the federal government. Interestingly, the first age discrimination law in Canada was developed in the province of British Columbia in 1964, three years prior to the ADEA. Subsequently, Canada enacted two federal laws, the Canadian Human Rights Act (CHRA) in 1977 and the Canadian Charter of Rights and Freedoms (CCRF) in 1982, which amended the Canadian Bill of Rights (1960). Both laws proscribe discrimination based on age, but, as in most other countries, the proscriptions also include race, ethnicity, national origin, and other classifications. An important point to note about Canada is that major court cases borrow from and often cite U.S. case law, although as we will witness below, they do not always follow it.

The Australian states and territories have a history of proscriptions against age discrimination similar to Canada, the major difference being

TABLE 12.1
Countries and Age Laws Considered in This Chapter

Country	Applicable Age Law(s)	Comment
United States	ADEA (1967)	Separate federal age law (and only for older workers)
Canada	CHRA (1977) and CCRF (1982)	Federal laws protecting age and other groups
Australia	AD Act (2004)	Separate federal age law
New Zealand	HRA (1993) and ERA (2000)	Separate regional age laws (but only for employees)
Ireland	Employment Equality Acts (1998, 2004 and 2008)	Age law based on EU doctrine
England	Employment Equality (Age) Regulations (2006) and Equality Act (2010)	Age laws based on EU doctrine

that cases did not emerge in its states and territories until the 1990s. More recently, Australia enacted the Age Discrimination Act (AD Act) in 2004, making it the only country other than the US with a separate federal age discrimination law. However, in our review of case law, we found no cases in which a claimant has successfully used the AD Act. Thus, as in Canada, most claims, successful or otherwise, follow from cases brought in the states and territories.

The primary sources for age discrimination protection in New Zealand are the Human Rights Act (HRA) of 1993 and the Employment Relations Act (ERA) of 2000. Interestingly, the HRA covers only existing employees. Therefore, applicants for employment that claim age discrimination must use the ERA.

Based on our review, Ireland was the first EU country with age discrimination proscriptions. These proscriptions are nested with Employment Equality Acts in 1998, 2004, and 2008. The 2004 Act was implemented in accordance with EU Directive 2000/78, which established a framework for equal employment opportunity throughout the EU.

Interestingly, although the UK has a relatively long history of addressing workplace discrimination, there was no legislation on the books relating to age discrimination until the Employment Equality (Age) Regulations in 2006. These regulations followed from EU Directive 2000/78, and more recently the UK implemented the Equality Act of 2010 to prohibit age discrimination in both goods and services.

Despite being the most recent entry into the age discrimination arena, the amount of case law in the UK (and the EU in general) has grown exponentially in recent years. According to statistics compiled by Lewis Silkin,[1] there were only 972 age discrimination cases in the EU in 2006/07, a number that grew to 2,949 in 2007/08, 3,801 in 2008/09, 5,200 in 2009/10, 6,800 in 2010/11, and 3,800 in 2011/12.

A final point to note is that all of the countries we studied, including the US, have a three-tier system that includes trial courts, appeals courts, and a highest court. In the US, trials are conducted in district courts, appeals are made to circuit courts, and the Supreme Court is the highest court in the land. In other countries, the most common name for the trial courts is tribunal, the appeals courts go by various names, and the highest court is called the High Court or the Supreme Court.

Our goal for the rest of the chapter is to capture what we believe are the major distinguishing features among the laws in various countries against the backdrop of the ADEA. To this end, we devote a short section below to the ADEA, focusing on broad comparisons to other countries. The second section samples case law from the various countries one country at a time, and we present our summary thoughts and conclusions in the last section, with an emphasis on providing what we anticipate are major developments in age discrimination case law in the future.

SECTION I: A PRIMER ON THE ADEA

Our goal in this section is to provide a brief overview of the ADEA that is broad enough to permit point-by-point comparisons with the other countries. To that end, we will limit many of the technical aspects of the ADEA so as to enable laypersons to better understand these comparisons. We will also attempt to capture major features of ADEA case law without going into exhaustive detail. Readers wishing to delve further into the technicalities of the ADEA and/or ADEA case law are directed to Gutman and colleagues (2010) and Gutman (2012).

Table 12.2 depicts six dimensions used by Gutman and colleagues (2010) to categorize all major U.S. anti-discrimination laws. Some of the dimensions are common to other U.S. laws. However, each one is somewhat different relative to other U.S. laws based on unique features of age discrimination as compared to discrimination against other groups.

TABLE 12.2
Six ADEA Dimensions

1. Protected Class	Age only: minimum age is 40; no maximum age. Age is a continuous dimension.
2. Covered Entities	Private, local, and federal employers; minimum of 2 employees; private lawsuits no longer permitted against state agencies, but the EEOC may sue state agencies on behalf of individual plaintiffs.
3. Covered Practices	Terms, conditions, and privileges of employment, segregation and classification, and retaliation.
4. Administrative Procedures	Plaintiffs have either 180 or 300 days from the point of an alleged violation to file a claim with the EEOC.
5. Remedies	Remedies include equitable relief (back pay, front pay, injunction, legal and expert fees) and liquidated damages.
6. Judicial Scenarios	Disparate treatment, facial discrimination, and adverse impact; statutory defenses include Good Cause, RFOA, BFBP, BFSS, and BFOQ.

D1: Protected Class

As noted in the introduction, the most obvious difference between the US and other countries is the age range for the protected class. The ADEA is an *older worker* statute with protections beginning at age 40. At its inception, there was a maximum age limit of 65. However, the ceiling age was raised to 70 in 1984 and eliminated entirely in 1987. In contrast, the comparison countries protect *both* younger and older workers beginning in most places at age 18, with or without upper limits depending on the country and/or the industry.

Common to all forms of workplace discrimination is the concept of similarly situated employees (or comparators). It is typical for protected class members to claim unfavorable treatment relative to comparators. However, unlike Title VII, which features discrete groupings (e.g., black versus white, females versus males), age is a continuous variable, and *age difference* is often more important than whether a complainant is over 40 and a comparator is under 40. This issue was first raised in *Loeb v. Textron* (1979) and turned into Supreme Court precedent in *O'Connor v. Consolidated* (1996). For present purposes, the important point is that we could find no cases in other countries specifying how large the age difference must be to determine if discrimination has occurred against older or younger workers.

Preference for older workers is generally prohibited in other countries because both older and younger workers are protected. However, there is nothing in the ADEA to prohibit preference for workers over 40 to those under 40. Moreover, in *General Dynamics Land Systems v. Cline* (2004), the Supreme Court upheld a health benefits plan for retirees with 30 or more years of service at age 50 or above even though the plan did not apply to comparators at age 49 years or below. Thus, the ADEA permits preference for older workers even if the younger comparators are also protected class members.

An additional and obvious point to note is that elimination of the maximum age in the ADEA meant elimination of mandatory retirement ages. Where it was once easy to forcibly retire older employees at the (then) applicable maximum age limits, such policies must be now justified by a statutory defense termed bona fide occupational qualification (BFOQ), which, in our opinion, is the most difficult of all defenses in the ADEA. It is important to note that mandatory retirement is perhaps the single most frequently litigated issue in other countries, and the rules vary across these countries.

D2: Covered Entities (Which Organizations are Covered)

At its inception, the ADEA covered only private entities with 25 or more employees. Coverage was then extended to federal, state, and local government agencies in 1974, and the employee number was reduced to 20. It should be noted that coverage of state entities was struck down by the Supreme Court in in *Kimel v. Board of Regents* (2000), meaning older workers no longer have a private right to sue state agencies. However, the EEOC has the independent authority to sue state agencies on behalf of older workers, and it has used it (see, for example, *EEOC v. Bd. of Regents of the Univ. of Wisconsin*, 2002).

An additional point to note is that Congress extended ADEA coverage to overseas subsidiaries of American companies in 1984 to counter a practice in which older workers were transferred overseas and subsequently fired (see, for example, *Goodman v. Heublein*, 1981 and *Cleary v. U.S. Lines*, 1984). This coverage, however, does not apply when there is conflict between the ADEA and foreign laws (see, for example, *Mahoney v. RFE/RL*, 1995).

The employee number is an essential ingredient in the ADEA and other U.S. anti-discrimination statutes as it protects "mom and pop" shops from being sued. For example, a pizza place with only a handful of workers could terminate an older employee without having to defend its practice. We saw nothing in any of the foreign statutes that mentions employee size. Thus, at least in theory, any employer in other countries, regardless of size, could be sued if it terminates an employee because he or she is too old (or too young).

D3: Covered Practices

The covered practices in the ADEA encompass any term, condition, or privilege of employment (e.g., recruitment, hiring, training, benefits, promotion, termination, and harassment). The ADEA also proscribes retaliation for complaining about an employer practice and/or filing a lawsuit, a practice that is commonly called "victimization" in most other countries. Additionally, as noted earlier, and as depicted in Table 12.3, there are three major exemptions to the mandatory retirement rules.

The first exemption permits mandatory retirement at age 65 for "bona fide executives" (BFEs), who have high-level management responsibilities, or "high policymakers," who directly influence company policies. Targeted employees must have guaranteed annual pensions of at least $44,000. Examples include college presidents (see *EEOC v. Wayne Community College*, 1983), division heads (see *Passer v. American Chemical Society*, 1990), and bank vice presidents (see *Morrissey v. Boston Five Cents Savings Bank*, 1995), but not corporate attorneys with minimal supervisory duties and who are not involved in "policy-creating" decisions even if they have fancy titles and high salaries (see *Whittlesey v. Union Carbide*, 1983).

The second exemption is for hiring and retirement ages for firefighters and law enforcement officers pursuant to "applicable state or local law." For example, courts have supported exclusion from hiring of police officers after age 35 (see *Kopec v. City of Elmhurst*, 1999; *Feldman v. Nassau County*, 2006) and mandatory retirement of police officers at age 55 (see *State Police*

TABLE 12.3
Mandatory Retirement Exemptions

Exemption 1	Forced retirement of bona fide executives at age 65 who are high policymakers and have annual pensions of $44,000 or higher.
Exemption 2	Forced retirement of firefighters and law enforcement officers at ages pursuant to state or local laws (usually age 55).
Exemption 3	Forced retirement of policymaking elected or appointed officials pursuant to state or local laws (usually at age 70).

v. *Difava*, 2003). To challenge such a policy, a claimant must prove that the law in question is a ploy (or "subterfuge") to evade the purpose of the ADEA, which is an extremely difficult proof.

The third exemption is for mandatory retirement of elected or appointed officials at the "policymaking level." This exemption followed three major challenges to mandatory retirement of judges at age 70 (*EEOC v. Massachusetts*, 1988; *Gregory v. Ashcroft*, 1991; *EEOC v. Vermont*, 1990). In its review of *Gregory v. Ashcroft* (1991), the Supreme Court ruled 7–2 that states have a rational basis for enacting such laws. Interestingly, the dissenters were the two oldest justices at the time (Justices Blackmun and Marshall), both over 70 at the time.

More generally, the proscriptions in this dimension are not unique to the ADEA, nor are exemptions for mandatory retirement. What makes the ADEA covered practices unique is that no other country pays as much attention to issues related to termination, as well as "collateral damages" associated with termination, most notably benefits, early retirement, and waiver of the right to sue. In particular, there are two key ADEA amendments worth noting.

The first amendment, in 1986, incorporated a core feature of the Employee Retirement Income Security Act (ERISA) into both the ADEA and the Internal Revenue Service Code to, among other things, guarantee pension contributions for employees choosing to work past age 65. The second amendment is the Older Workers Benefit Protection Act (OWBPA) of 1990, which addresses discrimination in benefits, discriminatory use of early retirement packages, and voluntary waiver of ADEA rights. There are no provisions we could find in any of the foreign countries that parallel the protections offered in these two amendments.

Two other points are worth noting. First, although the full range of terms and conditions of employment generalize across the globe, there are, for lack of a better term, quirks associated with some of these laws. For example, recall that New Zealand has two statutes that apply to age discrimination, the HRA of 2003 and the ERA of 2000. The quirk here is that the HRA applies only to existing employees. Therefore, claimants who claim discrimination in recruitment and hiring must use the ERA.

The second point relates to a regulatory exemption that originally permitted favoritism toward younger workers in apprenticeship training programs in the US. Other countries, most notably New Zealand, have prioritized opening up apprenticeship opportunities to older workers (see Harcourt, Wilkinson, & Wood, 2010).

D4: Administrative Procedures

In the ADEA, a claim must be filed with the EEOC and the EEOC must attempt to mediate and conciliate with the employer before the claimant can sue in court. What is unique is the amount of *independent* authority bestowed upon the EEOC in the US compared to enforcement agencies in other countries. For example, we have already seen that the EEOC can bring ADEA lawsuits against state agencies even though private citizens cannot. However, there are three other unique powers bestowed upon the EEOC

TABLE 12.4
Recent Settlements Forced by the EEOC

Allstate	$4.5 million: discrimination in layoffs against older workers in an RIF
3M	$3 million: discrimination in layoffs against older workers in an RIF
Hutchinson Sealing Systems	$210,000: termination of three older workers during an RIF
Advanced Components	$210,000: termination of 64-year-old sales manager
Kanbar Property Management	$140,000: termination of individual because of age
AT&T	$250,000: termination of individual because of age
Town of Elkton, MD	$235,000: termination of 70-year-old assistant town administrator
Metallic Products Corp	$60,000: unlawful mandatory retirement policy at age 70
Ruby Tuesday	$575,000: pattern or practice of discrimination in hiring
Western Energy Durango	$90,000: two engineers told they are too old to hire
Marymount Man. College	$125,000: refusal to hire 64-year-old professor because of age
Universal Toyota	$140,000: older workers not permitted to sell Scions due to age
MRA Systems	$130,000: retaliation and refusal to promote 61-year-old employee
K Mart	$120,000: age harassment, constructive discharge, and retaliation
Three Minnesota State Agencies	$574,000: policy prohibiting pension contributions at age 55
Western NY Fire Companies	$441,700: 35 firefighters discriminated against in pension benefits
Amityville Fire Dept.	$209,280: illegal pension policy for senior firefighters at age 65
Seldon Fire District	$263,000: policy prohibiting pension contributions at age 55

that we did not see in any of the other countries we studied. First, the EEOC has the authority to prosecute any of the claims it receives. In most other countries we examined, the enforcement authority is limited to the investigation/conciliation process. The lone exception is Canada, where the various human rights commissions bring cases to court if they feel they have merit. Second, unlike the other countries we examined, the EEOC does not have to wait for private claims to emerge; it may investigate and prosecute discriminatory practices on its own. The EEOC generally attempts to negotiate settlements before actually bringing a claim to federal district court. The settlements are substantial, sometimes in seven figures, and far exceed awards we saw in other countries.

Third, as discussed earlier, the EEOC is empowered to write regulations that have the force and effect of law in the courts. Again, we saw this in no other country we studied. The critical factor here is that regulations help courts decide cases. In contrast, outside of the US, courts are left to interpret the letter of the law on a case-by-case basis without the benefit of well-thought-out regulations.

D5: Remedies

The ADEA remedies are precise and include injunction, two years of back pay, reinstatement, front pay when reinstatement is not viable, lawyer and expert fees, and liquidated damages. Liquidated damages are awarded for *willful* violations, defined by the Supreme Court in *TWA v. Thurston* (1985) as an employer that "knew or showed reckless disregard for the matter of whether its conduct was prohibited by the ADEA."

There are three things worth noting apart from the sheer size of the monetary awards in the ADEA. First, the ADEA permits jury trials against private entities. We could not find even a single age discrimination case outside the US that featured a jury trial. This is particularly important because it makes sense that juries would likely be more sensitive to the plight of older workers than judges.

Second, we could not find even a single age discrimination case outside the US in which lawyer and expert fees were awarded. The most likely explanation here is that, particularly in Europe, at least in civil cases, all participants in court proceedings represent the court, which is British common law tradition. This is far different from the adversarial system in the US where each side is represented by counsel.

Third, we saw many age discrimination cases outside the US in which the loser has to pay court costs. Court costs, at least in theory, are only awarded in US cases when the claim is frivolous. This is extremely rare, and we could find not even a single ADEA case where an individual plaintiff had to pay court costs. Obviously, the potential for having to pay court costs can serve as a major barrier for making discrimination claims.

D6: Judicial Scenarios

Lastly, the ADEA features three judicial scenarios and five statutory defenses. The judicial scenarios are disparate treatment, adverse impact, and facial discrimination, and the statutory defenses are BFOQ, BFBP (bona fide benefits plan), BFSS (bona fide seniority system), Good Cause, and RFOA (reasonable factor other than age). The BFOQ and BFSS defences are Title VII transplants. However, the BFSS defense is rarely used in the ADEA as seniority rules generally favor older workers. The other statutory defenses are unique to the ADEA, although the Good Cause defense is rarely used because it is essentially subsumed under the RFOA defense.

Disparate treatment and facial discrimination fall under the label of "direct discrimination" in other countries. Other countries also use the label "indirect discrimination" for adverse impact. In disparate treatment scenarios, the plaintiff must compile direct evidence (e.g., written documentation, eyewitnesses) or indirect evidence (e.g., similarly situated comparators are treated less harshly) of the employer's motive to discriminate. In comparison, the motive to discriminate is irrelevant in adverse impact, where the plaintiff must identify a facially neutral selection procedure or policy and prove that it falls more harshly on older employees as compared to younger comparators. When it does, the defendant must then prove there is a nondiscriminatory RFOA that explains the adverse impact. In facial discrimination, the discriminatory motive is obvious (or clear on its face), and the question is whether that motive is justifiable. There are two such scenarios, one involving an employment practice (e.g., mandatory retirement ages), which requires the BFOQ defense, and one involving benefits, which requires the BFBP defense.

Another point to note is that civil trials in federal district court have precise three-phase scenarios with shifting burdens, something we did not see in any of the comparison countries. In Phase 1, the plaintiff must establish prima facie (or presumably true) evidence of a violation. Assuming success, the employer must defend the charge in Phase 2, and, assuming success, the plaintiff must prove pretext in Phase 3 (i.e., that the employer defense is an excuse for an illegal action). Also, unlike criminal trials, which use a higher burden of proof (i.e., beyond reasonable doubt), the plaintiff's ultimate burden in civil trials is to prove a violation with a preponderance of evidence (i.e., be more convincing than the defendant).

A final point to note is that the prima facie and defense burdens in discrimination cases are balanced, so that when the prima facie burden is light, the defense burden is light, and when the prima burden is heavy, the defense burden is also heavy. In general, the light-light relationship is featured in disparate treatment scenarios, whereas the heavy-heavy relationship is featured in adverse impact and facial discrimination scenarios.

Although the ADEA covers the full range of terms and conditions of employment, the dominant themes with regard to employment outcomes are termination and "collateral damage" associated with termination. The collateral issues are most often associated with RIFs and include discrimination in benefits, early retirement provisions, and waiver of the private right to bring an ADEA lawsuit. Most individual termination scenarios use disparate treatment rules, which refer to intentional discrimination. Class action lawsuits may use either disparate treatment or adverse impact rules. Impact refers to unintentional discrimination via facially neutral policies that produce disparate outcomes between groups. Facial discrimination scenarios use BFOQ rules for employment practices such as mandatory retirement and BFBP rules for discrimination in benefits.

It must be noted again that the goal in this chapter is to sample and illustrate, not to exhaust. Readers interested in the full range of employment practices, additional cases, and more thorough treatment of the cases from the United States are directed to Gutman and colleagues (2010). The following section focuses on issues from other countries.

SECTION II: SAMPLE EEO AGE ISSUES IN OTHER COUNTRIES

The goal in this section is to sample major cases in the non-U.S. countries we studied. Once again, our discussion is limited. Readers interested in more exhaustive coverage in these other countries are referred to the aforementioned website managed by Lewis Silkin (www.lewissilkin.com), which, in addition to Lexis/Nexis, served as a major source for us in obtaining court cases in each of the countries we studied. We will discuss the countries one at a time.

Canada

Canadian law uses the BFOR (bona fide occupational reasons) defense for mandatory cutoff ages and the bona fide pension plan defense for benefits. However, unlike the ADEA, where cutoff ages are addressed independently of each other with the BFOQ defense for cutoff ages and the BFBP defense for benefits, Canada's BFOR defense is superseded when mandatory retirement ages are connected to bona fide pension plans. When uncomplicated by pension issues, the BFOR defense is applied in similar fashion to the ADEA's BFOQ, though not always with the same case law rulings. Invariably, such cases involve safety issues.

Recall, for example, that in the ADEA, the BFOQ defense was used successfully for hiring ages for bus drivers (*Hodgson v. Greyhound*, 1974) under the "minimal risk" theory, but the same defense did not work for hiring ages for airline pilots (*Smallwood v. United Air Lines*, 1981). The *Smallwood* ruling was echoed in *Air Canada v. Carson* (1985) for hiring pilots at age 27, but the *Hodgson* ruling was rejected in *McCreary v. Greyhound* (1986) when Greyhound attempted to import its age 35 hiring cutoff to bus drivers. In *McCreary*, the court disagreed with the minimum risk to safety argument used in the ADEA case because "no procedures had been developed [by Greyhound] to assess drivers for the impacts of stressors."

Absent pension issues, the BFOR defense has applied to mandatory retirement ages in much the same way as the ADEA. For example, in *Ontario v. Etobicoke* (1982), two firefighters defeated a collective bargaining agreement (CBA) for mandatory retirement at age 60 on grounds that unions cannot waive the rights of older workers, a ruling similar to *TWA v. Thurston* (1985) in the ADEA. However, the Canadian Supreme Court found that a CBA calling for mandatory retirement of police officers at age 60 is a BFOR in *Large v. Stratford* (1995) and a Canadian appeals court found that mandatory retirement of airline pilots at age 60 was "reasonable" in *Air Canada Pilots Assn. v. Air Canada* (2012). This is the longest running mandatory retirement case in Canada and it is fraught with complexities that are beyond the scope of this chapter. Suffice it to say that Air Canada pilots are now allowed to fly past the age of 65.

In other cases with outcomes similar to the ADEA, a Canadian appeals court rejected a financial assistance program inapplicable to a 71-year-old blind man because it was applicable to disabled individuals under age 18 in *Ontario v. Roberts* (1995). Also, in *McKee v. Hayes-Dana* (1992), age discrimination was found when, in an RIF, an internal memo written by the company vice president stated that the company "hoped to keep people with career potential." In *McKinney v. University of Guelph* (1990), the Canadian Supreme Court upheld a contractual mandatory retirement age of 65 for university professors.

By 2008, mandatory retirement was outlawed in all Canadian provinces, as well as at the federal level in 2012. Unlike the ADEA, where mandatory retirement ages can only be justified by the BFOQ defense (except for exemptions), in Canada, the rules are different when mandatory retirement is tied to bona fide pension or retirement plans. Lower courts traditionally supported this rule, as did the Supreme Court in *New Brunswick v. Potash* (2008), where it was determined that a pension plan is bona fide if it is adopted in good faith and does not defeat protected rights. This was a divided 4–3 ruling in which the dissenting justices agreed pension plans should be bona fide, but argued that rules relating to mandatory retirement should require more than proof that the plan is not a sham.

The *Potash* ruling has been upheld in subsequent lower court rulings (see, for example, *Talbot v. Cape Breton*, 2009). However, there have been cases in which pension plans failed the sham defense (e.g., *Nilsson v. University of Prince Edward Island*, 2010; *Consell Scolaire v. Canadian Union of Public Employees*, 2012).

Australia

Unlike Canada, there is no dominant theme in Australian case law. There are cases that feature mandatory cutoff ages, but with different rules than Canada, and there are also cases that feature direct discrimination (disparate treatment) and indirect discrimination (adverse impact).

Mandatory cutoff based on age is illustrated in *Blatchford v. Qantas Airways Limited* (1997), where an applicant received four points if they were between the ages of 21 and 24, but only one point if they were over 32. Qantas argued that older applicants have shorter periods of employment and, as a result, there would not be time to recoup training costs. The court rejected this argument on grounds that exceptions to age discrimination laws cannot be based on "economic rationalism."

The cutoff for mandatory retirement is illustrated in *Qantas Airways Limited v. Christie* (1998), in which Qantas argued for an "inherent requirements" exemption for pilots at age 60. Their arguments included two factors: safety, and an international rule in the Convention on International Civil Aviation barring captains aged 60 or over from flying many routes they might be required to fly. The court rejected the safety argument, finding no evidence of medical incapacity at age 60 or above. However, the court accepted the international rule and found in favor of Qantas. Direct discrimination rulings are illustrated in *Webforge Australia Pty Ltd v. Richards* (2005) and *Talbert v. Sperling Tourism* (2011), while indirect age discrimination rulings are illustrated in *Dewan v. Main Roads* (2004) and *Hopper & Others v. Virgin Blue Airlines Pty Ltd* (2005).

A final point to note about Australia is the Fair Work Act (2009), which has a "reverse onus" burden. Thus, if a person makes an age discrimination claim, the burden (or onus) is on the employer to prove otherwise. This is obviously different than disparate treatment theory in the ADEA, where the burden of proof is on the plaintiff. That said, we found no cases that applied this burden to age discrimination, but would alert interested readers to stay tuned to see if such cases develop.

New Zealand

We chose to examine New Zealand because we expected to find multiple cases, as we did in other countries. However, after an exhaustive search via Lexis/Nexis and Google Scholar, among other search engines, we came up with only three cases relevant to the present discussion: *Totalisator Agency Board v. Gruschow* (1998), *Air New Zealand Ltd v. McAlister* (2012), and *Attorney-General v. IDEA Services Ltd* (2013). *McAlister*, which involved mandatory retirement of airline pilots, is the most important of these cases and will be discussed last.

Totalisator featured a claim of discrimination in hiring by a 41-year-old applicant who was refused a job because of his age. Ordinarily, such a case would be straightforward. However, it was an independent contractor that excluded the applicant, and the critical issue was whether an employer has vicarious liability for the independent contractor. The appeals court cited examples in which contracts between employers and contractors could be arranged for the purpose of escaping liability. However, the court felt there was insufficient evidence to make that determination and remanded the case back to the lower court. There is no doubt, in our opinion, that ADEA (and Title VII) case law would mandate liability for an employer for discrimination by an independent contractor, no examples needed and no questions asked.

The *IDEA* case featured a policy that provided "day services" for individuals with intellectual disabilities. The purpose of the day services program was to assist eligible individuals with life skills and vocational and work experience. The issue that was challenged was a cutoff age of

65 for these services. This policy was deemed discriminatory and was struck down.

The issue in *McAlister* was whether mandatory retirement of senior airline pilots at age 60 is a "genuine occupational qualification." McAlister, a senior pilot/flight instructor, was demoted to first officer when he reached 60. He needed to maintain his senior pilot status to remain a pilot instructor. At the time of his claim, the mandatory retirement age for airline pilots in the US was 60. There were opposing opinions in the two lower courts, but ultimately the Supreme Court of New Zealand ruled that age 60 was a genuine occupational qualification because of the need to fly over US space. However, the Supreme Court also ruled that Air New Zealand would need to prove it was reasonably unable to adjust its activities to accommodate the restriction, a decision that was remanded back to the lower courts.

As a postscript, TVNZ News in New Zealand reported recently that other senior pilots demoted or retired at age 60 sued Air New Zealand on grounds that the carrier knew the cutoff age of 65 was imminent and they were demoted anyway.[2] The report also states that the chief judge of the court hearing the case noted that the remedies claimed by the pilots in this case could amount to several million dollars.

Ireland

Early Irish age discrimination cases featured recruitment violations. For example, in what is reputed to be the first age discrimination claim upheld under Irish law (*Equality Authority v. Ryanair*, 2001), the defendant lost because of an advertisement stating, "we need a young and dynamic professional." Then, in *Cunningham v. BMS Sales* (2007), the defendant lost because an applicant refused to provide his age.

More recent age discrimination cases have focused on the mandatory retirement theme. Historically, mandatory retirement at a given age was acceptable in Ireland as long as it was written into the employment contract. For example, in *Leahy v. Limerick County Council* (2003), which featured mandatory retirement of firefighters at age 55, the claimant advanced what seemed like good arguments for why the requirement should be stuck down. However, it was not due to a contract provision.

More recent rulings are guided by EU Council Directive 2000/78/EC, which requires more than a contractual arrangement to set a mandatory retirement age. More specifically, that directive states:

Member States may provide that differences of treatment on grounds of age shall not constitute discrimination, if . . . they are objectively and reasonably justified by a legitimate aim, including legitimate employment policy, labour market and vocational training objectives, and if the means of achieving that aim are appropriate and necessary.

The first mandatory retirement case decided based on the directive was *Donnellan v. Minister for Justice, Equality and Law Reform* (2008), in which the High Court of Ireland ruled that a statute requiring mandatory retirement of Assistant Garda Commissioners at age 60 was "compatible and comfortable" with the directive because it was necessary to ensure "motivation and dynamism through the increased prospect of promotion." Clearly, such reasoning would not fly in the ADEA.

Similarly, in *Doyle v. ESB International* (2012), another case with logic questionable under the ADEA, a graphics designer faced mandatory retirement at age 65 and the court supported the defendant on grounds that it was important to ensure that vacancies were available to encourage recruitment and promotion of younger candidates.

In *Saunders v. CHC Ireland Limited* (2008), the company policy mandated retirement of helicopter winchmen at age 55. This policy was supported based on the *Donellan* ruling. However, it was based on what ADEA case law would consider more traditional grounds of safety for both winchmen and the public they serve.

There are other Irish cases in which mandatory retirement ages have been "objectively justified." However, in one recent case (*Mr Patrick Dunican and Mr Thomas Spain v. Offaly Civil Defence*, 2013), the court upheld a discrimination claim because it was based on a civil defense notice that did not specify retirement ages, and did not specify the various positions affected.

A final and very important point to note is that the aforementioned cases represent Irish interpretations of EU Council Directive 2000/78/EC. As far as we could tell, none of the cases have been appealed to the EU Court of Justice (ECJ). It will be interesting to see what happens if and when such cases are appealed to the EU court, particularly the ones in which objective justification arguments have been upheld.

United Kingdom

The UK's response to EU Council Directive 2000/78/EC was to enact the Employment Equality (Age) Regulations in 2006. The directive, coupled with the new regulations, induced a flood of age discrimination cases covering the gamut of terms and conditions of employment from recruitment to termination. However, most of the important cases, at least in our opinion, are related to mandatory retirement and unfair dismissal.

Regarding mandatory retirement, the UK had a historic default retirement age (DRA) of 65, meaning employers could force retirement at age 65 without fear of legal challenge. The new age regulations maintained the DRA, but with the stipulation that employees could request continued work, employers had to notify employees of that right, and the employers had to give such requests "good faith" consideration. The good faith defense sometimes succeeded (see *Bartram v. East Sussex County Council, Claversham Community College*, 2012) and sometimes failed (see *Compass Group v. Ayodele*, 2011), but by and large it was considered an easy defense.

The landscape was already changing at the time of the *Bartram* and *Compass* rulings as UK legislators re-evaluated the DRA and ultimately outlawed it in 2011. Employers can still enforce mandatory retirement, but only with proof that mandatory retirement is objectively justifiable, and the retirement age is a proportionate means of achieving the justification(s).

The impetus for this change was *Age UK v. Secretary of State for Business, Enterprise and Regulatory Reform* (2009), also known as the "*Heyday*" case (Heyday being a branch of a UK organization that launched the case). The case was brought in 2006 and was referred to the ECJ. The ECJ did not directly rule on *Heyday*, but advised that mandatory retirement had to be reasonably justified by a legitimate aim, and had to be appropriate and necessary. The ECJ indicated that this defense would require a "high standard of proof."

The *Heyday* case has yet to be resolved. However, the UK Supreme Court tested the post-DRA rules in *Seldon v. Clarkson, Wright & Jakes* (2012). Seldon was a partner in a law firm who was forcibly retired at age 65. The employment tribunal (ET) ruled that the law firm had three reasonable justifications: (1) giving associates opportunities for achieving partnership in reasonable time; (2) facilitating workforce planning; and (3) limiting the need to terminate underperforming partners, thus contributing to a congenial and supportive culture. The ET also ruled that the mandatory retirement age chosen was proportionate. The appeals tribunal (EAT) struck down the congeniality justification, but otherwise upheld the ET ruling. The Supreme Court reversed congeniality, but remanded on whether a mandatory retirement age of 65 was proportionate.

A critical factor in the Supreme Court's ruling was its reliance on the ECJ, which recognizes both intergenerational fairness (justification 1) and avoiding the need to terminate older workers for incapacity or poor performance (justification 3). However, it saw no proof of why age 65 was a proportionate means of achieving its justifications, thus leaving the ET with the responsibility of deciding this issue. The implication here is that while employers may find little difficulty in establishing justification, they might find it harder to prove that a specific age is proportionate means.

The proportionate means test in *Seldon* was subsequently adopted in lower court cases. For example, in *Engel v. Transports and Environment Committee of London Councils (TECLC)* (2012), a parking adjudicator's reappointment interval was timed to his 70th birthday, and was shorter than the normal five-year interval for three other younger adjudicators reappointed at the same time. The ET accepted TECLC's justifications, but ruled a retirement age of 70 was not proportionate, and TECLC did not consider less discriminatory methods for achieving its aims.

In *Kerr v. O'Hara Brothers Surfacing LTD* (2013), an unfair dismissal case, employees were placed in "gangs" that were rostered to surface roads and driveways. Kerr's gang was rostered for work, but Kerr was not included. He was told the work involved heavy lifting, for which he was too old. Kerr resigned after filing a grievance that was much delayed and ultimately rejected. Kerr then filed claims of unfair dismissal, direct age discrimination, harassment, and victimization (retaliation). The ET ruled that there was no proportionate means of assessing the aims of the heavy lifting requirement because the company had not performed a risk assessment. The ET also ruled that the ageist comments amounted to harassment, and the mishandling of Kerr's grievance amounted to victimization.

The UK Supreme Court also ruled on indirect discrimination in relation to retirement in *Homer v. Chief Constable of West Yorkshire Police* (2012). Homer was a 62-year-old legal advisor for the Police National Legal Database (PNLD). He was due to retire at the normal (but not mandatory) age of 65, but he hoped to achieve the top pay grade before doing so. However, the PNLD instituted a requirement to possess a law degree to reach the top grade, which Homer did not have. He claimed indirect discrimination, and the ET agreed. However, two appeals courts ruled that his situation was no different than any employee hoping to leave a job for any reason.

The Supreme Court reversed, ruling that people leaving for ordinary reasons have a choice that older employees did not have, and that different arrangements should have been made for employees appointed before the new policy. The Supreme Court also ruled that the aims of a discriminatory policy must be balanced against the impact on the affected group and, similar to adverse impact in the ADEA, this balance depends in large part on whether there are nondiscriminatory alternatives available.

Some Themes to Note

This global review of age discrimination protection and case law identified some interesting themes. For example, mandatory retirement systems appear to be a common area of challenge across countries, particularly in the aviation and broader transportation industries where there are obvious individual and public safety concerns. The protections themselves and maturation of case law vary meaningfully by country, which is not a surprise given that age discrimination protection is a relatively new concept in many countries as compared with the United States, where the ADEA has existed for almost 40 years.

Canada appears to provide similar protections to the US and has a mature body of case law, but many of the other countries have different legal scenarios and little available case law. For example, in Australia, the initial burden is on the employer to prove that they did not discriminate, as opposed to the US where the plaintiff has the initial burden to bring about a prima facie case. In New Zealand, there is very little case law to review. Case law from Ireland suggests that age protection in action at the court level is employer-friendly, such that many defenses that would not meet ADEA scrutiny won the case for the employer. As a final point, countries in Europe operate in the unique context of EU Council Directive 2000/78/EC, and as such are faced with balancing country-specific social values and legal context with broader EU considerations.

SECTION III: LOOKING TOWARD THE FUTURE

As this chapter has shown, age discrimination is complex. Based on our global review, it is clear that protection from age discrimination is of societal interest across multiple countries, yet how those protections play out and who is covered vary meaningfully across the globe. Table 12.5 summarizes these themes.

In light of what has been presented in this chapter, it is important to consider research and practice that would be particularly useful as it relates to age discrimination. This notion is particularly important given the aging workforce and changing nature of work. We see three major areas to consider:

1. enhancements to our understanding of age discrimination issues;
2. contemporary risk in organizational exits; and
3. the changing nature of social values and workforce demographics.

TABLE 12.5
Themes from Our Global Review of Age Discrimination

Theme	Description
Who is Protected	Some countries protect both older and younger workers, while others (including the US) protect only older workers.
Protection Specificity	Age protection in the United States was part of a well-orchestrated plan based solely on issues relating to older workers, and as such, the ADEA is a stand-alone protection for older workers. Other countries have broader statutes that protect age along with other classes such as gender and race/ethnicity.
Historical Context	In the United States, the ADEA has had 40 years of enforcement and case law to help us understand the operational reality and principles of age protection. The concept of protection from age discrimination is a much more novel concept in some countries, where laws and case law were only born in the last 10 to 15 years.
Enforcement Context	The ADEA was born with strong enforcement and regulatory controls, although those controls changed over time. Today, those controls are unmatched in any other country, primarily because of the EEOC's prosecution and investigative power. This is why many EEOC settlements never make it to court, yet are large in scope and effect.
Legal Scenarios	Legal scenarios in the United States are complex, and include disparate treatment, pattern or practice, and unintentional disparate impact (i.e., intention is not implied). The employer defenses are varied as well, and depend on the legal scenario. There are meaningful differences in legal scenarios and burdens of proof chronology across country.

Enhancing Our Understanding of Age Issues

Theory and practice can help to continue to enhance our understanding of age discrimination. From a theoretical perspective, Shore and Goldberg (2005) provided a review of theory and research associated with age discrimination in the workplace, and posited their own model of age discrimination. The model considers internal factors such as dyads, stereotypes, and organizational processes such as recruitment, selection, and training, as well as external factors such as the labor market, age norms, and age distributions. These factors may affect entry, exit, and existence points where discrimination may occur. The sheer complexity of the theory makes it challenging to test from a holistic perspective, but we suggest that researchers meet this challenge using both laboratory and applied settings.

From an applied perspective, we suggest a few sources of information that could be considered in expanding our understanding of age discrimination. The first relates to the practical realities of EEO enforcement. As an example, in the United States the EEOC releases a set of annual enforcement statistics that includes details on both claims and outcomes. These data can be useful, particularly when assessing patterns over time.[3] When evaluating fiscal year 2007 to 2013, a number of interesting patterns emerge. For example, the number of claims bounced up and down over time, likely in parallel to variability in all claims of discrimination. The worldwide economic recession and potential recovery may be one partial explanation for these trends. Interestingly, age claims generally represent between 20% and 25% of all claims made to EEOC. During the period in question, the highest percentage of age claims was found in 2008 (25.8%), while the lowest percentage was found in 2013 (22.8%). However, when evaluating the financial remedies EEOC collected on behalf of potential victims, the most money was collected in 2013. This suggests that EEOC may be becoming more effective when it comes to systemic age cases, and is doing more with fewer claims.

Another potential factor related to the increased financial remedies obtained may relate to disparate impact theory. Before the 2000s, there was substantial ambiguity regarding whether unintentional discrimination was allowable under the ADEA. As described in more detail by Gutman and colleagues (2010), *Smith v. City of Jackson* and *Meacham v. KAPL* represent a set of Supreme Court rulings confirming that disparate impact was a viable theory under the ADEA. These cases by definition affect a large class, and the legal community is likely up to speed on this contemporary issue.

Relatedly, it would also be beneficial to better understand existing age-based subgroup differences on procedures used to make selection decisions. Subgroup difference research associated with race and gender has dominated the personnel selection literature over the last few decades, with far less research focused on age differences. This topic is even more important in the United States now that disparate impact is viable under the ADEA.

Organizational Exits

Case law across countries and EEOC activity in the United States clearly signals that reduction in force initiatives and mandatory retirement and related pension issues will continue to be an area of activity on the age discrimination front. As such, employers will have to put more effort into developing reasonable layoff criteria and mandatory retirement policies in the future. This effort may include more research-based work analysis around critical work activities and worker characteristics needed for particular jobs, as well as clearer identification of the points on the performance continuum that differentiate successful performance from unsuccessful performance. Once these data are available, organizations can develop policies, procedures, and tools that differentiate employees or identify retirement ages based on job-related criteria. For jobs with public safety consequences such as transportation, physical ability and psychomotor capabilities should likely be explicitly considered.

The Changing Nature of Work

As Cascio (1994) noted some 20 years ago, the modern world of work is constantly changing. These changes include what work is performed, who is performing it, and the technological and other contextual factors defining how that work is performed. A consideration of the legal context makes understanding the modern world of work even more complicated, because of the changing nature of socially derived values as well as workforce demographics.

As an example of values-based differences across country, we found it particularly interesting that younger workers are protected in many of the countries we considered in this review, while the United States only protects older workers. The historical context for why the ADEA protected older workers is intuitive: that was the group being discriminated against at the time. This begs the question as to whether age discrimination could be happening to younger workers more often today in the modern economy.

That does not appear to be the case based on case law from other countries. Additionally, it is interesting to note that in many cases, age comparisons are between old and older workers that are all protected over the age of 40. Whether age 40 is currently a logical protection breakpoint is food for thought.

Cascio (1994) was one of the first to note changing demographics in the modern workforce. Today, the workforce is older than it has ever been in the past. We suggest that when this fact is paired with recent worldwide economic conditions, there are clear reasons why reduction in force and mandatory retirement issues dominate contemporary case law across country. One interesting point we noted from our case law review is that there are few age discrimination cases where organizational entry (via external employee selection or promotion to other jobs) is challenged.

Finkelstein, Burke, and Raju (1995) summarized age issues in selection, and noted technology challenges. Technological issues may be even more important to consider now at a time when virtual work is common, and many organizations administer employee processes related to hiring, promotion, and other organizational outcomes via computers, tablets, smartphones, and other technologies. It will be interesting to see whether there will be more age-related challenges to selection processes simply as a function of more: (1) older workers in the workforce; and (2) novel technologies leveraged by organizations for employee selection.

NOTES

1. www.agediscrimination.info/international/Pages/international.aspx (accessed January 15, 2015).
2. http://tvnz.co.nz/national-news/air-new-zealand-faces-big-bill-4102122 (accessed January 15, 2015).
3. For example, please refer to www.eeoc.gov/eeoc/statistics/enforcement/adea.cfm and www.eeoc.gov/eeoc/statistics/enforcement/charges.cfm (accessed January 15, 2015).

CASES CITED

Australia

Blatchford v. Qantas Airways Limited [1997] NSWEOT
Dewan v. Main Roads WA (2005) EOC 93-362
Hopper & Others v. Virgin Blue Airlines Pty Ltd [2005] QADT 13

Qantas Airways Limited v. Christie [1998] HCA 18, 193 CLR 280
Talbert v. Sperling Tourism [2011] NSWADT 67
Webforge Australia Pty Ltd v. Richards [2005] WAIRC 01264 (2005)

Canada

Air Canada v. Carson (1985), 6 C.H.R.R. D/2848 (Fed. C.A.)
Air Canada Pilots Assn. v. Air Canada (2012) F.C.J. No. 976
Consell Scolaire v. Canadian Union of Public Employees (2012)
Hodgson v. Greyhound Lines (CA7 1974) 499 F.2d 859
Large v. Stratford (City) [1995] S.C.J. No. 80 CASCC 1995/10/19 Supreme Court of Canada Judgments
McCreary v. Greyhound (1986) 1986 82 (CHRT). 1986-01-09. T. D. 1/ 86
McKee v. Hayes-Dana Inc. (1992), 17 C.H.R.R. D/79, supplementary reasons 19 C.H.R.R. D/511 (Ont. Bd. Inq.)
McKinney v. University of Guelph [1990] S.C.J. No. 122 CASCC 1990/12/06 Supreme Court of Canada Judgments
New Brunswick (Human Rights Commission) v. Potash Corporation of Saskatchewan Inc. [2006] S.C.C.A. No. 379 CASCC 2008/07/18
Nilsson v. University of Prince Edward Island (2010) P.E.I.H.R.B.I.D. No. 1
O'Brien v. Ontario Hydro (1984), 6 C.H.R.R. D/2512 (Can. Trib.), affd 7 C.H.R.R. D/3250 (Can. Rev. Trib.), affd 8 C.H.R.R. D/4184 (F.C.A)
Ontario v. Roberts (1995) BOI 95-032
Ontario (Human Rights Commission) v Etobicoke (Borough of) [1982] 1 S.C.R. 202
Smallwood v. United Airlines (CA4 1981) 661 F.2d 303
Talbot v. Cape Breton (2009) N.S.H.R.B.I.D. No. 3, 2009 NSHRC 1

Ireland

Cunningham v. BMS Sales Ltd [FEB/EE/2007/017]
Donnellan v. Minister for Justice, Equality and Law Reform and Ors. (Unreported, High Court, McKechnie J. 25 July 2008)
Equality Authority v. Ryanair [2001 E.L.R 107]
Leahy v. Limerick County Council [DEC/E2003/038]
Mr Patrick Dunican and Mr Thomas Spain v. Offaly Civil Defence DEC-E2013-027
Paul Doyle v. ESB International Limited [Dec – E2012-086]
Saunders v. CHC Ireland Limited DEC-E/2011/142

New Zealand

Air New Zealand Ltd v. McAlister (2012) 1 NZLR 153
Attorney-General v. IDEA Services Ltd (2013) 2 NZLR 512
Totalisator Agency Board v. Gruschow (1998) NZAR 529

United Kingdom

Age UK v. Secretary of State for Business, Enterprise and Regulatory Reform (2009) Case C-388/07

Bartram v. *East Sussex County Council, Claverham Community College* [2012] EqLR 384 (Apr 2012)
Compass Group plc v. Ayodele [2011] IRLR 802 (EAT)
Homer v. Chief Constable of West Yorkshire Police (2012) UKSC 15
Kerr v. O'Hara Brothers Surfacing Ltd, Watford Employment Tribunal (Employment Judge Lewis; A Scott, R Jewell) (2013) EqLR 296
Mr AJ Engel v. Transports and Environment Committee of London Councils, London Central Employment Tribunal, 26 April 2013, case number 2200472/2012
Seldon v. Clarkson, Wright & Jakes (2012) UKSC 16 SC

United States

Cleary v. U.S. Lines, Inc. (CA3 1984) 728 F.2d 607
EEOC v. Bd. of Regents of the University of Wisconsin (CA 7 2002) 288 F.3d 296
EEOC v. Commonwealth of Massachusetts (CA1 1988) 858 F.2d 52
EEOC v. State of Vermont (CA2 1990) 904 F.2d 794
EEOC v. Wayne Community College (CA6 1983) 723 F.2d 509
Feldman v. Nassau County (2006 CA2) 434 F.3d 177
General Dynamics v. Cline (2004) 40 US 581
Goodman v. Heublein Inc. (CA2 1981) 645 F.2d 127
Gregory v. Ashcroft (1991) 111 S.Ct. 2395
Int. Brotherhood of Teamsters v. United States (1977) 431 US 324
Kimel v. Board of Regents (2000) 528 US 62
Kentucky Retirement System v. EEOC (2008)
Kopec v. City of Elmhurst (CA7 1999) 193 F3d 894
Loeb v. Textron, Inc. (CA1 1979) 600 F.2d 1003
Mahoney v. RFE/RL (CA DC1995) 47 F.3d 447
Meacham v. KAPL (2008) 200 U. S. 321
Morrissey v. Boston Bank (CA1 1995) 54 F.3d 27
O'Connor v. Consolidated (1996) 116 S.Ct. 1307
Oubre v. Entergy Operations (1998) 118 S.Ct. 838
Passer v. American Chemical Society (D.D.C 1990) 53 FEP cases 1442
Smith v. City of Jackson (2005) 44 U.S. 22
State Police v. Difava (CA1 2003) 317 F.3d 6
TWA v. Thurston (1985) 469 US 111
Whittlesey v. Union Carbide Corp. (S.D.N.Y. 1983) 567 F.Supp 1320

REFERENCES

Cascio, W. F. (1995). Whither industrial and organizational psychology in a changing world of work? *American Psychologist, 50*, 928–939.
Finkelstein, L. M., Burke, M. J., & Raju, N. S. (1995). Age discrimination in simulated employee contexts: An integrative analysis. *Journal of Applied Psychology, 80*, 40–45.
Gutman, A. (2012). Age-based laws and regulations. In J. W. Hedge & W. C. Borman (Eds.), *Work and Aging Handbook* (pp. 606–628). New York: Oxford University Press.
Gutman, A., Koppes, L. L., & Vodanovich, S. (2010). *EEO Law and Personnel Practices* (3rd ed.). New York: Routledge.

Harcourt, M., Wilkinson, A., & Wood, G. (2010). The effects of anti-age discrimination legislation: A comparative analysis. *International Journal of Comparative Labour Law and Industrial Relations, 26*(4), 447–465.

Shore, L. M., & Goldberg, C. B. (2005). Age discrimination in the workplace. In R. L. Dipboye & A. Colella (Eds.), *Discrimination at Work: The Psychological and Organizational Bases* (pp. 203–226). Mahwah, NJ: Erlbaum Associates.

Sterns, H. L., Doverspike, D., & Lax, G. A. (2005). The age discrimination in employment act. In F. S. Landy (Ed.), *Employment Discrimination Litigation: Behavioral, Quantitative and Legal Perspectives* (pp. 256–293). San Francisco, CA: Jossey-Bass.

Part III

Multidisciplinary Viewpoints

Workforce aging issues have gained the attention of scholars in multiple disciplines as the development of effective strategies to mitigate the problems associated with maintaining a vital older workforce will no doubt require multidisciplinary efforts. Although our volume concentrates largely on the perspective of I-O and management scholars, we think that it is also useful to include a sampling of the perspectives of colleagues from other disciplines who have also addressed some of the issues raised in this volume. Thus, this section includes voices from gerontology, lifespan development, and demography.

13

How Individuals Navigate Social Mobility: Changing Capacities and Opportunities in Careers Across Adulthood

Jutta Heckhausen and Jacob Shane

UPWARD MOBILITY STRIVING IN DIFFERENT SOCIETIES

Industrialization, in concert with rapid technological developments, has allowed an increasingly specialized and differentiated division of labor (Durkheim, 1893/1977). Attaining professional and specialized careers now relies on extensive education and vocational training, necessitating strong and sustained motivational commitment on the part of the individual (Heckhausen, 2005). Individuals have to manage their commitment toward these career paths taking into account available opportunities that undergo substantial changes across adulthood (Heckhausen, 1999; Heckhausen & Schulz, 1999).

While industrialization and technological advancement continue to spread throughout the world, societies differ in subtle to radical ways regarding how they structure the opportunities for their members' social mobility and career development at different times in the life course. These differences exist along objective dimensions, such as the educational and welfare systems, and in terms of the permeability of career and education tracks (Blossfeld et al., 2007). Societal differences also exist along subjective dimensions, reflecting citizens' beliefs about the available pathways for careers and one's goals for upward social mobility (Kluegel & Smith, 1986; Shane & Heckhausen, 2013; Shane, Heckhausen, Lessard, Chen, & Greenberger, 2012). For example, the United States and most European countries share similar technological sophistication and industrialized development. However, the United States has more permeable educational and vocational systems at the expense of less structured and predictable career pathways, a weak welfare system, and high levels of social inequality. In contrast, many European countries implement a stronger welfare system and structured career pathways with more modest social inequality, but stricter boundaries between educational and vocational pathways (Blossfeld et al., 2007), and thus less opportunity for switching careers after young adulthood.

Reflecting these different social structures, U.S. citizens largely endorse a worldview consistent with notions of the American Dream wherein individuals believe that they have the opportunity to attain their career and social mobility goals if only they invest sufficient effort and have the required talent (Economic Mobility Project, 2007; Shane & Heckhausen, 2013). These enhanced perceptions of opportunities to attain upward social mobility lead to overly optimistic aspirations being normative and generally advantageous for attaining higher levels of education (Heckhausen & Chang, 2009) and income, despite standing in contrast to the limited social mobility prospects many U.S. citizens actually have (Corak, 2013; Economic Mobility Project, 2012). This increasing disconnect between objective and perceived opportunities poses a unique challenge to individual agency, and may ultimately undermine individuals' motivational commitment toward their career and social mobility goals (Heckhausen & Shane 2015). In other societies, such as Germany, individuals are tracked into different educational pathways early in their school years. Those pathways in turn direct young adults toward particular career paths. In this situation, prospects for upward social mobility are moderated and highly structured by the society, creating an environment where realistic career and social mobility goals are normative and generally adaptive (Heckhausen & Tomasik, 2002).

MAKING THE MOST OF CHANGING CAPACITIES AND OPPORTUNITIES ACROSS THE LIFESPAN

Across the lifespan, individuals have to respond to two major classes of influence on their careers, the biology of maturation and aging, and the way in which society structures access to and paths within careers. In order to successfully navigate the world of work throughout adulthood and its changing opportunities, individuals need a considerable degree of active striving for personal developmental goals and the self-regulation to select appropriate goals, engage with them, and to disengage and adjust goals as opportunities disappear or change over one's life-time (Heckhausen, 2005).

Changing Capacities

Work-relevant competencies and capacities undergo radical change during adulthood and old age. The changes do not happen in lock step, nor do they follow the same age-related trajectories (see principle of multidimensionality and multidirectonality) (Baltes, Lindenberger, & Staudinger, 2006). Some competencies undergo radical growth during young adulthood as individuals enter their careers and rapidly acquire new skills and knowledge as they build their professional expertise. Before these skills and knowledge systems mature into expertise, an individual has not reached his or her potential for a peak performance in a given career field. On the other hand, constituent competencies and sensory, cognitive, and executive functioning capacities such as multitasking start declining in early midlife (Li, Lindenberger, Freund, & Baltes, 2001; Lindenberger, Marsiske, & Baltes, 2000).

These maturation trajectories and the aging of constituent capacities collectively serve to constrain the age range when peak performance can be reached. Thus, individuals attain their highest level of vocational functioning when their constituent capacities have sufficiently developed through training and experience and at the same time have not been significantly eroded by aging-related functional decline. Obviously, different careers require different sets of capacities, skills, and competencies. For example, domains of competence relying strongly on advanced physical functioning involve steeper age-related growth but also steeper decline, leaving just a narrow window of appropriate age for a given career. Examples are athletic and physically demanding careers (e.g., wildfire fighters, military), which peak at early ages (Ericsson, 1990; Schulz & Curnow, 1988) and therefore require career exits in early or mid adulthood.

Individuals typically do not show loss of functioning in regular activities with few time constraints during midlife. However, some age-related losses in executive functioning start in midlife and begin to undermine performance in multitask management, as is required in careers that involve monitoring and managing multiple moving objects (e.g., air traffic controller) or diversely acting people (e.g., teacher). In advanced old age, aging-related losses become more prominent, especially under time constraints and with increased cognitive loads (e.g., Kray & Lindenberger, 2000; Mayr & Kliegl, 1993). However, expertise-related knowledge systems stay intact, and even fluid intellectual skills (e.g., memorizing nouns, mental rotation) can be reactivated by short training interventions or minimal practice (e.g., taking an intelligence test once) (Baltes, Sowarka, & Kliegl, 1989), and new fluid skills (e.g., a mnemonic technique) can be acquired as well (Baltes & Kliegl, 1992).

This complex landscape of changing competencies during adulthood provides a challenge to individual workers/professionals and their employers to maximize their potential at any given time in life. In addition, individuals have to manage the consequences of rapidly changing technology and swift innovation in most production- and service-oriented career fields. In many careers, vocational and professional training can become outdated very quickly. Therefore, individuals have to either systematically and regularly enroll in continued education in their profession, or move on to more supervisory and administrative roles in their workplace.

Changing Opportunities

Modern industrialized societies provide differentiated opportunity paths into vocational and professional careers, and associated opportunities for social mobility (see more detailed discussion of social mobility in prior section). The opportunities to grow one's competence within a given career strongly depend on the institutional constraints imposed upon these careers. Non-professional careers in skilled labor or service jobs have limited opportunities to expand one's competence after the initial period of establishing oneself in the career. In these fields, career entry unfolds after completing high school and some vocational training on the job or in a dedicated vocational training institution. Thereafter, neither further promotion nor further competence development can be expected, and in the ideal scenario the employee remains in this career until retirement, although globalization is rendering such long-term stability of careers unlikely (e.g., Sennett, 1998). Thus, most people in these career fields are unlikely to experience increases in mastery in their jobs after their mid or late twenties.

Professional careers (e.g., engineering, teaching, healthcare) provide somewhat more extended opportunities to expand one's competence and remain positively challenged in one's job, but by middle adulthood even these careers typically do not offer further potential for growth and increased mastery. This means that a few decades before the age-related changes in cognitive and executive functioning become a constraining factor, the societal organization of careers leaves little room for growth in expertise, thus rendering individuals under-challenged and potentially frustrated.

In sum, a major challenge for organizations and employers is to provide their employees sufficient opportunities to expand or transform vocational and professional work so that older employees remain engaged. Without such enrichments, workers and professionals alike will end up disengaged and frustrated at the later phases of their careers.

Engagement-Disengagement Cycles with Explicit Motives (Goals)

Opportunities for growth in work-related activities as provided by biological capacities and institutional opportunities at the workplace do not, in and of themselves, activate the individual worker or professional. For these opportunities to become fruitful, the individual worker has to realize the available potentials for growth in mastery and responsibility and adopt them as personal developmental goals.

The motivational theory of lifespan development proposes that goal selection, goal engagement, and disengagement are most adaptive when they act in accordance with goal-specific opportunities (Heckhausen, Wrosch, & Schulz, 2010). Most important life goals or developmental goals see waxing and waning opportunities across the adult lifespan. For example, biological changes set the ideal timing for bearing children to the twenties and early thirties, and women get consciously and unconsciously engaged with child-bearing goals during this time period and disengaged when their "biological clock" has run out (Heckhausen, Wrosch, & Fleeson, 2001).

When individuals decide for a particular goal, they move into a volitional phase of action, which typically involves a strongly goal-oriented and biased mindset supporting continued commitment to the goal and investment of resources toward attaining it (Heckhausen et al., 2010). When applied to careers, these goal engagements are long-term and involve sustained effort across the lifespan, and due to the increasing costs of education also involve a considerable monetary investment. Under these circumstances, it is extremely challenging to switch from a strong engagement with a particular career goal to disengagement, goal adjustment, and re-engagement with a new and modified career goal.

In vocational and professional careers, the timing of promotions is more or less tied to age ranges, a characteristic that varies across societies, and may be more pronounced in European compared to American contexts. Individuals vary in the extent to which they can tailor their goal engagement, goal disengagement, and goal adjustment to the changing opportunities across adulthood and to the opportunities available in their industry. Some individuals get motivationally entrapped in careers that no longer hold promise for themselves because of the sunken costs associated with previously invested time, energy, and money. Even under low-control circumstances, individuals may keep investing in improving their career and work situation with some success, but at the cost of compromised mental and physical health (Shane & Heckhausen, 2012).

EXPLICIT GOALS AND IMPLICIT MOTIVES AS DRIVERS OF CAREERS

Individuals are motivationally guided by both explicit and implicit motives (Brunstein, 2011; McClelland, Koestner, & Weinberger, 1989). Explicit goal engagement is a better motivational guide for settings with clearly structured assignments, such as within the education system and some highly structured and closely supervised jobs (Heckhausen & Heckhausen, 2011). Under circumstances where it is less clear what exactly is required for success, and if the individual has to ferret out his or her own opportunities and challenges, implicit motives should play a larger role in enabling individuals to succeed (Heckhausen, 2014).

Across the lifespan, most career transitions are from more to less structured. These transitions from more to less structured phases in careers can entail surprises regarding employee performance. Someone who showed exemplary performance during a highly structured phase of training may prove much less adept at seeking out opportunities for mastery when "set free" as a self-directed professional. Moreover, an individual's career development often requires self-initiated seeking and progress toward higher mastery challenges, which are more readily done by those who are propelled by a high implicit motive for achievement. We can therefore expect that individuals with strong and career-congruent implicit motives should be advantaged as they move into more mature stages of their career.

REFERENCES

Baltes, P. B., & Kliegl, R. (1992). Negative age differences in cognitive plasticity of a memory skill during adulthood: Further testing of limits. *Developmental Psychology, 28*, 121–125.

Baltes, P. B., Sowarka, D., & Kliegl, R. (1989). Cognitive training research on fluid intelligence in old age: What can older adults achieve by themselves? *Psychology and Aging, 4*, 217–221.

Baltes, P. B., Lindenberger, U., & Staudinger, U. M. (2006). Life span theory in developmental psychology. In W. Damon & R. M. Lerner (Eds.), *Handbook of Child Psychology: Vol. 1. Theoretical Models of Human Development* (6th ed.). New York: Wiley.

Blossfeld, H. P., Buchholz, S., Hofäcker, D., Hofmeister, H., Kurz, K., & Mills, M. (2007). Globalisierung und die Veränderung sozialer Ungleichheiten in modernen Gesellschaften. Eine Zusammenfassung der Ergebnisse des GLOBALIFE-Projekts [Globalization and the change of social inequality in modern societies: A summary of findings from the GLOBALIFE-project]. *Kölner Zeitschrift fu_r Soziologie und Sozialpsychologie, 59*, 667–691.

Brunstein, J. C. (2011). Implicit and explicit motives. In J. Heckhausen & H. Heckhausen (Eds.), *Motivation and Action* (2nd ed.) (pp. 230–249). New York: Cambridge University Press.

Corak, M. (2013). Income inequality, equality of opportunity, and intergenerational mobility. Institute for the Study of Labor, Discussion Paper No. 7540. Forthcoming in the *Journal of Economic Perspectives*.

Durkheim, E. (1977). *De la division du travail social* [*Über die Teilung der sozialen Arbeit*]. Paris: Übersetzung. Original work published in 1893.

Economic Mobility Project (2007). *Economic Mobility: Is the American Dream Alive and Well?* The PEW Charitable Trusts. Available at: www.pewtrusts.org/~/media/legacy/uploadedfiles/pcs_assets/2012/PursuingAmericanDreampdf.pdf (accessed January 9, 2015).

Economic Mobility Project (2012). *Pursuing the American Dream: Economic Mobility Across Generations*. The PEW Charitable Trusts. Available at: www.pewtrusts.org/~/media/legacy/uploadedfiles/pcs_assets/2012/PursuingAmericanDreampdf.pdf (accessed January 9, 2015).

Ericsson, K. A. (1990). Peak performance and age: An examination of peak performance in sports. In P. B. Baltes & M. M. Baltes (Eds.), *Successful Aging: Perspectives from the Behavioral Sciences*. New York: Cambridge University Press.

Heckhausen, J. (1999). *Developmental Regulation in Adulthood: Age-Normative and Sociostructural Constraints as Adaptive Challenges*. Cambridge: Cambridge University Press.

Heckhausen, J. (2005). Competence and motivation in adulthood and old age: Making the most of changing capacities and resources. In A. J. Elliot & C. S. Dweck (Eds.), *Handbook of Competence and Motivation* (pp. 240–258). New York: The Guilford Press.

Heckhausen, J. (2014). Motivational affordances in school versus work contexts advantage different individuals: A possible explanation for domain-differential gender gaps. In J. S. Eccles & I. Schoon (Eds.), *Gender Differences in Aspirations and Attainment* (pp. 346–362). London: Cambridge University Press.

Heckhausen, J., & Chang, E. S. (2009). Can ambition help overcome social inequality in the transition to adulthood? Individual agency and societal opportunities in Germany and the United States. *Research in Human Development, 6*(4), 235–251.

Heckhausen, J., & Heckhausen, H. (2011). Motivation and development. In J. Heckhausen & H. Heckhausen (Eds.), *Motivation and Action* (2nd ed., pp. 384–443). New York: Cambridge University Press.

Heckhausen, J., & Schulz, R. (1999). Biological and societal canalizations and individuals' developmental goals. In J. Brandstädter & R. Lerner (Eds.), *Action and Self Development: Theory and Research Through the Life-Span* (pp. 67–104). London: Sage.

Heckhausen, J., & Shane, J. (2015). Social mobility in the transition to adulthood: Educational systems, career entry, and individual agency. In L. A. Jensen (Ed.), *The Oxford Handbook of Human Development and Culture* (pp. 535–553). New York: Oxford University Press.

Heckhausen, J., & Tomasik, M. J. (2002). Get an apprenticeship before school is out: How German adolescents adjust vocational aspirations when getting close to a developmental deadline. *Journal of Vocational Behavior, 60*, 199–219.

Heckhausen, J., Wrosch, C., & Fleeson, W. (2001). Developmental regulation before and after a developmental deadline: The sample case of "biological clock" for childbearing. *Psychology and Aging, 16*, 400–413.

Heckhausen, J., Wrosch, C., & Schulz, R. (2010). A motivational theory of life-span development. *Psychological Review, 117*, 32–60.

Kluegel, J. R., & Smith, E. R. (1986). *Beliefs About Inequality: Americans' Views of What is and What Ought to Be*. Piscataway, NJ: Aldine Transaction.

Kray, J., & Lindenberger, U. (2000). Adult age differences in task switching. *Psychology and Aging, 15*, 126–147.

Li, K. Z. H., Lindenberger, U., Freund, A. M., & Baltes, P. B. (2001). Walking while memorizing: Age-related differences in compensatory behavior. *Psychological Science, 12*, 230–237.

Lindenberger, U., Marsiske, M., & Baltes, P. B. (2000). Memorizing while walking: Increase in dual-task costs from young adulthood to old age. *Psychology and Aging, 15*, 417–436.

Mayr, U., & Kliegl, R. (1993). Sequential and coordinative complexity: Age-based processing limitations in figural transformations. *Journal of Experimental Psychology: Learning, Memory, and Cognition, 19*, 1297–1320.

McClelland, D. C., Koestner, R., & Weinberger, J. (1989). How do self-attributed and implicit motives differ? *Psychological Review, 96*, 690–702.

Schulz, R., & Curnow, C. (1988). Peak performance and age among superathletes: Track and field, swimming, baseball, tennis, and golf. *Journal of Gerontology: Psychological Sciences, 43*, 113–120.

Sennett, R. (1998). *The Corrosion of Character*. New York: Norton.

Shane, J., & Heckhausen, J. (2012). Motivational self-regulation in the work domain: Congruence of individuals' control striving and the control potential in their developmental ecologies. *Research in Human Development, 9*(4), 337–357.

Shane, J., & Heckhausen, J. (2013). University students' causal conceptions about social mobility: Diverging pathways for believers in personal merit and luck. *Journal of Vocational Behavior, 82*, 10–19.

Shane, J., Heckhausen, J., Lessard, J., Chen, C., & Greenberger, E. (2012). Career-related goal pursuit among post-high school youth: Relations between personal control beliefs and control strivings. *Motivation and Emotion, 36*(2), 159–169.

14

Labor Force Transitions in Late Life: Between Agency and Structure

Kène Henkens

The current aging process is unprecedented—the scale at which it is affecting populations has never been so great or so enduring—and the era of young population structures will not return (Department of Economic and Social Affairs United Nations, 2010; Lee, Mason, & Cortlear, 2010). This structural development has not only made the sustainability of pension and social security arrangements a key issue for governments, but also influenced the way in which people organize their working lives and firms manage their workforces. Research over the past decades has focused on the driving forces behind early exit from employment and its consequences for organizations and individuals (Ekerdt, 2010; Wang, Henkens, & van Solinge, 2011). However, as Ekerdt (2010) states, "The trend toward earlier retirement is history." Exit routes have been closed, benefit levels are lower, and the duration of these benefits has shortened. These reforms have taken place within a macroeconomic context of increasing job and pension insecurity and an erosion of trust in governing institutions (Hershey, Henkens, & van Dalen, 2010).

The fundamental shift from an early exit culture (Ebbinghaus, 2006) to a culture in which extended labor force participation by older adults is the norm (Henkens & Schippers, 2012) raises many questions about how current and future generations of older adults are managing and will manage their late careers. Older workers, who are expected to work much longer than they had envisioned, are challenged to find ways to remain productive, while employers are equally challenged to offer opportunities to attain that goal.

In this short contribution, I will suggest a few directions for future research that might help us to get a deeper understanding of labor market transitions and choices of new generations of older adults. These directions are rooted in the life course perspective, which is a promising framework for interdisciplinary research.

A central tenet of the life course perspective is the principle of "human agency within structure," which implies that individuals have plans, make choices, and undertake actions within the opportunities and constraints of their social worlds, which are shaped by history and social circumstances (Elder & Johnson, 2003; Settersten & Gannon, 2005). Life course theory is multidisciplinary and integrates insights from economics, sociology, and psychology in order to explain the retirement process (Szinovacz, 2003). Economic research highlights that work-retirement processes are restricted by the availability of key resources such as money and time and that institutions are important in structuring labor force transitions (Wise, 2010). Sociological studies stress that life course transitions are socially embedded in relations with social network members inside and outside the workplace, while those in the field of psychology emphasize the importance of the precursors of differences in plans, attitudes, and behaviors, and the different phases of retirement decision-making (Feldman & Beehr, 2011).

For future research, three overarching research questions might be developed further to increase our insights in the driving forces of the roles older adults play in aging societies and the role of paid and unpaid work in particular:

1. What are the main patterns of work and other productive roles in which adults are engaged in at the end of their labor market careers, and how are these interconnected?
2. How are these patterns of productive behavior influenced by the multilayered contexts of institutional arrangements, household contexts, and employers' behaviors?
3. To what extent are these patterns of productive behavior the result of active planning and agency by older adults developing their own life courses?

PATTERNS OF PAID AND UNPAID PRODUCTIVE ACTIVITIES IN LATE CAREER

Labor market behavior interacts with other roles that people play within society; participation in volunteer work, grandparenting, and care obligations are connected with late-life labor force transitions (Kaskie, Imhof, Cavanaugh, & Culp, 2008; van Bavel & de Winter, 2013; van den Bogaard, Henkens, & Kalmijn, 2013). Some activities such as volunteering may increase human capital or social resources, which subsequently facilitates workforce opportunities, while others such as caring may reduce these opportunities due to time barriers and limited access to new networks (Carr & Kail, 2013). While fewer older adults seem to be opting for full retirement, increasing numbers of older workers continue to extend their working lives through continued careers or bridge employment (Wang, Adams, Beehr, & Shultz, 2009). Others are involved in some type of hybrid employment or part-time and phased retirement (Kantarci & van Soest, 2008). Furthermore, post-career transitions into self-employment are increasingly common (Hochguertel, 2010; van Solinge, 2013; Wang, Zhan, Liu, & Shultz, 2008).

Rather than focusing on paid work exclusively, scholars might address different types of paid and unpaid productive activities, investigate how these activities interact, and determine whether distinct patterns of paid and unpaid productive activities can be identified. For instance, do these paid and unpaid activities compete with each other given the existence of other leisure pursuits that can restrict the time available? Or do paid and unpaid productive activities reinforce each other? Studying socially productive behaviors in a comprehensive way, rather than in isolation, is a difficult yet promising way to move the research field forward.

THE IMPACT OF MULTILAYERED CONTEXTS

The life course approach emphasizes the contextual and social embeddedness of life transitions as well as the interdependencies between different domains of life (e.g., family, work, health). This holds in particular for older adults' late career transitions. Contextual influences on late career employment operate at the macro-level (institutional arrangements and pension regulations), at the meso-level of employers (organizational and labor market demand), and at the micro-level of the family (family and household resources, preferences, and actions). Future work might put more emphasis on the impacts of the multilayered contexts of institutional arrangements, employers' behaviors, and household constraints on decisions people take at the end of their career. Taking into account the impact of a multilayered context will enrich models that are overly reliant on individual resources.

Focusing on the contextual embeddedness serves as an important advancement of the existing literature because opposing forces may be at work. Strong contextual stimuli (e.g., retirement regulations) may have weak effects when the opportunities they aim to provide are countervailed by opposing organizational or household constraints. For example, institutional incentives to extend working life may be thwarted by a family or organizational situation that discourages continued work (Henkens, 1999). Future studies might want to look at how these different categories of determinants interact and how these possibly opposing forces shape the opportunities available to older workers.

One of the key actors in understanding the restrictions older adults face in the labor market is the employer. Employer policies and programs, on the one hand, allow employers to control the retirement process and, on the other hand, shape the opportunities for individuals' late-life work and retirement. The literature on employers' behaviors reveals a considerable variety in organizations' age management policies (Henkens & van Dalen, 2012; Taylor, Brooke, & Di Biase, 2010). This variety is reflected in the large differences in the extent to which organizations support delaying the labor force exits of their older workers (Henkens, van Solinge, & Cozijnsen, 2009), are willing to hire older workers in bridge employment (Karpinska, Henkens, & Schippers, 2011; Oude Mulders, Henkens, & Schippers, 2013), and are employing policies to maintain and enhance worker productivity (Conen, 2013; Goldberg, Perry, Finkelstein, & Shull, 2013; Munnell & Sass, 2008; van Dalen, Henkens, & Wang, 2014; van der Heijden, Schalk, & van Veldhoven, 2008). Employers have started to face unprecedented challenges, namely an aging labor force, one of the deepest recessions since the 1930s, and rapidly changing retirement regulations restricting early exit from work. So far, we have only limited insights in how employers deal with these challenges.

LIFE COURSE AGENCY OF OLDER WORKERS

Older adults' late careers options are shaped by different and often opposing stimuli coming from different contexts. An interesting question in this respect is to what extent older adults act as active agents in designing their future careers? To what extent do older adults plan their late careers and post-retirement activities? Moreover, if they make plans, what are they? And finally, what are the characteristics of those who are able to put their plans into practice, and which factors are important in (not) realizing these plans?

Several theorists have argued that in a world of alternative lifestyle options, life course planning is of key importance (Beck & Beck-Gernsheim, 2002; Giddens, 1991). Life course planning or life course agency is a means of preparing a course of future actions to shape one's future life course and has been defined as the ability to formulate and pursue life plans (Hitlin & Elder, 2006; Marshall, 2005; Shanahan & Elder, 2002). Although there is ongoing debate in the social sciences over the primacy of structure or agency in shaping human behavior (Liefbroer, 2007; Settersten & Gannon, 2005), empirical examinations of the importance of life course agency are rare (Hitlin & Elder, 2007). This also holds for research on late career transitions, where planning and agency are often implicitly assumed. Ekerdt (2010) contends, however, that it is unclear to what extent older workers are able to control the course of their late careers. An agentic view of the labor market transitions of aging workers may see their part-time and flexible work in less demanding jobs as a reflection of their career preferences. Transitions may, however, also result from restrictive contexts in which older adults are confronted with institutions, norms, and economic circumstances that structure—the lack of—late career employment. Moen and Flood (2013) expand this argument to other forms of public activities such as volunteering, arguing that the post-retirement life stage may be a new arena in which inequality may occur in the form of the social exclusion of some subgroups of older people from public activities valued by society.

The idea of agency and structure in retirement decision-making has mainly been studied in relation to discrepancies between retirement-timing intentions and behavior (Anderson, Burkhauser, & Quinn, 1986; Henkens & Tazelaar, 1997) and the notion of perceived involuntary retirement (Dingemans & Henkens, 2013; Szinovacz & Davey, 2005; van Solinge & Henkens, 2007). These studies have shown that a large proportion of earlier cohorts experienced retirement as a forced transition due to serious health problems, organizational restrictions, and mandatory retirement rules. In other cases, although retirement is not forced, it is not really voluntary either (Vickerstaff, 2006). For example, older adults may have certain health problems that make them feel that they must retire. Feldman and Beehr (2011) argue that much more research is needed on retirement transitions that are neither forced nor completely voluntary.

We might want to expand the research on life course agency by studying agency and planning not only with respect to the timing of transitions, but

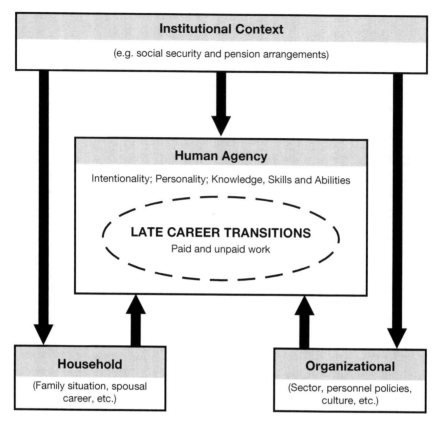

FIGURE 14.1
Overall graphical representation of agency within structure

also with respect to different pathways (e.g., phased exit, self-employment, bridge employment in different sectors) and post-retirement activities (e.g., volunteer work).

By connecting agency and contexts in a theoretical framework and in empirical tests (see Figure 14.1), we will be able not only to establish to what extent older adults actively design their late career life courses, but also to ascertain the characteristics of older adults who are successful in executing their plans. An interdisciplinary approach is also promising in the development of surveys to test our hypotheses. On the one hand, carrying out a large-scale nationwide survey—a strategy more often employed by economists and sociologists—reduces issues of sampling error that are common in many convenience samples used in retirement research in the field of psychology (Wang, 2012). On the other hand, paying attention to the validity and reliability of measures—which is common in psychology studies—is less common in the work of economists and sociologists. Future researchers might be more focused on ways to combine the methodological strengths of the disciplines, instead of being overly concerned about issues of scale construction and reliability (psychology) or national representativeness (economics and sociology). Perhaps we could all benefit from a more open-minded attitude when it comes to adopting the perspectives and methodologies of other disciplines.

CONCLUSION

The aging of society is one of the dominant developments in modern societies. Social integration of the new cohorts of older adults in society is not only important from the perspective of social well-being of these generations, but also from the perspective of a society that may need the use of this hidden pool of labor supply on the paid and unpaid labor market. To understand the decisions older adults take, as well as the restrictions that they face in their social worlds, scholarly research is highly relevant for science and society. To date, much is unknown about the new patterns of productive paid and unpaid activities that emerged as a result of the changing regulations on retirement and the ambitions of new generations of older adults approaching retirement age.

REFERENCES

Anderson, K. H., Burkhauser, R. V., & Quinn, J. F. (1986). Do retirement dreams come true? The effect of unanticipated events on retirement plans. *Industrial and Labour Relations Review*, 39(4), 518–526.

Beck, U., & Beck-Gernsheim, E. (2002). *Individualization: Institutionalized Individualism and its Social and Political Consequences. Vol. 13*. New York: Sage.

Carr, D. C., & Kail, B. (2013). The influence of unpaid work on the transition out of full-time paid work. *The Gerontologist*, 53(1), 92–101.

Conen, W. (2013). *Older Workers: The View of Dutch Employers in a European Perspective*. Amsterdam: Amsterdam University Press.

Department of Economic and Social Affairs United Nations (2002). *World Population Ageing: 1950–2050*. UN, available at: www.un.org/esa/population/publications/worldageing19502050 (accessed January 11, 2015).

Dingemans, E., & Henkens, K. (2014). Involuntary retirement, bridge employment, and satisfaction with life: A longitudinal investigation. *Journal of Organizational Behavior*, 35(4), 575–591.

Ebbinghaus, B. (2006). *Reforming Early Retirement in Europe, Japan and the USA*. Oxford: Oxford University Press.
Ekerdt, D. J. (2010). Frontiers of research on work and retirement. *Journals of Gerontology Series B-Psychological Sciences and Social Sciences, 65*(1), 69-80.
Elder, G. H., & Johnson, M. K. (2003). The life course and aging. Challenges, lessons, and new directions. In R. A. Settersten (Ed.), *Invitation to the Life Course. Towards New Understandings of Later Life* (pp. 49-81). New York: Baywood.
Feldman, D. C., & Beehr, T. A. (2011). A three-phase model of retirement. *American Psychologist, 66*(3), 193-203.
Giddens, A. (1991). *Modernity and Self-Identity: Self and Society in the Late Modern Age*. Palo Alto, CA: Stanford University Press.
Goldberg, C. B., Perry, E. L., Finkelstein, L. M., & Shull, A. (2013). Antecedents and outcomes of targeting older applicants in recruitment. *European Journal of Work and Organizational Psychology, 22*(3), 265-278.
Henkens, K. (1999). Retirement intentions and spousal support: A multi-actor approach. *Journal of Gerontology: Social Sciences, 54*(2), 63-74.
Henkens, K., & Schippers, J. (2012). Active ageing in Europe: The role of organisations. *International Journal of Manpower, 33*(6), 604-611.
Henkens, K., & Tazelaar, F. (1997). Explaining retirement decisions of civil servants in the Netherlands. *Research on Aging, 19*(2), 139-173.
Henkens, K., & van Dalen, H. P. (2012). The employer's perspective on retirement. In M. Wang (Ed.), *The Oxford Handbook of Retirement* (pp. 215-227). Oxford: Oxford University Press.
Henkens, K., van Solinge, H., & Cozijnsen, R. (2009). Let go or retain? A comparative study of the attitudes of business students and managers about the retirement of older workers. *Journal of Applied Social Psychology, 39*(7), 1562-1588.
Hershey, D. A., Henkens, K., & van Dalen, H. P. (2010). What drives retirement income worries in Europe? A multilevel analysis. *European Journal of Ageing, 7*(4), 301-311.
Hitlin, S., & Elder, G. H. (2006). Agency: An empirical model of an abstract concept. *Advances in Life Course Research, 11*, 33-67.
Hitlin, S., & Elder, G. H. (2007). Time, self, and the curiously abstract concept of agency. *Sociological Theory, 25*(2), 170-191.
Hochguertel, S. (2010). Self-employment around retirement age (No. 10-067/3). Tinbergen Institute discussion paper.
Kantarci, T., & van Soest, A. (2008). Gradual retirement: Preferences and limitations. *Economist-Netherlands, 156*(2), 113-144.
Karpinska, K., Henkens, K., & Schippers, J. (2011). The recruitment of early retirees: A vignette study of the factors that affect managers' decisions. *Ageing & Society, 31*(4), 570-589.
Kaskie, B., Imhof, S., Cavanaugh, J., & Culp, K. (2008). Civic engagement as a retirement role for aging Americans. *The Gerontologist, 48*(3), 368-377.
Lee, R., Mason, A., & Cortlear, D. (2010). Some economic consequences of global aging: A discussion note for the World Bank. Health, Nutrition and Population Discussion Papers. Washington, DC: World Bank.
Liefbroer, A. C. (2007). De maakbare levensloop? In T. van der Lippe, P. A. Dykstra, G. Kraaykamp, & J. Schippers (Eds.), *De maakbaarheid van de levensloop* (pp. 9-20). Assen: Koninklijke van Gorcum BV.
Marshall, V. W. (2005). Agency, events, and structure at the end of the life course. *Advances in Life Course Research, 10*, 57-91.

Moen, P., & Flood, S. (2013). Limited engagements? Women's and men's work/volunteer time in the encore life course stage. *Social Problems*, 60(2), 206–233.

Munnell, A. H., & Sass, S. A. (2008). *Working Longer: The Solution to the Retirement Income Challenge*. Washington, DC: Brookings Institution Press.

Oude Mulders, J. O., Henkens, K., & Schippers, J. (2013). Organizations' ways of employing early retirees: The role of age-based HR policies. *The Gerontologist*, advance access.

Settersten, R. A., & Gannon, L. (2005). Structure, agency, and the space between: On the challenges and contradictions of a blended view of the life course. *Advances in Life Course Research*, 10, 35–55.

Shanahan, M. J., & Elder, G. H. (2002). History, agency, and the life course. In R. A. Dienstbier & L. J. Crockett (Eds.), *Agency, Motivation, and the Life Course* (pp. 145–186). Lincoln, NE: University of Nebraska Press.

Szinovacz, M. E. (2003). Contexts and pathways: Retirement as institution, process, and experience. In G. A. Adams & T. A. Beehr (Eds.), *Retirement. Reasons, Processes and Results* (pp. 6–52). New York: Springer.

Szinovacz, M. E., & Davey, A. (2005). Predictors of perceptions of involuntary retirement. *The Gerontologist*, 45(1), 36–47.

Taylor, P. E., Brooke, L., & Di Biase, T. (2010). European employer policies concerning career management and learning from a life-span perspective. In G. Naegele (Ed.), *Soziale Lebenslauf Politik* (pp. 474–497). Wiesbaden: VS Verlag.

van Bavel, J., & de Winter, T. (2013). Becoming a grandparent and early retirement in Europe. *European Sociological Review*, 29(6), 1295–1308. Advance online publication. DOI: 10.1093/esr/jct005.

van Dalen, H., Henkens, K., & Wang, M. (2014). Recharging or retiring the older worker? Uncovering age-based strategies of European employers. *The Gerontologist*, advance access.

van den Bogaard, L., Henkens, K., & Kalmijn, M. (2014). So now what? Effects of retirement on civic engagement. *Ageing and Society*, 34(7), 1170–1192.

van der Heijden, B. I., Schalk, R., & van Veldhoven, M. J. (2008). Ageing and careers: European research on long-term career development and early retirement. *Career Development International*, 13(2), 85–94.

van Solinge, H. (2013). Who opts for self-employment after retirement? A longitudinal study in the Netherlands. *European Journal of Ageing*, 11(3), 261–272.

van Solinge, H., & Henkens, K. (2007). Involuntary retirement: The role of restrictive circumstances, timing, and social embeddedness. *Journals of Gerontology Series B-Psychological Sciences and Social Sciences*, 62(5), 295–303.

Vickerstaff, S. (2006). Entering the retirement zone: How much choice do individuals have? *Social Policy & Society*, 5(4), 507–517.

Wang, M. (Ed.) (2012). *The Oxford Handbook of Retirement*. Oxford: Oxford University Press.

Wang, M., Zhan, Y., Liu, S., & Shultz, K. S. (2008). Antecedents of bridge employment: A longitudinal investigation. *Journal of Applied Psychology*, 93(4), 818–830.

Wang, M., Adams, G. A., Beehr, T. A., & Shultz, K. S. (2009). Career issues at the end of one's career. Bridge employment and retirement. In S. G. Baugh & S. A. Sullivan (Eds.), *Maintaining Focus, Energy, and Options Through the Lifespan* (pp. 135–162). Charlotte, NC: Information Age.

Wang, M., Henkens, K., & van Solinge, H. (2011). Retirement adjustment. A review of theoretical and empirical advancements. *American Psychologist*, 66(3), 204–213.

Wise, D. A. (2010). Facilitating longer working lives: International evidence on why and how. *Demography*, 47(1), 131–149.

15

Optimizing Older Workforces

Laura L. Carstensen, Michaela E. Beals,
and Martha Deevy

Work is changing in important ways as we enter the 21st century. Rather than seeing retirement age continue to fall, as it did throughout the second half of the 20th century, retirement age has begun to tick upward. In 2000, 32.4% of people aged 55+ were in the labor force; by 2010, this number had climbed to 40.2% (Toosi, 2012). Surveys of boomers find that a significant number expect to work past traditional retirement age (Helman, 2014), and the evidence so far suggests that their expectations may well come to pass.

Not only are people working longer, workforces are becoming more age-diversified than ever before in history. Such changes not only reflect the global demographic trends underway, they also reflect changes in work practices and norms. In stark contrast to conceptions of retirement as the "prize" awarded after decades of hard work, large numbers of workers are coming to see retirement as an outdated concept or a signal to pursue a different, often emotionally rewarding kind of work. If wisely addressed, we expect that working longer will be beneficial for individuals, employers, and societies. The benefits for societies are obvious. Greater workforce participation positively affects gross domestic product, and lesser reliance on federal programs and pensions strengthens these respective funds. Below, we consider potential rewards of longer working lives for workers and employers.

Working longer holds appeal to workers for multiple reasons, with financial need topping the list among Americans who are notably ill-prepared to begin to rely on their savings for income. Yet another significant number of workers say that they are continuing to work because they like their work. Indeed, across income, education, gender, and race, older workers are the most satisfied workers in the workforce (Benz, Sedensky,

Tompson, & Agiesta, 2013), and the line between work and retirement is becoming increasingly blurred, with retirees more routinely coming in and out of the workforce for part-time and flexible opportunities. For others, retirement represents a chance to pursue "encore careers" or "second acts," where workers opt for lesser pay but greater satisfaction in social entrepreneurship (Freedman, 2008).

A growing body of research suggests that working longer confers more than just financial security. Increasingly, studies that control for health and other factors that influence continued active engagement find that work in paid or volunteer positions during later adulthood contributes to physical, social, and emotional health (Bonsang, Adam, & Perelman, 2012; Carlson et al., 2009; Fratiglioni, Paillard-Borg, & Winblad, 2004; Jenkinson et al., 2013; Rohwedder & Willis, 2010), presumably due to the way such work facilitates engagement physically, cognitively, and through social integration (Fried et al., 2004).

Of course, considering the fact that life expectancy at retirement age has doubled since 1965, retirement age, now 62, remains relatively young. In order for wide-scale changes in retirement practices to occur, employers will need to embrace older workers and workforces. Although there is some evidence that this may be the case in parts of Europe where workforces are shrinking, in the United States there is little evidence for enthusiasm on the part of employers to employ older workers. At the Stanford Center on Longevity, we have been working with major employers in an effort to help prepare for the changing demographics of the workforce. We held two workshop-style conferences (April 2013 and January 2014) with attendance from numerous employers, academics who study work and aging, and nonprofit representatives who think about public policy responses to these issues. Proceedings can be accessed at: http://longevity3.stanford.edu/publications/. The qualitative findings reveal a simple but not unexpected result: when employers think about older workforces, they express considerable unease about cost, pipeline issues, and sluggish productivity related to physical and cognitive decline. Are these concerns warranted? Some of the concerns we hear are rooted in unfounded stereotypes about older people, similar to those that authors in the present volume document. Others reflect real issues in workplace practices that must be addressed in order to optimize older workforces. First, we consider evidence that physical and cognitive decline are *unlikely* to influence productivity during working lives.

Perhaps the greatest concern employers have is the perception that older workers exhibit lower productivity than younger workers due to age-related physical and cognitive decline. Concerns that older employees are too *infirm* to work effectively fail to acknowledge historical improvements in physical health (Börsch-Supan, 2013), functional adaptions to chronic physical changes that do occur with age (MacArthur Foundation Research Network on an Aging Society, 2009), and the fact that as the American manufacturing sector contracts, fewer jobs are as physically demanding today as compared to the past (Eugene Steuerle, Spiro, & Johnson, 1999). Research based on scores of workers and thousands of observations of workers in a German auto manufacturing plant found that productivity increased up to retirement age (see Börsch-Supan, 2013). German luxury automaker BMW has reconfigured assembly lines in one of its plants to suit older workers, installing larger computer screens with bigger type, providing employees with special shoes to ease aching feet, and adding chairs to some parts of the line so workers could perform tasks while sitting down (Loch, Fabien, Bauer, & Mauermann, 2010).

There is reason to think that concerns about cognitive abilities are also exaggerated in light of existing evidence. Although the precise relationship between aging and work performance remains poorly characterized, research does not support the claim that job productivity steadily worsens due to cognitive decline. On the contrary, knowledge-based job performance increases with age. It is true that certain cognitive skills decline with age, such as comprehension, abstraction, processing speed, and processing accuracy. However, other types of intelligence, such as general knowledge, vocabulary, language skills, thinking strategies, social competence, and emotional regulation, improve with age and largely offset performance until declines are substantial (Carstensen, 2014). In knowledge-based jobs, one can predict steady gains with age and experience. Even in nonprofessional or low-complexity jobs, however, increases in knowledge and expertise compensate for age-related declines in cognitive processing speed (Salthouse, 1984).

Despite little evidence for decline in performance related to cognitive abilities, we expect that motivational changes on the part of employees and employers may be related to performance of older workers (see Kanfer & Ackerman, 2004; Kanfer, Beier, & Ackerman, 2012). In our view, however, motivation is likely affected by time horizons more so than chronological age. There is considerable evidence in the lifespan psychology literature that time horizons affect motivation (Carstensen, 2006). When time is perceived as open-ended and future paths are uncertain, people tend to pursue goals related to novelty, new learning, and exploration; in contrast, when endings are perceived, goals shift to ones about emotional meaning and satisfaction (Carstensen, Isaacowitz, & Charles, 1999). A recent article by Stroebe (2010) provided an illustration based on academic productivity over historical time, before and after mandatory retirement. When retirement was anticipated in the early 60s, academic performance, as measured by publications and grants, declined steadily after age 45. Post-mandatory retirement, older academics publish more and run the best-funded laboratories. In other words, people prepare for endings. When they are perceived, workers prepare; when they are not perceived, workers (at least selectively) continue to invest. A recent report from the Sloan Center on Aging & Work at Boston College is consistent with this interpretation. They found that workers who worked past retirement age became more, rather than less, engaged and satisfied with their jobs (Brown, Auman, Pitt-Catsouphes, Galinsky, & Bond, 2010). Again, selection effects are at play, but the fact remains that older employees do not necessarily "grind down" at predictable ages.

Time horizons of employers also matter. We were told by employers who attended our workshops that managers stop investing in training older workers and shift important tasks to younger workers when they view older workers on the way out, not because they question the older workers' abilities, but because investments in younger workers will pay off longer. We expect that research on the effects of time horizons on job performance and new models of part-time work may be fruitful.

What are the real barriers to longer working lives? We maintain that the greatest barriers to longer working lives are practical. Many are structural. As Alicia Munnell and Steven Sass noted in their 2008 book *Working Longer*, older workers are expensive; they generally have higher wages than their younger counterparts and their health insurance costs more. Further, government policies regarding retirement plans and healthcare programs can sometimes act as disincentives to employing older workers (Munnell & Sass, 2008). Creating further challenges for employers, the shift from defined benefit to defined contribution retirement plans resulted in undersaving for many workers and relatedly made it harder for employers to predict retirement transitions, thus making workforce planning quite difficult. Companies worry that when senior management stagnates, even if effective, mid-level employees leave the company when they see little chance for promotion. Despite clear macroeconomic evidence that greater workforce participation among older workers is not detrimental to younger workers (Munnell & Wu, 2012) (i.e., the lump of labor fallacy), in some companies older workers inevitably create "chokepoints" in the pipeline that influence the career trajectories of mid-level employees. Other challenges may be psychological. Rather than reflect cognitive and physical decline, however, we expect that they are more likely motivational. Structural changes to work practices, gradual retirements, and allowing workers to increasingly focus on projects they value may not only reduce the problem, but enhance the performance.

In summary, work and retirement norms at play today are ones that evolved around young workers and workforces. The challenges that we face reflect a mismatch between antiquated norms and the abilities of today's workers. Arguably, the most striking omission in the conversations underway about work today is consideration of the strengths of older workers, the potential of mixed-aged teams, and the ways in which younger workers may be advantaged by the mentorship of seasoned employees. With thoughtful consideration about ways to redesign work life to reflect an aging population, productivity will not inevitably decline; in fact, we expect that it may improve.

REFERENCES

Benz, J., Sedensky, M., Tompson, T., & Agiesta, J. (2013). Working longer: Older Americans' attitudes on work and retirement. *Research Highlights*. NORC Center for Public Affairs Research. Available at: www.apnorc.org/PDFs/Working%20Longer/AP-NORC%20Center_Working%20Longer%20Report-FINAL.pdf (accessed August 15, 2014).

Bonsang, E., Adam, S., & Perelman, S. (2012). Does retirement affect cognitive functioning? *Journal of Health Economics, 31*, 490–501.

Börsch-Supan, A. (2013). Myths, scientific evidence and economic policy in an aging world. *Journal of the Economics of Ageing, 1*, 3–15.

Brown, M., Auman, K., Pitt-Catsouphes, M., Galinsky, E., & Bond, J. T. (2010). Working in retirement: A 21st century phenomenon. *The Sloan Center on Aging & Work*. Available at: http://familiesandwork.org/site/research/reports/workinginretirement.pdf (accessed August 15, 2014).

Carlson, M. C., Erickson, K. I., Kramer, A. F., Voss, M. W., Bolea, N., Mielke, M., McGill, S., Rebok, G. W., Seeman, T., & Fried, L. P. (2009). Evidence for neurocognitive plasticity in at-risk older adults: The Experience Corps program. *Journal of Gerontology: Medical Sciences, 64*(12), 1275–1281.

Carstensen, L. L. (2006). The influence of a sense of time on human development. *Science, 312*, 1913–1915.

Carstensen, L. L. (2014). Our aging population: It may just save us all. In P. Irving & R. Beamish (Eds.), *The Upside of Aging* (pp. 3–18). Hoboken, NJ: Wiley & Sons.

Carstensen, L. L., Isaacowitz, D., & Charles, S. T. (1999). Taking time seriously: A theory of socioemotional selectivity. *American Psychologist, 54*, 165–181.

Eugene Steuerle, C., Spiro, C., & Johnson, R. W. (1999). Can Americans work longer? *Straight Talk on Social Security and Retirement Policy No. 5*. Washington, DC: The Urban Institute.

Fratiglioni, L., Paillard-Borg, S., & Winblad, B. (2004). An active and socially integrated lifestyle in late life might protect against dementia. *Lancet Neurol., 3*, 343–353.

Freedman, M. (2008). *Encore: Finding Work that Matters in the Second Half of Life*. New York: Public Affairs.

Fried, L. P., Carlson, M. C., Freedman, M., Frick, K. D., Glass, T. A., Hill, J., McGill, S., Rebok, W., Seeman, T., Tielsch, J., Wasik, B. A., & Zeger, S. (2004). A social model for health promotion for an aging population: Initial evidence on the Experience Corps model. *Journal of Urban Health: Bulletin of the New York Academy of Medicine, 81*(1), 64–78.

Helman, R. (2014). The 2014 retirement confidence survey: Confidence rebounds—for those with retirement plans. *EBRI Issue Brief, 397*, 25–27.

Jenkinson, C. E., Dickens, A. P., Jones, K., Thompson-Coon, J., Taylor, R. S., Rogers, M., Bambra, C. L., Lang, I., & Richards, S. H. (2013). Is volunteering a public health intervention? A systematic review and meta-analysis of the health and survival of volunteers. *BMC Public Health, 13*, 773–783.

Kanfer, R., & Ackerman, P. L. (2004). Aging, adult development and work motivation. *Academy of Management Review, 29*, 440–458.

Kanfer, R., Beier, M. E., & Ackerman, P. L. (2012). Goals and motivation related to work in later adulthood: An organizing framework. *European Journal of Work and Organization, 22*(3), 253–264.

Loch, C. H., Fabien, J. S., Bauer, N., & Mauermann, H. (2010). How BMW is defusing the demographic time bomb. *Harvard Business Review*, March, 99–102.

MacArthur Foundation Research Network on an Aging Society (2009, Fall). Facts and fictions about an aging America. *Contexts, 8*(4), 16–21.

Munnell, A. H., & Sass, S. (2008). *Working Longer: The Solution to the Retirement Income Challenge*. Washington, DC: Brookings Institution Press.

Munnell, A. H., & Wu, Y. (2012). Are aging baby boomers squeezing younger workers out of jobs? Issue in brief (pp. 12–18). October 2012. Available at: http://crr.bc.edu/wp-content/uploads/2012/09/IB_12-18-508.pdf (accessed August 15, 2014).

Rohwedder, S., & Willis, R. J. (2010). Mental retirement. *Journal of Economic Perspectives, 24*(1), 119–138.

Salthouse, T. (1984). Effects of age and skills in typing. *Journal of Experimental Psychology, 113*, 345–371.

Stroebe, W. (2010). The graying of academia: Will it affect productivity? *American Psychologist, 65*, 660–673.

Toosi, M. (2012). Labor force projections to 2020: A more slowly growing workforce. *Monthly Labor Review*, January 2012. Available at: www.bls.gov/opub/mlr/2012/01/art3full.pdf (accessed January 15, 2013).

Part IV

Editor Viewpoints

Many edited volumes end with a final, summative chapter by all the editors. In our joint opening chapter, we shared our common vision of the topic. As we moved toward the end of this project, however, we realized that we held slightly different, though complementary, views about the about the major themes that emerge from this volume. Thus, rather than summarizing the themes across chapters in a single voice, we thought it would be more interesting to the reader if we each provided short commentaries about the major themes from our individual points of view. Although unconventional, we believe that these brief summative commentaries offer the reader an opportunity to better understand the complexity and rich set of research opportunities afforded by slightly different takes on the material contained in this volume.

16

Employment Transitions in Late Adulthood

Ruth Kanfer

Demographic trends, macroeconomic conditions, and changes in the nature of work have spurred interest in the older worker. Increasing population longevity and reduced birth rates have led policymakers to delay or eliminate fixed-age mandatory retirement as a means of stabilizing workforce size. At the same time, organizations concerned with talent shortages and organizational knowledge transfer have explored the use of exit strategies that extend the employee retirement process over time (e.g., bridge retirement). In theory, such trends are expected to provide support for sustained employability and a longer working life, and there is growing evidence that older individuals are increasingly delaying retirement or re-entering the workforce. In practice, however, it is unclear how labor policy changes and organizational practices affect the worker transition process, sustain employability, and promote worker well-being following labor force exit. Although organizations may offer bridge employment options, human resource management practices are often slow to change (see de Lange, Kooij, & van der Heijden, this volume), leading to older worker feelings of disenfranchisement and work dissatisfaction. Organizations have often taken a reactive rather than proactive approach to the development of programs and practices that promote sustained employability (such as older worker socialization, training, and development), mitigate disruptive intergenerational conflict in increasingly age-diverse work teams, and support the hire of qualified older workers. Taken together, these local work experiences may encourage older worker exit from the job and/or the workforce despite broader organizational goals to attract, train, and retain such workers. In summary, while there is wide consensus on the desirability of a longer high-quality working life for many people in developed countries, the development of effective, coordinated strategies for accomplishing such a goal remains largely elusive. This volume seeks to address this issue from a person-centric perspective, namely by examining the impact of work on older worker experiences, goals, attitudes, and behaviors.

THE PSYCHOLOGY OF LATE ADULTHOOD EMPLOYMENT TRANSITIONS

In many developed countries, employment transitions during late life are volitional. Even individuals who are required by law to retire at a particular age (e.g., pilots) may subsequently seek employment or work in other positions or industries. The initiation and management of the transition process from full employment to full workforce withdrawal depends critically on personal characteristics and the perceived constraints and affordances of environments in which the worker lives. As such, understanding why, when, and how older individuals initiate, extend, or reverse the employment exit process is an essential first step in the development of sound public and organizational policies to sustain employment and employability. The chapters in this volume address these questions from a variety of perspectives, and provide a wealth of insights and suggestions for new and promising research directions on the topic of the older worker.

As the authors in this volume attest, a multitude of factors affect the older individual's work experiences and transitions in and out of employment. During late adulthood, the most pervasive (though not necessarily the most potent) influences originate in broad age-graded societal laws and social norms, and work-related expectations, along with the associated institutionalized arrangements that exist for the provision of medical and financial support of retired people (see Guttman & Dunleavy, this volume). Such expectations and norms influence both the individual and those who work with that person (see Rudolph & Zacher, this volume). These norms and expectations, whether they are bounded by nation, ethnicity, or organization, contribute to the formulation of beliefs that in turn motivate a plethora of behaviors and work practices that affect the individual's sense of identity, competencies, and well-being, as well as the decisions and behaviors that others (in and out of the workplace) make about the individual's workability.

During the past few decades, however, there has been a growing dissociation between human capabilities in later adulthood (due to increased longevity, improved healthcare, and changing work demands), and institutionalized norms regarding older worker participation in the labor force. In many developed countries, workers often outlive mandated retirement ages by two or more decades. As a consequence of shifting societal, organizational, and individual needs, there has been upheaval in both the manner by which older workers transition out of the workforce and the individual's experiences during this process. For many older workers, the transition is no longer an abrupt exit from work ("retirement"), but rather a prolonged process characterized by movement into bridge retirement positions or exit from one line of work into a different type of work. As Zhan and Wang (this volume) note, for some individuals the process is characterized by "voluntariness" with respect to workforce exit; for others, the process is "involuntary." Understanding the distal and proximal factors that contribute to the individual's perception of voluntariness in this transition and the individual's proactivity in this process represents a major challenge for researchers concerned with understanding adjustment and well-being following retirement.

The chapters in this volume underscore the multi-level complexity of understanding individual attitudes and behaviors associated with work and retirement in later adulthood. Consistent with dominant models of human behavior, most contributors of this volume adopt a broad person X situation perspective that typically includes consideration of personal attributes (such as health, knowledge, skills, motives, and personality traits) and situational factors (such as socioeconomic trends and work demands). In addition, however, several chapters (Beier; Czaja, Sharit, Charness, & Schmidt; Rudolph & Zacher; Heckhausen & Shane, this volume) also point to the importance of self-related attributes (such as self-regulation, learning self-efficacy, work centrality, social identity) that change as a function of work experiences over time, and explore how these variables contribute to different employment choices and end-of-work and retirement adjustment trajectories. Other chapters (e.g., Dieffendorf, Stanley, & Gabriel, this volume) highlight fundamental age-related changes in cognitive and affective competencies and the way these age-related changes may affect the individual's attempts to manage their work (e.g., job crafting) and the choices made among different employment options at different points in time. Taken together, these chapters highlight the importance of the temporal dimension and the need for focusing on the impact of person X situation interactions *over time*. Going one step further, the chapters provide a compelling argument for going beyond basic person attributes, such as cognitive and non-cognitive traits. Specifically, such variables focus on delineating the emergent psychological properties of the "whole person" over a cumulative lifetime experience of work.

The chapters in this volume also extend our conception of the "situation" component. Several authors (see Ilmarenin & Ilmarinen; Peiró, Hernández, & Ramos; Henkens, this volume) point to the importance of taking a more comprehensive view of context. For example, traditional accounts of retirement decision-making and age bias in the workplace have typically focused on distal factors, such as sociocultural norms and/or proximal workplace factors, such as supervisor support. Adopting a person-centric perspective, Ilmarinen and Ilmarinen, and Henkens (this volume) argue that greater attention must be given to the role of the family context on older worker transitions and the individual's non-job-related social environment. Although the primacy of these contexts in affecting worker transition decisions and behavior may vary over time and as a function of culture, the chapters in this volume call attention to the notion that in the real world, work behavior cannot be divorced from other aspects of an individual's life. As a consequence, researchers studying older worker employability and retirement must take into account more than the immediate work context.

FINAL COMMENTS

Our volume highlights the point that human aging reflects a biological process, not an end. As the nature of work changes and healthcare improves, an older adult's employability is determined less by biology than by person and environmental variables and their interactions over time. Consistent with this view, a growing number of researchers have begun to examine workforce aging issues using context-grounded person variables, such as functional age and subjective age (see Zabel & Baltes, this volume). In contrast to chronological age indices that provide distal, undifferentiated measures of functioning across the lifespan, context-grounded conceptions of age capture the joint contributions of biological and psychosocial influences and so provide a more proximal measure of the individual's beliefs and attitudes toward work.

There has been increasing sophistication in our understanding of the impact of the work environment on older worker motivation at work. Heckhausen and Shane (this volume), for example, point to the importance of evaluating the congruence between one's job and implicit and explicit career motives. Other authors note the need for additional theory and research to investigate the impact of specific, new, and increasingly popular organizational strategies for training (such as reverse mentoring and multimedia training) (see Czaja, Sharit, Charness, & Schmidt, this volume) and work accomplishment (such as the use of teams, virtual technologies, and open office environments) (see Kunze & Boehml; Zabel & Baltes, this volume). As Zabel and Baltes note, new training and work strategies may exert multiform effects on older worker motivation and satisfaction, through both the increased demands they place on new learning as well as the opportunities these strategies afford for rewarding social interactions. Coordinating theories of aging to distinct elements of modern sociotechnical work systems is urgently needed in order to identify the features of new workplaces that promote and/or discourage early job exit among older workers.

LOOKING AHEAD

The study of late adulthood employment transitions is a new area of organizational inquiry that demands an understanding of work from the individual's perspective. As such, fruitful research programs require consideration of how age-related changes and forces operating in different dimensions of the individual's environment interact to affect worker goals, attitudes, and behaviors. The chapters in this volume extend our understanding of the unique experiences and issues that individuals confront as they enter later adulthood, the possibility and expectations of retirement, and different pathway options for reformulating their role at work and their participation in the labor force. We hope that the current volume makes a contribution to helping organizations and individuals more effectively address these formidable challenges.

17

An Aging Workforce: The Contribution of Work, Industrial, and Organizational Psychology

Franco Fraccaroli

AN INTERDISCIPLINARY AND GLOBAL APPROACH

Reading many chapters of this book, starting from the introduction, it is possible to find strong evidence that the relationship between age and work is evolving, and further, that large changes are expected in the near future (20–30 years). This is true not only for the older generation of workers, but also for the younger, as shown in the chapter of Peiró, Hernández, and Ramos in this volume. The demographic transition, with two main global phenomena (reduction of birth rates and improvement of life expectancy), is now affecting the so-called advanced economies (USA, Japan, Europe) (Phillips & Siu, 2012). But it is also expected that the next 20 years will unsettle the developing economies such as China, Brazil, and Eastern Europe (Kinsella & He, 2009). We are at the leading edge of a global change that requires the intervention of a global science able to transfer knowledge from one context to another (Truxillo & Fraccaroli, 2014). At the same time, this global science needs also to be equipped to understand cultural differences (e.g., the meaning of working in different cultures), and to explain differential effects of specific norms (e.g., laws related to work and retirement are very peculiar for every country) and the level of economic development (e.g., large economic differences also inside the so-called developed economies, such as the level of youth unemployment or in the employment of people over 55). What is expected (and is already underway), following this demographical scenario, is a drop of the working age population, a radical improvement of the dependency ratio (the relationship between people over 65 and people at working age), and an extension of the lifespan after retirement. This is the picture that could be derived from demographic research and projections. As a consequence, it is assumed from an economic point of view that there is a need to lengthen the working lifespan and postpone retirement, also with the objective of preserving the equilibrium of the national pension systems. As Skirbekk, Loichinger, and Barakat (2012, p. 63, added emphasis) point out:

> Workforce aging is not necessarily an economic liability ... The major challenge associated with aging population ... is to what extent an older age structure will result in a growing share of those retired; or alternatively, whether the capacities of older cohorts will be *used* in the labor market, allowing dependency ratios to stabilize in spite of population aging.

THE ACTIVE ROLE OF INDIVIDUALS COPING WITH SOCIAL CHANGES

What is dominant in some demographic and economic approaches is an emerging "apocalyptic" point of view related to the future. That means building models and predictions on the basis of logical fallacies unleashed to produce the illusion of a valid model (Cronshaw, 2012). False dichotomies, such as "dependent" (over 65) and "non-dependent" (15–64) people, are still considered in the literature despite the large inter-individual differences within these artificially created demographic groups. There are a large number of people over 65 still working and/or living with their own resources (see Zhan & Wang, this volume). At the same time, there are a large number of people of "working age" that are not working and/or are dependent on their parents (sometimes also over 65) for either financial or family support, or on other social support systems. Moreover, a stereotypical view of aging is widespread in the demographic and economic literatures as a declining process but is an underestimation of the individual capacity for adjustment. Little attention is devoted to the capacity of individuals to proactively adapt and act on the new social scenario, despite the data showing that people are changing their attitudes, behaviors, and strategies related to emerging aging issues. People are ready to work longer, to save more money for their old age, to postpone retirement, and to develop a work career after retirement (Wang, Olson, & Shultz, 2012). All these factors—individual, societal, economic—could be better understood through a psychological perspective on aging. For these reasons, we have tried to promote with this book an I-O psychology perspective that should be integrated in an interdisciplinary body of research on aging and work, and that also will drive much needed future research.

Many chapters of this book are able to show how important the adoption of a work/industrial and organizational psychological approach is in studying the relationship between age and work and to consider age diversity in organizations. A W-I-O psychological perspective assumes that:

1. cognitions, motivation, and attitudes are not simply exposed to a linear and generic decline with age;
2. interpersonal differences are a key issue for understanding how people grow in the workplace along their life trajectory;
3. people adopt individual, family, and collective (strategic) behaviors to cope with the changes during the late career and the transition to retirement;
4. jobs, organizations, and careers could be adapted to older workers' characteristics, needs, and motives; and
5. there are identifiable antecedents to successful retirement in terms of psychological well-being and health, many of which are under the control of the individual, organization, and society.

STUDYING DIFFERENCES

Many suggestions are inspired by the different perspectives developed in the chapters. They could be considered as a plan for the future research on this topic. First, there is a need to develop comprehensive models that are able to explain the different experiences of aging in the workplace and the transition to retirement through a lifespan perspective. SOC (selection, optimization, and compensation) and SES (socio-emotional selectivity) theories are widely used in this field, and they have been applied to obtain some interesting results to help interpret how individuals could redefine goals and change behaviors in different life stages (Yeung & Fung, 2009; Zacher & Frese, 2011). These theories were originally developed to understand the process of successful aging. They are not specific for an application to the workplace context. What we need is not simply to apply these theoretical models to the workplace, but also to try to develop them in relationship with the specific context (aging in workplace) and in a specific stage of life (late career and transition to retirement). The chapter of de Lange, Kooij, and van der Heijden in this volume gives an example on how SOC theory could be enlarged considering HR practices and their impact on aging workforces.

A second line of development of research in the field of older workers and retirement transition is related to analyzing differences. It is well established that the experience of late career in terms of performance, engagement, satisfaction, and well-being depends on a series of personal, organizational, family, and societal variables. There is not a common trend of aging in the workplace that could be explained by the simple aging process (i.e., chronological age). Older workers are not a homogeneous entity in terms of their psychological experience. There is no room to enter into more details here. But from the Czaja, Sharit, Charness, & Schmidt chapter, we learn that particular attention should be devoted to different types of job demands. The implications of this approach are clearly important to understand the capacity of older workers to cope with different levels of job demands (in terms of physical, cognitive, and emotional efforts) and to define possible training programs specifically devoted to older workers. Similar considerations could be made for the transition to retirement. The handbook recently edited by Wang (2013) largely explains how this process depends on a large set of factors that could affect the way people are able to adjust to the transition, derive satisfaction from the new occupational situation (retirement, part-time job, bridge employment), and define a new social identity and maintain an acceptable level of activity and interest. The chapter of Zhan and Wang in this volume gives insights for a new research agenda. Studying differences in this field means also consideration of the individualization and de-standardization of the life course and careers (Sargent, Lee, Martin, & Zikic, 2013). The careers of people are less linear and univocal related to the past; modern careers include interruptions, suspensions, several changes, late entry in the labor market (particularly for women), return back to the education system, and/or temporal experiences in bad jobs. These are some examples of the possible strong differences between the career path of people that could have some effects on the timing and the strategic choice of retirement. Then, to understand the retirement process, it is more and more important to consider the great heterogeneity in the career path during their lifespan (the so-called kaleidoscope careers).

A USE-INSPIRED APPROACH

A more deep attention to these variables (type of job, job demands, career patterns) could also help I-O psychology to be more equipped in giving advice to people that are taking decisions about older workers and retirement (unions, policymakers, institutions). Thus, we go back to the subtitle of this book and to the introductory chapter: a use-inspired approach. For instance, there is a great deal of work concerning the policies of retirement age (Baruch, Sayce, & Gregoriou, 2014). Some countries (such as the USA and the UK) decided to abolish fixed retirement ages; other countries, such as Finland, tested some solutions on job/retirement based on work ability of people (and not only based on chronological age) (see the Ilmarinen & Ilmarinen chapter in this volume). Other European countries have mandatory retirement ages and continue to adopt early retirement strategies to solve problems in private firms or to promote generational turnover in public sector. Usually, the main arguments used to support these different strategies are based on demographic data (also in terms of organizational demography), or economical reasoning. But as shown in the Baruch and colleagues (2014) study, there are also some ethical issues such as fairness, equal opportunity, and individual rights that should be considered in the definition of the legal age for retirement. In this case, values, beliefs, and fairness perceptions of people are central variables to be considered.

REFERENCES

Baruch, Y., Sayce, S., & Gregoriou, A. (2014). Retirement in a global labour market: A call for abolishing the fixed retirement age. *Personnel Review, 43,* 464–482.

Cronshaw, S. F. (2012). Aging workforce demographics in Canada. In J. W. Hedge & W. C. Borman (Eds.), *The Oxford Handbook of Work and Aging* (pp. 98–114). Oxford: Oxford University Press.

Kinsella, K., & He, W. (2009). *U.S. Census Bureau, International Population Reports, P95/09-1, An Ageing World: 2008.* Washington, DC: U.S. Government Printing Office.

Phillips, D. R., & Siu, O. I. (2012). Global aging and aging workers. In J. W. Hedge & W. C. Borman (Eds.), *The Oxford Handbook of Work and Aging* (pp. 9–32). Oxford: Oxford University Press.

Sargent, L. D., Lee, M. D., Martin, B., & Zikic, J. (2013). Reiventing retirement: New pathways, new arrangements, new meanings. *Human Relations, 66,* 3–21.

Skirbekk, V., Loichinger, E., & Barakat, B. (2012). The aging of the workforce in European countries. In J. W. Hedge & W. C. Borman (Eds.), *The Oxford Handbook of Work and Aging* (pp. 60–79). Oxford: Oxford University Press.

Truxillo, D. M., & Fraccaroli, F. (2014). The science of a global organizational psychology: Differing approaches and assumptions. In R. L. Griffith, L. Foster Thompson, & B. K. Armon (Eds.), *Internationalizing the Curriculum in Organizational Psychology* (pp. 41–55). New York: Springer.

Wang, M. (Ed.) (2013). *The Oxford Handbook of Retirement.* Oxford: Oxford University Press.

Wang, M., Olson, D. A., & Shultz, K. S. (2013). *Mid and Late Career Issue. An Integrative Perspective.* New York: Routledge.

Yeung, D. Y., & Fung, H. H. (2009). Aging and work: How do SOC strategies contribute to job performance across adulthood? *Psychology and Aging, 24,* 927–940.

Zacher, H., & Frese, M. (2011). Maintaining a focus on opportunities at work: The interplay between age, job complexity, and the use of selection, optimization and compensation strategies. *Journal of Organizational Behavior, 32,* 291–318.

18

Developing "Best Practices" for Organizations: A Gap in the Current Aging Research

Donald M. Truxillo

A good case has been made throughout this volume for the societal importance of the aging workforce in the coming decades of the 21st century. These demographic changes have led to increased concern among the governments of industrialized countries and in the popular press. In the I-O psychology literature, age is beginning to be seen as not only a statistical control variable—its traditional role—but also as a topic worthy of study in itself. In this volume, we have asked some of the leading researchers in this field to describe the current state of the field, and also to provide guidance for future research in this area.

The chapters in this volume provide excellent recommendations for where the research needs to go in order to understand the aging workforce. In reviewing these chapters and looking to the future, one key question for our field—across all areas of aging workforce research—is what organizations can actually *do* to support workers across the work lifespan, facilitate people working side by side, extend the work lives of older people who either choose to work or who must work longer, and address the health and well-being of people working beyond "traditional" retirement ages.

Although our field has done much to understand the psychological issues related to the aging workforce, we have done rather less on developing and testing specific interventions and policies based on this research. Such an approach would provide a set of "best practices" for employers and societies and would raise the visibility of I-O psychology as a profession. Notably, one chapter in this book is focused specifically on such interventions (Zabel & Baltes), providing a framework to guide future research. In this section, I consider some issues associated with the implementation of age-related interventions in organizations. Specifically, I differentiate interventions that can help all workers versus those that can help older workers specifically. I also note the challenges of implementing these interventions in actual organizations, and conclude with a discussion of the need for a lifespan view of interventions, specifically differentiating interventions that support older workers from those that may head off aging issues earlier in the career.

ALL WORKERS OR JUST OLDER WORKERS?

One common question employers ask about age-related workplace issues is: "What can be done to help older workers and to keep people working longer?" But there are really two ways to approach answering this question: (1) Which interventions help workers *regardless* of their age, including older workers? (2) Which interventions are specifically effective for older workers per se (i.e., and may be less so for younger workers)? We address each of these issues below.

Which Practices Help Workers of All Ages?

The I-O literature can offer a number of interventions and policies that help workers of all ages. An example would be organizational interventions that support work-life balance. The I-O literature already shows that workplace policies and supervisor support for workers' outside obligations can have salutary effects on worker health and well-being (Kossek, Hammer, Kelly, & Moen, 2014). This is likely true for workers of all ages: although people may have substantially different outside obligations and interests at different life stages, workers of all ages seem to benefit from such policies. In other words, although people's non-work responsibilities may change as they age (e.g., care responsibilities for young children versus aging parents versus grandchildren), all people can benefit from these kinds of workplace supports for their non-work lives. In this sense, our field can provide substantial guidance for supporting workers of all ages—including those who are in the final decades of their work lives.

Which Practices are Especially Helpful to Older Workers?

The second question implies that some interventions benefit older workers specifically because they are *different* from younger workers. In other words, what is it that organizations need to do differently for people in their later years versus workers just starting their careers? In fact, the bulk of the I-O psychology research on aging takes this approach of considering differences between older and younger workers, focusing on age differences in terms of motivation, abilities, interests, and careers, and whether these differences affect their work attitudes, performance, and health. But applying this research in terms of interventions, policies, and workplace practices is tricky. There are three challenges associated with the issue of translating our research on age differences into workplace interventions.

First, *how can organizations implement practices that treat people of different ages in ways that are fair to all of them?* That is, how can an organization provide different resources to people of different ages, even if the research were to show that people of different ages need different resources? For example, an SOC-based intervention for older workers might involve helping late-career workers select job tasks that better fit their optimized skills to compensate for other weaknesses. But does this mean that older workers are able to hand off less desirable tasks to their coworkers? If so, this could create interpersonal and perhaps legal issues. At this point, our best approach to addressing this challenge may be to consider flexible, sustainable HR policies that address the needs of workers at different life stages (de Lange, Kooij, & van der Heijden; Kunze & Boehm, this volume). Certainly, we need to keep our eye on developments on the legal front regarding age-related protections and accommodations (Gutman & Dunleavy, this volume).

Second, can the findings from much of our age research—which is based on differences in older and younger workers' perceptions of what they need—translate into effective organizational interventions? In other words, much of our research has focused on what people of different ages perceive their work environment to be, rather than on objective characteristics, but this may not provide sufficient guidance for best practices about the objective work environment. As an example, using a job design framework, we may be able to show that older workers perceive certain job features (e.g., skill variety) as more attractive than others (e.g., task variety). But redesigning a workplace based on these perceptions might be an inferential leap, as what constitutes skill variety and task variety is largely in the eye of the beholder. In short, we may need more research that looks at objective aspects of the situation in order to provide best practices to organizations.

A third challenge with translating our literature into actual interventions that specifically help older workers is that much of the literature on the aging workforce is based on cross-sectional comparisons between people of different ages. However, we also know there are substantial differences among people within the same age group. In fact, these between-individual differences seem to increase with age. Further, the research from developmental psychology suggests that there are substantial intra-individual changes taking place, and that people have different developmental trajectories. As an example, while the mean conscientiousness of older people is generally higher than that of younger people (e.g., Roberts, Walton, & Viechtbauer, 2006), there is still considerable variability within older people in terms of conscientiousness, and in fact there are quite a few older people who are less conscientious than their younger counterparts. In short, *it will be challenging to develop organizational interventions and policies for older workers in general, as they are not completely different from younger people, and there is considerable variability within older workers across a spectrum of individual differences.* In this sense, it may be better to focus our research on variables that are associated with age such as specific cognitive skills (Beier, this volume) or subjective age (e.g., Zabel & Baltes, this volume), rather than focusing strictly on chronological age itself.

THE CHALLENGE OF CHANGING THE SOCIAL CONTEXT

A separate challenge for translating research findings into practice is the social context. Although making physical changes to accommodate older workers is often cited as being costly to organizations—which it is—changes to the social context may provide their own challenges to organizations as well. For example, reducing age stereotyping and improving the age diversity climate (Kunze & Boehm; Rudolph & Zacher, this volume) are both valuable goals for improving organizational life for people of all ages. Despite their clear value, it can be difficult to actually bring about such changes in organizations except by very slow, painstaking work. This would include buy-in from the top, changes in organizational communication, and training supervisors and teams on these issues. Thus, specific guidance as to how to change the social context on an organizational level is needed so that organizational decision-makers will have a blueprint about how to bring such changes about.

OTHER BEST PRACTICES ISSUES

I conclude with a few additional remarks in terms of developing best practices for organizations to address the aging workforce. First, there may be a number of issues related to the aging workforce that our field is not addressing. One prime example is the issue of knowledge transfer within organizations, an issue associated with the large-scale retirements of the baby boomer generation. Another example is better preparing workers for retirement from an economic standpoint. There is relatively little I-O research on these important issues, and researchers should be providing organizations with some guidance on these topics. Second, any recommended best practices to support an aging workforce should be described with care, including the use of fidelity tools to facilitate dissemination to other organizations.

Finally, one way to frame age-related best practices may be to break them down into the categories of those that solve the problems older workers are already having, versus those that help workers adjust throughout their work life spans, helping them to avoid age-related problems later on. One way to conceptualize this issue is to consider workplace aging practices as primary, secondary, or tertiary practices (Truxillo, Cadiz, & Hammer, in press), as has been done in the health literature. *Primary interventions* would be those that might address an issue before it becomes a problem, such as developing a supportive social context for workers of all ages and backgrounds. *Secondary interventions* would help to control problems that are developing, such as helping workers apply SOC strategies that can best fit their abilities to the job. *Tertiary interventions* would accommodate problems that already exist, such as a job reassignment for an older worker in a physically demanding job. In short, best practices for addressing the aging of the workforce may be developed to address problems before they develop, or developed to help workers in their final years on the job. Developing these different types of interventions will require that we, as I-O psychologists, consider longitudinal designs not just in terms of months, but in terms of years and decades—a significant shift for our field. But the payoff to organizations—and to society—would be best practices that could be applied across the career to help workers adjust to what looks to be a longer work life than has ever previously existed.

REFERENCES

Kossek, E., Hammer, L., Kelly, E., & Moen, P. (2014). Designing work, family & health organizational change initiatives. *Organizational Dynamics, 43*, 53–63.

Roberts, B. W., Walton, K. E., & Viechtbauer, W. (2006). Patterns of mean-level change in personality traits across the life course: A meta-analysis of longitudinal studies. *Psychological Bulletin, 132*, 1–25.

Truxillo, D. M., Cadiz, D. E., & Hammer, L. B. (in press). Promoting the health and well-being of an aging workforce. *Annual Review of Organizational Psychology and Organizational Behavior*.

19

Now That We Know What . . . How?

Lisa M. Finkelstein

The editors of this volume set out with the goal to truly be guided by the meaning and spirit of *frontiers* in the execution of this book. We gave our contributors a specific mission: focus on what can and should be done in research and practice to constructively address the implications of aging workforces for societal policymakers, organizations, and the individuals who work and live in them. In other words, we asked that they cast their eyes not backward (by way of comprehensive review), but rather forward to a research agenda built to meet the needs of our changing world of work. Each contributor took on this challenge with enthusiasm and careful thought, and after seeing the final product, I am so pleased to say, "mission accomplished." Although I am feeling re-energized and intrigued by the research agendas herein, I must admit that a bit of apprehension remains, as there are still a host of practical issues to sort out as we face the challenges of a multi-age workforce. To put it succinctly: now that we know what we should do . . . exactly *how* can we pull this off?

In this commentary, I would like to pinpoint some key research and practice obstacles that I foresee us facing going forward. Some of these have been touched on by the authors, while others have not. My purpose is not to end this volume on a pessimistic level, but rather to rally the troops, so to speak, to take these ideas and use them to move research and practice forward.

RESEARCH OBSTACLES

Although by no means exhaustive, the biggest mountains that I see on the horizon are: (a) cross-cultural research team formation; (b) the need for complex and time-/resource-consuming research methodologies; and (c) access to relevant and willing research participants. These, of course, are important issues that I-O psychologists grapple with in a host of topical domains; here, they are examined not only in the general sense, but also particularly in relation to studying aging and work.

Cross-Cultural Research Team Formation

As can be seen from the chapters in this book, the multi-age workforce is a pressing worldwide concern, but the particular issues being faced in different parts of the globe are not of universal priority. Moreover, aging itself is not only a physical phenomenon, but also a psychological, social, and cultural one as well. In some ways, then, it would make sense for researchers to focus on their local workplace aging issues and nuances to have the highest likelihood of a locally relevant contribution. While this might be true to some extent, to fully tackle the challenges of a multi-age global workforce we must also discover ways to work together on projects that will speak to the complexities faced by global communities and organizations.

Future research sections of papers and chapters quite often suggest cross-cultural research as an important next step, but this may seem like a lofty endeavor easily suggested but not often pursued. Part of the reason for this is that many of us are not trained in how to get such collaborations off the ground; many people probably have no idea what to do first.

Attending international conferences and networking with other researchers, of course, can be extremely beneficial, but going from a brief meeting at a symposium or coffee break to an in-depth collaboration is a big, effortful, and sometimes risky leap. I believe it would be quite helpful if conferences had more research incubators where people not only meet and exchange ideas, but also begin the planning and detail stages of projects so they are more likely to pick up momentum. Sessions and workshops on forming effective cross-cultural collaborations hosted by those with a track record would be very welcome. Unlike more local collaborations, cross-cultural collaborations require a shared understanding of funding opportunities and requirements, IRB expectations, tenure and promotion pressures, and typical roles of graduate student collaborators, among other issues.

Complex Research Strategies

Not only do the research ideas throughout this book call for cross-cultural approaches, but they also often call for an increased complexity in research design. Many more specific approaches could be described here, including challenges inherent to the multi-level designs that so many of our chapter authors suggest (cf., Hitt, Beamish, Jackson, & Mathieu, 2007), but for space considerations I consider two specific methodological challenges: longitudinal designs and person-centric designs.

Longitudinal Designs

An even more common refrain at the end of articles and chapters than the suggestion for cross-cultural research that was noted above is the call for longitudinal designs. Again, this is a direction that has been suggested in myriad substantive areas of work psychology. Ployhart and Vanderberg (2010) pointed out how often organizational theory is crafted to represent inherently longitudinal processes, yet researchers settle to test those theories in a cross-sectional manner. The processes specified in a theory, particularly in relation to order and time, ultimately do not receive a fair test. I am hard pressed to think of an area where the unfolding of time is more central than with aging; in essence, it is another metric for time. And like in other areas, we aging and work researchers have settled for comparing individuals of various ages rather than truly looking at the process of aging as experienced by the worker over his or her career.

Longitudinal research has more complexity to sort out than cross-sectional designs, to be sure, and the depth of those issues have not always been clear because there seem to be so few models of long-range longitudinal research to follow. Fortunately, there are accessible resources for planning, conducting, and analyzing such work (Ployhart & Vanderberg, 2010 mentioned above is a prime example).

A practical issue that cannot be ignored is the ratio of commitment to payoff that researchers perceive in undertaking long-term longitudinal work. The tenure and promotion system in many universities has been lamented for providing a structure that reinforces and incentivizes quick and tried-and-true research over more complex, time-consuming, and interesting work (Daft, 1983; Davis, 1971). To expect that to change overnight would be naive to say the least, but could we not begin to see this as an "and" rather than an "or" decision? As a graduate student and untenured academic, create a program of research that is rigorous and systematic, and includes a substantial percentage of studies that could be executed within the time constraints of probationary periods, and commit to a project or two—in a team of others—that is comprehensive and long term. Additionally, if as a field we can think creatively of ways to develop metrics by which to judge participation in longitudinal work at its early stages, we may be able to further incentivize involvement among early scholars.

Person-Centric Approaches

Although not all of the ideas in the current volume are person-centric, a goal was to at least consider the person-centric perspective. As we age, we may expect to pass through similar stages of development and decline, but we also experience such a path in ways that are unique to our many experiences, work-related and otherwise. As described in Chapter 1 and other sources (cf., Weiss & Rupp, 2011), such an approach moves its focus to the person as they experience work. It may focus on the moment-to-moment experiences of a worker, or look at how the experience of working changes over time and contexts. Although Weiss and Rupp and others (e.g., Liu, Zhan, & Wang, 2011) have noted that methodologies for person-centric research have not yet been fully developed, systematized, or likely taught widely, ideas are emerging. The more immediate approaches ("What is it like at work right now?") to understanding the cognitive, affective, and behavioral experiences of workers of different ages and in contexts comprised of people of different ages require methods that allow participants to report experiences in situ. Those that are more dynamic longitudinal in nature—tracing individual workers as they age and compile different experiences—may require more intensive narratives.

Not only do we, as a field, need to focus on developing rigorous methodology to fully answer person-centric questions, but we must also disseminate practical guidance for using such methods to graduate students and more seasoned researchers alike. Again, systematic and focused programming at conferences, units in classes, and workshops will be needed.

Access to Relevant and Willing Participants

Advances in Internet survey technology have facilitated access to a wider range of willing participants and have streamlined and often reduced expenses in the data collection process itself. Additionally, working with cross-cultural teams potentially allows access to a wider network of potential research participants. All of this is good news. Yet, as discussed above, the research advances put forth in this book will often require more complex methodologies that may be particularly taxing to participants in several ways.

Longitudinal research obviously requires an extensive commitment in participants. This is true for all kinds of topical areas, but we are studying *aging*. Aging (though it does not always feel that way) is a very long process in research-study terms. Not only do the researchers need to be willing to commit to a very long-term enterprise, but the participants do as well. The researchers can clearly see what the benefits could be for taking on such a project, but what are the benefits to the participant? Fair compensation for participants for a long-term commitment will likely require hefty resources, and benefits to participation must be articulated clearly from an ethical standpoint, as well as to entice participants to last for the long haul. It is important to point out as well that person-centric studies, even those not longitudinal in design, may likely require a lot from participants in order for researchers to garner the rich information that is the hallmark of these types of methods.

PRACTICE OBSTACLES

The emphasis in this book, like any other *Frontiers* series book, is mainly on inspiring research, but putting findings into practice is always a goal, and indeed this book is use-inspired in its framing. A great deal of attention has been given to the sources, nature, and solutions to the science-practice gap in our field (e.g., Cohen, 2007; Rynes, 2012). I would like to direct the reader's attention to two particular challenges early in the process of turning research to practice: (a) reaching the appropriate audience; and (b) providing a usable message.

Reaching an Appropriate Audience

Research findings have no shot at contributing to improved practice if they are never seen in the first place. The first hurdle is to reach the audience who could use them. Researchers who are inspired to carry out studies to help with the issues created in our multi-age workforce do have an advantage of doing work where there is a current widespread interest. When embarking on this work, think not only of the academic outlets for this research, but also to outlets that practitioners will access. Cohen (2007) and Rynes (2012) include several useful suggestions, such as contributing to newsletters and websites, writing white papers, and speaking at practitioner-attended events.

Providing a Usable Message

Reaching the audience is only half the battle; being able to communicate the specific usefulness of findings in a clear and actionable way is vital. Some excellent recommendations by Rynes (2012) include using language that is persuasive and not hedging, terminology that is shared by the audience, and a tone that it is collaborative. Additionally, written works or talks that state general principles and illustrative examples are more likely to resonate. A mindset where we start to actively plan a dissemination strategy, and write short and useful implications pieces in addition to journal articles as a part of our routine research processes could really make a difference.

CONCLUDING THOUGHT

In my roles both as instructor and as symposia discussant, I have tried an exercise with my class/audience that I am now attempting to translate into a concluding paragraph, so bear with me. So often I think we engage in discussions about confounding problems and general solutions that are at such a high level that it is very taxing to take what are sometimes very good ideas and actually do something with them. So my challenge to my classes/audience, and now my challenge to you, is to think about something you could actually do *right now*, literally, as soon as you put this book down to face down one of the obstacles described here. Could you sign up for a longitudinal methods course, look online for the next international meeting of aging researchers, or ask a practitioner friend how to make your aging research more applicable? Whatever action it is, start some momentum, and together we can work toward a maximally successful multi-age workforce.

REFERENCES

Cohen, D. J. (2007). The very separate worlds of academic and practitioner publications in human resource management: Reasons for the divide and concrete solutions for bridging the gap. *Academy of Management Journal, 5,* 1013–1019.

Daft, R. L. (1983). Antecedents of significant and not-so-significant research. In T. S. Bateman and G. R. Ferris (Eds.). *Method and Analysis in Organizational Research* (pp. 3–14). Reston, VA: Reston Publishing.

Davis, M. (1971). That's interesting: Toward a phenomenology of sociology and a sociology of phenomenology. *Philosophy of Social Science, 1,* 309–344.

Hitt, M. A., Beamish, P. W., Jackson, S. E., & Mathieu, J. E. (2007). Building theoretical and empirical bridges across levels: Multilevel research in management. *Academy of Management Journal, 50,* 1385–1399.

Liu, S., Zhan, Y., & Wang, M. (2011). Person-centric work psychology: Additional insights into its tradition, nature, and research methods. *Industrial and Organizational Psychology, 4,* 105–108.

Ployhart, R. E., & Vandenberg, R. J. (2010). Longitudinal research: The theory, design, and analysis of change. *Journal of Management, 36,* 94–120.

Rynes, S. J. (2012). The research-practice gap in I/O psychology and related fields: Challenges and potential solutions. In S. W. J. Kozlowski (Ed.). *The Oxford Handbook of Organizational Psychology, Vol. 1* (pp. 409–452). Oxford: Oxford University Press.

Weiss, H. M., & Rupp, D. E. (2011). Experiencing work: An essay on a person-centric work psychology. *Industrial and Organizational Psychology, 4,* 83–97.

Author Index

Ackerman, P. L. 115, 224–225
Adams, G. A. 243
Alavinia, S. 67
Allen, J. 145
Ambady, N. 197
Anderson, S. 88
Armstrong-Stassen, M. 63
Ashforth, B. E. 86

Baltes, B. B. 343
Barak, B. 33
Barakat, B. 345
Barger, P. B. 194
Baruch, Y. 348
Bashshur, M. R. 88
Bauer, T. N. 87, 88
Beehr, T. A. 325
Boehm, S. A. 30, 236, 274
Bos-Nehles, A. 71
Bruch, H. 30, 274
Burke, M. J. 306

Campion, M. A. 258
Cartensen, L. L. 113, 210
Cascio, W. F. 305–306
Chan, A. W. 33
Chiu, C. K. 33
Chu, C. W. L. 30, 32
Cohen, D. J. 360
Costanza, R. 52
Czaja, S. J. 172, 347

de Grip, A. 145
de Lange, A. H. 64, 347
der Heijden, B. I. J. M. 347
Dikkers, J. S. E. 64–66
Docherty, P. 54

Earl, J. K. 244
Egri, C. P. 67
Ekerdt, D. J. 321, 325
Ekman, P. 182
Elfenbein, H. A. 197
Erdogan, B. 87, 88

Feldman, D. C. 83, 243, 258, 325
Finegold, D. 63
Finkelstein, L. M. 259, 306
Fiske, S. T. 259
Flood, S. 325
Fox, S. 274
Frey, C. B. 144
Fugate, M. 86, 100

Gebert, D. 29, 275
Giles, H. 274
Goldberg, C. B. 304
Grandey, A. A. 194
Greenberg, D. H. 97
Guest, D. 71
Gutman, A. 286, 294, 304

Hackman, J. R. 52
Hamermesh, D. 168
Heckhausen, J. 342–343
Heidkamp, M. 171
Henkens, K. 66, 237, 342
Hernández, A. 88, 344
Hershey, D. A. 237
Holling, C. 52
Hu, M. 270

Ilmarinen, J. 56–57, 342
Ilmarinen, V. 342
Iweins, C. 273

Author Index

Jahoda, M. 85–86
Jansen, P. G. W. 64–66
Johnson, S. L. 196
Joshi, A. 29, 270

Kanfer, R. 64–66, 115, 224–225
Kearney, E. 29, 275
Kessler, E. M. 273
King, E. B. 259
Kinicki, A. J. 86
Kluve, J. 97
Kooij, D. T. A. M. 64–66, 211, 347
Kubicek, B. 244
Kunze, F. 30, 274

Lam, K. C. 30, 32
Lawrence, B. S. 263
Leccardi, C. 99
Leung, C. S. Y. 244
Levenson, R. W. 187, 188
Li, J. 30, 32
Liao, S. 30, 32
Liu, B. 270
Loichinger, E. 345

McCann, R. M. 273–274
Marías, J. 94, 99
Mathieu, J. E. 243
Michalopoulos, C. 97
Moen, P. 325
Mohrman, S. 63
Morton, K. R. 233
Müller, A. 67
Munnell, A. 333

Neuman, G. A. 214
Ng, T. W. H. 243, 258
North, M. S. 259

Oldham, G. R. 52
Ortega y Gasset, J. 90
Osborne, M. A. 144
Osland, J. 67

Patel, P. C. 36
Patten, B. C. 52
Peiró, J. M. 87, 88, 90, 344
Pfeffer, J. 52
Pinquart, M. 240

Ployhart, R. E. 358
Posthuma, R. A. 258
Pugh, S. D. 196–197

Raju, N. S. 306
Ramos, J. 344
Rau, B. L. 243
Redman, T. 33
Robertson, P. J. 209–210
Robins, P. K. 97
Roh, H. 29
Rudolph, C. 57
Rupp, D. E. 90, 93, 359
Russell, T. A. 197
Ryan, K. M. 259
Rynes, S. J. 360, 361

Sass, S. 333
Schindler, I. 240
Schippers, J. 66
Searcy, T. 173–174
Shane, J. 342–343
Sharit, J. 172, 347
Shiota, M. N. 187–188
Shore, L. M. 304
Shultz, K. S. 233, 244
Silkin, L. 286
Skirbekk, V. 345
Smith, A. 165
Snape, E. 33
Spreitzer, G. M. 63
Stern, W. 89–90
Stokes, D. 17
Staudinger, U. M. 273
Stroebe, W. 333

Taylor, S. 67
Thatcher, S. 36
Truxillo, D. M. 87, 88, 221

Ursel, M. D. 63

van Dalen, H. 66, 237
van Dijk, H. 29
van Engen, M. L. 29
van Knippenberg, D. 29
Vandenberg, R. J. 358

Wang, M. 240, 244, 341, 347
Waters, L. 86

Weckerle, J. R. 233
Weiss, H. 90, 93, 359
Winefield, A. H. 88

Zabel, K. L. 343
Zajac, D. M. 243
Zhan, Y. 341, 347

Subject Index

abilities *see* cognitive abilities; interpersonal skills; work ability
acting: deep 183–184, 186–187, 189; surface 184, 186–188
activities 94, 322–323
adaptability 57, 86, 100–101
ADEA 283–284, 286–294
affect 17, 90, 181–183, 187, 193–194
affective events 181, 182, 183, 187, 193
affectivity *see* disposition
age climate 271
age conceptualizations 211, 214
Age Discrimination Employment Act *see* ADEA
age diversity 3–4, 8, 13, 35–38, 44, 215–216, 253, 272–274
age grading 254, 261, 263, 264, 340
age inclusivity 42, 152, 235–236
age-related changes 13–16, 64, 115–116, 163, 190–192, 315–317
age-related interventions 101, 142, 151, 196–197, 209–229, 350–351
age stereotyping 30, 33, 39, 257–260, 264, 265, 266–267, 271–272, 274, 353
Age UK v. Secretary of State for Business (2009) 300
agency 86, 95, 99–102, 322, 324–327
agentic 99–102
Air New Zealand Ltd v. McAlister (2012) 298
applied psychology *see* I-O psychology; person-centric approach
appraisal 186–187, 193
Asia 31–33
attitudes 142
attributes *see* cognitive abilities; emotions
audience 360
Australia 284–285, 296–297

autonomy 121–122, 220–224
awareness 152

best practices 350–354
BFEs 289
bias *see* discrimination
big data 268–270
biography 99
BLS 160–161
BMW 160, 332
bona fide executives *see* BFEs
bridge employment 230–231, 240–246, 341
Bureau of Labor Statistics *see* BLS
BYOD 165

Canada 284, 292, 295–296
career 347; development 220; identity 100–101; path 12–13, 86, 97–99, 313–314, 316–318
case law *see* employment law
categorization-elaboration 29, 273
change *see* age-related changes; training
chronological age 211, 218, 224; *see also* age related change
climate *see* operational environment
cognitive abilities 14–15, 163, 187, 191–192, 332; intellectual 115–116, 170–171, 222
collaboration *see* teams
collectivism 31–32, 100, 222–223
communications 273–274
community colleges 170
companies *see* organizations
compensatory strategies 120, 123–124, 128
competence 141–142, 147, 149, 315–316
complexity 112

Subject Index • 367

conceptualizations of age 115, 209, 211, 215, 217–219, 221–222, 223, 225
configural approach 234–235
conflict 254–257, 259, 261–272, 274–275
congruence 95
consumer technology 165
contact hypothesis 274–275
context 55, 90–91, 138, 345–346, 353; retirement 235–238, 245, 323–326, 342
contractors 297
control 70, 87
coping 87, 101–102
covered practices 289–290
critical thinking 170–171
cross-cultural research 31–32, 356–358
culture 12–13, 45; interventions 216, 219, 222–223, 225–226; organizational 43; research 357; teamwork 30–33
customers 183–185, 193–196
CVS 219

databases 268–270
decision-making 28–29, 215, 235
deep acting 183–184, 186–187, 189
deficit hypothesis 33
demography 5–7, 159–161, 214, 217, 220–221, 223–224, 306
deprivation 86
desired work 37–38
development *see* sustainability; training
differences 347
discrimination 30, 35, 118–119, 168–169, 304–305; *see also* employment law; stereotypes
display rules 181–182, 184, 194
disposition 182–183
diversity 3–4, 8, 13, 35–38, 44, 215–216, 253, 272–274; *see also* intergenerational
division of labor 34
Donnellan v. Minister for Justice (2008) 299
downsizing 138–139
dynamism 16–17

e-learning 164
economics 7–9, 167, 215, 218–219, 221–222, 224; downsizing 138–139; life course 322, 326–327; teamwork 33–35
The Economist 108

education *see* overqualification; training
EEO law *see* employment law
eldercare 218
emotional labor 180–191, 196–198; research 191–196
emotions 101, 116, 117, 180–191, 196–198, 273
Employee Retirement Income Security Act *see* ERISA
employment 86, 100–101, 166–169; bridge 230–231, 240–246, 341; policies 93; transitions 339–343; *see also* labor market; unemployment
employment law 302–306; ADEA 283–284, 286–294; Australia 296–297; Canada 295–296; Ireland 298–299; New Zealand 297–298; UK 299–302
engagement 57, 112, 118, 121, 137, 142, 161, 217, 221, 224, 235, 243, 318, 331, 347; engagement-disengagement cycles 317–318
entrepreneurship 100
equal opportunities *see* employment law
equity theory 87
ergonomics 175
ERISA 290
ethics 54, 87, 154
ethnicity 159
EU 6, 33–34, 100, 160–161, 167, 298–302, 313–314
Eurostat 6
exchange 116, 184–185
experience 166, 187–189, 193
expression 189–191, 194
external environment 237–238

family 96–97, 100, 138, 236–237
faultline 29, 36–38, 40, 44
Finland 148–151
firefighters 289–290
flexibility 84, 100, 121, 217–219
focal approach 19
formal support *see* support systems
functionalism 85–86, 221, 224
future research 28, 210, 225–226, 254–255, 346; on age diversity 35–36, 39–40, 42–43; on age stereotypes 259–260; on career development 220–222; on collectivist cultures 222–223; example

directions 266–267; on flextime policies 217–219; in HR 67, 71–73; on intergenerational conflict 262–263, 265, 272, 274–275; on labor force transitions 321–322, 327; and physical setting interventions 223–225; on retirement and bridge employment 231, 235–236, 238, 239–241; on sustainability at work 54; suggested research topics 126–127, 212; on team building 214–216; in youth unemployment and underemployment 92, 100, 102

gender 36–37, 44, 244
generational conflict 9; *see also* intergenerational conflict
generational differences 254–257, 265–271; *see also* intergenerational
Germany 27, 120–121, 314, 332
globalization 84, 137–138, 216, 316, 344–345; corporations 12–13; teamwork 30–43, 45–46
goals 40, 64, 116, 317–318
Good Work—Longer Career 148–151
Google 268–269
government policy 237–238
Gregory v. Ashcroft (1991) 290
growth 115–116

health 54, 137–139, 141–143, 167, 175–176, 221, 331
Homer v. Chief Constable (2012) 301
house model *see* work ability
HR 35, 42–43, 45, 62–67; sustainability 67–73; unemployment 93–94
HR bundles 64–67; functions of 67–68, 69; research into 72
HR practices: actual vs. perceived 62–64
human capital 86–87
human resources *see* HR

I-O psychology 4–5, 19, 230–231, 283, 346, 350–352
identities 32–33, 35–36, 91–92, 274; career 100–101; social 29, 215, 262–263, 270–271
ILO 54
implicit age grading 263

implicit motives 318
India 223
informal economy 96
institutions *see* collectivism; organizations
intellectual abilities 115–116, 170–171, 222; cognitive 14–15, 163, 187, 191–192, 332
interdisciplinary research 326–327, 344–346
interface 175–176
intergenerational: conflict 261–272, 274–275; exchange 253–257, 273; stereotypes 257–260
International Labor Organization *see* ILO
interpersonal skills 117–118, 180, 188; *see also* emotional labor
interventions 101, 196–198, 209–211, 214–226, 274, 350–354
intra-individual change 16, 353
Ireland 285, 298–299

Japan 6–7, 34
jobs 93, 117–118; *see also* work
job attitudes 192
job characteristics 111–113, 128
job crafting 70, 73, 102
job demands 4, 159–176, 347
job design 111–112, 121, 220–223
job fit 70, 87, 88, 97, 111, 146
job obsolescence 9–10, 144–145, 147
job performance 113–114; PJ fit 111–114, 116, 118–122, 124–129
judicial scenarios 293–294

Kerr v. O'Hara Brothers Surfacing LTD (2013) 301
knowledge 166, 332; experience 166, 187–189, 193; work 4, 34, 117, 161, 163; *see also* cognitive abilities
KSAOs 112–116, 119–120, 122–128

labor market 34, 144–146, 167, 237, 322–323; ILO 54; labor force 160–161, 321–327; outsourcing 12–13; unemployment 83–85, 88, 93, 98; *see also* diversity; emotional labor
late adulthood 13–16, 18, 185; employment transitions 340–341, 343
law *see* employment law

Subject Index • 369

leadership 40–42, 44–45, 262, 275
leader-member exchange theory 261–262
learning 10–11, 165–166, 172; *see also* training
levels of analysis 3–19, 345–346
life: agency 322, 324–326; course 322–327; expectancy 331; learning 10–11; spheres 94–96, 118–119, 128
lifespan psychology 7–8, 245, 275, 332–333; HR 70–71; interventions 215, 217–218, 224–225; social mobility 314–318; *see also* SOC; SST
longevity 18, 241, 339, 341
longitudinal research 239–240, 244–245, 358–360
loss 115

McCreary v. Greyhound (1986) 295
macroeconomics 33–35, 237
management 142–143, 147, 289; *see also* HR; organizations
meaning of working study *see* MOW
Medicare 169
mentoring 173
message 361
middle aged workers 125
mobility 37–38, 99–100; social 313–318
moral issues *see* ethics
motivation 142, 150, 225, 317–318, 332; bridge employment 242–243
MOW 94
multigenerational 14, 263
multi-nationals *see* globalization

needs 95, 234
Netherlands 66, 167, 237–238
New Brunswick v. Potash (2008) 296
New Zealand 285, 290, 297–298
noise 224–225
non-work demands 18, 109–110, 118, 128
non-work life 219, 242
norms 42–43, 91–92, 263, 334, 340–341; display rules 181–182, 184

OADR 5–6, 33–34, 160
obsolescence 144–145, 147
office 223–225
old-age dependency ratio *see* OADR

older workers 8–9, 114–116, 351–353; agency 324–327; emotions 185–196; law 287–288; optimizing 331–334; stereotypes 257–260; work ability 143; workplace changes 160, 164–175
Older Workers Benefit Protection Act *see* OWBPA
operational environment 135–139, 147, 153, 154
optimization *see* productivity
organizational environment 138–139, 142–143, 162–176, 223–225, 235–237, 271
organizations 17–18, 118–119, 333–334; age 211, 263; bridge employment 242–243; changes 137, 161–176; employment policies 93–94; interventions 216–219; law 288–289; level 30, 44, 62, 153, 219, 274, 353; PJ fit 120–122, 129; teams 28–30, 42–43; work ability 142–143, 148–151; *see also* HR; interventions; retirement; work
outsourcing 12–13
overqualification 88–89, 145–148; *see also* underemployment
OWBPA 290

participants 359–360
PE fit 57, 68, 72, 87–88, 238; job fit 111–114, 116, 118–122, 124–129; relational demography 262
pensions 6–7; *see also* retirement
perceived age 37, 124–125
performance 18–19, 113–114, 154, 164–165, 331–334
person-centric approach 13–18, 89–102, 231–235, 342, 359–360
person-environment fit *see* PE fit
person-job fit *see* PJ fit
physical abilities 14, 15–16, 115, 127, 221, 222
physical interventions 223–225, 332
physical setting 210, 223–225
PJ fit 111–114, 116, 118–122, 124–129
police 289–290
population *see* demography
positivity effect 116
postmodern values 92

Subject Index

power distance 31
practices 289–290, 350–354, 360–361; see also organizations
practice recommendations 43–45, 102–103, 129, 152–155, 175–176, 196–198, 225–226, 244–246, 348, 354, 360–361
priority 54
privacy 224–225
production 137
productivity 18–19, 113–114, 154, 164–165, 331–334
professional competence see competence
progress 55
projected old-age dependency ratio see OADR
protected class 287–288
psychology 3–4; age 125; life course 322, 326–327; social 85–87; transitions 340–342; see also IO psychology; person-centric approach
Public Workforce System see PWS
PWS 169–172

qualitative research 246

rationalization 137
recession 167–168
regulations see employment law
relational demography 261–262
relative deprivation 86
remedies 292–293, 304
reorganization 116
research 4–5, 350–354, 356–360; discrimination 303–306; emotional labor 191–196; HR 71–73; interdisciplinary 326–327; interventions 212–213; organizations 30, 42–43; teams 28–30, 35–42; work 92, 124–128; work ability 152–154
resources 54, 244
resources theory 56, 59
retirement 230–240, 244–246, 323–327, 330–333; mandatory 18, 288–290, 295–302, 305; state policy 6–8, 160
return on investment see ROI
rewards 40, 44–45
risk 142–143

ROI 143
roles 39, 322–323
rules see norms

Saunders v. CHC Ireland Limited (2008) 299
SAVI 188
Seldon v. Clarkson, Wright & Jakes (2012) 300–301
selection optimization and compensation see SOC
self-categorization 262–263, 270–271
self-regulation 86, 95
service sector 180–182, 194–198
SEST see SST
signaling theory 62
skills 141–142, 163, 315–316; interpersonal 117–118, 180, 188; obsolescence 144–145, 147; technology 37–38; see also emotional labor
smartphones 165
SOC 64–68, 70, 112–113, 120, 346–347; interventions 210, 215, 218, 221, 223–225; retirement 241, 244–245
social: exchange 62–64, 184–185; identity 29, 215, 262–263, 270–271; intervention 214–216; mobility 313–318; psychology 85–87; support 96–97, 237–238
social context 55, 90–91, 138, 345–346, 353; retirement 235–238, 245, 323–326, 342
socio-emotional selectivity see SST
socialization 162, 339; organizational 42–43, 100, 256; work 85, 91–92, 100
sociology 322, 326–327
space 223–225
SST 113, 116, 118, 186–188, 346–347; interventions 210, 214–215, 218, 223–225; retirement 233–234, 244–245
stability 55, 57
stereotypes 257–260, 265, 271–272; see also discrimination
strength and vulnerability integration see SAVI
stress 138–139
structure see labor market; organizations; social context

subgroups 29, 34–35, 234–235, 305
subjective age 37, 124–125
successful aging 19, 73, 241–242, 346
supervisor 142
support systems 96–97, 237–238
surface acting 184, 186–188
sustainability 50–57, 62, 67–73

tasks 38–40, 221
teams 4, 27–30, 164, 273; building 214–216; global 30–43, 45–46; virtual 12, 216
technology 4, 44, 306; emotional labor 197–198; interventions 216, 219–225; and performance 38, 44, 144–145, 161, 162–163, 164–165, 169, 174, 176, 198, 305; skills 37–38, 144–145; social mobility 313–314; training 9–12, 161–165, 172–174
TFL 40–42, 44, 70–71, 275
time 97–99, 239–240, 333, 341
Title VII (US) 283–284, 287, 293, 297
Totalisator Agency Board v. Gruschow (1998) 297
trade unions 148–149
training 8–9, 122–128, 141–142, 166–175; emotions 196–198; technology 10–11, 44, 145, 161–165
traits *see* cognitive abilities; interpersonal skills; work ability
transformational leadership *see* TFL
Twitter 269–270

UK 66, 285–286, 299–302
UN 51
underemployment 85–89, 145–148; youth 83–85, 89–103
unemployment 8–9, 34–35, 85–89, 159–160; youth 83–85, 89–103
upward mobility 313–314
USA 6–7, 34, 238, 313–314; employment law 283–294; job demands 159–160, 169–171

use-inspired 17, 348, 360
utility 64–65

values *see* motivation
victimization 289
virtual teams 12, 216
voluntariness 233, 341

WAI 139–141
welfare *see* support systems
well-being 3, 52, 53, 92, 96, 136, 184, 260, 347; employee 11, 143, 182, 185, 238; of older workers 176, 350; physical 121; psychological 86, 88, 147, 239–240, 346; in/after retirement 17, 239–241, 244, 245, 341; social 327; work 148–149, 150, 151, 339, 351
Western culture 30–35, 222
WIA 169–171
work 8, 117–118, 305–306, 330–331; demands 56, 67, 141, 341; design 111–112, 121, 220–223; desired mode 37–38; location 11; socialization 42–43, 91–94; sustainability 50–57, 62, 67–73; *see also* jobs; organizations
work ability 56–57, 135–139, 141–155; WAI 139–141; *see also* job attitudes
work environment 138–139, 142–143, 162–176, 223–225, 235–237, 271
workers 119–120, 160–161, 321–327, 351–353; aging 3–4, 8, 13–17, 108–109, 330–331; HR 62–68; middle aged 125; *see also* older workers; young people
workforce changes 5–7, 16
Workforce Investment Act *see* WIA
workplace changes 164–165, 168
workplace interventions *see* interventions

young people 196, 273–274, 287–288, 334; stereotypes 258, 272; unemployment 8–9, 83–85, 89–103
youthfulness 32–33

eBooks
from Taylor & Francis

Helping you to choose the right eBooks for your Library

Add to your library's digital collection today with Taylor & Francis eBooks. We have over 50,000 eBooks in the Humanities, Social Sciences, Behavioural Sciences, Built Environment and Law, from leading imprints, including Routledge, Focal Press and Psychology Press.

Choose from a range of subject packages or create your own!

Benefits for you
- Free MARC records
- COUNTER-compliant usage statistics
- Flexible purchase and pricing options
- 70% approx of our eBooks are now DRM-free.

Benefits for your user
- Off-site, anytime access via Athens or referring URL
- Print or copy pages or chapters
- Full content search
- Bookmark, highlight and annotate text
- Access to thousands of pages of quality research at the click of a button.

Free Trials Available

We offer free trials to qualifying academic, corporate and government customers.

eCollections

Choose from 20 different subject eCollections, including:

- Asian Studies
- Economics
- Health Studies
- Law
- Middle East Studies

eFocus

We have 16 cutting-edge interdisciplinary collections, including:

- Development Studies
- The Environment
- Islam
- Korea
- Urban Studies

For more information, pricing enquiries or to order a free trial, please contact your local sales team:

UK/Rest of World: **online.sales@tandf.co.uk**
USA/Canada/Latin America: **e-reference@taylorandfrancis.com**
East/Southeast Asia: **martin.jack@tandf.com.sg**
India: **journalsales@tandfindia.com**

www.tandfebooks.com